The Paradox of Myanmar's Regime Change

This book analyzes Myanmar's contemporary political history, arguing that Myanmar's so-called "democratization" has always been a calculated regime transition, planned by the military, with every intention that the military remain the key permanent political actor in Myanmar's political regime.

Using the period since Myanmar's regime change in 2011 as an extended case study, this book offers an original theory of regime transition. The author argues that Myanmar's ongoing regime transition has not diverged from its authoritarian military roots and explains how the military has long planned its voluntary partial withdrawal from direct politics. Therefore, Myanmar's "disciplined democracy" contains features of democratic politics but at its core remains authoritarian. Providing an original contribution to the theoretical literature on regime change by developing a theory of trial and error regime transition, the book engages with and challenges the popular democratization theory by arguing that this theory does not sufficiently explain hybrid regimes or authoritarian durability. Additionally, the book adds to an alternative understanding of how the regime transition was initiated by examining the historical evolution of Myanmar's post-colonial regime and offers a fresh perspective on contemporary political developments in Myanmar.

An important contribution to the study of authoritarian durability and the dynamics of regime change in Southeast Asia, this book will be of interest to academic researchers of comparative politics, international relations, and Southeast Asian studies.

Roger Lee Huang is Lecturer in Terrorism Studies and Political Violence in the Department of Security Studies and Criminology at Macquarie University, Australia.

Routledge/City University of Hong Kong Southeast Asia Series
Edited by Federico Ferrara and Mark R. Thompson

For more information about this series, please visit: www.routledge.com/Routledge-City-University-of-Hong-Kong-Southeast-Asia-Series/book-series/CUHK

The Paradox of Myanmar's Regime Change

Roger Lee Huang

Routledge
Taylor & Francis Group

LONDON AND NEW YORK

First published 2020
by Routledge
2 Park Square, Milton Park, Abingdon, Oxon OX14 4RN

and by Routledge
605 Third Avenue, New York, NY 10017

First issued in paperback 2022

Routledge is an imprint of the Taylor & Francis Group, an informa business

Publisher's Note
The publisher has gone to great lengths to ensure the quality of this reprint but points out that some imperfections in the original copies may be apparent.

British Library Cataloguing-in-Publication Data
A catalogue record for this book is available from the British Library

Library of Congress Cataloging-in-Publication Data
Names: Huang, Roger Lee, author.
Title: The paradox of Myanmar's regime change / Roger Lee Huang.
Description: NY : Routledge, 2020. | Includes bibliographical references
  and index.
Identifiers: LCCN 2019059779 | ISBN 9780367337971 (hardback) |
  ISBN 9780429322013 (ebook)
Subjects: LCSH: Regime change—Burma—21st century. | Political
  stability—Burma—21st century. | Democratization—Burma—21st
  century. | Authoritarianism—Burma—21st century. | Burma—Politics
  and government–21st century.
Classification: LCC JC489 .H83 2020 | DDC 320.9591—dc23
LC record available at https://lccn.loc.gov/2019059779

ISBN: 978-1-03-240011-2 (pbk)
ISBN: 978-0-367-33797-1 (hbk)
ISBN: 978-0-429-32201-3 (ebk)

DOI: 10.4324/9780429322013

Typeset in Times New Roman
by Apex CoVantage, LLC

Contents

Acknowledgments

The foundations of this book began nearly a decade ago at the end of my time working at Lingnan University, Hong Kong. My colleagues Brian Bridges and Baohui Zhang encouraged me to apply for the Hong Kong PhD Fellowship scheme, and thus began my journey into academic research. Kyaw Yin Hlaing and Jonathan London were instrumental in the early stages of developing my research for this project. I had the privilege of studying the political economy of Southeast Asia with Robert Taylor who shared interesting stories of his Myanmar adventures. Mark Thompson's supervision of my PhD was critical to the completion of my doctoral thesis, and thus in turn, this book. Mark ensured that I kept on track with my writing, and our conversations have helped me immensely in thinking critically about political regimes. I would also like to thank my colleagues Valerie Yap, Nadira Lamrad, Sarah Aubry, Brad Williams, Federico Ferrara, Nick Thomas, and Justin Robertson – who provided useful suggestions and feedback while I was at the City University of Hong Kong.

Win Ma Ma Aye, Nodoka Hasegawa, Peter Sai Hom Kham, and Martin Shin have always helped me in more ways than they know during my research trips in Myanmar. During my fieldwork, I was very lucky to meet Nay Lin Htike, who assisted with several important interviews. Many others, including Zin Mar Lwin, Sithu Pe Thein, Sai Kyaw Win, Mya Thet Titsar, Mya The Titsar, and Khin Zaw Win have been generous with their time, knowledge, and insight. I am extremely grateful to all interviewees, friends, and acquaintances for their trust to conduct interviews and for their patience with my questions.

Lee Jones and two anonymous reviewers provided useful critiques on an earlier draft of this book, and their reviews have undoubtedly helped to sharpen my analysis. John Buchanan meticulously read chapter seven and provided valuable comments. I am also grateful to my colleagues at Macquarie University for their support and encouragement, including Ben Schreer, Head of the Department of Security Studies and Criminology. The collegiality and kindness of my colleagues helped ensure the completion of this book through much needed distraction in the form of lunch and coffee breaks. Maryam Khalid, Alex Simpson, and Jonathan Symons have reviewed different parts of the manuscript and provided useful feedback. Jonathan Symons has also been a reliable barista, routinely offering me a decent cup of strong coffee. At Routledge, my thanks to Dorothea Schaefter, for supporting the book project, and Alexandra de Brauw, who made sure I kept on track with my manuscript.

Finally, this book would not have been possible without the love and support of my family. I am grateful to my parents who have always supported my academic interests. My partner Amy Barrow, and our daughter Sophia Huang, are my greatest cheerleaders, and I am lucky that they were willing to put up with my erratic schedule in the final stages of completing this book. I am extremely grateful to Amy, who despite her own academic endeavors has provided much needed emotional and intellectual support throughout the journey. All errors, oversimplifications, shortcomings, and views are, of course, mine alone.

Roger Lee Huang
Sydney, 2019

Acronyms and abbreviations

21UPC	21st Century Panglong
AA	Arakan Army
AAPP	Assistance Association for Political Prisoners (Burma)
ADB	Asian Development Bank
AFPFL	Anti-Fascist People's Freedom League
AI	Amnesty International
ANP	Arakan National Party
ARSA	Arakan Rohingya Salvation Army
ART	antiretroviral therapy
ASEAN	Association of Southeast Asian Nations
BCP	Burma Communist Party
BGF	Border Guard Force
BSPP	Burma Socialist Program Party
B4P	Business for Peace
CBO	community-based organization
CMEC	China-Myanmar Economic Corridor
CNPC	China National Petroleum Company
CPCS	Centre for Peace and Conflict Studies
DKBA	Democratic Karen Benevolent Army/ Democratic Karen Buddhist Army
EAO	ethnic armed organizations
EU	European Union
FESR	Framework for Economic and Social Reforms
FFM	The Independent International Fact-Finding Mission on Myanmar
GAD	General Administration Department
GDP	gross domestic product
GONGO	government organized non-governmental organization
HIV/AIDS	human immunodeficiency virus/acquired immunodeficiency syndrome
HRW	Human Rights Watch
ICESCR	International Covenant on Economic, Social and Cultural Rights

ICG	International Crisis Group
ICJ	International Court of Justice
IDP	internal displaced people
IFI	international financial institutions
IMET	International Military Education and Training
IMF	International Monetary Fund
INGO	international nongovernmental organization
KIA	Kachin Independence Army
KIO	Kachin Independence Organization
KKO	Klo Htoo Baw Karen Organization
KMT	Kuomintang/Chinese Nationalist Party
KNDO	Karen National Defense Organization
KNLA	Karen National Liberation Army
KNU	Karen National Union
LGBT	lesbian, gay, bisexual, and transgender
MEC	Myanmar Economic Corporation
MNDAA	Myanmar National Democratic Alliance Army
MNHRC	Myanmar National Human Rights Commission
MNLA	Mon National Liberation Army
MP	member of parliament
MPC	Myanmar Peace Center
NAM	Non-Aligned Movement
NCA	Nationwide Ceasefire Agreement
NDA-K	New Democratic Army-Kachin
NDF	National Democratic Force
NDSC	National Defense and Security Council
NGO	nongovernmental organization
NLD	National League for Democracy
NLM	New Light of Myanmar
NRPC	National Reconciliation Peace Centre
NUP	National Unity Party
ODA	official development assistance
OECD	Organization for Economic Cooperation and Development
PRC	People's Republic of China
RC	Revolutionary Council
RCSS	Restoration Council of Shan State
RFA	Radio Free Asia
RMB	renminbi
SLORC	State Law and Order Restoration Council
SME	small and medium enterprise
SNLD	Shan Nationalities League for Democracy
SOP	standard operating procedure
SPDC	State Peace and Development Council
TCG	Tripartite Core Group
TNLA	Ta'ang National Liberation Army

UEC	Union Election Commission
UK	United Kingdom of Great Britain and Northern Ireland
UMEHL	Union of Myanmar Economic Holdings Limited
UN	United Nations
UNHRC	United Nations Human Rights Council
UNODC	United Nations Office on Drugs and Crime
UNSC	United Nations Security Council
US	United States of America
USDA	Union Solidarity and Development Association
USDP	Union Solidarity and Development Party
UWSA	United Wa State Army
WB	World Bank

1 Introduction

Myanmar's puzzling transition

Ever since the military coup of 1962, Myanmar's *tatmadaw* (armed forces) has consistently deflected challenges to its rule and maintained repressive military control over the state apparatus. When the military-backed Burmese Socialist Program Party (BSPP) government (1962–1988)[1] collapsed at the height of anti-government protests in 1988, the result was an internal coup that returned the *tatmadaw* to the forefront of direct governance under the State Law and Restoration Council (SLORC), renamed as the State Peace and Development Council (SPDC) in 1997. During this prolonged period of direct military rule (1988–2011), the *tatmadaw* promised a multiparty "democratic" political system, while all the while expanding the military's capacity and scope both as an institution and as government. Despite the *tatmadaw*'s consolidation of power over the state apparatus and national politics, the military regime nevertheless continued to push a transitional plan for the "flourishing of a genuine, disciplined multi-party democratic system" (Ministry of Information 2008: 3). Following through with its seven-step roadmap to a disciplined democracy, first declared publicly in August 2003, the military junta voluntarily dissolved itself on March 30, 2011. The nominal election of the Union Solidarity and Development Party (USDP) government ended more than two decades of direct military rule. However, the first notionally elected president of the new "disciplined democracy" was Thein Sein, a recently retired general who had also happened to be the last prime minister of the SPDC.

Many critics initially perceived the military's seven-step roadmap to a disciplined democracy as a cosmetic attempt to disguise and civilianize military rule (i.e., Maung Zarni 2012). Yet, the dissolution of the SPDC led to real, albeit limited, regime change in post-junta Myanmar. In line with the military-drafted Constitution, new political institutions emerged during the Thein Sein's administration (2011–2016), leading to the diffusion of power, greater pluralism, and new opportunities for civilians to participate in formal politics (Kyaw Yin Hlaing 2012: 206–210). This military-driven regime transition has led a number of observers to suggest that the once highly authoritarian regime is undergoing what Samuel Huntington refers to as regime "transformation" (1991: 114; e.g., Ganesan 2017: 196). Other commentators observe that the elite-led "nascent democracy" (Holliday 2013: 100) is moving "beyond electoral authoritarianism" (Farrelly 2015).

Myanmar's so-called "democratization" gained further traction after the Thein Sein administration, in accordance with the 2008 Constitution, held a relatively fair general election on November 8, 2015. The result was a landslide electoral victory for Aung San Suu Kyi and the National League for Democracy (NLD). With the advent of a popularly elected NLD-led coalition government in 2016 under President Htin Kyaw,[2] a Suu Kyi loyalist, Myanmar entered a new era of genuine power sharing, albeit an asymmetrical relationship where the military is constitutionally guaranteed expansive powers including institutional autonomy, free from civilian oversight.

The 2015 election marked the first time since the 1962 coup that a military outsider had been able to hold the country's top office and form a government in conjunction with the *tatmadaw*. Just days after the start of the new NLD-dominated parliament, a fast-tracked bill established a new post of State Counsellor and appointed NLD leader Aung San Suu Kyi to the post. The new post circumvented constitutional restrictions barring Aung San Suu from the presidency, while giving her prime minister-like powers as the *de facto* head of the civilian government. Despite the military's protest against the bill, the NLD's defiance did not lead to the *tatmadaw* unraveling the disciplined democratic system of its own design. Myanmar's regime change therefore cannot simply be explained as "the menu" for institutional manipulation to sustain authoritarian rule (Schedler 2002). While under the military's disciplined democracy, the army remains independently powerful with control of the security apparatus, in the civilian sphere of politics, the elected NLD leads the executive and legislative branches of government.

Robert Taylor, an expert on Myanmar's political economy, has consistently argued that there is a "long-term continuity and logic to the course taken by the military" (2012a: 221). That is, the military has consistently viewed itself as being the responsible, non-partisan guardian and builder of the contemporary Myanmar state (Taylor 2009: 498). Even under the "greatly liberalized political atmosphere" in post-junta Myanmar, Taylor maintains that there is "more continuity than change in Myanmar's political system" (Taylor 2013: 394–395). If one considers the *tatmadaw*'s rule as being uninterrupted since 1962,[3] Myanmar's military regime has lasted for nearly half a century, and remains to this day only partially civilianized. Why then would the powerful *tatmadaw*, coming from a position of strength, voluntarily dissolve the junta in 2011, and critically, allow its political adversary to form a government in 2016? Further, is Taylor's account of continuity rather than change accurate, given that since the implementation of the country's new Constitution in 2011, there have been dramatic policy reversals and a genuine sharing of power between elected civilians and the military?

Regime change fundamentally concerns the reconfiguration of political power, and the transformation of existing institutions or the creation of new ones. Under the military's disciplined democracy, new political institutions have been established, while the political role of an existing one – the *tatmadaw* – is institutionalized by the new Constitution. Post-junta Myanmar is no longer the same type of repressive, highly authoritarian military regime of its recent past. The relatively rapid changes taking place since 2011, in particular the ascent of the NLD opposition into government following a relatively fair[4] 2015 general election, has been characterized by some observers as a "failure of authoritarian learning" (Dukalskis and Raymond 2018). This line of reasoning assumes that the post-junta reforms have superseded the transitional plan of the *ancien régime*, with the military effectively losing control of the political processes. Therefore in this view, Myanmar as a "hybrid regime," with the co-existence of democratic practices and the old legacy of authoritarian military politics is assumed to be an ongoing, incomplete process of democratic transition (Egreteau 2016: 15).

This book challenges this conventional democratization account. It argues that the liberalization of socio-political space during the Thein Sein years can best be understood as a non-democratic regime transition that has thus far followed a trial-and-error regime logic, shaped by the corporate interests and vision of the *tatmadaw*. The advent of the NLD-led administration in 2016 may not be the preferred or expected outcome of the military designers, yet it does not signal the beginning of democratization. Myanmar's unconventional political trajectory may have allowed outsiders access to the corridors of power, yet politicians can only access the civilian sphere of politics that the military has voluntarily relinquished direct control of. By design, the *tatmadaw*'s disciplined democracy is a *bona fide* hybrid regime. Therefore, any political actor that wishes to engage in and participate in formal politics must abide by the military's pre-determined rules of the game, as set out by the military-drafted Constitution. The *tatmadaw* remain the final arbiters of decisions and powers related to the structural foundations of Myanmar's disciplined democracy

Regime change under the Thein Sein administration (2011–2016)

For over two decades, the *tatmadaw* ruled over Myanmar as a highly authoritarian military regime, where formal regime power was monopolized by a small group of high ranking military officials with a clear hierarchical chain of command (Kyaw Yin Hlaing 2008: 163–173). Socio-political pluralism was exceptionally limited, and the repressive government did not tolerate public dissent. Prior to the dissolution of the SPDC, Freedom House described Myanmar in 2011 as one of the "worst of the worst" regimes, where citizens were denied even the most basic civil and political rights. After more than two decades of direct junta rule however, the military imposed a restructuring of its regime, and through a deeply flawed electoral process installed a new hybrid civilian–military government under the notionally elected Thein Sein presidency in 2011.

From the onset of his presidency, Thein Sein signaled that politics under the new government would be different from its recent repressive past. At his inaugural address, President Thein Sein signaled a renegotiation of state-societal relations. Thein Sein not only spoke positively about the role of non-state actors but also openly appealed for civic participation and assistance from intellectuals, NGOs, and even international organizations, to contribute to the development of a modern, democratic Myanmar (*NLM* 2011a). This immediate tonal shift would later help shape Thein Sein's reputation both domestically and abroad as a reformist president, with one foreign correspondent dubbing him as the "listener-in-chief" (Robinson 2013). Many observers and activists at the time were convinced that the new government would indeed govern differently, and their faith seemed justified when Thein Sein unilaterally suspended the controversial Myitsone Dam on September 30, 2011, ostensibly as a response to public demand (Interviews and discussions with activists in 2012). The China-backed hydro-electricity project had long faced opposition from affected communities, as well as from a small circle of environmentalists. However, it was only in the more relaxed political environment under new administration that activists became emboldened to mobilize a nationwide "Save the Ayeyarwady," anti-Myitsone Dam campaign (Chan 2017: 680–683).

Within a year of the implementation of the military's disciplined democracy, the Thein Sein administration has pushed through a series of legal reforms, which significantly altered state-societal relations. Many basic civil and political liberties, long denied to Myanmar citizens, were suddenly legal and tolerated. Citizens begin to form labor unions, participate in industrial actions, and mobilize in protest against unpopular government decisions. Previously taboo subjects – talk of human rights, public discussion of politics, and criticism of the government – became acceptable, albeit within limits. The new government also introduced economic reforms to encourage foreign investments and private sector growth. The liberalization of the telecommunications sector significantly changed how the general populace accessed and exchanged information. By the latter half of 2011, a series of presidential amnesties had released hundreds of political prisoners (Nakanishi 2013: 314). In early 2013, the government also created the Remaining Political Prisoner Scrutiny Committee to address the issue of political prisoners, leading to the President's (dubious) declaration at the end of the same year that political prisoners no longer remain incarcerated (Mathieson 2015).[5] The viability and credibility of disciplined democracy was further bolstered by Aung San Suu Kyi's entry into parliament after the April 2012 by-election. This development convinced many observers that Myanmar was on a trajectory toward democratic transition.[6] By the end of Thein Sein's tenure, socio-political space has expanded significantly, with partisan politics normalized and the country's international reputation largely rehabilitated. The military backed Thein Sein administration evidently felt comfortable enough with the socio-political changes, that it oversaw a relatively fair and open electoral contest in 2015. This allowed the longtime opposition to win in a landslide, and the formation of the NLD-led government, thus further demonstrating that Myanmar was certainly no longer the same type of regime of yesteryear.

Myanmar's perplexing regime change

Regime change is a complicated issue that has been one of the most challenging puzzles explored in the social sciences (Bermeo 1990; Bunce 1995; O'Donnell and Schmitter 1986; Teorell 2010). Despite the wealth of literature, political scientists often find themselves unable to sufficiently explain – let alone predict – the rise, fall, and evolution of political regimes (Howard and Walters 2014). In particular, Myanmar's unusually durable military authoritarianism has long been characterized as an anomaly in the so-called era of democracy (Kyaw Yin Hlaing 2009). It is generally assumed that when the military foray into the realm of formal politics and direct governance beyond its defensive duties, they often fragment into distinct cliques, forming centrifugal forces that lead to the ultimate collapse of the military regime. That is why military regimes are considered the least durable type of non-democratic regimes (Geddes et al. 2014: 159). The *tatmadaw* however, has long dominated Myanmar's politics, and even after enduring several internal purges, which have at times included the removal of senior members and whole branches of the *tatmadaw*, the military continues to maintain its institutional unity and remains the most coherent political force in the country (Win Min 2008b: 1018–1037).

The speed and direction of liberalization introduced under the civilianized Thein Sein government has been described by Dan Slater as a "sudden transformation" that has caught some scholars, policymakers, and the popular press by surprise (Slater 2014: 172). Although the civilianization of military governments, and the return of the military to the barracks is by itself not a unique phenomenon, the case of Myanmar stands out, as it is a top-down initiated, planned voluntary regime change that has been undertaken by a remarkably unified military regime, from a position of strength. Conventional explanations such as internal pressure (elite defection, factionalism within the state, a restive society that could challenge regime survival) or exogenous shocks (international pressure or threats, societal mobilization against the state, natural disasters) fail to explain the rationale behind the elite-led transformation in Myanmar (Taylor 2013; Jones 2014b, 2015).

Prior to the advent of Thein Sein's presidency in 2011, most political science literature on Myanmar was generally pessimistic about the chances of regime transition, or change. For example, much has been written about the persistence of military rule over the state apparatus (Callahan 2009; ICG 2001), and by most pre-2011 accounts, the prospects for regime change in Myanmar, especially with a weak, factionalized opposition appeared bleak (Casper and Taylor 1996: 88–90; Kyaw Yin Hlaing 2008).

In the aftermath of the so-called 2007 "Saffron Revolution," Win Min, an expert on the Myanmar military, suggested that after the 2010 elections, military hardliners were expected to hold on to power, and the SPDC leaders Than Shwe and Maung Aye would likely remain as active members of the *tatmadaw* (2008a: 45). Since the dissolution of the SPDC in 2011, neither retired generals remain in government. Sussane Prager-Nyein (2009) correctly argued that the 2008 Constitution and the 2010 general election would allow the *tatmadaw* to institutionalize its dominant role over its state and society, but she assumed this would come at the expanse of "shrinking citizenry." These earlier works provided excellent accounts of why the *tatmadaw* remains in control and is resistant to change, but their focus was to explain authoritarian durability, and as such, they did not account for the rationale behind regime change in the absence of any exogenous shocks or regime failures.

The limits of democratization theory and Myanmar's regime change

Given the significant reconfiguration of political power following the advent of the NLD government in 2016, most observers have explained post-junta politics from the perspective of democratization theory (e.g., Barany 2018; Egreteau 2016; Kipgen 2016; Ganesan 2017). As an extension of the ideological debates from the Cold War, democratization theory often conceptualizes regimes based on two broadly polarized ideal-types – ones that are authoritarian or authoritarian-leaning as opposed to their more liberal-leaning democratic counterparts (Schmitter and Karl 1991). In the democratic transitions literature, the process of change is generally examined as a linear transition from an authoritarian form of governance to a more "democratic" one (Gans-Morse 2004).

This book challenges the applicability of this theory to Myanmar and argues that the end of direct military rule does not make Myanmar a democracy in transition. The main limitation of the democratization literature is the way in which regimes that choose to liberalize are conceptualized as pursuing democratization, while regimes that persist with authoritarian rule are seen as anomalies in the "an age of democratization" (Brownlee 2007). This democratic transitions approach reduces regime change to two opposite poles and conceptualizes regime change as a linear process. The transitions paradigm perpetuates the view that when autocrats liberalize they are necessarily moving their regimes toward democratization, and that any illiberal backsliding during the transition should be understood as democratic regression. In this manner, democratization studies view durable authoritarian regimes as puzzles; but their preoccupation with understanding why these non-democratic regimes have failed to democratize do not sufficiently explain what is actually transpiring when authoritarian regimes liberalize without "democratization" (Albrecht and Schlumberger 2004). By assuming and categorizing regimes as either "liberal and democratic" or "illiberal and authoritarian," much of the nuance of the regime change process and the actual nature of the state and regimes is lost in the polarizing lens of democratization theory.

Although since 2011, the *tatmadaw* has significantly liberalized its political system, it never intended to introduce a "Western-style" liberal democracy. The dissolution of the military regime, and the partial transferal of power to a hybrid civilian–military coalition government is "Myanmar's way to Democracy," akin to the *tatmadaw*'s previous attempt to implement the Burmese way to Socialism (Huang 2017: 28). In this sense characterizing Myanmar's transition to a self-proclaimed disciplined democratic system as a process of democratization is a normative, teleological, and unsatisfying explanation.

In the absence of any identifiable "shocks" to the SPDC, many analysts have abandoned structural and institutional explanations and have instead relied on the agency of political elites to explain how reforms are unfolding in Myanmar. In one of the first articles published about post-junta politics, Kyaw Yin Hlaing, a former advisor to President Thein Sein suggested that a group of liberal-minded reformists within the government was critically leading the country in its "early stages of democratization" (2012: 206–210). Similarly, Tin Maung Maung Than, commenting on the 2012 by-elections, suggested that "personalities" will likely trump "institutions" as Myanmar continues to liberalize (2012). Marie Lall also agrees broadly with this elite-agency account, crediting Thein Sein as instrumental in pushing for a "more inclusive participatory "democratisation process" by working with civil society actors and organizations, and reconciling with Aung San Suu Kyi and the NLD (Lall 2016: 6–7, 71–73)

This "elite pact" explanation has also been popular among many seasoned Myanmar observers as well as journalists (Callahan and Steinberg 2012: 2, Egreteau 2016: 15; Fuller 2012; Osnos 2012). Popularized by the classic work of scholars such as Guillermo O'Donnell, Philippe Schmitter, and Laurence Whitehead, the "elite pact" literature argues that democratization can occur when ruling elites create political openings (1986: 48). This literature defines an elite pact as

> an explicit, but not always publicly explicated or justified, agreement among a select set of actors which seeks to define (or, better, to redefine) rules governing the exercise of power on the basis of mutual guarantees for the "vital interests" of those entering into it.
>
> (O'Donnell et al. 1986: 37)

Regime change is assumed to have taken place when the political establishment and their challengers compromise and agree to this "pacted transition." Exceptional leadership skills are sometimes considered vital to a successful transition, but more often, the emphasis is on the process of bargaining and elite negotiations between soft-liners and hardliners within and between the establishment and their challengers (Przeworski 1991: 105–153).

According to many observers, the historic meeting between Thein Sein and Aung San Suu Kyi on August 19, 2011 marked the beginnings of an elite pact (Callahan and Steinberg 2012: 2). The widely reported meeting was peppered with highly symbolic images, which suggested to most observers that the government was serious about fostering a different type of politics. An official portrait released by the state media placed Thein Sein and Aung San Suu Kyi next to one another, as equals. Between the two leaders, a portrait of Aung San was featured prominently in the background. This was particularly meaningful, given that for decades the junta had proscribed all images of Aung San Suu Kyi and deliberately limited references to Aung San in the public space.[7] Months after the initial meeting, the Thein Sein government would actively amend the party registration law in time for the NLD to re-register, compete, and win the April 2012 by-elections by a landslide. With Aung San Suu Kyi now a new parliamentarian in Myanmar's disciplined democracy, it was sufficient to convince the broader Western-centric community that Myanmar was undergoing "democratization," demonstrated by the normalization of US-Myanmar relations a few months after the election (Bünte and Dosch 2015: 12–13). *Foreign Policy* magazine also recognized Thein Sein along with Aung San Suu Kyi as the top "Global Thinkers" of 2012. Even the International Crisis Group (ICG) awarded the former general a peace prize in 2013.

Focus on the actions of elite actors is a particularly favorable approach among scholars who document and explain the Thein Sein administration's reformist agenda (2011–2016). Kyaw Yin Hlaing (2012) discusses the role of soft-liners ousting their more conservative colleagues within the USDP, in particular focusing on the efforts of Thein Sein and Shwe Mann, the speaker of the lower house, in ensuring that the new government did not simply "function like its predecessor" (*ibid*: 209). Marie Lall credits the instrumental role of Thein Sein in winning "an epic battle of wills . . . between reformers and the hardliners" during the first parliamentary recess in the summer of 2011 (2016: 65). This is a view supported by Renaud Egreteau, who argues that subsequent negotiations between an elite circle of military and civilian elites "allowed the transitional process to unfold a few years" later, paving way to the 2015 general elections (2016: 15). In his opinion the "procedural transition," into what he refers to as "caretaking democratization," became possible only after a group of retired, high ranking SPDC officials agreed to an "incomplete and fragile 'pact,'" therefore opening up the space for the "vast enterprise of political change" (*ibid*: 5; 20–21).

This is indeed the common perception among many who have engaged personally with these political elites. For example, one keen observer of Myanmar politics commented that Shwe Mann must have had a real "desire to change," although he admits this is strange, given that Shwe Mann was previously the third highest ranking official in the repressive SPDC government (Interview with a veteran Yangon-based journalist, January 22, 2014). Nyo Ohn Myint, a former anti-military activist, explained that many former dissidents returned to Myanmar and worked with the Thein Sein government because they believed in the sincerity of the President's reformist agenda (Interview on January 6, 2014; this is an opinion that is shared by a large majority of the interviewees that I spoke with between 2011 and 2015). Even scholars, who disagreed with the "elite pact" narrative, nevertheless continue to repeat the mantras of the transitions paradigm, suggesting that an elite compromise would be the most viable path for Myanmar's democratization (Diamond 2012; Kipgen 2016: 153–154).

Clearly, elite agency plays a vital role in any political change: the retirement of the junta's top two leaders Than Shwe and Maung Aye, and the succession of Thein Sein as the first "civilian" president in post-SPDC Myanmar is necessary to explain the timing of regime transition (Taylor 2013: 396–397). However, the first post-junta government was staffed with the same regime players that were already in the top echelon of the preceding SPDC regime, and there is no evidence to suggest that these "new" leaders under the first post-junta government were intrinsically liberalizers or reformers who had previously merely put up with the repressive policies of their SPDC superiors. Surprisingly, in these elite-centric pacted transitions literature, there has also been a lack of critical analysis on the role of the Commander-in-Chief Min Aung Hlaing, the top representative of the *tatmadaw*.

I argue that the agency of the reformist elites only became possible *after* the dissolution of the military junta, following the relaxation of several structural constraints that had long discouraged socio-political pluralism. Even if there was a "desire to change" within some factions of the military leadership, Myanmar's regime transition is not the product of an "elite pact." Within the *tatmadaw*, there is no evidence of elite defection or fragmentation that led to the regime insiders to compromise with regime challengers. This also explains why Shwe Mann and his allies, the so-called liberals who had worked together with the executive branch in the early Thein Sein years, were forcefully expelled from USDP leadership positions in 2015, after Shwe Mann repeatedly threatened the interests of the *tatmadaw* (Htoo Thant and Swan Ye Htut 2016).

Clearly, the NLD's participation in the military-led political process is a significant departure from the half a century in which the military maintained authoritarian control of the formal powers of the state. The NLD's ascent to government in 2016 was certainly unpredictable even in the final SPDC/SLORC years. However, when re-examining the basic political positions of the USDP and NLD, the elite pact thesis is not convincing. For years, one of the NLD's key demands has been for the military to recognize the 1990 electoral results and transfer power to the NLD. Throughout her time as opposition leader during the SLORC/SPDC years (1988–2011), Aung San Suu Kyi consistently rejected the *tatmadaw*'s political legitimacy and rebuffed the military's Constitution and its seven-step roadmap to a disciplined democracy. In 2010, the NLD refused to re-register as a legal political party and boycotted the general elections.[8] Therefore, Aung San Suu Kyi's decision to re-register and participate in the 2012 by-elections, and to join parliament, were all reversals of the opposition's previously held positions.

Through these reversals, the NLD legitimized the military's "disciplined democracy" and accepted the military's rules of the game, which include the constitutional protection of a set of undemocratic military privileges. Beyond facilitating the NLD's return to the legal fold and participate in disciplined democracy, the pro-military establishment has not sought to amend the constitution to dismantle the expansive political role of the *tatmadaw*.

In short, the NLD has had to compromise and accept the limits to their electoral, partisan powers as dictated by the *tatmadaw*'s version of "democracy." Although regime outsiders have now been allowed to join as coalition partners in a joint civilian–military government, they still do not have any real bargaining powers to negotiate the further retreat of the military from politics, which would require fundamental institutional changes beginning with the amendment of the 2008 Constitution. The entry of the opposition into partial position of power is therefore not indicative of an elite pact. Rather, the NLD have been strategically co-opted, turning their role as potential spoilers to disciplined democracy, into one of recognized players working within the parameters of the new hybrid regime.

Myanmar post-2011 regime transformation is the product of a long planned unilateral decision made by the military establishment. Post-SPDC politics is not the product of a successful liberal-minded faction overcoming the control of the more conservative elements of the military leadership, nor is it the story of sophisticated democrats overcoming their former military oppressors. President Thein Sein and his allies may be the key actors driving the post-2011 reforms, yet the "timing and nature" leading to the government change "is not dictated by incumbent elites alone" (Jones 2014b: 784).

In any case, as Valerie Bunce argues, elite action should not be solely viewed as the result of political agency, as there are underlying structural reasons which cannot be explained based purely on the actions of individuals and their personal preferences (2000: 707–710). Were we to focus only on this moment of change (i.e., politics after 2011), and key personalities, this would capture only a "snapshot" of institutional change and may overstate the role of elite agency in regime change without considering the fact that social processes are gradual and unfold over time (Pierson 2004; Mahoney and Thelen 2010).

In a democratic regime, popularly elected civilians in general, should have control over political decisions, while the military's role should be limited to policy implementation and operation. This is not the case under Myanmar's disciplined democratic system. In Myanmar's disciplined democracy, the Constitution highlights the importance of the military in affairs of the state. Not only are they guaranteed permanent political positions in both the executive and legislative branches of government, the armed forces also have independent powers, free from civilian oversight. Under Myanmar's disciplined democracy, irrespective of the legitimacy and outcome of elections, the Constitution enforces a civilian–military coalition government, where the military still holds decisive powers in matters of national security. Further, there is also a growing consensus among democratization theorists and advocates that democracy should be understood, as more than just the existence of electoral, multiparty politics; democratic regimes should also embrace greater respect for transparency, human rights, and a strong civic culture (Carothers 1994; Hollyer et al. 2011). These important features of a liberal democracy continue to be wanting in Myanmar, even after the advent of the popularly elected National League for Democracy (NLD) government in 2016 (David and Holliday 2018: 98). In short, post-2011 political developments in Myanmar is not "democratization."

Soft authoritarianism, hybrid regimes, and the regime survival thesis

The initial optimism that the NLD-led government would lead to greater liberal socio-political reforms has never materialized, leading many observers to turn away from the democratization narrative and suggest that Myanmar's violent "colonial and military oppression," (Wells 2018: 13) is failing the "new democracy" (Fisher 2017; Pedersen 2019; Ibrahim 2018).

Political scientists have been compelled to reexamine these "illiberal democracies" that are liberalizing without democratizing. They have sought to describe them via new terms such as "hybrid regimes," "electoral authoritarianism," and "soft authoritarianism" (Bunce 2000: 732; Diamond 2002; Brownlee 2009; Zakaria 1997). In the emerging soft authoritarianism subfield, scholars typically argue that liberalizing authoritarian regimes may adopt the language of democrats and allow greater liberty; however, limited political liberalization is not intended as a step toward genuine democratization (Brownlee 2007: 9; Levitsky and Way 2002: 54–55). For these observers, authoritarian's elections, including Myanmar's elections since the military came to power in 1962, have predominantly been motivated by the regime's interest to legitimize and, to a lesser extent, manage its rule (Morgenbesser 2016: 87–88).

As Milan W. Svolik argues, the introduction of "democratic" institutions, such as the establishment of legislatures, political parties, and elections, allows dictators to co-opt the "most capable and opportunistic" citizens, strengthen the regime, and help "serve quintessentially authoritarian ends" (2012: 13). In other words, liberalizing authoritarian regimes are an innately different kind of regime from democracies, as they do not allow any meaningful sharing of power from those outside the political establishment (*ibid*: 23–24). The central premise of "soft authoritarian" literature is that the autocrats' decision to liberalize is a reaction to societal discontent and public pressure, external challenges, and international influence (Svolik 2012: 4; Brownlee 2007: 32).

Not unlike the democratic transitions literature, the soft authoritarianism literature suggests that non-democratic regimes undertake socio-political reforms for the purpose of regime survival in response to prolonged socio-political crisis, with the intention of re-affirming the connection between the political establishment and their support base or co-opting some regime challengers into the regime. The aim is not to revolutionize the existing power structure nor surrender power to regime outsiders (Tanneberg et al. 2013; Schedler 2002: 36). It is assumed that by liberalizing some aspects of the regime, this would allow the survival of their regimes, and delay (or deny) democratization (Albrecht and Schlumberger 2004). Under this model, "hybrid regimes" may lose control of the transition process and face collapse, but only when the political establishment is unable to maintain elite cohesion, thus leading to political "defections and instability" (Brownlee 2007: 32).

There is a general consensus that the army's constitution was designed specifically to institutionalize the political role of the military in Myanmar (Bünte 2014; Croissant and Kamerling 2013). However, given that regime outsiders can access political power through electoral politics, some scholars have positioned Myanmar's regime development as a transition into "electoral authoritarianism" (MacDonald 2013; Farrelly 2015), "illiberal democracy" (Naing Ko 2018: 36), or limited liberal democracy (David and Holliday 2018: 201). For Adam MacDonald, Myanmar's transition to electoral authoritarianism reasserts the "primacy of the old order" (MacDonald 2013: 21). Others have suggested that the transition is a "transformative bargain" to "placate" the political opposition (Chambers 2014: 118), or a calculated strategy for a renegotiation of state-societal relations under a diminished authoritarian regime (Huang 2013: 258).

The basic assumption of these authors is undoubtedly accurate: the partial liberalization of Myanmar's political regime is a form of regime maintenance. The idea that Myanmar is turning into some form of hybrid regime or electoral authoritarianism may help to explain political developments following the advent of the nominally civilianized Thein Sein government in 2011, but it does not offer a convincing rationale explaining the military's partial withdrawal from politics. The hybrid/soft authoritarianism literature largely assumes that any change in power dynamics is a reaction by regime elites to counter institutional failures or to negotiate a peaceful transferal of power in pursuit of elites' self-preservation.

This literature therefore does not provide a compelling account of why the powerful SPDC, in the absence of any credible threats to its survival, elected to dissolve itself in 2011. Further, it also does not explain why the Thein Sein government and the military sanctioned a relatively fair electoral process in 2015, which allowed the victorious NLD opposition the right to control both houses of parliament, as well as to secure election of the country's first NLD President. Alexander Dukalskis and Christopher Raymond's explanation for example, that the NLD's electoral victory reflects the "failure of authoritarian learning," simply does not account for the logic and rationale of the military's disciplined democratic system (Dukalskis and Raymond 2018: 545–546). Myanmar's new constitutional order may not be a liberal democracy, but it has also moved beyond the concept of soft authoritarianism, as citizens are not only passively consenting "to the legitimacy of the regime" (Nasir and Turner 2013: 340) but rather regime outsiders have been granted partial access to formal politics and power via the polls. The decision to transform from a pure military junta into a hybrid military-civilian government with features of democratic politics is not merely a strategy for regime survival; the military hierarchy has not "lost" control of the "transition" process, nor has there been an effective elite defection leading to regime collapse. The NLD opposition's 2015 electoral victory and their ascent into government in 2016 may not have been the preferred outcome of the military establishment, yet these political changes are in line with the transitional plan and design of the *tatmadaw*. The reconfiguration of power may have changed the dynamics of the regime, yet the basic rules of the game of the military's disciplined democracy remain intact.

Democratic transitions theory and soft authoritarianism literature's reliance on elite choice and calculation from the perspective of regime survival does not consider the importance of ideas, identity, and the broader institutions that shaped and governed the rationale behind non-democratic, yet genuine regime changes. Although material interests and a desire to maintain power certainly are critical factors in the calculation of the military establishment, serious consideration must be given to the *tatmadaw*'s institutional identity as self-prescribed guardians of Myanmar's nation-state. The power sharing arrangement between elected civilians and unelected military is the disciplined democracy as planned by the *tatmadaw*. This hybridism therefore is a partially civilianized, diminished authoritarian regime. There might be some democratic features and a partially elected government, yet the special prerogatives reserved for a powerful and unelected military demonstrates that Myanmar remains a non-democratic regime.

Endogenous theory of regime change: the military's interests remain key

Given that exogenous shocks or external factors cannot explain the cause of Myanmar's voluntary regime change, we might presume that the key to understanding Myanmar's perplexing regime change lies in endogenous, evolutionary factors (Taylor 2012b). Many analysts therefore have focused on the role and interests of the military institution to explain this transitional process. Aurel Croissant and Jil Kamerling explain that the new constitutional order institutionalizes military dominance and allows for power-sharing arrangements among the ruling elites (2013: 121). This parallels the view of Marco Bünte, who argues that the new "quasi-military rule" addresses internal pressures by allowing a smooth generational change in the military leadership (2014: 756).

Although Lee Jones does not reject the premise of the institutionalization of military dominance argument, he argues that this explanation does not address the "transition's timing or substance" (2014b: 782–783). Jones rejects the *sui generis* argument as suggested by some scholars and suggests that Myanmar's disciplined democracy parallels other cases of military withdrawal from politics (2014b: 795). Citing an older literature on military regimes, Jones points out that military juntas generally position themselves as interim governments and often hand over power to reliable civilian partners once they have addressed the crisis that purportedly led them to directly intervene in politics in the first place (*ibid*: 783). From the perspective of the military, partisan politics have long been impotent when addressing the "centrifugal forces" driven by center-peripheral conflicts and ethnic separatist movements, which threatened the territorial integrity and stability of the Myanmar state (*ibid*: 785). Two decades of intensified state building under the SLORC/SPDC ensured that the military has expanded the state's reach into the ethnic borderlands and with an enhanced coercive ability to ensure the *de jure* territorial integrity of the Myanmar state. Satisfied that it has control over the country's political economy, and confident that it has a failsafe Constitution that will protect its ideological and corporate interests, the *tatmadaw* leadership therefore allowed the "transition" to a disciplined democracy (*ibid*: 795–796).

This book argues that the key to understanding Myanmar's regime transition lies in understanding the character and nature of the *tatmadaw* both as an institution and as a government. The decision to voluntary dissolve the SPDC ruling junta, and the transition to its version of democracy therefore should not be understood as merely a regime survival technique. Although the disciplined democracy seeks to institutionalize the dominant role of the military in any future governments, the soft authoritarianism literature does not fully account for the fact that regime outsiders have genuine access to partial state and political power. In other words, the NLD, long considered challengers of the military regime, has now, by accepting the rules of the game of a disciplined democracy, been co-opted as part of this hybrid civilian–military regime. The regime transition in post-2011 Myanmar is a genuine (if limited) regime change, which has followed a trial and error process that led to this type of regime maintenance.

Background, methodology, and purpose of the book

The book grew out of a doctoral thesis developed from 2011 to 2016, which included over 100 qualitative research interviews conducted with multiple stakeholders in Myanmar during six separate field trips from the early stages of quasi-civilian rule in 2011 to the general election in November 2015. These interviews provide a series of "compelling narratives" rather than "final truths" (Silverman 1994: 114). These individual narratives, of both elite and grassroots actors, are not intended to quantify the impact of regime change other than exploring perceptions of what factors have influenced regime change, as well as considering what type of regime Myanmar is transitioning from and to. This is not to diminish the value of these perspectives, which are likely to be shaped by stakeholders' understandings (Kenny 1994: 1) of the role of the political parties, civil society, international actors, as well as the military establishment. Importantly, these narratives enrich existing research on Myanmar's military regime by providing a more nuanced understanding of the determinants of Myanmar's regime transition, which is informed by multiple stakeholder perspectives.

In the early stages of the fieldwork, Kyaw Yin Hlaing and some students of Myanmar Egress, a prominent capacity training organization, connected me with several different civil society actors. In addition, I have maintained contacts from my time as an intern with United Nations Office on Drugs and Crime (UNODC) from August 2006 to February 2007. Through a process of snowball sampling, I was able to conduct both formal and informal interviews, as well as discussions with a variety of interviewees during a series of field visits to Myanmar. Most of the interviews were conducted in Yangon, the commercial center and the largest city in Myanmar. However, several interviews were also conducted in Mandalay, Naypyidaw, Bangkok, and Hong Kong. My interviewees include a wide variety of key actors including civil servants and ex-military officers, local and international NGO staff, local and international journalists, activists, consultants, academics, diplomats, entrepreneurs, politicians, lawyers, and other professionals, who are either involved in or have important insights about the regime and current reforms.

When possible, and with the permission of the interviewees, some interviews were audio recorded. Over the course of the field research, informants were increasingly open to the idea of being audio-recorded with more informants agreeing to be recorded in the latter stages of the research, a few years after reforms began. This also suggests that people had become much more comfortable and outspoken in the liberalized environment of post-SPDC Myanmar.

The in-depth, semi-structured interviews are supplemented by firsthand observations and informal conversations with a wide range of individuals. These conversations often took place, for example during my various taxi rides, where drivers sometimes shared information about their livelihood, as well as their opinions on the political developments in the country, the progress of the reforms, as well as on key political personalities – especially figures such as Aung San Suu Kyi, Thein Sein, Shwe Mann, and Than Shwe. Although these discussions do not inform the main theoretical analysis, they do provide some anecdotal examples of popular attitudes and sentiments about political developments in the country. Further, these conversations are an important reminder of how open Myanmar is now compared to my own experiences living in Yangon in 2006 under highly repressive conditions. Prior to 2011, it was extremely rare for ordinary citizens to publicly express their opinions and personal views to foreigners, particularly on issues that touched upon the *tatmadaw* or politics.

While in the field, I also attended as many events as possible and observed events firsthand as they developed. I attended information seminars, report launches, press conferences, political party events and meetings, capacity training classes, and social gatherings with Myanmar activists. I have also visited interviewees at their houses and offices, as well as in local teashops, cafes, and restaurants. During these informal meetings and gatherings, I was able to freely exchange ideas and observed firsthand the sentiments of the informants. Some of these unplanned, informal, but in-depth conversations have also been recorded in my field notes.

On Election Day 2015, I hired a car and, accompanied by some friends and informants, traveled around Yangon to observe the polls informally. Through the interpretation of a Burmese friend, I was able to chat with some Union Election Commission (UEC) staff and volunteers, and I also engaged with a few voters to listen to their views on the election. In one case, a male voter approached me and asked me to "watch the ballot," as he did not seem to trust the process. However, most of the electorates I observed were patient and enthusiastic about participating in the polls. I also witnessed several elderly voters that were assisted by their friends or family and UEC staff to cast their ballots. Overall, the UEC staff appeared welcoming and did not question or challenge my presence observing the elections, and I did not enter the actual voting area reserved for voters. However, in two polling centers, a few UEC individuals were more hesitant and unsure about our presence at the polling center, and in one case in Insein Township, we were not allowed to approach closer to the polling center. Overall, given that I was not an official, government sanctioned electoral observer, I was able to have remarkable access to witness the voting at a reasonable distance. All in all, we were able to observe more than ten polls, including downtown areas, neighborhoods with a high concentration of Muslim voters, as well as two polling sites in the Insein suburbs. Throughout Election Day, and in the aftermath of the voting, I made several visits to the NLD Headquarters to observe the reaction of NLD supporters during the counting of the polls, which lasted a few days after the election on November 8, 2015.

After the election, I also attended the international press briefings by two key international observation teams – the European Union Election Observation Mission and the Carter Center.

Since returning from the field, I have maintained regular contact with several informants through email exchanges and social media (Facebook in particular). I have continued to follow developments through monitoring prominent Myanmar-focused news websites such as the *Myanmar Times, The Global New Light of Myanmar, The Irrawaddy, Democratic Voice of Burma*, and *Mizzima News*, among others. This allows me to keep up to date and informed about important developments in Myanmar.

In addition to these qualitative interviews, the book brings together the major literature on Myanmar's political development to offer a systematic overview of ongoing regime transition in Myanmar. The book analyzes key scholarship, reports, critical documents, and news articles on Myanmar, and it builds upon existing regime-centric theory – that is democratic transitions, soft authoritarianism, and military regime theories – to provide an explanation of Myanmar's non-democratic regime change. In particular, the book adopts a historical institutionalist approach, given that there is a growing consensus that structural variables, particularly political and economic institutions, may provide better explanations of the origins of political order, as well as how historical institutional arrangements may help explain political change (Acemoglu and Robinson 2012; Mahoney and Thelen 2010).

With regard to the study of Myanmar under the SLORC/SPDC, there is a general agreement that an institutional equilibrium has been established under the *tatmadaw* tutelage, thus most Myanmar specialists have long utilized structural conditions to explain the stability of Myanmar's military authoritarian regime (Kyaw Yin Hlaing 2009; Taylor 2009). Given the seemingly perplexing reversal of policy direction since 2011 and genuine, albeit conditional liberalization of the country's repressive politics, much of the first wave of scholarship examining post-2011 changes has abandoned structural accounts and has instead turned to elite-focused, agency-centric explanations to study Myanmar's recent political developments. Although these narratives certainly give us insight on the agency of the stakeholders in the reform process, they do not sufficiently explain the broader structural conditions that allow the reconfiguration of power and the renegotiation of state-societal relations since 2011.

This book builds a regime-centric theoretical approach to explain how agency and structure both reinforce Myanmar's regime transition in a path-dependent manner through tentative experimentation by the *tatmadaw*. By understanding the type and nature of Myanmar's military regime, this book builds a trial and error regime-centric model of regime change to explain Myanmar's transformation from a highly authoritarian military regime into a partially civilianized hybrid regime.

This book thus addresses some of the shortcomings of political science literature, which has generally been unable to predict and explain endogenous regime changes. A regime is an institutional complex, which is a "historically-emergent system of structured interests, rules, and compliance procedures that governs social life and expectations within a given setting" (London 2012: 5). Political life can be structured and influenced by institutions and ideas, which affects political outcomes. Based on this understanding of institutions, this book proposes an endogenous theory of regime change, which builds upon the regime typologies developed by Juan Linz and Alfred Stepan (1996).

Myanmar's post-2011 regime change is a long-term process driven by the *tatmadaw* following the collapse of the BSPP regime in 1988. The key driver of Myanmar's regime change is the military institution, yet the military's agency is structured by the attributes of the regime – both ideational and materialist factors – as well as by how it interacts with external actors, that is regime outsiders such as society (i.e., non-state actors) and the broader international community. These structural factors – economic, social, and political realities – limit the range of options and strategy choices available to the *tatmadaw*.

The *tatmadaw* has consistently demonstrated that they are not sophisticated politicians and find electoral politics difficult to master. Despite their underwhelming instincts in electoral competition, the *tatmadaw* continues to view themselves as the ultimate praetorian "guardians" of the nation-state (Egreteau and Jagan 2013: 43–44). Myanmar's military regime may have been governed by "war fighters," however they are made of politicized, nationalistic military officers who fashioned themselves as legitimate state builders (Callahan 2003).

The post-2011 constitutional system that guides Myanmar's disciplined democracy may have created new arenas for civilian–military cooperation and competition in politics and governance; however the role of the military remains predominant. By providing a historically specific explanation of why Myanmar's military has enacted this partial regime change, this book will offer insight into how the military's disciplined democracy, that is, a hybrid regime, has operated, and actually consolidated, since the advent of the NLD-led coalition government in 2016.

Overview of the book

This book is divided into eight chapters. Following this introductory chapter, Chapter 2 develops the theoretical framework that structures the analysis. The works on ideal regime type from Linz and Stepan (1996) will serve as a foundation of the theory, which engages with the literature on military regime theory as well as conceptual approaches from historical institutionalism. In particular, the chapter examines how Myanmar's military regime is informed by its anti-colonial, praetorian ethos. The chapter explores how the *tatmadaw* developed into a durable authoritarian regime that has adapted and evolved based on the various challenges faced by the regime. Fundamentally, Myanmar's regime transition went through a trial and error process, and the current transition reflects the continuity, or the evolution, of Myanmar's military regime.

Chapter 3 applies the trial and error model to explain how the military developed into a strong, authoritarian, military regime. The chapter begins by identifying how Myanmar's military was able to remain highly cohesive while balancing its dual roles as a defensive force and a government. In particular, unlike other military regimes in the region (for example contemporary Thailand or Indonesia under Suharto), Myanmar's junta never successfully co-opted other societal actors into any position of autonomous power, although it did utilize its allies (such as the *tatmadaw*-backed cronies) to further its agenda. By analyzing how the military has been able to achieve this strength, this chapter suggests that Myanmar's regime change should be understood as a conscious evolution. The military has adapted its regime type to reflect changing circumstances without forfeiting its dominant control over politics and the state. This chapter concludes with a discussion of how Myanmar's military regime developed through a trial and error process, including a chronological account of the evolution of the military regime from its early foundational roots as the Revolutionary Council in 1962 up to its transition to a "disciplined" democracy in 2011.

Chapter 4 re-examines the literature on civil society and argues that Myanmar's non-state actors played an indirect role in shaping Myanmar's post-2011 regime transition. The chapter begins with a critique of the concept of "civil society." The chapter then examines how Myanmar society adapts to and struggles against Myanmar's authoritarian rule. Tracing the evolution of associational life in Myanmar since the emergence of the State Law and Restoration Council (SLORC), Chapter 4 argues that although civil society has been gradually developing since 1988, there is far more continuity than the so-called change that is taking place in Myanmar's public sphere. The focus of this chapter is to rethink the way relations change between state and society under military rule. As such, in this chapter I argue that it was the military state's domination over its disciplined society, rather than any bottom-up process of change, that allowed the military to introduce political reforms. The submission of Myanmar's subdued, depoliticized society was a precondition that allowed the military to introduce its version of multiparty democracy, confident that the military would still be able to manage the transition and superimpose its agenda and vision upon the partially civilianized state.

Chapter 5 examines the role of the broader international community and how it has influenced Myanmar's reform project. This chapter examines the role of external pressure on the decisions of the regime. The main claim pushed forward in this chapter is that the long-lasting pariah status of the regime has limited Myanmar's foreign policy options and trading partners. US-led sanctions thus pushed Myanmar to form closer regional ties with its immediate neighbors. Inevitably, the changing external conditions – the end of the Cold War, the emergence of a rising China in the global stage, the role of Association of South East Asian Nations (ASEAN), and the growth of a neoliberal global environment – have all played a conditional role in the strategic calculations of the military regime, and thus influenced how, when, and why Myanmar is undergoing a regime transition. However, these external factors did not cause Myanmar's regime change; rather they serve as secondary considerations that provided the incentive structure for the regime to adopt some of the more liberal features of political reforms *after* the military regime decided to liberalize.

Chapter 6 serves as a test case of the theory and discusses in detail Myanmar's transition from a direct military government (1988–2011) into a diminished form of civilianized authoritarian regime (2011–2016) and the consolidation of "Myanmar's Way to Democracy" (Huang 2017). The chapter explains how the regime has developed during President Thein Sein's administration (2011–2016) and identifies the key features of this new political arrangement. This chapter also accounts for political developments in the lead up to, and in the aftermath of, the elections, explaining how the electoral results, although allowed the partial transition of power to the country's main opposition party, confirms the consolidation of the military's version of a disciplined democracy; that is, a partially civilianized hybrid regime.

Chapter 7 provides an update on political developments in Myanmar since the partial transferal of power to Aung San Suu Kyi-led NLD government in 2016. This chapter examines some of the major thematic political developments under the NLD-led coalition government. In particular, the chapter will explain widespread policy continuities under the new government. It argues that despite tensions between the civilian and military authorities, the NLD-led government has not diverged from the military drafted constitutional system – a "disciplined" Myanmar democracy. The chapter concludes with some preliminary assessment of key unresolved political issues, including the military's continued dominance in the country's political economy, with implications for the unresolved peace negotiations, the intensification of fighting in the ethnic peripheries, and the resurgence of authoritarian practices under the NLD-led government.

The concluding chapter draws together the key arguments explored throughout the book. The chapter returns to the discussion of Myanmar's post-2011 regime transition and demonstrates that even with the partial transferal of power to a popularly elected NLD government in April 2016, Myanmar is not "democratizing," nor has the military's vision of its disciplined democracy been undermined. Despite civilian–military tensions, there appears to be a resurgence of authoritarian practices, while the military has also seen renewed popularity with Bamar-Buddhist nationalists. The chapter situates these current developments in Myanmar in relation to the broader phenomenon of the resurgence of strongman politics and authoritarian practices in Southeast Asia. The chapter concludes by considering some of the critical issues that have developed during the transition, and how these may or may not derail the junta's "genuine, disciplined multi-party democratic system."

Notes

1 The military initially ruled directly as a Revolutionary Council (RC) from 1962–1971, although the senior leadership of the RC were all BSPP members.
2 President Htin Kyaw resigned ostensibly for health reasons on March 21, 2018 and was succeeded by Myint Kyaw.

3 Although the military regime introduced a BSPP single-party state structure from 1974–1988, the party apparatus was merely an extension of the military institution, as all positions of power were dominated by high ranking active or retired military officials, and there was significant overlapping between military and party state duties. In other words, even if the military had theoretically ruled indirectly under the BSPP government (1974–1988), the reality is that the BSPP was never able to develop as an autonomous political force in its own right, and was dependent on the military for its existence, including for example, party leadership and personnel.

4 The 2015 general elections cannot be considered free, as there were as systematic exclusion of selective communities (in particular the Rohingya, as well as a number of other minority groups) from being able to participate in the 2015 elections as either candidates or voters.

5 However most independent investigations suggest that in the lead up to the 2015 elections, the government has increased their persecution of citizens for political offences. A Human Rights Watch report (2016) identified at least 600 individuals either serving time for political offenses or are facing politically motivated charges at the end of the Thein Sein presidency.

6 Although a number of opposition parties have participated and won seats in the 2010 general elections, much of the US-led international community did not seriously consider Myanmar's regime change as genuine until Aung San Suu Kyi and the NLD began to participate in parliamentary politics. Some observers argue that this inclusion of Aung San Suu Kyi and the NLD into disciplined democracy is in part the Myanmar' government's response to the *quid pro quo* diplomacy shaped during US Secretary of State Hillary Clinton's visit to Myanmar in 2011 (Liow 2017: 144–147).

7 Aung San was always a sensitive and awkward figure for the SLORC/SPDC, as he has long been considered the founding father of the *tatmadaw* as well as the Myanmar nation-state, yet at the same time he was Suu Kyi's father.

8 NLD members that disagreed with the leadership's decision splintered into a new National Democratic Force party and competed and won a number of seats in the 2010 general elections.

2 Myanmar's trial and error praetorian regime

Introduction

In contemporary Myanmar, the military has established itself unquestionably as the hegemonic institution in the post-colonial political economy. Since taking direct control of the state apparatus after the 1962 coup d'état, the *tatmadaw* has remained united in its concerted state (and regime) building project. In 2011, the military, arguably at the height of its powers, partially withdrew from direct governance, and implemented its vision of a disciplined democracy with features of partisan politics – all the while maintaining the authoritarian powers of the military. By 2016, the military had further reduced its influence over partisan politics following the partial transfer of power to regime outsiders with the ascent of a popularly elected civilian-led coalition government in 2016 under the National League for Democracy (NLD). The 2015 electoral outcome that brought the NLD into government may not be the preferred outcome of the *tatmadaw*, yet the institutional arrangements created by the country's third Constitution, already in place since 2011, suggests disciplined democracy continues to follow the political framework designed by the *tatmadaw*.

Institutions incorporate rules – both formal and informal – as well as norms, ideas, and organizations, which govern the behavior of strategic actors (Thelen and Steinmo 1992: 2). Regime change therefore fundamentally concerns the reconfiguration of political power, and the creation of new institutions or the transformation of existing ones. Political agency is structured, and conditioned by institutions, which affect political outcomes (Lieberman 2002: 699). Building on the concept of ideal regime types exemplified by the classic works of Juan Linz and Alfred Stepan (1996), this chapter proposes an endogenous theory of regime change. By examining the path-dependent process of institutional change, this chapter develops a trial and error approach to explain how regimes transition and change. This endogenous, trial and error mechanism of regime change corrects the existing literature's excessive focus either on the moment of change based on the agency of elite actors or factions, or on explanations that rely on institutional failures or exogenous shocks.

By focusing on the institutionalized role of the military in the development of Myanmar's post-colonial regime, this chapter argues that Myanmar followed an evolutionary, path-dependent process of military-enforced regime change through tentative experimentation. Driven by the *tatmadaw*'s political agenda, the military has followed a trial and error path of regime change. In each instance of Myanmar's post-1962 regime change, the *tatmadaw* has consistently preserved and institutionalized its political role as the ultimate "praetorian" dictating the rules of the game of each iteration of Myanmar's political regime (Egreteau and Jagan 2013: 19–20). The post-2011 regime change continues to follow this pattern.

This chapter first provides a general overview of how regimes are conceptualized and how such a conceptualization can be applied in the context of Myanmar's regime development. The chapter then develops a trial and error model to explain the path-dependent logic of Myanmar's regime change. Revisiting the classic literature on military regimes and the importance of ideas and identity in understanding the behavior of military institutions, the chapter then incorporates the "praetorian" ethos thesis, to explain the ideational factor that explains the *tatmadaw*'s behavior. Through a cycle of trial and error, the military has consistently pushed forward with its regime building and maintenance agenda. The military's partial exit from politics in 2011, and the transformation of Myanmar's authoritarian military regime, into a "disciplined democratic" hybrid regime demonstrates a remarkable path-dependent continuity in the military's methods to regime building.

Regimes and regime typologies: contextualizing Myanmar's regime type

A regime is essentially a system of governance. It is generally accepted that the distribution of, and access to political power and material resources are essential for understanding how regimes operate (Calvert 1987: 18). In Robert Dahl's classic definition, "power" is understood to be a "relation among people," and inevitably, those who have the ability to control, command, and influence play a significant role in shaping outcomes (Dahl 1957: 202–203). Given that in the contemporary political system the state is seen as the basic unit where formal and legitimate political power resides, those that have control of and/or formal access to the state apparatus can be part of the political establishment. According to James Mahoney, groups in a position of authority can use their position to further reinforce the existing institutional arrangements to their benefit:

> The institution initially empowers a certain group at the expense of other groups; the advantaged group uses its additional power to expand the institution further; the expansion of the institution increases the power of the advantaged group; and the advantaged group encourages additional institutional expansion.
>
> (2000: 524)

Regimes, therefore, produce "self-reinforcing" mechanisms that allow "increasing returns," which further rationalize and justify institutional "lock-in," perpetuating the durability of existing institutional arrangements (Thelen 1999: 392). In contemporary Myanmar, the *tatmadaw* is undisputedly the most powerful, enduring organization that has long been the main driver in shaping Myanmar's successive post-colonial regimes. Following the 1962 coup d'état, the *tatmadaw* was the state. In its dual role as a coercive organization and as government, the *tatmadaw* was able to develop its capacity as the most powerful institution vis-à-vis all other challengers. By the time of the *tatmadaw*'s partial withdrawal from power in 2011, the military was the definitive hegemonic institution, deeply entrenched in the country's political economy.

One way to understand the logic of these institutional complexes is to analyze how political regimes make and implement decisions. Based on the Weberian concept of regimes, Juan J. Linz and Alfred Stepan developed a typology of ideal regimes. They identify four main types of non-democratic regimes – authoritarian, totalitarian, post-totalitarian, and sultanistic – which can be differentiated by four key attributes: pluralism, ideology, leadership, and mobilization (Linz and Stepan 1996: 41–42). Based on these regime categories, one can thus theorize how decisions are made, how resources are distributed, the behavior and rationale of the regime, and state-societal relations. Since the 1962 coup, Myanmar has been under the rule of a military-backed highly authoritarian regime, with occasional totalitarian tendencies in its early years (Huang 2013: 250–252). Since 2011, the military's implementation of a new military-drafted constitution allows features of civilian-led partisan politics alongside the unelected authoritarian powers of the *tatmadaw*. This conditional regime change, therefore, situates Myanmar's disciplined democracy as a form of hybrid regime.

In much of the earlier regime-centric literature, hybrid regimes were conceptualized as unsustainable "halfway houses," with the high likelihood of transitioning to a more democratic form of governance (Huntington 1991: 174–175). However, as discussed in the introductory chapter, by focusing on the "democratization" potentials of these hybrid regimes, transitologists often miss the reality that many hybrid regimes are in a state of equilibrium. Contrary to earlier predictions, hybrid regimes have in fact demonstrated remarkable resilience and should not be considered as regimes in transition, but as a "particular type of regime" (Bogaards 2009: 415).

All political regimes regularly engage in routine regime maintenance. Regime maintenance is essential for non-democratic regimes, as institutional failures could lead to the displacement or transformation of the regime. Involuntary regime change in non-democratic settings may lead to the purge and destruction of institutions and actors that have supported the regime. Autocrats and their supporters may face prosecution and have their assets seized if they fall out of power and could potentially face the risk of death. Some of the most haunting deaths of dictators in contemporary times for example include the execution by firing squad of Romania's Nicolae Ceauşescu in 1989, the hanging of Iraq's Saddam Hussein in 2006, and the violent death of Muammar Gaddafi in the streets of

Libya in 2011. As a result, autocratic leaders and the institutions that support non-democratic rule, generally resist "political openings" for as long as possible, in order to preserve their own political survival (Bratton and van de Walle 1997: 83). A voluntary relinquishing of power in the absence of a threat to regime survival therefore is relatively unusual and rare.

Regimes rely on a combination of coercion, patronage and legitimacy to maintain political stability (Gandhi and Przeworski 2006; Gerschewski 2013). Since regimes are institutional complexes, both formal and informal institutions shape their attributes. Informal institutions for example often play a critical role in sustaining authoritarian regimes' rule (Levitsky and Way 2010: 27–28). While official strategies of coercion and societal control may prove effective, especially for totalitarian regimes, for other types of non-democratic regimes, such strategies could incur high costs for the political establishment at the expense of the regime's reputation, legitimacy, and material interests. Many authoritarian regimes adopt informal mechanisms of coercion and co-optation alongside formal controls, in order to allow the regime a degree of deniability for their repressive tactics. Authoritarian regimes thus may employ vigilantes to attack political challengers, harass dissidents, stuff ballot boxes, buy votes, selectively interpret and enforce the law against opponents, and build patronage networks through institutionalized corruption such as "[b]ribery, blackmail, proxy ownership, and other illicit exchanges" (*ibid:* 28).

Myanmar, during the SLORC/SPDC junta years (1988–2011), was a highly authoritarian military regime. It had a clear leadership hierarchy based on the military's chain of command, informed by a pragmatic nationalistic mentality. Socio-political pluralism was critically restrained, with an absence of genuine partisan politics. The military state cultivated support through patronage and routine state-led mobilization, while societal mobilization was actively suppressed. For over two decades, the junta utilized a variety of both formal and informal strategies of political repression to restrict the powers of regime outsiders (Kyaw Yin Hlaing 2013). Potential detractors were ousted from the military state, citizens were actively monitored, and foreign agents and diplomats were scrutinized closely (Selth 2019: 619). By the 1990s, the *tatmadaw* had developed a reputation as one of Asia's most efficient intelligence apparatus with a sophisticated surveillance network. The appalling human rights conditions in Myanmar infamously led the country to be described as one of the "outposts of tyranny" in 2005 by then US Secretary of State Condoleezza Rice. Under direct military rule, the *tatmadaw* also built an extensive military-capitalist network, with the *tatmadaw* involved actively in practically every sector of the political economy (McCarthy 2019: 12–20). Since the collapse of the single-party Burmese Socialist Program Party (BSPP) state, the *tatmadaw*, apart from the 1990 elections, had long postponed elections from taking place. When the ruling junta finally allowed elections – first, for the 2008 national referendum on the military-drafted Constitutional Charter, followed by the 2010 general elections – they were effectively "rigged" to ensure the delivery of an electoral outcome in support of the *tatmadaw*'s political agenda (Englehart 2012).

Conceptualizing institutional change: from regime transition to regime change

Regimes are generally resistant to change, and so it is common to observe "path-dependent institutional stability and reproduction" (Capoccia and Kelemen 2007: 341). Regime change is a relatively rare phenomenon and usually occurs in brief moments of "critical juncture," where momentous change is suddenly possible (*ibid*). During such momentary breaks from the *status quo*, the regime's structural constraints are significantly weakened, leading to "punctuated equilibrium" (Peters et al. 2005: 1278). In this transitory phase, strategic actors have greater agency to determine whether institutions change, survive, or collapse (Mahoney and Thelen 2010: 7). Political actors may have access to a wider range of policy choices, but the "initial conditions" and "general law," which preceded the period of critical juncture continues to structure the strategic options available to change agents (Goldstone 1998). Decisions and actions taken during this temporary state of flux may have greater ramifications, yet any dramatic breaks from the previous institutional arrangement, short of a revolutionary change, suggest that most institutional change continues to be guided by a path-dependent process.

A regime change is a systematic transformation of institutions. Ordinary shifts in formal and informal rules and procedures does not constitute a regime change. However, when norms and principles have changed beyond merely the alteration of routine procedures, then it is reasonable to argue that a regime transition is taking place. This moment of regime transition can be captured by the concept of critical juncture. It is during this moment of fluidity, that the interaction between new and old/existing institutions can determine if, how, and when a new "equilibrium" emerges. When a new pattern of institutional arrangements is established and normalized broadly, it signals that the period of regime transition has ended and a change of regime has taken place. To use a popular political science metaphor, when the large majority of strategic actors consent to the new "rules of the game," then a new regime is established. Consent, however, does not mean an absence of institutional contradictions, competitions, or weakness. Beyond active support for the new regime, consent here includes passive recognition, or the inability, or reluctance of strategic actors to challenge forcefully the "new" *status quo*, including, for example, the limited capacity for actors to restore *status quo ante*.

At the time of writing, eight years have passed since the dissolution of the SPDC, which marked the formal beginning of Myanmar's disciplined democracy. Yet, inexplicably, a vast amount of literature continues to refer to post-2011 political developments in Myanmar as an ongoing "transition" (Girke and Beyer 2018). In part, as discussed in the introductory chapter, the concept of "transition," largely influenced by democratization theory, has become a fashionable, popular "shorthand" to explain socio-political liberalization in Myanmar (*ibid*: 224). However, the post-2011 *tatmadaw*-led liberalization has significantly reconfigured political power and created new institutions to the extent that regime outsiders have become co-opted as a critical part of the "new" regime. Beyond mere rule changes, there has been an observable norm shift, and the "game" being played is a distinctly different one from pre-2011 days. While socio-political pluralism remains conditional, it has vastly expanded in this new "disciplined" democratic game. Under the Thein Sein administration (2011–2016), the first post-junta government organized relatively fair elections, which has institutional-ized genuine, albeit conditional partisan politics, as an important feature of the new regime. Previous regime outsiders, notably the NLD, have become part of the political establishment. After serving as loyal opposition following the 2012 by-elections, the NLD ascent into a position of authority following their triumph in the 2015 general elections (see Chapters 6 and 7). The powerful *tat-madaw* may have retained significant powers and a prominent political presence, but the NLD, as the new ruling party since 2016, has gained access and control of genuine, formal powers, parallel to those of the military. The fragmentation of state power has meant that post-junta policies are decided in a "less hierarchical and more complex" manner (Lall 2016: 56–57).

Regime outsiders, including non-state actors, have, since 2011, gained condi-tional access to legally sanctioned space to mobilize and the potential to interact with and influence the decision of policymakers. Although a number of well-armed ethnic armed organizations (EAOs) in the peripheries have refused to directly participate in Myanmar's disciplined democracy, and a good number of EAOs are actively in combat against the Myanmar state, thus far, the majority of non-insurgent political actors have generally accepted the new rules, norms, and principles, however unwillingly, of the military's "disciplined democratic" game. That is, even if several stakeholders remain unsatisfied with the existing constitutional arrangements, the majority have essentially agreed to pursue reforms within the parameters of the established rules of the game. Contrary to some observers' view that Myanmar is transitioning "toward an uncertain 'some-thing else'" (Egreteau 2016: 27), a clear path-dependent process of regime change has already taken place. In the military-enforced "disciplined democ-racy," the military has retained an active prominent political role, yet there are also features of electoral, parliamentary politics, and conditional, but meaningful, pluralism, attributes that are markedly different from the highly authoritarian military years. Myanmar's disciplined democracy is not a regime in transition. This legal sharing of political power between elected civilians and the autono-mous military achieves an equilibrium that was carefully designed by the *tatma-daw*. In other words, the institutional arrangements and attributes of disciplined democracy positions post-junta Myanmar as a hybrid regime.

For over half a century, the *tatmadaw* actively constructed the institutions and structures that support a highly authoritarian regime. It had taken on the role of caretaker government in 1958–1960, before deciding to take control of the state apparatus through a coup d'état in 1962. From that period, until the *tat-madaw*'s partial withdrawal from politics in 2011, the powerful military had been the main driving force determining the direction of Myanmar's regime develop-ment. Therefore, the post-2011 regime change, which has diminished some of the regime's most authoritarian impulses, is often seen as a paradox. The same autocrats, mostly retired and active military officers that had long supported authoritarian institutions, became the principal agents of regime change, by introducing controlled reforms that allowed expanded socio-political pluralism post-2011. During this critical juncture, the greater fluidity brought about by significant institutional changes and development allowed political elites to enact several systematic, dramatic policy changes. These broad socio-political directly contradict decades of highly authoritarian rule. However, a focus on elite agency does not sufficiently explain how changing conditions allow for this flux and for a punctuated equilibrium to alter the *status quo*.

Without the loosening of existing structural controls, the "new" leaders of Myanmar's disciplined democracy, comprising the same autocrats of the "old" regime, would not have had the agency to push for socio-political liberalization. Even with the greater fluidity, political agency is still structured by the parameters of what is possible in its operating environment. A careful examination of the "initial conditions" that preceded the post-2011 regime change suggests that Myanmar's so-called dramatic changes in fact evolved through a path-dependence process of change that has not diverged from the praetorian rationale of the *tatmadaw* establishment (see Chapter 3). Although the post-junta leadership introduced broad reforms that some considered more liberal and far-reaching than their former superiors (i.e., Than Shwe and Maung Aye) may have desired, these unfolding developments, including the tolerance for partisan politics, were only possible because of the new institutional patterns established by the military's Constitution. The roots of the 2008 Constitution can be traced to the end of the BSPP state, when BSPP Chairman Ne Win floated the idea in 1987, and again in the midst of nationwide anti-government protests in 1988, that provisions for greater social-economic, multiparty system may be necessary to address the failures of the single-party socialist system.

The *tatmadaw*'s political role may have diminished, yet the newly liberalized space has not challenged the fundamental powers of the military as stipulated by the Constitution. Under this new hybrid regime "equilibrium," the transitologist's democratization was never part of the military's agenda but rather reflected the path-dependent continuum logic of the *tatmadaw* in preserving its corporate interests, while imposing its version of "Myanmar's way to democracy" (Huang 2017, this point will be further developed in Chapters 6 and 7).

It is, therefore, important to consider how institutions shape and structure ideational factors, especially the self-identity of institutional agents. In a comparative case study of how modern economic policies were respectively made by the British and French states in the twentieth century, Peter Hall (1986) demonstrated that the form and character of institutions – in this case the type of state – was vital for understanding the decision-making process and the outcome of the policy regimen adopted. Taken from an organizational behavior point of view, James March has argued that actors in an organization largely adhere to the "logic of appropriateness" that shapes their behavior and action (March 1994). Actors who adhere to the rules and norms of the institution benefit from their conformity and further reinforce the legitimacy and rationale of the system (Thelen

1999: 392). As such, agency cannot merely be explained as a materialist calculation; rather, the actions of agents are "matched to situations by means of rules organized into identities" (March 1994: 57–58).

In other words, the importance of ideas, and their ability to be "prime movers of history," should not be ignored and require serious consideration when accounting for political action (Lieberman 2002:699). In this view, ideas can be understood as the main driver of political agency, as they are "casual beliefs," which guide actors to determine how to resolve particular problems by defining their "goals and strategies," which are then translated into political decisions and action (Béland and Cox 2010: 3). One way of incorporating identities and ideas into the analysis of political change, is to consider from an organizational perspective, how organizations are bounded rationally, that is, how leaders act despite incomplete information, and make decisions that "minimize decision-making costs rather than maximize goal attainment when coping with policy choices" (Peters et al. 2005: 1285). Therefore policymakers often make decisions based on what is readily available in their "immediate environment of existing policies, rather than engage in a more comprehensive search for an optimal policy" (*ibid*).

This explains why, prior to 1988, socialism was the undisputable guiding ideology that informed the actions of the first generation of post-colonial Myanmar political elites in their fight for independence and nation-building (Steinberg 1982: 124). Not unlike nationalist movements elsewhere in Asia, Marxism not only ignited the passions of Bamar nationalists but was also seen as a pragmatic ideological tool that was useful to challenge the ailing British imperialist order and its exploitative economic policy (Shwe Lu Maung 1989: 21). Aung San, the assassinated "father" of the *tatmadaw* and the post-colonial Myanmar nation-state, was also the founder of the Burmese Communist Party. Yet, he was not a "doctrinaire Marxist but remained a nationalist and a pragmatist, willing to employ whatever means deemed necessary to obtain Myanmar's independence" (Tin Maung Maung Than 2007: 34). Nevertheless throughout his career as noted in his public speeches and writings, Aung San held socialism as the solution for Myanmar's problems, and his martyred status turned him into the "ultimate authority on Myanmar's socialist future" (*ibid*: 31). In particular, Aung San set out the course for a strong state intervention in the economic development of independent Myanmar at the Sorrento Villa Conference on June 6, 1947, which formed the broad socialist blueprint for Myanmar's national economic plans until 1988 (Maung Maung 2015 [1962]:135–139). Ne Win would later cite Aung San as his inspiration for building a BSPP single-party state structure (Maung Maung 1969: 298). This is consistent with Jeffery Pfeffer and Gerland Salancik's observation made in 1978 that "political decisionmakers often do not experience directly the consequences of their actions" and that "decisions are most frequently applied across the board to entire classes of individuals and organizations, going well beyond the time and place of the original problem" (Pfeffer and Salancik 1978: 191).

Therefore, in order to understand the seemingly dramatic post-2011 regime transition and change, it is important to identify what the "initial conditions" and "general laws" were that shaped the agency of the *tatmadaw*. The ideas driving and shaping the organizational culture of the *tatmadaw*, and their justification and logic in preserving the military's political role provide an important starting point for understanding the path-dependent process of Myanmar's regime change. As the next chapter will demonstrate, Myanmar's turn away from single-party state socialism is rooted in the critical juncture of 1988, when the military re-evaluated their role and strategies to maintain the unity of the state and the stability of the military regime. The next section, therefore, explores the self-rationalizations the military has developed to justify its long legacy of political control.

Military regimes and the praetorian logic

As institutional complexes, regimes are assumed to be bounded rationally, that is, they are guided by the logic of its institutions (Dequech 2001: 920–921). Regime agency therefore can be said to be informed by a set of legitimized norms, rules, and structures shaped by the characteristics of the regime, or what is commonly referred to in the organizational literature as standard operating procedures (SOPs) (DiMaggio and Powell 1983: 151). Army experts have long considered institutional cohesiveness as an important feature that can determine the strength of a military organization, including the efficiency, success, or failure of a military operation (Shils and Janowitz 1948). Former US Army Chief of Staff Edward Meyer defines military cohesion as "the bonding together of soldiers in such a way as to sustain their will and commitment to each other, the unit, and mission accomplishment, despite combat or mission stress" (Manning 1991: 457). A cohesive military force thus, can "cooperate effectively, overcoming their reluctance as individuals to accept the mental and physical stress of combat, including the possibility of violent death and subordinating individual welfare to that of the group" (Guilmartin 1997: 24). The *tatmadaw* regime, unlike most contemporary military regimes, critically, was able to maintain its military cohesion, even after formally entering the realm of governance and national politics, while excluding meaningful civilian participation.

The main distinction in military regimes is the dominant role of the military in state governance (Alagappa 2001). In Weberian ideals of modern states, authority derives from rational-legal norms, and the military is only one part of the state. It usually plays a supplementary role as a coercive agent of the state involved only in issues of national security, subordinate to some form of civilian oversight (Huntington 1985: 80–85). In a military regime, however, the armed forces are the primary agent of the state. As such, political power is institutionalized in the hands of the army, while the role of civilian authority is limited and subordinated to that of the military establishment. Military regimes also have the advantage of the actual power they hold in command of direct coercive force (Feit 1972: 255). On top of their control over arms, militaries, in general, are better organized based on the "principles of hierarchy and discipline" (Sundhaussen 1984: 547), especially when compared to their civilian counterparts, and are often regarded as prestigious with a "highly emotionalized symbolic status" (Finer 2002: 6).

Military regimes typically emerge as a response to some form of crisis within the state through a military coup (Feit 1972: 255). In general, the motivation, or pretext for the military to take control of the state, stems from a belief that the state is at the point of collapse, and thus it is up to the military to save the nation (Janowitz 1964: 27–37). In the face of a weak civilian government, the military may often see themselves as being state builders that are more capable than, and sideline their civilian counterparts (Huntington 1985: 61). In situations where the military is the most unified political institution, they may develop a "new professionalism" mentality in order to justify their expanded responsibilities from being defenders against external military threats, to becoming responsible for the "internal security and national development" of the state (Feit 1972: 18). In this sense, some scholars argue that a praetorian ethos guides military regimes – that is the belief that the military is the only institution capable of defining and safeguarding the interests of the nation (Perlmutter 1969).

Praetorianism chiefly describes the political role of the military, and the ethos incorporates the idea that "[s]ocial and economic decisions become inseparable from military decisions" (Wiseman 1988: 231). Perhaps one of the most important features of a praetorian regime is that justification to rule is based on those who have the ability to govern, not those who "should" govern (Egreteau and Jagan 2013: 26). After all, military regimes generally assume power via a coup with the use of illegitimate force, and thus their entry into politics is through purely military means (Finer 1985: 16). However, most military regime theorists have argued that militaries generally capture political power, "without intending to retain it permanently" (Brooker 2009: 203). Praetorian theorists therefore argue that once the initial threats that had justified military intervention are eliminated, the army is more likely to return to the barracks, as they are confident that the general conditions have improved to the extent that the principal objectives of the military's initial justification for taking over power are satisfied (Huntington 1992: 584; Perlmutter 1974: 8–9). Lee Jones has advanced this line of argument in his explanation of Myanmar's post-2011 regime change, and rightfully argues that the *tatmadaw*'s partial withdrawal from power derived from the confidence that it has designed a "constrained electoral regime," which would continue to champion the military's interests while containing the diminished threats to the stability of the state (2014b: 784).

Eric Nordlinger further provides a nuanced model of the different forms of praetorian regimes: ruler, moderator, and guardian (1977: 20–29). Praetorian rulers come into power in general to maximize the military's power in order to establish "direct and permanent military control" (Perlmutter 1974: 9). Praetorian moderators "act as highly politicized and powerful pressure groups" who are keen to influence political outcomes but are not necessarily interested or committed to direct governance (Nordlinger 1977: 22–24). Finally, praetorian guardians typically seek to rule provisionally as a response to avert an imminent crisis to the state (*ibid*: 25–27). As Renaud Egreteau and Larry Jagan have demonstrated, the *tatmadaw* appears to have taken all three praetorian forms in contemporary Myanmar (2013: 43–44). During the early parliamentary years (1948–1958), the *tatmadaw* acted as a praetorian moderator while focusing on its defensive and internal security roles but also acted as the arbitrator during the polarizing partisan politics under the Anti-Fascist People's Freedom League (AFPFL) administration. The 18-months caretaker government between 1958 and 1960 saw the emergence of the *tatmadaw* as "praetorian guardian," which supported the restoration of order and stability, and the brief return of electoral politics in 1960 (*ibid*). Finally, in 1962, the *tatmadaw* became, for the first time, a fully fledged "praetorian ruler," taking over all aspects of politics and governance, with totalitarian-like tendencies. Based on this theoretical model, the military enforced regime change in 2011 has returned the role of the *tatmadaw* to that of "praetorian guardians." That is, although they maintain an active political presence, they have delegated the duties of everyday governance to civilianized institutions.

This repeated pattern of direct military intervention in Myanmar's politics suggests that a praetorian-oriented theory is useful for understanding the rationale of the military authoritarian regime established by the *tatmadaw*. As the next chapter will explore further, the military clearly saw itself as the prime agent responsible for building the post-colonial Myanmar state. Its early experiences fighting multiple insurgencies, and later fear of a possible Chinese invasion, motivated its self-appointed role as the leading institution to provide "a stable political order that safeguards national security" (Pedersen 2008: 112). At least since 1962, the *tatmadaw* has taken the lead in shaping political outcomes at each "critical juncture." In each case of "punctuated equilibrium," the military has been the principal institution that determines the timing and form of a new equilibrium (i.e., regime change). As will be further explored in Chapter 7, the electoral defeat of the military establishment in 2015 may not have been the preferred outcome of the *tatmadaw*; nevertheless it is the military's willingness to abide by its own rules of the game, that allowed the partial transferal of power to its former foes, the NLD.

Regime change through trial and error

Thus far, this chapter has set out to combine regime typologies and a historical institutionalist approach to build a trial and error framework that explains the dynamics of endogenous regime change with reference to the role of ideas and regime identity. In the case of Myanmar, even with a dominant military institution that has largely pacified its main national challengers, the *tatmadaw*'s powers are not limitless, and the regime does not exist in a vacuum. Although the military clearly is the main determinant of the structures and agency shaping Myanmar's regime change, the role of "political conflict" must be considered to provide a "dynamic conception of agency," (Peters et al, 2005: 1277). The role of regime outsiders – particularly the role of non-state actors (often conceptualized as "civil society") and international institutions (the international political economy and the "neoliberal" order) – will be examined in this framework and are discussed in detail in Chapters 4 and 5. The rationally bounded military leadership have clear, identifiable objectives, but they also have to adjust and adapt to changing domestic and international circumstances in achieving their ultimate political goal.

A trial and error framework of institutional change takes the role of ideas and coherent political agency seriously. The basic framework can be simplified as follows: the regime leadership based on an internally generated "logic of appropriateness" (i.e., the *tatmadaw*'s praetorian ethos), collectively decides on the political action to be taken in order to achieve the regime's political agenda. The "initial conditions" that a regime finds itself in determines the strategic options available, and the possible path it can elect to take in achieving a particular political agenda (in this case the military's active project of constructing a "disciplined democracy"). The decision is then turned into action, with institutional agents implementing the ideas, structured by the regime's SOP.

Through a process of trial and error during policy implementation, regime insiders can follow through by either staying on course until regime goals are eventually achieved, or they can diverge from their original path, compromise, and alter their goals. There is always the possibility that the regime may abandon their political action altogether; or in the regime's least desirable scenario, the regime leadership may concede decision-making power to new actors, to create new sets of actions with new goals (i.e., internal factionalism leading to a new leadership or regime collapse, replaced by regime outsiders).

Regimes often re-adjust expectations and strategies conditioned by contingency events such as political, economic, or societal crises (Jessop 1990: 205). Political outcomes thus are not deterministic; they are dependent on the dynamics of the power relationships between contesting groups (Mahoney and Thelen 2010: 8–9). For resilient non-democratic regimes, conflicts and challenges to its political agenda may lead the political process to take dives and turns, yet if they remain committed to their political agenda and endure the detour, they may eventually reach the conditions to deliver their preferred political outcome. This path explains Myanmar's trial and error political trajectory.

In Myanmar's case, political conflict primarily comes from regime outsiders, and not in the form of internal contradictions. The military is not a monolithic organization, yet it has established a system of formal and informal rules – with a clear defined hierarchical command to ensure that internal tensions are kept in check and that rivalries are never allowed to develop to the extent that they could lead to the fragmentation of the *tatmadaw*'s unity (Kyaw Yin Hlaing 2008). The main challenges therefore facing the military regime derive from non-state groups and international actors that have attempted to challenge the *tatmadaw*'s political reform process. However, given the particularly insular nature of Myanmar's military authoritarianism, the actions of regime outsiders are often interpreted by the military establishment as interference, obstacles, or errors that need to be addressed and resolved for the military to return to its chosen path toward political reform. The praetorian-oriented *tatmadaw* regime has diminished the threat of political challengers through coercion and co-optation, and it has, at least in the period between 1962 and 2011, always adopted an insular position and refused to allow regime outsiders to influence the decision-making process. Just as the military had for decades pushed forward its version of a Burmese way to socialism (1962–1988), the subsequent direct military years (1988–2011), and the contemporary "disciplined democratic" regime (2011–present) reflect the evolutionary change of Myanmar's political regime and the shifting praetorian role of the *tatmadaw*.

The unfolding regime transition follows a praetorian logic, that is, the military follows its SOP and pushes through its regime change agenda in a linear manner. Once the military leadership has come up with a collective vision of what post-socialist Myanmar would look like – in the form of the basic principles of the yet drafted Constitution – it had proceeded to create the conditions in its bid to achieve its political vision. As the military became increasingly confident of its rule, Myanmar's disciplined society was allowed incremental growing socio-economic pluralism, although the military continues to have tight control over political space. This "pragmatic" authoritarian response ensured the survival and gradual consolidation of the military regime. Along the way, in its bid to create the conditions that are deemed suitable for the implementation of its regime change, the military has faced several challenges or "errors" in its plan. Thus, the regime has undergone a long, drawn-out trial and error process, where episodic setbacks to its transition plan, such as the Depayin massacre in 2003, mass "Saffron Revolution" protests in 2007, and the 2008 Cyclone Nargis, were resolved by standard military responses, which meant that any perceived threats to the plan were eliminated. Following the removal of these perceived threats, the military regime was able to get back to its envisaged track toward developing its "democratic" regime. In short, not unlike the 26-year Burmese way to socialism project, post-2011 marks the beginning of Myanmar's way to democracy.

This book thus argues that Myanmar's post-2011 regime transition and change has followed a trial and error process guided by the praetorian logic of the *tatmadaw*. The changing domestic conditions and the changing norms of the broader international political economy were not the determinants of Myanmar's regime change, yet they have created the external structures that limit the strategic options of the *tatmadaw*. Nevertheless, the military has maintained remarkably coherent and coordinated efforts in realizing its version of "disciplined" democracy. The establishment of the new post-2011 institutions, and the shifting of power relations within regimes insiders, as well as vis-à-vis the expanded pool of legitimized political actors (i.e., the NLD and other minority political parties), have created a new "disciplined democratic" equilibrium.

Although neither the *tatmadaw* establishment nor the new ruling NLD party, are satisfied with the new political arrangement, all the major strategic stakeholders have, in principle, acquiesced to the same "rules of the game" of "disciplined democracy." Even with a non-military preferred party coming into a position of power in 2016, this electoral result is not the result of an "elite pact" between regime insiders and the opposition. The electoral results could be explained as the unintended consequence of "ambiguous compromises" that does "not reflect the goals of any particular group" (Mahoney and Thelen 2010: 8), however, the reality is that the hybrid governance structure, as designed by the military, has now become institutionalized. Even with the popularly elected NLD and its head Aung San Suu Kyi at the helm of civilian politics, neither the constitutional-based patterns of political arrangement, nor the praetorian logic guiding the role of the *tatmadaw*, has changed (see Chapter 7).

Conclusion

This chapter identifies the dominant institutional role of the *tatmadaw* in shaping Myanmar's post-colonial regime development through a trial and error process of regime change. The *tatmadaw*'s durability as the hegemonic institution in Myanmar's political structure has been guided by its praetorian ethos. Therefore, the seemingly paradoxical liberalization of Myanmar's political regime since 2011 has in fact followed a much more coherent, path-dependent process reflective of the *tatmadaw*'s evolving political agenda and interests. The regime change is not a direct reaction against centrifugal forces. The *tatmadaw* remains largely united and coherent, while all credible external challengers have been systematically weakened and external pressure has made little impact on the stability of the SPDC government. The establishment of a hybrid regime post-2011 is a continuation of the military's limited, planned trial and error strategy to impose its principal political objective that is the institutionalization of the *tatmadaw* as a dominant, permanent political actor in the *tatmadaw*-imposed Myanmar way to democracy. Although the military establishment has allowed for the significant liberalization of its political economy, the *tatmadaw* retains a monopoly over the coercive powers of the regime, while civilian stakeholders are restricted to access to a number of policy directions that continue to fall in the military's sphere of politics, as determined by the Constitution.

The military-enforced regime change is not *sui generis*; however, the circumstances of its voluntary withdrawal is unusual, as it is not guided by a fear of breakdown of authoritarian rule. In order to understand why formal military rule ended in Myanmar on March 30, 2011, it is vital to understand the role of the military in Myanmar politics, and the type of political regime Myanmar was prior to the transition. Not unlike other authoritarian regimes, the *tatmadaw*-led government was challenged routinely by the wider society and the international community, as well as from within its own ranks occasionally. Myanmar's authoritarian regime, however, maintained military cohesion and secured regime continuity. The next chapter traces systematically how the military has emerged as the principal actor at the center stage of national politics in contemporary Myanmar, and how it has established an enduring military presence in Myanmar's post-colonial regime development.

3 The evolution of Myanmar's military regime

Introduction

Upon Myanmar's independence in 1948, the post-colonial state immediately faced a critical juncture. Faced with several insurgencies, the *tatmadaw* asserted itself quickly as the central institution in state building, as it was often the only organization that represented the national government in the conflict-prone peripheries. In addition to dispersing violence against rebel groups, it also had to take on the additional role as state administrator in conflict areas (Callahan 2003). Although independent Myanmar (then Burma) began as a parliamentary "democracy," the weak and fragmented party politics, and the existential security challenges confronting the state, meant that the *tatmadaw* quickly established its dominant institutional role in the political hierarchy. Prime Minister U Nu may have been the popularly elected *de jure* head of government; however, throughout much of his tenure, "many of the highest decisions of state ... were cleared with the top military leadership" (Butwell 1961: 75). By 1958, a decade after formal independence, the *tatmadaw* felt bold enough to coerce U Nu to "invite" army chief Ne Win to form a temporary "caretaker government" for a period of six months (U Nu 1975: 327). The caretaker government would later extend its rule for another year, before organizing and allowing relatively free and fair general elections in 1960. The temporary restoration of parliamentary politics, with U Nu back in power, was ended, this time seemingly indefinitely, when the military launched a "formal" coup d'état on March 2, 1962, and established the Revolutionary Council (RC).

At the time of the coup, the founding of another junta was not particularly remarkable, especially given the earlier precedence of direct military rule under the caretaker government (Lovell and Kim 1967: 117). Military regimes were relatively common during the Cold War and found in diverse geographic settings stretching from Latin America to Africa, Europe, and Asia. However, unlike its contemporaries, the *tatmadaw*'s ascent to direct political power in 1962 turned out to be exceptional. It has long been one of the few "stylized facts" of political science, that military regimes are generally short-lived and are the least secure type of authoritarianism (Kim and Kroeger 2018: 4). Contrary to this trend, the *tatmadaw* demonstrated remarkable resilience and political continuity. For over half a century, the military maintained control of the state apparatus and excluded regime outsiders from any genuine access to political power. Brief interruptions and critical challenges to military rule, most notably the popular protests in 1988, have led to the occasional military-imposed regime change. Prior to 2011, each iteration of the military-enforced government change, whether the nominal civilianization of the RC into the Burmese Socialist Program Party (BSPP) in 1971, the establishment of the State Law and Order Council (SLORC) in 1988, or the reconfiguration of SLORC into the State Peace and Development Council (SPDC) in 1997, the *tatmadaw* establishment monopolized all forms of formal political authority.[1]

In other cases, such as neighboring Thailand, where the military has maintained a strong legacy of political interference, such rule is often punctured by periods of civilian rule, and respective militaries have had to share some powers with their non-military counterparts (Croissant and Kuehn 2009). In Myanmar, genuine sharing of power with civilian outsiders only became possible after 2011, following the SPDC's self-dissolution. Although the military attempted to co-opt non-military forces in the 1970s following the transformation of the RC into a BSPP single-party state, party leadership positions continued to be dominated by active and retired military men. The socialist party never genuinely developed its own independent powers separate from the *tatmadaw* hierarchy.

Non-*tatmadaw* outsiders only came to genuine, albeit limited, positions of power following the 2015 general elections.[2] The military had near uninterrupted control of the state either directly or indirectly for over five decades. Further, unlike common rationales for military withdrawal from politics, Myanmar's case stands out because the *tatmadaw* voluntary transformed itself, in the absence of any credible threats to regime survival. The *tatmadaw*'s post-2011 approach to disciplined "democracy" shares remarkable similarities with how the military had imposed its Burmese way to socialism from 1962 to 1988. The *ancien régime* that embraced authoritarian rule was also the initiator of Myanmar's post-2011 change into a partially civilianized, hybrid regime (as will be explored in Chapters 6 and 7). Collectively, the highly cohesive *tatmadaw*, structured by its praetorian ethos (see Chapter 2), have decided to continue to "march in unison, but in a different direction"[3] toward conditional liberalization in the form of "disciplined democracy."

This chapter begins by situating the 1962 coup that established the Revolutionary Council as a "critical juncture," which led to a path-dependent process of subsequent evolution of different versions of Myanmar's military regime. Bounded by its praetorian ethos, the *tatmadaw* established a strong legacy of a politicized military that is determined to take the lead in building a stable and united Myanmar nation-state. The chapter then unpacks how the *tatmadaw* has been able to maintain its remarkable unity and cohesion, while minimizing potential internal contradictions within the military hierarchy. The chapter traces how the military-dominated regime has evolved since 1962, when the military embarked on a journey toward the Burmese way to socialism, until the ultimate collapse of the socialist state building project in 1988. The chapter explores the significance of the military's return as "praetorian rulers" fully in control of the political development process at the forefront of governance post-1988. The chapter concludes that the *tatmadaw* maintained and built a strong military regime, before ultimately initiating its own strategic regime change, to fulfill its much delayed and long promised transition to its version of a "disciplined" democracy in 2011.

The initial conditions: origins of Myanmar's praetorian-led regime

Ever since Myanmar became independent, the *tatmadaw* has played a fundamental role in the decisions of the state. In the opinion of Dorothy Guyot, the *tatmadaw*, founded initially as an anti-colonial guerrilla force during the Japanese occupation, was "a political movement in military garb" (1966: 51). As Tin Maung Maung Than suggests, the founding members of the *tatmadaw* were "first and foremost nationalists of socialist persuasion" and did not share the "old professionalism" of the Western military tradition of staying away from formal politics (2001: 163). Given its historical roots as a nationalist force, the *tatmadaw* was never simply an instrument of war but was a political institution invested in the administering of the state (Taylor 2009: 236). Its early experiences fighting against multiple insurrections meant that the *tatmadaw* had to transform itself into a capable instrument of war, which went beyond the use of violence. Especially in the conflict areas, the military generally took on the role as state builders while the post-colonial civilian bureaucracy was just in the infancy of its development (Callahan 2003: 18). The first generation of the *tatmadaw* hierarchy included several political heavyweights involved in the independence movement. The upper echelon of the military therefore saw the role of the military "as a permanent part of the state apparatus, with enduring interests and permanent functions that transcend the interests of the government of the day" (Linz and Stepan 1996: 67). These nationalistic military men reproduces that praetorian ethos into the younger generation of military officers, preparing their successors to take over governing duties as "the triumphant elite of the future" (US Embassy 2009).

Since its founding in 1962, Myanmar's first ruling junta demonstrated several features that are quite different from its regional counterparts. During the Cold War most regimes in East and Southeast Asia faced threats from communist insurgencies. However, unlike their pro-US right-wing counterparts – Sarit Thanart's Thailand, Suharto's Indonesia, and Park Chung-Hee's South Korea – the RC in Myanmar was decidedly leftist and a strict follower (and a founding member) of the non-aligned movement (NAM). Unlike the right-wing military regimes that embraced a US-centric position and adopted state-led market-oriented industrialization working with indigenous and foreign capitalists, the RC chose a self-isolationist neutralist policy, purged the pre-coup social structure, and adopted an autarkic socialist economy. The particularly bitter experience during the British colonial era, as well as the violent confrontations against ethnic minority groups during the Japanese occupation molded a xenophobic, nationalist army, which regularly produced "[n]arcissus-like propaganda" inspired by its leftist-nationalistic ideology (Egreteau and Jagan 2013: 42). Although it faced a credible communist threat, the RC adopted a socialist position that was further to the left than the left-leaning U Nu government it had replaced (Badgley 1965).

Socialism was already a popular ideology at the critical juncture of Myanmar's independence. The most active nationalists and politicized elites, including political adversaries, and many military officers embraced the socialist agenda and philosophy as the solution to redress decades of exploitative British colonialism in Myanmar (Steinberg 1982: 124). Socialism served as a convenient policy direction that the RC could use to further justify and articulate its rule. The RC's Burmese way to socialism aimed to prevent the monopolization of the leftist ideology by the communist insurgents, while combining traditional Buddhist ideas, in order to appeal to the general masses (Aung-Thwin and Thant Myint-U 1992: 67–71). In essence, the junta leaders merely adopted existing policies in the immediate environment as a matter of convenience, "rather than engage in a more comprehensive search for an optimal policy" (Peters et al. 2005: 1285).

The state-led political violence that followed under Ne Win's rule was also not unique in Southeast Asia at the time. In comparison, the Suharto-led 1965 coup in Indonesia led to a period of intense systematic anti-communist massacres that have been described as Indonesia's "genocide" (Melvin 2017) and far surpassed the level of violence witnessed in Myanmar during the same period. What was different however, was that the RC, at least in its early years, was more akin to a quasi-totalitarian regime than an authoritarian one (Mya Maung 1992). Compared to the more authoritarian strategies of its regional Thai and Indonesian contemporaries, the RC made systematic, totalitarian-like efforts to control all aspects of society. In particular, the *tatmadaw*, informed by their praetorian ethos, was hostile to socio-political pluralism and viewed partisan politics as messy and detrimental to the interests of the nation-state. The impact of long running insurgencies and the arrival of the Chinese Nationalist Kuomintang (KMT) remnants into its territory meant that the state saw security challenges everywhere and viewed "social forces and the citizenry" as "potential enemies" (Callahan 2003: 17). The *tatmadaw*'s general distrust of civilian outsiders endured and led to a much-prolonged military rule.

In the various incarnations of military authoritarianism, the *tatmadaw* had subdued non-state forces and dominated the state apparatus, while avoiding externally imposed regime change. The very *raison d'être* for the *tatmadaw* was to ensure stability, unity, and the territorial integrity of the Myanmar state, although it may not always have a well thought-out strategy to deliver their political agenda (Prager-Nyein 2009: 645).[4] Given its long dual role as both a defensive organization and a political institution against various perceived threats to the disintegration of the Myanmar state, it was clear that the praetorian driven *tatmadaw* self-rationalized itself as, in the words of a US diplomat, "the only guarantor of that unity and stability" (US Embassy 2009).

Maintaining a cohesive, hierarchical military regime

In the first iteration of Myanmar's military government, the founding RC set the foundations for a relatively disciplined and coherent hierarchical military regime. The RC leadership was based on the hierarchy of the *tatmadaw*, staffed with high-ranking military men and supported by a cabinet of eight ministers, seven of which were also active military officers (Nakanishi 2013: 101–102). At the time of the 1962 coup, General Ne Win had already been military chief since 1949, after his predecessor Smith Dun was relieved of his duties. This meant that on top of Ne Win's nationalist credentials as one of the "Third Comrades" of the Burmese Independence Army, and later, commander-in-chief of the Burma National Army, he was already a veteran of the armed forces and the most senior military officer in the RC and the armed forces. With the RC under a clear chain of command, Ne Win had no credible military equals that could challenge his leadership. Until his retirement from all formal positions of power in 1988, Ne Win was the clear hegemon of the military state, who institutionalized a highly coherent armed forces by ensuring factionalism that led to the collapse of military regimes elsewhere did not become a problem in Myanmar (Kyaw Yin Hlaing 2008: 175).

A year before the coup, Ne Win consolidated his authority over the military by purging potential contenders from position of power. A restructuring of the *tatmadaw* allowed the Ministry of Defense tighter control over all military activities. The new Northwestern and Central Commands – the only units that had the organizational capacity to threaten the central government – were placed under the command of Ne Win loyalists San Yu and Sein Win (Callahan 2003: 202). Of the original 18 field commanders, only five remained in their posts after the purge (*ibid*: 200). According to Mary Callahan, the 1962 coup bore all the hallmarks of a "unified, bureaucratized military, in which orders issued from Rangoon were followed with remarkable regularity throughout the territory" (2003: 203).

Although military regime's ideology may have evolved over time, yet prior to 2011, the essential power structure remained largely the same, with formal power in the hands of a small inner circle at the highest echelon of the politicized military command (Maung Aung Myoe 2009: 16–42). In the socialist years, this power was centered on the members of the RC, later the BSPP and the dictatorship of Ne Win (Lintner 1989: 55). After the collapse of the BSPP and the subsequent resignation and retirement of Ne Win, the *tatmadaw* launched a self-coup under the banner of the SLORC, with Saw Maung taking over as the new junta leader. The erratic leadership of Saw Maung, however, became increasingly detrimental for the stability of *tatmadaw*, an error that was eventually rectified by an internal purge in 1992. Saw Maung's ouster, ostensibly for health reasons, appeared to have the support of the collective leadership of the *tatmadaw* and allowed Than Shwe's elevation to the position of SLORC Chairman. Not unlike Ne Win, Than Shwe maintained the military's unity through careful balancing of the various military factions but also vigorously defended the integrity of the chain of command. In the initial years as SLORC Chair, Than Shwe did not have the same type of authority that Ne Win enjoyed in his long tenure. After incidents of insubordination, including an alleged spat with the Minister of Trade Tun Kyi, Than Shwe, with the support of his subordinates Maung Aye and Khin Nyut, respectively the second and third highest-ranking SLORC officials, launched a purge in 1997, replacing a number of senior SLORC veterans with a younger generation of military officers (Kyaw Yin Hlaing 2008: 168–169). Under the rebranded SPDC, Than Shwe was able to assert a clear vertical chain of commands, and with all of his contemporaries removed, he became the most powerful and senior officer of his generation that remained in active service. Than Shwe was able to further strengthen his influence over the SLORC by making almost every critical personnel decision, as he is known to hand pick loyal officers for promotion to crucial positions (Nakanishi 2013: 301–307). A retired colonel indicated that all the key players that have succeeded in positions of power in 2011, such as President Thein Sein, Speaker of the Lower House Shwe Mann, and the new army chief Min Aung Hlaing, were pre-determined and chosen prior to Than Shwe's retirement (Interview with the author, retired colonel, Yangon, January 20, 2014; also see account by Soe Thane 2018: 18–19).

Despite the personal authority of Myanmar's dictators, the military regime maintained a form of hierarchical rule that centered on the coherence and the collective interests of the *tatmadaw*. It was not a sultanistic type regime that was predominantly dependent on the powers of an enigmatic dictator that has led to the factionalization and split of the ruling elites witnessed elsewhere – for example Indonesia under Suharto (Slater 2010a). The hierarchical nature of the *tatmadaw* regime meant that dictators like Ne Win and Than Shwe derived authority primarily from the "charisma of office," based on their position as the supreme commander of the army (Taylor 2009: 368). These political hegemons' dictatorial powers, therefore, were not unrestricted and limitless but were structured by the institutional culture and the established standard operating procedures (SOPs) of the *tatmadaw* (Kyaw Yin Hlaing 2009: 274). The influence and powers of the top leadership is supported by their military ranks and their official capacity as military commanders, and their influence, is dependent on the network of loyal subordinates. Although "Chairman" Ne Win may have been the closest to achieving near absolute dictatorial-like powers, Myanmar's military leaders never developed a popular personality cult of sultanistic or totalitarian-like regimes. Policies determined by the very top of the leadership required the collective backing of the *tatmadaw* high command and are adhered to, as detractors are at risk of being ostracized by the organization. In the words of former navy chief Soe Thane, it is simply the *tatmadaw*'s tradition that "orders given above are to be obeyed" (2018: 18).

Further, once these former dictators no longer hold an official position within the military or the state, they no longer carry the same type of authority that they once wielded. This explains Ne Win and his family's eventual fall from grace in 2002, when more than a decade after his retirement, the former dictator died in relative obscurity and was not afforded a state funeral following a failed coup attempt by members of his family (Nakanishi 2013: 279). The SLORC's first chairman Saw Maung was never able to genuinely assert his leadership as the paramount leader of the junta, as he lacked the anti-colonial credentials of Ne Win, but more critically he was not the most senior military officer in the SLORC (Kyaw Yin Hlaing 2008: 163). After a four-year trial as SLORC Chairman, Saw Maung, clearly an error, was removed in 1992, as his unpredictability was deemed a liability, detrimental to the stability of the military regime. Finally, despite continued speculations about Than Shwe's post-retirement activities since 2011, there has been no evidence that he has retained any genuine power of influence in Myanmar's "disciplined" democracy (Kyaw Phyo Tha 2015).

Minimizing the centrifugal forces of factionalism

The *tatmadaw*'s long domination over the state apparatus is due largely to the early foundational setup as a highly coherent, hierarchical military regime, with well-institutionalized SOPs. Although factionalism has occasionally threatened the unity of the *tatmadaw*, the regime leadership has been able to successfully apply its formal and informal institutional controls to govern the behavior of regime insiders. As a hierarchical organization, insubordination, and any open internal rivalries that threatened the collective interests of the *tatmadaw*, were intolerable offenses. Kyaw Yin Hlaing identified two key practices that have minimized internal conflict within the *tatmadaw* to ensure its continued survival. The first is the creation and maintenance of "discrete domains," which above all else, ensure senior officers limit their activities within the domains assigned by their superiors (*ibid*: 275–283). In doing so, officers are discouraged from getting involved in other colleague's activities and spheres of influence. Offenders to this rule were routinely purged to prevent the institutionalization of critical factional rivalries that could undermine the stability of the *tatmadaw*. The second tradition is one of patronage. Officers are enticed to remain committed to the *tatmadaw* and loyalists are well rewarded even after retirement. This institutional culture of obedience and unity is established to maintain the network of support even after officers leave active service. Those officers who do not abide by the military's rules are, along with their families, excommunicated from the military network and denied access to the most basic rights and services (*ibid*: 283–287).

This explains why no genuine liberal factions emerged during the military's long rule, due to the risk of being punished as traitors to the *tatmadaw* (*ibid*: 274, 286). Some earlier analysts had initially labelled Khin Nyunt as a moderate reformist for his willingness to reach out to ethnic armed organizations (EAOs) and advocating greater engagement with "Western" governments and organizations. However, as Kyaw Yin Hlaing's research suggests, the former prime minister was no genuine democrat, had no interest in working with regime opposition, and his actions were motivated by practical considerations for regime maintenance (2009: 286). When Khin Nyunt formally unveiled the seven-step roadmap to disciplined democracy in 2003, some analysts had interpreted this plan as a personal initiative of the former prime minister. As will be discussed later, however, the roadmap persisted even after Khin Nyunt's downfall in 2004. The SPDC leadership went out of its way to endorse publicly the roadmap in the state-run *New Light of Myanmar* and declared that the transitions plan did not belong to any individual and was, in fact, a state directive (Selth 2019: 620).

Elite individuals such as the former top ranking SPDC general Shwe Mann were able to reinvent themselves as liberal reformers only *after* the 2011 regime change and after their formal retirement from the military. However, Shwe Mann's decision to diverge from the political plan of the *tatmadaw* by realigning his interests with longtime opposition leader Aung San Suu Kyi and the National League for Democracy (NLD) earned him the scorn of his former colleagues, leading to his eventual purge from the military-backed Union Solidarity and Development Party (USDP) in 2015. To add insult to injury, the *tatmadaw* accused Shwe Mann publicly of harming the military's image, and rejected him as a "brother" of the Defense Services Academy, effectively disowning the once powerful general from the military network (Lun Min Mang and Htoo Thant 2016). A memoir written by Soe Thane, who served as a senior minister in Thein Sein's government, would later call out the "traitors" that collaborated closely with the opposition as "turncoats" (Aung Zaw 2019a). The *tatmadaw* continues to view Shwe Mann's collaboration with the NLD as a betrayal and has made repeated attempts to derail his post-USDP career (*ibid*).

The extent of which the leadership at the highest echelon of the *tatmadaw* largely remained loyal to the military institution can best be demonstrated by two anecdotal cases: the 1963 purge of the second highest ranking RC member Aung Gyi, who was repeatedly imprisoned after his dismissal, and the house arrest of SPDC military intelligence head and prime minister Khin Nyunt in 2004. In the case of Aung Gyi, although he would become a vocal critic and opposition leader against the BSPP government, he remained loyal to the *tatmadaw* institution. Aung Gyi initially helped found the NLD on September 27 1988, and even served as its first chairman. However, Aung Gyi remained supportive of the *tatmadaw* publicly and shared the same antagonism the military held against the communists (Lintner 1989: 223). Citing the alleged infiltration of communist members into the NLD, Aung Gyi left the party in December to form the Union National Democratic Party (*ibid*: 59, 101–103, 124–125, 217). Even though he was critical of Ne Win and the BSPP policies, he did not fault the military institution publicly for the country's woes.

At the time of his purge, Prime Minister Khin Nyunt was the chief of military intelligence and the third highest-ranking SLORC official. Khin Nyunt's growing ambitions, and the intelligence service he commanded, often over-stretched into the domains of other military factions and threatened the *tatmadaw*'s cohesion (Kyaw Yin Hlaing 2008: 171–172). In October 2004, a month after a clash openly pitted local intelligence personnel against army units in the town of Muse, Khin Nyunt was removed from all positions of power, and the entire military intelligence branch was dismantled. The spectacular purge of Khin Nyunt demonstrates the military's remarkable resilience and adherence to its own SOPs and customs. Even though the ruling junta was aware that the purge would damage the regime's short-term ability to monitor dissident activities, the insubordination of Khin Nyunt and the military intelligence under his command were deemed to be greater threats to the unity of the military and therefore had to be stopped and punished (Selth 2019: 620, 627).

Since Khin Nyunt's downfall and eventual release, the former prime minister has not only refused to criticize the *tatmadaw* or his former colleagues but has actively defended the policies of the SLORC/SPDC years while attacking a journalist's work as counter-productive by "digging into the actions of the country's former leaders" (*The Irrawaddy* 2015a). In his 2015 autobiography, Khin Nyunt also wrote fondly of the "mutual respect" and friendly relationship he had with Than Shwe, who had ordered his purge (Gleeson 2015). Despite the fallout, Khin Nyunt has continued to adhere to the norm of not openly criticizing the *tatmadaw*.

Having discussed the attributes and institutional culture that govern the behavior of the *tatmadaw*, the remainder of this chapter will trace how the military regime has evolved since its founding in 1962, the process that led to its policy position changes, and its eventual transition and change to its version of a "disciplined" democracy since 2011.

The Revolution Council and its experimentation with the Burmese way to socialism

When the RC took power in 1962, they introduced the idea of resolving Myanmar's problems through a revolutionary path toward building "unity, stability, and equity" (Taylor 1986: 79–92). As self-appointed praetorian rulers, the *tatmadaw* initially attempted to maximize its rule with the indication that direct military rule may be indefinite. In the early years of the RC, the immediate agenda was to suppress any internal challenges to the survival and independence of the Myanmar state (Taylor 1989: 208). The 18-member RC abolished the 1947 Constitution and dissolved the parliament, choosing to rule directly. As Yoshihiro Nakanishi argues, although the coup leaders clearly intended to launch a socialist revolution and rule the country on a long-term basis, "they did not have any clear idea of a political ideology for their new regime," although it was clear the coup leaders have rejected the decade long parliamentary "democratic" system (Nakanishi 2013: 91). Though the RC issued The Burmese Way to Socialism policy statement on April 30, 1962, official ideology for the new regime was not drafted until November, four months *after* the founding of the BSPP (*ibid*).

The RC's official ideology, *The System of Correlation between Man and his Environment*, was adopted the in January 1963. The actual text of the ideology, drafted by Chit Hlaing, apparently had little input from the RC and was based largely on his earlier work as an anti-communist propagandist for the military (*ibid*: Chapter 3). This signified that the RC needed the state ideology to justify its broad socialist vision, though it was largely unconcerned with the actual content of the ideology. The RC, assured of its superiority to rule the state, did not have a committed blueprint on how to govern but saw its political duty as necessary. Given the popularity of socialism in Myanmar, the RC saw its BSPP state ideology as a useful set of "non-divisive" concepts that could help the *tatmadaw* in its ambition to establish a strong, unified nation-state (Taylor 2009: 358).

Although the military leadership had broad lofty socialist ideals, above all else, it saw itself as the prime defender of the stability and unity of the Myanmar nation-state. The military's attempt to implement its socialist revolution from above reflected the trial and error pattern of regime building that would become institutionalized under *tatmadaw* authoritarian rule. The decision of the high command to implement its Burmese way to socialism instituted a policy "lock-in," and the socialist experiment persisted for 26 years.

Under the Burmese socialist ideology, the RC justified its attempt to control all aspects of social life (Trager 1963: 321). Early attempts to co-opt the country's three major political parties failed, and the RC established its own party, the Burmese Socialist Program Party (BSPP), on July 4, 1962, four months after the coup (Nakanishi 2013: 92–93). All political parties were subsequently abolished by the 1964 National Security Act, essentially transforming Myanmar into a *de facto* single-party state that was controlled by the military (Mya Maung 1992: 22). The RC also tried to silence all opposition to its rule, especially in the urban centers. Infamously, the military brutally repressed student protests, destroyed the iconic Rangoon University Student's Union building, and commenced a prolonged shutdown of universities (Silverstein and Wohl 1964: 50). The RC went as far as dictating the private lives of its citizens. The increasingly totalitarian-like regime issued a series of orders banning popular activities that were perceived to be immoral (Thant Myint-U 2007: 293–294). The military intended to remove all external influences and pre-coup socio-economic structures, while only the regime's ideologically approved activities were permitted (Taylor 2009: 298).

On the economic front, the RC implemented an extreme form of economic nationalism, with the intention of nationalizing all of the country's major businesses (Lissak 1976: 171–172). Although, the *tatmadaw* became an important economic agent during its reign as caretaker government (1958–1960), their claimed economic competence during the 18-month tenure did not carry over to the RC. Part of the reason was a split in policy direction within the RC. Aung Gyi, the second most senior member of the RC, responsible for economic policies during the caretaker government, was forced to resign from the RC and the *tatmadaw*, as he was against the nationalization plan that was eventually adopted (Steinberg 2001: 20). Myanmar's rejection of the market-oriented colonial economic structure would be especially detrimental toward its economic development, as the country was shut "off from the world economy" (Mieno 2013: 95).

The economic failures of the 1960s nationalization policy would soon force the RC to scale back its earlier totalitarian-like ambitions. The RC never had absolute control over its territory as various EAOs and the Burmese Communist Party (BCP) continued to threaten the authority of the government (Lintner 1989:

64–71). In response to the continued economic failures, Ne Win acknowledged that there was a need to eventually transition to civilian rule at the BSPP's First Party Seminar in 1965 (Nakanishi 2013: 112).

Significantly, by 1971, at the first BSPP congress, the party sought to rectify earlier errors made in their socialist experiment. Realizing their role as praetorian rulers was not bringing Myanmar closer to a socialist utopia, the regime leadership begin to shift their role into becoming praetorian guardians. The RC therefore began the process of civilianizing the regime by transforming the BSPP from an elite, insular cadre party, to become a mass popular-based political party. The government also relaxed some control over the private sector, and took on the task of drafting a new constitution (Steinberg 1982: 165). Nevertheless, despite some key revisions of its economic policy, the government continued to exclude foreign direct investments as a route toward industrialization and economic development (Brown 2013: 150). To reform its failing policies, the RC began to co-opt and tolerate non-state forces, which led, ironically, to the further decay of the regime's socialist vision. In an effort to self-correct its own errors, the regime pushed out the senior members that were the most committed to the socialist revolutionary ideals, while those that remained in power were no longer genuine believers of the Burmese way to socialism (Kyaw Yin Hlaing 2003: 35).

First attempt at civilianization: the BSPP years

Direct rule by decree under the RC had failed to deliver the military's agenda, which led the military to change tracks and make provisions to civilianize the state in 1971. The RC agreed to a draft a new constitution, which was completed after two years and was put up to a referendum in 1973. The government recorded an official approval rate of 90.19 percent, although approval rates in the ethnic peripheries were largely lower than in the Bamar-centric centers (Silverstein 1977: 134). The purpose of the new charter, according to Robert Taylor, was a genuine attempt by the military to address the various ethnic-based conflicts in Myanmar with the aim to foster "national unity" (1979).

The implementation of the second constitution of Myanmar in 1974 saw the dissolution of the RC and the *de jure* recognition of the BSPP single party state structure. All the senior members of the abolished RC retired from the military and took on "new" role as civilian officials of the BSPP government. Instead of General Ne Win leading the party under the RC, as was the norm following the 1962 coup, theoretically at least, the BSPP was to lead the state under the leadership of Chairman Ne Win (Taylor 2009: 317). The BSPP also began a membership drive and transformed the previous insular, cadre-based elite party into a mass political party with reportedly more than two million members from diverse sectors of society, including pre-coup political figures, career civil service servants, opportunists, and job seekers (Shwe Lu Maung 1989: 95).

Nevertheless, even with the expanded membership, the BSPP never turned into a genuine autonomous organization, as all critical party positions remained in the hands of military officers (Nakanishi 2013: 112). The adoption of the 1974

Constitution, and the restructuring of the bureaucracy, did not shift the regime away from its praetorian, military roots. The BSPP structure continued to reflect the military's hierarchy to ensure that the "chain of command was not compromised" (Tin Maung Maung Than 2007: 162). At all levels, party positions were held by commanding military officers, and civilians without any previous military background never played any significant role in the party.[5] Despite lacking a formal political role, the military remained deeply involved in state governance. For example, 70 percent of BSPP Central Committee members in 1981 were active or retired military officers (Taylor 2009: 321).

Although the party derived its powers from its direct linkage to the *tatmadaw*, the party-military divide also introduced a new element of tension within the regime. A particular grievance and a source of tension was the field command-headquarter divide, where those fighting in the peripheries felt that the BSPP leadership, including senior army officers in Yangon were uncommitted to providing adequate resources to the counterinsurgency operations (Callahan 2003: 210). An unsuccessful coup attempt by a group of "Young Turks" in 1976, combined with a series of public protests and continued economic mismanagement further exposed increasing tension within the state (Tin Maung Maung Than 2007: 162).

At the 1977 third party congress, some party congress members apparently tried to manipulate the new voting system to remove Ne Win from the Central Committee (Nakanishi 2013: 133–141). This was an apparent attempt by a faction of the BSPP leadership to "reassert control over the state's functions" (Tin Maung Maung Than 2007: 162). Ne Win and his loyalists responded by purging 113 party congress members (Nakanishi 2013: 133–141). Those that were purged largely belonged to a group of high-ranking party members whose careers no longer depended upon the *tatmadaw*. These members were tied to party executive positions, and their career advancement could only be made within the party. By 1978, Ne Win had abandoned his plan to further develop the BSPP into a real political institution. The BSPP was thus turned "into an organization for distributing benefits to the tatmadaw" (*ibid*).

Both the BSPP party and the BSPP state apparatus continued to rely upon the military for personnel, and thus, over time, the party and the state became alternative routes for career advancement for military officers (Tin Maung Maung Than 2001: 165). This alternative channel for promotion had two contradictory legacies. The expanded career options for military personnel served as a reward system from within the state bureaucracy, which strengthened the foundations for a coherent, strong military regime (*ibid*: 167). However, the staffing of the state bureaucracy with underqualified military-cum-bureaucrats meant the deterioration of the state's capacity to govern and the continued downward spiral toward economic disaster (Bertrand 2013: 206). Similar trends can be observed in the post-2011 regime change, with retired military men going into alternative careers as USDP politicians, or as retired senior civil servants in the various ministries (Wade 2015). The military's trial and error approach to implement its Burmese way to socialism failed to deliver its socialist vision, but it further institutionalized the *tatmadaw*'s praetorian politics.

The collapse of the BSPP

By the 1970s, the failing economy meant that for most people, including government officials, had to turn to the black market for everyday commodities (Kyaw Yin Hlaing 2003: 24). The size of the shadow economy was estimated at US$ 3 billion in 1987, covering as much as 40 percent of the country's GDP (Perry 2007: 60–61). As the BSPP government had limited ability to regulate its borders, a vibrant underground economy led to the development of various contraband and illicit drug industries in the peripheries filtering into Myanmar's urban centers (Chang 2013; Meehan 2011). The BSPP's attempt to co-opt societal forces to achieve its socialist agenda never materialized, and non-state actors had to find a variety of means to ensure their own survival. Toleration of the illegal black market trade was so prevalent that it was well known that state agents from all levels of the regime developed various degrees of patron-client relations with prominent black market traders. These illegal traders actively sponsored state activities including local public construction projects such as schools and hospital buildings (Kyaw Yin Hlaing 2003: 45–49). The regime also began to gradually back away from its earlier isolationist policies by allowing a limited opening up of its economy. In order to reduce its budget deficit, the regime actively sought foreign aid and assistance from international organizations such as the World Bank (WB) and the Asia Development Bank (ADB), as well as invited limited foreign investments for mining projects and oil exploration (Holliday 2011: 52).

Two demonetization campaigns in the 1980s, which were intended for the state to re-assert control over the economy, had the opposite effect of accelerating the financial collapse of the BSPP state. The 1985 demonetization campaign took out the 20, 50, and 100 kyat notes from circulation and put a cap of 5,000 kyats per household for the exchange of disused notes for new legal tender (Brown 2013: 154–156). The 1987 demonetization policy went further by wiping out the 25, 35, and 75 kyat notes, but this time with no provisions for legal tender change, thus wiping out 60 to 80 percent of all money in circulation (*ibid*). The already fragile state-societal bond reached a breaking point. The chaos that came about from pent-up societal frustration led to a popular uprising and general unrest in 1988, which led to Ne Win's resignation from the state and the party. Several weeks of anarchy followed, with civil servants, including the police, and some low-ranking members of the military joining nationwide strikes and demonstrations against the government. A senior civil servant who had supported the protestors and voted for the NLD in the 2015 general election, described the 1988 protests as out of control "mob rule," one of the "scariest experiences" of his life (Interview with the author, senior civil servant, Naypyidaw, November 17, 2015). There is some suggestion that after the initial crackdown in August, the military kept back from maintaining order as a calculated tactic to create a general societal breakdown, which would allow justification for the internal coup that eventually followed. In this narrative, the military deliberately created a state of disorder in the final weeks of August 1988, therefore creating the conditions where the masses would prefer authoritarian-imposed order to anarchy (Ferrara 2003: 322).

In any case, the mass rejection of military rule had the unintended consequence of provoking the return of the *tatmadaw* in the form of the SLORC. Given that this was the same praetorian army that saw itself as being the most competent organization, the military quickly justified their crackdown as a restoration of law and order (hence the junta's name), while "state and regime security ... remained the top government priority" (Taylor 2009: 395). Although the military prevailed in their control of the state, under the SLORC government, three significant changes took place. First, the change of government allowed a "generational change among political leaders from the first to second generation of officers" (Nakanishi 2013: 279). Second, the purge of the BSPP ideology and policies allowed a shift from autarkic-socialism to a market-oriented economy with promises for a multiparty "democratic" system. Third, unable to have its own preferred party elected in the 1990 election (discussed later), the SLORC junta chose to govern directly, no longer relying on any proxies that it had briefly experimented with after the promulgation of the 1974 BSPP constitution. The *tatmadaw*'s return to direct politics allowed the *tatmadaw* to rid itself of the "locked-in" socialist vision that had long structured Myanmar's post-colonial economic policy. A complete policy reversal from socialism to a market-oriented economy became possible when the long failing equilibrium was punctuated by exogenous shocks brought about by the regime's self-made socio-economic disaster. However, instead of an external-imposed regime change, the *tatmadaw* was able to reassert its control and led an internal regime transition directly from a military-backed socialist state system into a direct military rule with a turn to a market-oriented economy and promises of a multiparty "democracy."

The return of direct military rule: regime continuity and change

The decision to introduce a regime change toward a disciplined, democratic system in 2011 has its roots as far back as 1987, a year before the ultimate collapse of the BSPP. In August of the year, Ne Win admitted to the failure of the socialist project and floated the idea of economic and political reforms, including the possibility of amending the 1974 Constitution (Steinberg 2001: 3). Soon thereafter, in the latter half of 1987, the government implemented in an "inconsistent and haphazard manner," a series of economic reforms as a necessity for political preservation (Taylor 2009: 381). Most notably, the control of a variety of agricultural commodities, especially rice, was relaxed. This policy change had an immediate but temporary effect of alleviating rural discontent, but it did little in the way of addressing the systematic problems of the failing socialist economy. This implied change of policy direction from the very top of the political hierarchy, although not immediately accepted by the collective BSPP leadership, would nevertheless inform the general direction of the *tatmadaw* after it returned to the forefront of governance in the form of SLORC/SPDC.

A year later, at the height of the 1988 protests, the BSPP Congress met for the last time, as Ne Win officially resigned from all official positions of power and put forward a referendum proposal for citizens to decide whether the country should return to multiparty political rule. Although the BSPP Congress rejected Ne Win's final proposal as BSPP Chair, the prospects that Myanmar may need to embrace change of politics and accept some form of multiparty system became a serious policy consideration.

Ne Win's immediate successor, General Sein Lwin imposed martial law days after coming into office and ordered the violent crackdown of protestors in Yangon. However, just 17 days into his tenure, Sein Lwin resigned from the government and was succeeded by Dr. Maung Maung, a long time civilian collaborator of the BSPP regime (Lintner 1989: 152–153). As the last BSPP President, Maung Maung tried to save the state by promising quick reforms and called for multiparty elections. The mobilized protestors ignored Maung Maung's overtures, thus finally setting the stage for the *tatmadaw* to launch an internal coup, which led to the dismantling of the BSPP regime and the return of direct, authoritarian military rule (Maung Maung 1999: 221–226).

In the last days of the BSPP regime, the BSPP bureaucracy might have been in disarray, but the chain of command within the *tatmadaw* remained clear, as coup leaders Saw Maung and Khin Nyunt were known to have consulted the former dictator at his private residence before launching the 1988 coup (Interview with a retired colonel, January 20, 2014).[6] Despite the political turbulence, and at times breakdown of communication within the BSPP government, the military hierarchy largely remained intact and the army united. When the *tatmadaw* launched its coup on September 18, the new ruling junta quickly and pragmatically dismantled and purged the remnants of the BSPP state. Paradoxically, the attempt by the protestors to dislodge the military-backed state had the unintended consequences of re-igniting the *tatmadaw*'s instincts to return to direct governance as praetorian rulers. The disorder during the 1988 protests strengthened the *tatmadaw*'s long-held institutional belief that it was the only non-partisan organization capable to hold the country together (Taylor 2009: 389).

Although the SLORC government inherited a failing state and an unstable regime, the *tatmadaw* leadership remained united in their commitment to rebuild the state. The regime's decision to reverse its autarkic-socialist policy direction coincided with the coming end of the Cold War and the gradual opening up of other Asian socialist economies such as China and Vietnam. The triumphant neoliberal zeitgeist created a favorable policy option for the *tatmadaw* to adopt a gradual liberalization of its political economy as a corrective to its 26-year failed single-party state socialist error. A year before its collapse, the BSPP government had already begun implementing economic liberalization, beginning with the domestic agricultural market (Okamoto 2008: 17–18). This pragmatic turn in part is due to the absence of any committed socialist ideologues after series of purges but also reflected the bounded rationality of the praetorian motivated *tatmadaw*. After the establishment of the SLORC, the new government quickly introduced a number of *ad hoc* economic reforms, such as the further relaxation of agricultural exports, and courting foreign investments openly, including provisions for foreign companies to have full ownership in their Myanmar-based operations (Brown 2013: 176). However, the junta only endorsed its full commitment to a market-oriented economy several months after the implementation of these economic reform measures. In March 1989, the junta revoked the 1965 Law of Establishment of the Socialist Economic System, therefore formally ending the BSPP system (*ibid*). A couple of months later, the junta also formalized plans to hold elections by issuing SLORC Law No. 14/89, which laid out the groundwork for multiparty elections (discussed in detail in the following section). No longer constrained by the single-party socialist ideology of its BSPP predecessor, the SLORC/SPDC government turned to more pragmatic authoritarian practices and allowed the re-emergence of limited pluralism gradually.

Re-building the *tatmadaw* regime

Throughout the two decades of the military's return to direct rule, state and military ranks were largely congruent, and the military maintained a high level of regime coherence. It was in the opinion of a former exiled rebel-turned advisor to the Thein Sein government, a "very strict, very pure military regime" (Interviewed on January 6, 2014). The *tatmadaw* took active measures to further expand its scope, size, and capabilities in its dual role as a military organization and as government. The *tatmadaw* underwent a significant upgrade of its military hardware, doubled its troop numbers, while at the same time further extending the reach of the military state into previous conflict areas through a series of bilateral agreements with insurgent groups (Selth 2002: 253, 2008a: 281–286). Not unlike the RC/BSPP Ne Win years, the SLORC/SPDC also adhered strictly to the military's hierarchical order, and overcame both internal and external challenges to the military's unity, including a successful restructuring of the junta following a systematic purge in 1997 when SLORC was transformed into the SPDC (Taylor 2009: 394–395). The growing powers of regional commanders, and signs of growing insubordination, had led to the reshuffling of the military command. The re-packaged SPDC allowed the remaining senior leadership to further centralize powers and ensured the long-term stability of the ruling junta.

Continuing down its "new military professionalism" path, the *tatmadaw* further expanded its duties beyond its primary role as dispensers of state-sanctioned violence and trained its cadets to become "engineers, technicians, economic experts, medical doctors, male nurses, pharmacologists and the like," often at the expense of the underfunded and mismanaged national education (Prager-Nyein 2009: 646–647). By reserving the best opportunities and concentrating resources within the *tatmadaw*, the military reinforced its self-perpetuating praetorian belief that the *tatmadaw* is a superior institution, and the most competent, and only, non-partisan protector of Myanmar's national interests.

In order to address the bankrupted state, the SLORC in the 1990s demonstrated an "impressive ... legislative energy" by pushing through a series of rapid economic reforms including the privatization of state-owned industries and the legalization and promotion of a wide-range of new industries and businesses that had long been prohibited by the BSPP (Brown 2013: 177). This included a determined push for a new "open-door policy," introducing a wide range of reforms to attract foreign investors and international trade, a complete overturn of the two decades of isolationist policy of its BSPP predecessor (Mieno 2013: 96). The ruling junta also fostered a small group of prominent entrepreneurs actively, with the intention of establishing these cronies as industry leaders to help develop the country's woeful industries (Maung Aung Myoe 2009: 163– 190). Unlike the "money politics" prevalent in Southeast Asia (Aspinall 2015: 299–313), Myanmar's cronies did not develop an independent source of political power, as their fortunes were linked to the status of their military patrons. Under the SLORC, the military also established two mammoth military conglomerates, which became actively involved in every sector of Myanmar's economy, with special tax exemption privileges (McCarthy 2019: 14). These economic advantages and career opportunities further incentivized the military to retain its privileged position of power.

The result was, the emergence of a "state-mediated capitalism" that enriched various military officers, as well as their crony business partners (Jones 2014a: 145). In the ethnic peripheries, the SLORC/SPDC state enabled the rise of "ceasefire capitalism," which allowed the gradual primitive accumulation of wealth for ceasefire insurgent leaders, as well as the regional *tatmadaw* commanders through the exploitation of the country's resources and cross border trafficking (Woods 2011: 751). Unlike the BSPP yesteryear, senior military officers and their crony associates lived a life of luxury and flaunted their wealth openly (Callahan 2007a: 40). The emergence of a new class of nouveau riche commanders and crony capitalists contrasted starkly with the increasing wealth gap of the rank and file and the broader society.

A very long transition: the 1990 elections and the long road to the 2008 constitution

When the military launched a self-coup on September 18, 1988, the newly established SLORC suspended the 1974 Socialist Constitution, defended its rule as provisional, and declared almost immediately that multiparty elections promised earlier by the purged BSPP government would be honored (Lintner 1989: 216– 218). After governing as praetorian rulers, first, directly, in the form of the RC, later, indirectly, with the additional layer of the BSPP state apparatus as nominal praetorian guardians, the collapse of the RC/BSPP government saw the junta return to its praetorian ruler roots, albeit the junta argued that it would eventually return to a praetorian guardian/arbitrator role. The military although clearly intended to maintain its powers and control over the state and society, but it appeared that they were also willing to introduce gradual and controlled pluralism. Days after the coup, SLORC passed the Political Parties Registration Law, thus officially ending the BSPP single-party state socialism and opening up a new legal space for political parties to form. It soon became evident, however, that the *tatmadaw* was making policies in an *ad hoc* fashion. SLORC had a broad objective that was to develop Myanmar into some form of multiparty, market-oriented system. Yet, similar to when the RC first took over the state apparatus in 1962, the SLORC in 1988 had no comprehensive blueprint for how the *tatmadaw* was to implement its post-socialist multiparty "democracy." The leadership's decision to hold elections and the military's SOP meant that SLORC continued to collectively carry out its duties to organize elections. On May 31, 1989, SLORC Law No. 14/89 was issued, which set out a detailed legal framework governing the rules and regulations in preparation for the country's first multiparty "democratic" general elections since 1962. Known as the *Pyithu Hluttaw* Election Law, the law clearly stated the election was to vote for representatives for a *Pyithu Hluttaw*, which is a national legislative body.

The military decree covered several bureaucratic and technical concerns, but it did not specify a timeline for when the *Pyithu Hluttaw* would convene. Also missing were specifics about the purpose and powers of the new *Pyithu Hluttaw* (Tonkin 2007: 39). In other words, although SLORC soldiered on with its promises to hold elections, they did not set out the new rules of the game, nor did they provide clear ideas about how the post-BSPP "democracy" would operate. Just days after the passage of the election law, SLORC publicly revised the purpose of the planned elections. According to Derek Tonkin, the records of the 43rd SLORC Press Conference on June 9 1989 shows that the junta decided that the election was, in fact, for drawing up a constitution.[7]

The junta also maintained that it had no intention to hold on to power indefinitely, and that transferal of power to a new government would take place "as soon as possible," but only after the "people" approved a new constitution (*ibid*). It appeared that the junta decided to change tracks after it realized that there was no legal mechanism that would safeguard the military's core institutional and national interests. The junta later clarified its key political objectives guiding the military's transition plan. These four objectives, propagated in all public spaces for the next two decades, were: stability of the state, community peace and tranquility, prevalence of law and order; national reconsolidation; emergence of a new enduring state constitution; and the building of a new modern developed nation in accordance with the new state constitution (Tin Maung Maung Than 2007: 340).

Significantly, the military followed-through its initial decision to call for elections, a policy continuity from the final days of the BSPP government. Yet, broadly reflective of the trial and error process of implementing its regime change, the *tatmadaw* continued to persist with its electoral plan with imprecise ideas of what the regime change would look like. Further, the SLORC announced some vague outline of how and when it would eventually implement "democracy" in Myanmar. Although, the military unilaterally decided to change the purpose of the election, the junta continued to allow the political parties to carry on with their campaigns. The junta's authoritarian instincts meant that during the electoral campaign, opposition groups and parties faced harassment, which included the arrest of several key opposition figures. Despite targeting the opposition unfairly, the SLORC government also provided substantial material help for all registered parties. At a time when petrol was normally sold for 100–150 kyats a gallon on the black market, all registered parties were entitled to purchase 70 gallons of petrol per week from the government, at an official rate of 16 kyats a gallon (Lintner 1989: 164). Additionally, each party was entitled to four telephone lines at a time when it normally took several months for private citizens to have a telephone installed in their private residence. Contrary to the later, well-orchestrated irregular elections in 2010 (likely after learning from its mistakes from the 1990 elections), which saw the installment of the military-backed USDP following its landslide victory, despite various flaws, the 1990 general elections allowed much of the electorate a reasonable environment in which to cast a relatively free and fair vote.

The result, to the surprise of the SLORC the NLD was able to deliver a landslide victory was a shock to the military leadership. Under Aung San Suu Kyi's absentee leadership, the NLD won 59.87 percent of the votes and managed to win 392 out of 485 seats, or 80.82 percent of all seats, while the National Unity Party (NUP), the successor to the BSPP, won only 21.16 percent of the votes, which translated to ten seats (*ibid*: 34). The electoral defeat of the NUP is particularly telling of the military's behavior and actions. Despite the general perception and assumption that the NUP was aligned with the military, the NUP did not receive any significant special treatment from the military (Holliday 2011: 7, 64). Once the military have decided to formally divorce itself from the socialist project, it ended all formal backing for the BSPP, which led to the political irrelevance of the successor NUP in subsequent years. The NUP may have been the preferred party of the *tatmadaw*, but similar to the 1960 elections under Ne Win's caretaker government, the *tatmadaw* likely miscalculated the electoral appeal of its preferred party. Further, the strong institutionalized belief that the *tatmadaw* is a non-partisan organization contributed to its relative electoral neutrality in 1990.

As one interviewee, a former critic turned advisor of the Thein Sein government, explained, the *tatmadaw* made no backup plan in the event of a NUP electoral defeat and had no concrete transition plans to a civilian government that it was not able to control (Interview with the author, Yangon, January 6, 2014). The uncertainty and constant change of position in the early days of the SLORC rule suggests that the *tatmadaw* was consistently reevaluating its strategy. On July 27, 1990, two months after the NLD delivered a landslide victory, the junta issued SLORC Order No. 1/90, which further clarified the junta's position that those who won in the 1990 elections would serve as delegated to draft a new constitution (Pedersen 2008: 130). The same decree also emphasized that the SLORC military government has the sole right to exercise all the powers of the state: judicial, legislative, and executive, at least until a new election were held after the implementation of the then-to-be-drafted constitution. Various competing political parties largely ignored these pronouncements by the SLORC, and the NLD was quick to demand that the SLORC hand over official power to the newly elected members after the elections (Tonkin 2007: 40–51).

The SLORC's position was that without a constitution in place, power could not be transferred, since there was no legal framework to prevent the state from breaking apart. In the view of the *tatmadaw* elite, the 1947 Constitution[8] that the NLD had suggested could be re-adopted was a flawed one, given that this was the constitution that "permitted minority states to secede" (Jones 2014b: 786). The confusion and stalemate between the NLD and the *tatmadaw* after the 1990 elections gave pretext for the SLORC to suspend, indefinitely, the transfer of power to any civilian authority.

Nevertheless, the military did follow through the motion of a longwinded constitutional drafting process. The National Convention (NC) for the drafting of the constitution officially began on January 9, 1993. Only 99 out of the 702 NC delegates were elected politicians from the 1990 elections, while the remaining members were mostly township-level officials handpicked by the military (Lian H. Sakhing 2014: 204). Of these, 86 were NLD members (Reynolds et al. 2001: 97). The NC was very much a military-controlled process. Delegates met irregularly with frequent suspensions, and was suspended in November 1995 after all 86 NLD members were expelled (Diller 1997: 29).

On June 7, 1996, the SLORC issued Law No. 5/96, "The Law Protecting the Peaceful and Systematic Transfer of State Responsibility and the Successful Performance of the Functions of the National Convention against Disturbances and Oppositions," which outlawed any public criticism of the NC, with offenders subjected to a potential prison sentence ranging from five years to a maximum of 20 years (Freeman et al. 1997: 42). One interviewee, a retired military officer who was present during a discussion in 1995 between Than Shwe and a divisional commander, the senior general contextualized these tensions around constitutional reform, suggesting that there was no time frame for drafting the constitution, and that it could have taken up to "twenty or thirty years" (Interview with the author, a retired colonel, Yangon, January 20, 2014).

There were other indicators that the military was making long-term plans to eventually implement a political transition. Development of a planned new capital in the center of the country appeared to have been underway since as early as 2002, yet these plans were shrouded in secrecy, with the public only learning about the capital's relocation in late 2005, when the junta suddenly announced its decision to move the capital. The considered attempt and scale of building a grand capital with massive administrative buildings, as well as several public spaces, including the Uppatasanti Pagoda, a replica of its more famous Shwedagon Pagoda in Yangon, indicated that the *tatmadaw* was serious about fulfilling its own political agenda. Even as the military regime was consolidating its powers over state and society, it continued to advance its own political transitions plan based on the decisions of its own political hierarchy, with no observable input from regime outsiders.

The significance of the seven-step roadmap to disciplined democracy

The National Convention (NC) to draft the constitution reconvened in 2004, following the August 30, 2003 announcement of a seven-step "roadmap to democracy" by then Prime Minister Khin Nyunt (See Table 3.1). The reconvened NC met on May 17, 2004, with an expanded delegation of 1,076 members, which included representatives from 25 ethnic ceasefire groups, but was boycotted by the NLD (Lian H. Sakhing 2014: 205).

These constant delays were seen by critics of the regime as a pretext for prolonging the introduction of real political reforms (Charney 2009: Chapter 9). However, as one interviewee, a former anti-regime activist, suggested that while Khin Nyut's roadmap may have been a response to the Depayin massacre when Aung San Suu Kyi's entourage was attacked by pro-government groups, it was also a genuine transition plan (Interview with the author, former critic and advisor to the Thein Sein government, Yangon, January 6, 2014). Certainly, Khin Nyunt's purge and the dismantling of the entire military intelligence apparatus in October of 2004 did not derail the regime's roadmap.

By 2005, the SPDC government began plans to re-civilianize its governance structure by transferring power from direct military rule to civilian bureaucrats at the sub-state level (Callahan 2007b: 7). Finally, 14 years after the NC first met, the proceedings were concluded on September 3, 2007, followed by a largely flawed referendum on May 10, 2008, just barely a week after the devastating Cyclone Nargis struck Myanmar.

In effect, the *tatmadaw* was able to force through its carefully controlled constitutional drafting process, introducing the military's version of the Myanmar's way to democracy, albeit through a long, drawn-out process. The last three stages of the seven-step roadmap concluded with the holding of the country's first general elections in over 20 years on November 7, 2010, which led to step six, the convening of the USDP-dominated bicameral *Pyidaungsu Hluttaw* (National Parliament), thus allowing for the final step of the roadmap toward a disciplined democracy – the advent of the Thein Sein administration in 2011.

Despite speculations of the role of "exogenous shocks," such as the 2007 "Saffron Revolution" and the 2008 Cyclone Nargis, as determinants that have led to Myanmar's post-2011 regime change, there is no evidence of this (as will be discussed in Chapters 4 and 5). The long, drawn-out NC proceedings concluded days before the infamous crackdown on the "Saffron Revolution" mass protests (Holliday 2011: 82). Robert Taylor asserts that the 2007 protests were in fact an opportunity for the *tatmadaw* "to suppress its most vehement opponents until the new order was in place" (Taylor 2013: 394). Further, the junta had already indicated that 2008 would be a critical year for the beginning of political reforms (Taylor 2009: 489). Despite the intensification of international pressure, the SPDC regime resolved to follow through with its seven-step roadmap toward a disciplined, flourishing democracy based on its own timeframe and without engaging the country's main opposition parties. This is best demonstrated by the SPDC regime's insistence to go ahead with the largely orchestrated constitutional referendum on May 10, 2008, just days after the disastrous Cyclone Nargis.[9]

SPDC held a largely flawed election in November 2010, where the military-aligned USDP won 80 percent in the lower house and 77 percent in the upper house of the new parliament (ICG 2011). Key members of the USDP were all

Table 3.1 Seven-step Roadmap to Discipline-flourishing Democracy

The seven-step Roadmap to a Disciplined Democracy	Steps taken by the SPDC corresponding to their self-declared roadmap
(1) Reconvening of the National Convention that had been adjourned since 1996.	The National Convention (NC), suspended since 1996, reconvened on May 17, 2004 and met at the Nyaunghnapin Camp, which was built specifically for the purpose for the NC. The first session of the NC concluded on July 9, 2004.
(2) After the successful holding of the National Convention, step by step implementation of the process necessary for the emergence of a genuine and disciplined democratic system.	1 The NC met for their second session on February 17 2005 until March 31, 2005. 2 Naypyidaw, the purpose-built capital was officially revealed to the public, and government offices and civil servants begin to move to the capital on November 6, 2005. The capital's official name was announced to the public on March 27, 2006 (Armed Forces Day). Officially written in English as *Nay Pyi Taw*, it is generally translated as "abode of kings" or "royal abode." 3 The NC met for the third session from December 5, 2005 until January 31, 2006, where the delegates "adopted the detailed basic principles of the chapters on the sharing of the executive and judicial powers" (*New Light of Myanmar* 2006). 4 The NC met for the fourth session between October 10, 2016 and December 29, 2006. Further chapters of the Constitution were completed. 5 The NC met for the final session on July 18 2007 and announced on September 3, 2007 the conclusion of the NC with the completion of drafts of the remaining chapters of the Constitution and the adoption of the "Fundamental Principles and Detailed Basic Principles" of the Constitution.
(3) Drafting of a new Constitution in accordance with basic principles and detailed basic principles laid down by the National Convention.	A 54-member Constitution-Drafting Commission met on December 3, 2007 to formally draft the Constitution based on the principles agreed upon by the NC. The Constitution was officially declared completed on February 19, 2008.
(4) Adoption of the Constitution through national referendum.	A national referendum was held on May 10, 2008, just weeks after the devastating Cyclone Nargis. In the worst hit

The seven-step Roadmap to a Disciplined Democracy	Steps taken by the SPDC corresponding to their self-declared roadmap
	townships, the referendum was postponed to May 24, 2008. According to the government the turnout rate was 98.12 percent, with 92.48 percent of voters supporting the Constitution.
	Leading up to the 2010 elections, there was also an accelerated process of privatization of state assets (Ford et al. 2016: 27; *The New York Times* 2010).
(5) Holding of free and fair elections for *Pyithu Hluttaws* (legislative bodies) according to the new Constitution.	The SPDC Government held Myanmar's first election in 20 years on November 7, 2010. The USDP won the overwhelming majority of the votes in an electoral process that was deemed largely unfree and unfair by the Western-centric international community, including the United Nations (MacFarquhar 2010).
(6) Convening of *Hluttaws* attended by Hluttaw members in accordance with the new Constitution.	The elected members of the bicameral *Hluttaws* attended their first parliamentary session on January 31, 2011. The *Hluttaws* enacted the 2008 Constitution and proceed to elect Thein Sein as the first President based on the 2008 Constitution.
(7) Building a modern, developed, and democratic nation by the state leaders elected by the Hluttaw; and the government and other central organs formed by the Hluttaw.	Thein Sein inaugurated as President on March 30, 2011, thus leading to the official dissolution of the SPDC and the beginning of a disciplined flourishing democratic system – Myanmar's way to democracy.

Source: *New Light of Myanmar* (adapted).

members of the recently retired upper echelon military officers of the SPDC regime. By 2011, Thein Sein, the last prime minister of the SPDC, became the new President of post-junta Constitutional Myanmar, in charge of an amended political system that continues to privilege and protect the core interests of the *tatmadaw*.

The main ideational and normative interests of the military were articulated as original principles in SLORC Order No. 13/92, which, above all else, retained the military's role to participate in the politics of the state and the preservation of the political unity of the nation-state. These basic principles listed in 1992 have been retained in their entirety and became the "consistent objective" of the 2008 Constitution.[10] In essence, despite all talks of crises and challenges against the *tatmadaw* regime, the military was able to introduce transition from above based on the conditions that it had always promulgated. The 2008 constitution kept all the key objectives and core institutional interests that the military had announced two decades earlier when it established the SLORC. This remarkable military continuity in politics took several twists and turns, yet in each military-imposed systematic political change, the *tatmadaw* has succeeded in determining the rules of the game and institutionalized its role in government.

Conclusion: *tatmadaw*'s path to a disciplined multiparty democratic system

When the military took full control of the government in 1962, it was evident that the *tatmadaw* did not have a comprehensive blueprint as to how it would govern. With a broad political agenda, a formal ideology was drafted after the 1962 coup to justify the *tatmadaw*'s authoritarian rule. The guiding socialist ideology was an easy choice at the time, and there was little disagreement among the major political stakeholders on the potential of state-led economic nationalism to redress decades of exploitative British *laissez faire* economic policy. Lukewarm attempts to civilianize the RC and transform into a BSPP single-party state in the 1970s never materialized, and the BSPP remained a hollowed out party reliant on the *tatmadaw* for personnel and leadership.

The 1988 popular uprising may have punctuated the 26-year socialist equilibrium, yet regime outsiders were unable of capitalizing upon the opportunity to force an external-led regime change. Although the socialist revolution failed, direct rule by military men prevailed for another 23 years. The turn toward a market-oriented economy and the expansion of military capitalism during the SLORC/SPDC years further entrenched the military's dominant position and privileged the militarized state. Consistently, since 1962 until 2011, power remained concentrated in the hands of the military establishment, and even today, the military has only partially withdrawn from formal politics, as will be discussed in detail in Chapters 6 and 7. Nevertheless, by the time Thein Sein became president of a nominally civilian Myanmar in 2011, the regime was no longer the same as the one that had emerged from the chaos of 1988.

The top-down, military-enforced regime change in 2011 would reconfigure power relations significantly within the new disciplined democratic system, yet its transitions process, and the military's approach to implementing its version of democracy, share parallel similarities with the military's earlier attempt to implement its Burmese way to socialism. In both the socialist project and the current attempt to build a disciplined democracy, the military has determined the rules of the game, cautiously designed a Constitution, and backed its game with the coercive powers of the military. This chapter has suggested that the *tatmadaw* is a remarkably resilient institution. Although periodically facing a range of trials – from economic mismanagement, internal dissent, natural disasters, and even occasional elite in-fighting – the military has remained unified and continues to be the dominant force shaping political developments in the country. In short, although Myanmar today is a different type of regime from its SLORC/ SPDC years, the military remains deeply embedded in the political process. However, instead of direct praetorian rule, the *tatmadaw* has shifted to the role of praetorian guardians since 2011. Outside of its core interests on issues of national security, the military are no longer directly engaged in the activities of day-to-day governance. The post-junta liberalization effort by a constitutional, nominal, civilian government in 2011 is thus a continuation of the gradual socio-political reforms that first began in 1988.

Notes

1 Although opposition parties and partisan politics became possible in 2011, genuine sharing of power arguably only occurred in 2016, after the landslide electoral victory of the National League for Democracy (NLD) in the 2015 elections.

2 Although opposition parties were allowed to participate in parliamentary politics since 2011, their limited numbers meant that their actual powers were limited, and any legislation would require the support of the ruling pro-military establishment.

3 I am indebted to Mark Thompson for this idea. Coincidentally, this is exactly the language used by Commander-in-Chief Min Aung Hlaing, who has stated in an interview that the military is "marching toward a multi-party democracy," as a direct response to what the people have demanded (RFA 2015).

4 The publicly stated "Three National Clauses" of the military which for years were published daily on all military publications and official newspapers are non-disintegration of the Union, non-disintegration of national solidarity, and the perpetuation of sovereignty.

5 The clear exception is Maung Maung, a lawyer, and briefly president of the BSPP, who was a close confidante to Ne Win. However, Maung Maung has served previously in the Burma Defence Army during World War II (Taylor 2008: 7).

6 This account mirrors the same assertion in Robert Taylor's works (for example, see: Taylor 2009: 387). Yoshihiro Nakanishi (2013: 274–275), however, challenges this assertion and cites in his interviews that it was some critical members of the BSPP's Central Executive Committee that directed the *tatmadaw* to stage a coup. Although there is a discrepancy between the two accounts, neither narratives dispute my main point, which is that the military leadership was united overall and decided collectively to stage a coup.

7 Five days earlier, the Chinese Communist Party (CCP) had cracked down violently on student-led protests in Beijing, with thousands reported missing or killed in what is known as the Tiananmen Square Massacre. It would not be surprising if the *tatmadaw* and the CCP may have learned from each other's experiences during this critical period of societal unrest.

8 The 1947 Constitution was drafted as the legal foundation for Myanmar's independence from British rule in 1948. The 1947 Constitution gives the Karen (*Kayin*), Karenni (*Kayah*), and the Shan states the right to secede from the Union after ten years of implementation of the Constitution. The Kachin State and the Chin Special Division were not given this right to secede. In any case, the military was unlikely to ever concede to secession of any part of the country, thus making the country's first Constitution, especially objectionable to the *tatmadaw*.

9 Although in some of the worst-hit areas, the referendum was postponed until May 24, 2008.

10 Since 1992, the *tatmadaw* have announced publicly core sets of principles and key national objectives when the regime issued SLORC Order No. 13/92. These were: 1) non-disintegration of the Union, 2) non-disintegration of national solidarity, 3) consolidation and perpetuation of sovereignty, 4) emergence of a genuine multiparty democratic system, 5) development of eternal principles of justice, liberty and equality in the state, and 6) participation of the *tatmadaw* in the leading role of national politics of the state (SLORC Order No. 13/92).

4 A disciplined society for a disciplined democracy

Introduction

When the military launched an internal coup and established the SLORC on September 18, 1988, the *tatmadaw* recognized that the BSPP single-party state and its socialist ideology had failed. As part of its initial efforts to organize the 1990 elections, the junta issued SLORC Law No. 6/88 a week after the coup, which formally opened the doors for non-state groups and political parties to apply and register as lawful organizations in Myanmar (Kyaw Yin Hlaing 2009: 160). The decree also stipulated that organizations that were deemed a threat to political stability or those that engaged in activities perceived to be anti-government would be banned, and any person associated with illegal organizations would be subjected to a possible prison sentence of up to five years (Chua and Gilbert 2015: 7).

Although the SLORC government established its authority by suppressing protestors and restoring the authority of the state, the emergence of a more pragmatic authoritarian regime meant the expansion of limited pluralism, where a new legal platform allowed the existence of non-state groups in the public arena, even if their space is severely restricted. The end of the BSPP's formal indiscriminate ban on all associational life thus marks a significant policy shift but is also indicative of the attitude of the state vis-à-vis non-state groups and partisan politics – they are to be tolerated, as long as they remain in the legal framework as designed by the *tatmadaw* government.

Reflecting on the evolving priority and praetorian logic of the authoritarian military regime, the SLORC/SPDC in its bid to reconsolidate the military's control over the state apparatus while also expanding the state's presence to the peripheral regions, dedicated its resources and attention to state security and the preservation of the Union's territorial integrity. In order to finance the state, the military regime eagerly sold is natural resources, with the large majority of foreign investments involved in the extractive industries, primary in the mining, oil, and gas sectors (Bissinger 2012: 24). Human security was largely ignored by the state, and even the most basic welfare concerns of its general population were generally unaddressed (James 2005).[1] The SLORC/SPDC in its self-declared three national clauses – non-disintegration of the union, non-disintegration of national solidarity, and the perpetuation of sovereignty (which were propagated as permanent slogans in billboards and newspapers throughout the country) aimed to maintain political stability. – Any deviation or challenges from society were perceived as a diversion from the military's regime transition plan and were treated as "errors" to be corrected.

By the late 1990s, Myanmar's disciplined civil society had gradually re-emerged under this authoritarian context. The authoritarian nature of the military regime meant that in order for civil society groups to operate prior to 2011, they had to establish cordial relations with the government, or at least with individual agents of the regime (Seekins 2009: 730). As long as these non-state actors focused on areas that were not considered contentious or contrary to the interests of the *tatmadaw* regime, they were allowed conditional autonomy. The state's inability to develop an organic bond with its society, meant that Myanmar's civil society developed a "horizontal solidarity" to address the social-welfare gap left by the weak infrastructural power of the state (Seekins 2009: 728–730).

Due to the military's historical antagonism and suspicion of popular mobilization and partisan politics, the gradual liberalization of society was severely limited by a series of laws and updated mechanisms of societal control that continued to curb the political rights of its citizens, and it effectively arrested the development of any credible, organized political opposition against military rule (Taylor 2009: 419–433). In any case, the primary concern of the general populace was communal survival, and thus societal force failed to develop independently as an effective political counterweight force against the high "despotic power" of the state (Prasse-Freeman 2012: 378). Under routine state suppression, society was largely depoliticized, but a relatively vibrant yet *disciplined* civil society had developed by the early 2000s.

This chapter will address the evolution of state-societal relations since the return of direct military rule in 1988 until the regime change in 2011. For the purpose of this book, I frame civil society, as all associational life, which includes non-state groups, formal and informal, including political society such as political activists, dissidents, human rights defenders, and pro-establishment groups. The chapter begins with a broad overview of the theoretical limitations of a normative definition of civil societies. It then examines some of the earlier literature on Myanmar's civil society and discusses how civil society developed under the SLORC/SPDC government.

Through trial and error, by way of suppressing, co-opting, or ignoring various societal forces, the regime was eventually able to find willing civilian partners to develop the type of civil society that is desirable from the military regime's perspective, best exemplified by the emergence of the so-called Third Force. These so-called Third Force organizations attempted to mediate between the state and society by operating within the political parameters permitted by the regime. These Third Force organizations are the archetype of *disciplined* civil society that the military regime aimed to shape in order to introduce Myanmar's way to a disciplined democracy. The Third Force became an important component of the regime's plan to push ahead with its agenda leading up to the 2010 general elections and the subsequent 2012 by-elections (Lidauer 2012).

Ultimately, adversary politics and the country's disciplined civil society were unable to pressure the regime to democratize. In fact, it was the ability of the military state to emasculate its political opposition and to ensure that its society was disciplined, which gave the regime confidence to push ahead and complete its seven-step roadmap, and thus commence its voluntary transformation from a highly repressive military authoritarian regime into a partially civilianized, hybrid regime in 2011.

Rethinking civil society

The study of civil society is especially popular within democratization theory. Its basic normative assumptions suggest that the prevalence of autonomous, non-state groups and a strong political opposition are essential to the process of regime liberalization, democratization, and the strengthening of democratic institutions (Diamond 1999). Despite its popularity as a theoretical and practical concept both in academia and policy circles, the actual definition of "civil society," including its membership, remains heavily contested (Foley and Edwards 1996). Within Western-centric policy circles as well as among transnational (and domestic) activist networks, the prevailing "civil society-democratization" paradigm has dominated much of the thinking of the role civil society is considered to play. Historically rooted in European liberal traditions, some have argued that civil society is essentially a product of modernity and thus a "contingent historical phenomenon" (Keane 1998: 145–146). However, associational life as a phenomenon, in its many forms, has historically existed in the non-Western world prior to the advent of colonialism, industrialization, and modernization. By contextualizing civil society as a normative concept rooted only in a Western-centric perspective, this approach ignores the reality that non-state indigenous associations, such as religious and ethnic organizations have long played a critical role in state-society relations outside of the European context, for example throughout Myanmar's history even before the advent of colonialism (McCarthy 2012: 5–7).

An argument popular with (Western-centric) policymakers and pro-democracy activists is that civil society is a vital institution that can help promote civility, "trust," and "social capital," thus serving as a political "counterweight" against the state, which could theoretically lead to "good governance" and democratization (for example see: Foley and Edwards 1996: 39; Calvert and Burnell 2004; Diamond 1999: 222–223; Mercer 2002; Newton 2001; Putnam 1993). Particularly during times of political or economic crisis, which often result in diminished resources for regime insiders to maintain political equilibrium, democratization theory hypothesizes that regime outsiders – political opposition and civil society can often force the regime to withdraw from power or concede to greater political liberalization or democratization (Reynolds et al. 2001; Haggard and Kaufman 1997; Williams 2011). This theoretical framework, however, is normative and assumes that political opposition and civil society groups are generally positive for society and constructive for political liberalization, democratization, and democratic consolidation.

While civil society may play a role in determining the dynamics of regime change, it is not always in the direction of democratization. Omar Encarnacion, for example, makes a compelling case refuting the allegedly democratizing effects civil society is perceived to possess and points out that civil society can at times actually help to strengthen authoritarian rule (Encarnacion 2006). Instead of an uncritical assumption of civil society as being wholly conducive to democracies, Encarnacion convincingly argues that the nature of civil society and its effects on "democracy" are largely determined by the political context. This assertion is backed by Sheri Berman's research, where she reminds us that the particularly rich associational life under the Weimar Republic actually led to the rise of the Nazis and the eventual collapse of the weak democracy (Berman 1997). As Berman argues, it was precisely the existence of a strong civil society that provided "training ground" for the Nazis to mobilize popular support and eventually gain control over the state apparatus, something that she suggests would be unlikely if associational life had been weaker (*Ibid*: 402). Similarly, the collapse of communism in Hungary and the decline of the infrastructural power of the state essentially left a vacuum that traditionally supported those that would be the most vulnerable to social transformation. As a result, at least during the early years of Hungary's democratization process, "uncivil society" in the form of extremism and Skinhead culture captured significant support from the youth population. Mass disillusionment based on the failures of the communist ideology and its associated youth movements would leave a legacy that created a generation of youth indifferent to or dissatisfied with the state and political parties (Kurti 2003: 37–53). A legacy of mistrust of associational life under communist rule also explains why many post-communist societies in Eastern Europe did not see an expansion of civil society activities in the early years during their political transition processes (Howard 2003).

Even some of the most prominent advocates of civil society, such as Robert Putnam, admit that "social capital" may not always be beneficial or have a "civilizing effect" on society, citing the example of the destructive capabilities of terrorist networks (Putnam 2007: 138). Thus, on the opposite side of the same coin, "civil society" can be uncivil, with friction from opposing groups sometimes leading to violent confrontations (Kopecký and Muddle 2003). In Thailand, for example, civil society actors have increasingly mobilized to partake in contentious politics that are partisan in nature (Thompson 2008). NGOs in Thailand that profess liberal, democratic views have paradoxically expressed skepticism of electoral politics and aligned with authoritarian forces, leading to the country's democratic regression (Kuhonta and Sinpeng 2014: 338).

In order, therefore, to understand the role of associational life under an authoritarian context, civil society needs to be stripped of its normative assumptions – they are non-state organizations, but they are neither good nor bad for society, nor are they necessarily positive or negative for democratization or political liberalization. The development of associational life is thus contextual and depends on the attributes of the regime, which shapes how its society develops (Mutebi 2006: 177–179). This is especially relevant given that empirically, there has been plenty of evidence of the close affiliation between civil society groups, political parties, and the role of the state (Berman 1997; Putnam 1993; Kyaw Yin Hlaing 2007b: 150–155). Further, evidence suggests that many civil society groups are reliant on the funding or policies of the state, both domestic and foreign (Henderson 2002; Rosenblum and Lesch 2011; Maung Zarni 2012). Foreign aid and assistance in the form of official development assistance (ODA), and international funding of INGO and NGO activities are generally considered an extension of a country's foreign policy (Pishchikova 2007; Sardamov 2005). "Democracy promotion" activities are often considered a form of foreign interference in domestic politics, and depending on the power dynamics, the effects of such promotion in illiberal regimes varies (Risse and Babayan 2015).

The Myanmar context

Due to the unwillingness of the highly authoritarian military regime to compromise to any form of "genuine" democratization in the aftermath of the 1988 crackdown, much of the first wave of civil society literature on Myanmar offered pessimistic and defeatist views about the prospects of Myanmar's civil society (Liddell 1999; Fink 2001; Steinberg 2001). Based on a "civil society-democratization" paradigm, which has dominated the thinking of many transnational advocacy networks and (Western-centric) policymaking circles, the earlier assessment of the state of Myanmar's associational life often understated their existence and failed to recognize their function under authoritarian rule. Zunetta Liddell writing just before the turn of the millennium suggested that the emergence of civil society in Myanmar appeared to be "grim," and at best, weak, an assertion that David Steinberg, a longtime Myanmar specialist appeared to support (Liddell 1999: 67; Steinberg 1999). The resilience of Myanmar's authoritarian military regime vis-à-vis critical opposition politics and high profile transnational activism campaigns contributed to the belief that after 1962, a "genuine" civil society simply could not exist under authoritarian Myanmar (McCarthy 2012: 2).

Further, the normative claim that civil society by nature should be civil, progressive, and liberal has been a domineering paradigm that generally does not consider organizations that do not explicitly demonstrate such qualities as a part of civil society (Kyaw Yin Hlaing 2007b: 144). This is an inherently a teleological argument that does not help to explain the existence of a vibrant, relatively independent associational life outside of the "civil" or "democratic" context. Kyaw Yin Hlaing (2004: 389–390) a sharp observer of Myanmar's social movements pointed out that:

> Most Burma-watchers failed to acknowledge the existence of civil society organizations because they thought that only formal organizations could function within the limits set by the government. In their opinion, civil society could not exist if there was no legitimate official space for civil society organizations.

In one of the first publications on Myanmar's contemporary civil society, the International Crisis Group (ICG) recognized the existence of an underdeveloped civil society but emphasized the political insignificance of these civic groups (2001). The ICG report recognized that Myanmar's nascent civil society at the turn of the millennium was neither liberal nor necessarily pro-democracy. However, in its report the ICG implied that a growing civil society would play a significant and positive role in democratization and national reconciliation in Myanmar and continued to advance the normative claim that an emerging civil society should be promoted (*ibid*).

Thus, those that argued a causal relationship between civil society and political democratization failed to recognize what did exist, i.e., the growth of a disciplined civil society or controlled associational life under authoritarian rule. Other observers have recognized the existence and diversity of civic organizations in Myanmar and taken a more nuanced approach, but they still believe in the normative value of these NGOs as well as how the international community can support a bottom-up approach to foster democratic culture in Myanmar through these grassroots organizations (Holliday 2011: 192). There is a tendency to view civil society as a "cure all" solution to address the failings of a state, which confuses correlation with causation (Posner 2004: 252).

Earlier literature concerning the dire state of Myanmar's associational life under military rule should not be dismissed entirely; however, more recent literature suggests a much more vibrant civil society that has been gradually appearing in the public sphere since the late 1990s (Kramer 2011: 11). Given the significant disconnect between earlier theoretical assumptions about civil society's "democratizing effect" and the actual empirical evidence, there is a need to understand this "re-emergence" of Myanmar's associational life outside of the democratization paradigm.

Associational life includes a myriad of organizations that engage in very different goals, strategies, and relations vis-à-vis the state, as well as with one another and the broader society. Recognizing the diversities and complexities of different civil societies, there is now a growing literature that argues against the exploration of civil society based purely on the democratization paradigm but rather understands all forms of associational life as they exist, under their respective political contexts (Cavatorta 2013; Jobert and Kohler-Koch 2008; Springer 2010). In the context of Myanmar, civil society developed not as an oppositional force to the state but rather supplemented the shortcomings of the regime's weaknesses.

Conceptualizing Myanmar's associational life

More recent literature has since challenged the pessimistic assertions about the state of Myanmar's civil society. One of the first empirical studies published about the state of Myanmar's civil society documented a dynamic associational life where NGOs are active throughout different parts of the country and engaged in a wide-range of activities (Heidel 2006). Based on his work in Myanmar with Save the Children UK, Brian Heidel argued that civil society "never died," with

NGOs and CBOs (community-based organizations) surviving for decades even during the most authoritarian periods (2006: 60). Heidel estimated that by 2004, there were 270 active local NGOs and more than 214,000 community-based organizations (*ibid*: 15). Heidel's work is supported by Kyaw Yin Hlaing's (2007b) research, which traces the roots of Myanmar's associational life as far back as to British colonial times. According to Kyaw Yin Hlaing, hundreds of organizations survived during the height of the BSPP repression, and some even managed to continue to open their offices by "skirting the regime's rule" by reinventing themselves, going underground, or organizing informally (2004).

A number of different types of organizations were allowed to remain intact even during the height of BSPP repressions (Kyaw Yin Hlaing 2007b: 159). Despite the BSPP's formal nationalization of the economy, the country's largest business lobbyist group the Union of Burma Chamber of Commerce and Industry (later renamed the Union of Myanmar Federation of Chambers of Commerce and Industry) was able to keep their offices open by maintaining a working relationship with local authorities through bribery or as donors in support of state activities (*ibid*: 158). Another business organization, the Mandalay Traders, Brokers, and Industrialists Association, disguised itself as a religious organization and with the full knowledge of the BSPP government, could function "in the way it did during the pre-socialist days" (*ibid*). Religious groups also continued their activities and proved to be an important social institution, as long as they stayed away from politics (Desaine 2011: 45).

According to Stephen McCarthy, this type of "traditional civil society," due to the indigenous source of customary power these groups possess, are potentially the most effective organizations that could politically challenge military rule (McCarthy 2012: 6). These groups had the ability to mobilize their networks to pool together resources for welfare and protection, as well as to respond to crises.

This is best demonstrated during times of crisis, when the mobilization of non-state groups and their informal networks may appear seemingly out of nowhere, in very public arenas. This was the case during the 1988 and 2007 popular anti-government protests, as well as the mass societal response to the 2008 Cyclone Nargis humanitarian disaster (Kyaw Yin Hlaing 2007b: 144; Paung Ku 2010). The remainder of this chapter turns to the analysis of how civil society re-emerged under SLORC/SPDC rule before discussing the role of civil society in Myanmar's transition leading up to the formal regime change in 2011.

Restoring law and order: controlling society through suppression and co-optation

When the SLORC returned the military to the forefront of politics, the government was in a fragmented state. The primary concern of the *tatmadaw* was therefore to restore law and order, and to rebuild the military and the state apparatus against an unruly society. As a military regime with weak bonds to its society, political stability was built on the despotic power of the authoritarian military regime, and regime survival and state security was paramount. Thus, the relationship between the state and its society was one based on coercion and indifference. Societal demands including the basic welfare needs of its general populace were largely left unaddressed and were at best secondary concerns to the regime. The military also readily exercised enough despotic power to ensure that non-state groups and the general populace complied with the authoritarian system and prevented opposition groups from organizing into a coherent political force.

Apart from physical coercion, the *tatmadaw* adopted other strategies of control. A series of formal and informal techniques were used to threaten or co-opt the political opposition. The state also tolerated societal initiatives that addressed welfare concerns, which were deemed unthreatening to regime security. The military junta took strict control of the population's capacity to mobilize politically seriously, with citizens closely monitored by a powerful intelligence regime (Selth 2019: 619). SLORC Law No. 2/88 banned

> gathering, walking, marching in procession, chanting slogans, delivering speeches, agitating, or creating disturbances on the streets of five or more people ... regardless of whether the act is with the intention of creating a disturbance or of committing a crime or not.

In the lead-up to the 2010 general elections, the regime passed Directive 2/2010 to regulate electoral campaigns, which prohibited citizens from "holding flags or marching and chanting slogans in procession."

The censorship system established since the days of the RC continued to be utilized by the government in order to control information and the media. The Printers and Publishers Registration Law of 1962 was established to limit and censor journalism. The 1964 Library, Museum and Exhibition Monitoring Act continued to frame how the government censored the works of artists and cultural workers (Carlson 2016: 130). Communication was prohibitively expensive, with private fixed lines and mobiles costing thousands of US dollars. Ownership of telephones, fax machines, and even computer modems was regulated, as the Burma Wireless Telegraphy Act of 1933 was amended in 1995 and 1996 to make it an illegal offense for individuals to own these devices without official permission (Holliday 2011: 73). Despite these control mechanisms, arbitrary but essentially weak enforcement meant that the state was unable to enforce an absolute censorship and information control over its society. The most evident example of weak law enforcement to control information has been the widespread access to satellite televisions and shortwave radio broadcasts. The government was unable to jam these broadcasts, and illegal and unregulated satellite dishes could be found in major urban centers, and even in rural communities. The authorities never made any serious attempt to suppress bootlegged materials and contrabands. Smuggled books, magazines, newspapers, and pirated video-cassettes (later DVDs) were delivered regularly to private residences or sold openly on the streets.

Given that student politics have historically played an important role in Myanmar's political development – including for example their anti-imperialist roots, as well as their ability to mobilize and challenge the BSPP state in 1974 and 1988 – the military government enacted various methods to weaken the autonomy and capacity of the country's university system. Universities have repeatedly been shut down whenever students attempt to organize anti-regime activities. Further the government also reorganized the university system, first by relocating many universities to suburban areas away from the city center, and second by encouraging the development of distance learning, making it a more common experience for most university students than traditional university settings (Seekins 2005b: 268). The semester was shortened, and the duration of studies was also cut down to three years from four, while exams were made easy, thus devaluing the quality and value of university degrees (Kyaw Yin Hlaing 2007b: 166). The result was that reading groups – which formed a critical underground network for political mobilization in the 1988 protests – were difficult to find by 2002 (Boudreau 2004: 162).

The other prominent societal force – the Buddhist monastic order – was also regulated heavily by the military regime. In the initial years of the SLORC rule, activist monks remained defiant against military rule, and after a monk and some students were shot and killed by soldiers during a protest in Mandalay, thousands of monks demonstrated in Mandalay. Under the leadership of U Yewata, the *Sangha Samaggi* (Monk's Union) of Mandalay, declared a rare religious boycott or "overturning the bowl," refusing to accept alms from the military or their family members – thus denying them the ability to accumulate "merit" (AAPP 2004: 14).

The SLORC government responded by passing SLORC Law 6/90, which demanded the revocation of the religious boycott and dissolved all independent *sanghas*. Following this, the very next day, SLORC Law 7/90 was passed, which prohibited monks from participating in any political activities and gave the state the right to disrobe and try monks in a military court (McCarthy 2008a: 302). SLORC Law 7/90 also decreed that only state *sangha* organizations would be legal, while all future development in monastery land and the conducting of religious ceremonies would require the permission of government-approved local *sangha* committees (*ibid*: 303). After the passage of these laws, the SLORC proceeded to suppress and disrobe many of the protesting monks, claiming that they were "bogus" or "rouge" monks, allowing the state to imprison them without affording them traditional rights or the respect generally reserved for the monkhood, a strategy that was repeated again, for example, in the aftermath of the 2007 "Saffron Revolution" crackdown (*ibid*: 310).

Apart from physical coercion, and formal control over the clergy, the SLORC/SPDC government also resorted to buying the support of senior monks and important monasteries, such as bestowing leading Buddhist clergymen with new titles, as well as making big donations, including expensive cars and luxury items (*ibid*: 305–306). Monasteries that developed cordial ties with the government thus received benefits from the state. As a result, the more senior monks and established monasteries were generally more conservative and did not criticize the government (Seekins 2009: 729–730).

On the other hand, the 2007 "Saffron" protests demonstrated that many *sanghas* continued to remain informally outside of the state orbit, retaining the ability to mobilize popular support and to organize protest movements against the state. The movement leadership was however, largely confined to younger monks, who may have shared a closer connection with their laymen followers and thus were conscious of their everyday hardship (McCarthy 2008a: 308).

Similar to the crackdown of the 1990 Mandalay protests, the SPDC government raided several monasteries after suppressing the 2007 Saffron protests, labelling and disrobing supposedly fake monks. Irrespective of whether the monks had a legitimate grievance or not, the military regime viewed all anti-government activities indiscriminately and readily cracked down on the protesting monks, leading to many deaths and imprisonment, while ensuring that the state's political agenda and transitions plan remained unchallenged (Zöllner 2009).

Outside of the religious sphere, the junta also regularly interfered with secular organizations often replacing the leadership of cultural, professional, and vocational associations with regime supporters (Tin Maung Maung Than 2013: 82). The military regime co-opted or rewarded societal elites such as artists, academics, and even former student leaders by giving them special access and rent – such as luxurious goods, business licenses, mobile phones, electricity, and heavily discounted land for purchase (Carlson 2016: 131). Additionally, the military also attempted form a direct channel of connection to grassroots communities by supporting or creating government-organized non-governmental organizations (GONGOs). GONGOs are essentially an extension of the state apparatus, and their presence often comes at the expense of limiting autonomous civil society space in the grassroots communities (CPCS 2009: 149). Their prime function is to recruit supporters for the state through patronage and coercion, and as an alternative channel for the state to control society. The leadership of the GONGOs generally parallels to the upper echelon of the military government, as they are usually staffed with active and retired military officers or their family members (Prager-Nyein 2009: 643). After the purge of Prime Minister Khin Nyunt in 2004, for example, his wife also had to resign as head of the Myanmar Women's Affairs Federation (Taylor 2009: 447).

The most important of these GONGOS was the Union Solidarity and Development Association (USDA), the military's *de facto* civilian arm. The USDA was founded on September 15, 1993, which corresponded with the government's advances on the constitution making front, as 104 "basic principles" had just been endorsed by the National Convention Convening Committee, laying the groundwork for the beginnings of constitutional drafting (*ibid*: 446). The USDA can be seen as a corrective of the SLORC's earlier self-induced "error," as SLORC Law 6/88, which allowed the creation of new organizations and political parties, also stipulated that civil servants including military personnel were prohibited from joining any political party.

The creation of the USDA, which eventually claimed to have 24 million members, thus allowed the military regime to circumvent its own law and was used to advance the *tatmadaw*'s political agenda. The USDA, which would become the Union Solidarity and Development Party (USDP), was always designed to eventually transform itself into a formal political party to represent the military's interests (Ei Ei Toe Lwin 2015). By 2010, USDA members and their assets were transferred to the newly founded USDP in time for elections on November 7 of the same year.

The military regime regularly utilized the USDA to mobilize support whenever the state needed a public demonstration to support the regime's agenda and policies (Charney 2009: 190). The USDA was also a useful extension of the regime's intelligence and coercive network and was involved in the routine monitoring and suppression of opposition groups (Win Min 2010: 112). Notably, the USDA has its own civilian militia, the *Swan Arr Shin*, a group accused of launching the Depayin Massacre in 2003, as well as attacking a group of monks in Pakkou on September 5, 2007, which was cited by some as the catalyst for the monks' "Saffron Revolution" (Horsey 2008: 17–18).

The state's willingness to use coercive force to silence its critics meant that the country lived under what Monique Skidmore refers to as a "politics of fear" (2004). A system of surveillance and societal control effectively created the perception of an omnipresent state and a climate of fear, which was an efficient way to silence dissent and halt the development of organized opposition against the state's authority. It is also well known that the Special Intelligence Branch of the police, popularly known as the "special branch" regularly monitor activities that are deemed potentially threatening to the government. Surveillance is also not necessarily clandestine, as the point is to instill fear and uncertainty, as well as to make sure people do not get out of line (Author's personal observation and conversations with interviewees in Yangon 2006–2015).

Foreign residents in Myanmar have also been routinely monitored, with some having been deported by the government on arbitrary charges. For example, Christina Peterson, a teacher with the American Center in Yangon was deported in December 2009 after giving a talk about environmental issues to the US Consulate in Mandalay. According to Peterson, no official reason was ever given for why she was deported, although she suspects that she was mistaken for a US female journalist who was traveling in the same area. Although Christina Peterson was deported, her sibling, who had been visiting at the time of Peterson's deportation, was allowed to stay in Myanmar (Personal correspondence with Christina Peterson, May 7, 2015).

Decades of state repression and control have thus ensured that activists are well aware that the state would be able to crack down on dissent "without suffering too much external costs for its actions" (Cavatorta 2013: 7). Although public frustration has routinely manifested itself into anti-government protests, most notably in 1988 and 2007, societal forces have been unable to temper the military's resolve to tighten its rule over society.

The emasculated opposition and a *sustainable* legitimacy crisis

Domestic challenges to military rule by leading activists groups such as the 88 Generation (composed of former student leaders in the 1988 protests) and the NLD, and later the 2007 "Saffron Revolution," exposed the military's general lack of legitimacy inside the country. Externally, active campaigns by transnational activist networks and the Myanmar diaspora, popular anti-military accounts shaped by the Western-centric media, and the small but influential literature on what Heather MacLachlan refers to as the "I-bravely-went-to-Burma-and-talked-to-regular-people-and-heroically-emerged-to-tell-the-tale," helped to reinforce the perception of Myanmar as a totalitarian-like state, which further delegitimized the military government in the US-centric international community (MacLachlan 2011: 11).

While Myanmar under the military regime is one of the most repressive states with a poor track record on human rights and political liberty, this reductionist one-dimensional portrayal of the realities of Myanmar's socio-political conditions has not aided understandings of the complex socio-political situation in Myanmar. Although the military government is generally viewed as illegitimate, they were nevertheless able to provide enough socio-political order and some improvement in the materialist conditions to establish an authoritarian equilibrium for 23 years. Incidentally, other regimes in the region with a history of authoritarian rule and poor human rights records, such as Thailand or Cambodia, were never subjected to the same kind of US-led isolation. The reputational blow from multiple anti-junta "pro-Burma" democracy campaigns, however, was not enough of a factor to pressure the regime to democratize. Two decades of oppositional politics failed to achieve what the US sanctions regime set out to do. In short, despite the trial posed by opposition challenges and a relatively successful campaign to isolate the junta from the US-centric international community, it was a *sustainable* legitimacy crisis that the regime was able to manage effectively (see Chapter 5).

The military had a low threshold for public criticism, yet it did not eliminate opposition to its rule completely. The military government, for its part, did not revert to a blanket ban on political parties and associational life, although as discussed earlier it did engage in various tactics to try to weaken these opposition groups. Leading activists and political figures routinely faced government repression and imprisonment, the most well-known example being the on-again-off-again house arrest of Aung San Suu Kyi. By 2009, there were an estimated 2,100 dissidents held in 43 prisons and 50 labor camps (HRW 2009b: 2). Of the original 95 political parties that competed in the 1990 election, only ten parties survived into the mid-1990s (Taylor 2009: 420). The majority of the parties were simply deregistered or forced to dissolve after continued government harassment (Diller 1997: 34–35). Interestingly, the NLD, although significantly emasculated, was afforded legal entity until September 2010, when it was deregistered after the party's decision to boycott general elections.[2]

The way the junta responded to political opposition evolved through its trial and error approach in pushing forward with its regime construction exercise. During times of routine regime-construction or maintenance, the government has appeared more confident and more tolerant of challenges toward its regime – yet the government has also reverted back to a "zero-tolerance policy" when dealing with more serious challenges that have nationwide implications (Kyaw Yin Hlaing 2013: 233).

For over two decades, the country's main opposition groups advocated a non-violent resistance against military rule with the aim of pressurizing the regime to recognize the 1990 electoral results. The NLD, and later the 88 Generation, rejected the government's political reform plans consistently, while the military also refused to make any political concessions to its challengers and insisted that it was the only legitimate driver of Myanmar's political transformation. The lack of compromise led to the NLD walkout and its subsequent expulsion from the government-controlled National Convention in 1995. The NLD also boycotted the reconvened National Convention in 2003. Leading up to the final stages of the military's roadmap, both the 88 Generation and the NLD advocated a "no" vote in the government-orchestrated 2008 constitutional referendum, and the NLD later decided to boycott the 2010 general election. Given the opposition's lack of leverage over the authoritarian military regime, the military simply decided to carry on with its transition plan by sidelining the country's opposition forces.

Temporary peace and the ceasefire economy

In the peripheral ethnic areas, the military was incapable of ending the long-running civil war. This "error" of ethnic politics is perhaps one of the most significant challenges to the military's political plans. The *tatmadaw* developed a new strategy to temporarily resolve the large majority of the conflicts by concluding a series of ceasefire agreements with various armed ethnic groups, including new armed groups that have splintered from the collapsed Burmese Communist Party (BCP) (Keenan 2012: 50–52). This allowed Myanmar to have the longest period of relative peace across the country since its independence (Taylor 2009: 433–445). Though "ceasefire capitalism" provided material benefits and relative peace for ceasefire groups, the largest beneficiary was the *tatmadaw* (Woods 2011). With the suspension of conflict, the *tatmadaw* was able to tighten its control and expand its presence throughout the country's territories including in contested ethnic regions. The SLORC/SPDC became the first regime since the country's independence to establish the closest resemblance of a "unified" Myanmar. Within a few years after the 1988 coup, the reach of the state was felt practically throughout the whole country in the form of the *tatmadaw's* presence, a picture vastly different from the days of the BSPP era (Callahan 2007b).

The inability of the military state to either incorporate or eliminate armed ethnic groups, and the difficulty of reconciling their differences, meant that ethnic groups, both ceasefire groups and armed insurgents, remained a serious challenge for the *tatmadaw* (Kyaw Yin Hlaing 2014a: 56–61). However, by the 1990s, the ability of these ethnic rebels to seriously threaten overall regime stability greatly diminished, especially following the collapse of the BCP and the reduced strength of the various rebel groups such as the once formidable Karen National Union (KNU) (South 2008, 2011). Fighting was localized and limited to the conflict zones, and thus ethnic rebels have had a limited political reach with only indirect influence over national politics. As explained by one interviewee, a chairman of an ethnic minority party, the large majority of these peripheral ethnic groups' agenda has been focused on the push for greater autonomy, or a "genuine, federal" Myanmar, where the central government will respect the demands of the local populace (interview with chairman of an ethnic minority party, Yangon, January 18, 2014).

Strong regime, weak state

The SLORC/SPDC government was never able achieve popular support to its rule, however two decades of coercion and tight social control meant that that the military state was able to ensure basic political stability. The SLORC/SPDC government had strong coercive powers, but Myanmar shared all the common attributes of a weak state, one "that rigidly controls dissent … but at the same time provides very few political good" (Rotberg 2004: 5). Myanmar's failure to industrialize has been well documented (Tin Maung Maung Than 2007), and chronic economic mismanagement led to the predatory military state's dependency on resource extraction in lieu of a rational Weberian bureaucracy to sustain itself (Perry 2007; Turnell et al. 2009). As a result, Myanmar's "crippled" bureaucracy "has difficulty accomplishing even basic tasks necessary to maintain the regime, such as collecting revenue and supplying the army" (Englehart 2005: 623).

Myanmar's contemporary civil society thus emerged in response to the weak capacity of the state, and was able to develop a degree of space in the public arena to address two particular gaps unfulfilled by the state: the social-welfare sector and ethnic-peripheries in the ceasefire, or disputed border, areas (Kramer 2007, 2011; Lorch 2006, 2008; South 2008). Given that the military junta had allowed a more formal, legal platform for associational life to develop, NGOs began to grow in numbers, as well as increase the range of activities in which they were involved. By the late 1990s, the government's confidence in its ability to contain political opposition and move forward with its gradual liberalization allowed the emergence of some of the most prominent local NGOs that remain active today. Some of the largest and most well-known local NGOs were all founded around this period, beginning with Pyi Gyi Khin (1997), the Metta Development Foundation (1998), Shalom (Nyein) Foundation (2000), and the Free Funeral Service Society (2001) (Smith 2007b: 72; Steinberg 2006: 192–163; Interview with Kyaw Thu, Co-Founder of the Free Funeral Service Society, Yangon July 7, 2011; Interview with a Co-Founder and Chair of a NGO, Yangon, July 8, 2011).

The SLORC junta's shift away from the BSPP isolationist policy also meant a drive to encourage foreign investors and organizations, including INGOs to setup operations inside the country. These INGOs and foreign donors began to seek local groups for project implementation (Kramer 2011: 6). Thus, when these foreign organizations and donors entered Myanmar, the supposedly non-existent "civil society" was re-discovered and reshaped by these external actors (Maung Zarni 2012). All of these INGOs, which begin to enter the country in the 1990s had to develop ties with their government counterpart, and the memorandum of understanding (MOU) that they have to sign with the individual ministries largely frames their mandate inside the country (Saha 2011: 8).

The Myanmar government issued its first ever "Guidelines for UN agencies, International Organizations, and NGOs/INGOs" in 2006, where one of the provisions included the requirement for INGOs to register with the Ministry of Home Affairs (ICG 2006: 9). Most organizations continue to work within the MOU framework, and very few INGOS register formally with the Ministry of Home Affairs as required, although they continue to operate inside the country (*ibid*). These INGOs, prior to 2011, were engaged largely in basic service delivery services and the development of communal capacitates to address communal needs – such as food security and basic health (Dorning 2006: 193).

Addressing the welfare gap: the development of horizontal solidarity and "unity in poverty"

Given that the military regime did not address the population's "mundane needs for food, housing, and the like," Burmese society has had to develop its own "strategies of survival," which also allowed individuals to develop an interdependent relationship with other individuals in the community, leading to the development of a "group identity and collective action" (Migdal 1988: 27). In other words, societal forces came together to address the welfare gap unaccounted for by the military regime.

The state was fixated on maintaining control over its society – but this was only in respect of control over political affairs and in areas considered to be linked to national security, otherwise the central state remained remarkably uninvolved in the lives of its citizens (Prasse-Freeman 2012: 379–380). Myriad indigenous groups, especially traditional religious organizations, took over the role as the prime providers of welfare relief for their respective constituents. In particular, religious organizations, which had long had a tradition to provide education for their respective communities as well as a source of welfare relief, re-emerged under the military government (Heidel 2006: 8–12). Through that process, the Burmese populace developed a "horizontal solidarity" that counter-balanced the inadequacy of the state and strengthened communal and kinship ties (Seekins 2009: 728–730). This strong "horizontal solidarity" meant that contrary to the assumptions of democratization paradigm, "social capital" was strong in Myanmar, even under the authoritarian military regime (*ibid*). A report by the

Tripartite Core Group (TCG) (2008: 2–3) examining the aftermath of the 2008 Cyclone Nargis for example explained that:

> Despite, or perhaps because of, the many challenges of Delta life, communities are relatively socially cohesive and have strong capacities for collective problem solving and decision-making. While the usual inter-group cleavages exist ... village activists tend to cut across such boundaries. There are a number of reason for the strength for social capital. First, development resources from high levels are scare. This accentuates the importance of working together at the community level and carefully prioritising resources for public goods. Second in the absence of a state or employer safety net, community members support each other in times of need, something particularly evident in their response to Nargis.

Although social capital and "trust" are difficult to quantify and measure, surveys conducted by international agencies often rank Myanmar as being one of the most generous, or charitable, countries in the world, with reportedly 91 percent of the population making donations and 51 percent claiming to have participated in voluntary services to the community (Charities Aid Foundation 2017: 10, 25). Part of this can be also explained by the role of Buddhist traditions, where communal life in many of the country's majority Buddhist populace continue to center around religious festivals and activities (Kramer 2011: 9).

Despite the evidence of strong "horizontal solidarity" as a communal survival strategy, the inability for the development of "vertical solidarity" with the indifferent state has meant that this solidarity was "unity in poverty" (Cooper 2014: 188). This also partially explains why, despite the ongoing interethnic and interreligious conflicts that contribute to the ongoing localized civil war in parts of peripheral Myanmar, with the exception of the Rakhine and Shan States, in the 2015 polls the masses were overwhelmingly united in support of the NLD, as a rejection against the failures of military rule (Thawnghmung 2016).

Molding a disciplined civil society

Although heavily regulated by formal laws and monitored by the government, civil society gradually developed in the 1990s, and had a significant presence by the 2000s. These groups have relative autonomy and cannot be considered as direct agents of the state. Thus, in Myanmar's authoritarian context, the restrictions and legacy of military rule have led to the emergence of a subordinated, disciplined civil society. This disciplined civil society emerged even before the regime leadership announced its seven-step roadmap to a disciplined multiparty democracy in August of 2003.

Civil society expanded progressively both in numbers as well as in the scope of activities since the SLORC/SPDC government repealed its formal ban on associational life. Civil society has demonstrated a limited role in influencing the politics of the regime, and it is not the cause of Myanmar's regime transition.

Nevertheless, civil society serves a functional role to help buffer societal discontent, as well as reassure the military-backed state that not all societal forces are detrimental to regime stability.

Prior to the reforms, Myanmar's civil society had consistently shied away from outright political activities that would be viewed unfavorably by the state, and thus these organizations have long been overlooked by many Myanmar watchers (Lorch 2006: 133). The high cost of participating in politics encouraged the more politically aware individuals to participate in civic affairs as a part of Myanmar's depoliticized civil society without confronting the state directly (Desaine 2011: 61). As secondary associations, NGOs understand the parameters that limit the type and range of activities their organizations can partake in. Thus, successful civil society organizations during the SLORC/SPDC years were explicitly non-political and mainly worked in areas related to the delivery of welfare services to constituents (Prasse-Freeman 2012: 380).

Myanmar's civil society has been limited to an instrumental role, to fill the void that the state is unwilling or unable to provide, such as material and social services to critical sectors of the local population. NGOs historically operate under particularly harsh conditions in Myanmar, and until very recently kept mostly a low profile. Nevertheless, NGOs have been allowed to engage in a range of activities, as long as these projects are considered non-political or non-threatening to the security-obsessed military state. For NGOs to succeed, these groups need to work within the framework designed by the state to limit the political impact of civil society.

NGOs are thus pressured to demonstrate that their activities pose no threat to the regime and have had to inform and seek approval from the local authorities routinely about the activities they wish to conduct (Taylor 2009: 449). Although the government has shown no hesitation to shut down "unlawful" organizations and imprison dissidents, the regime did not indiscriminately apply these draconian measures to all non-state actors. Often, many of the more well-known or established organizations are led by elite leaders that have close links with the regime or are trusted by national or local authorities. In fact, various local NGOs operate while violating junta laws, and most of these groups remained unregistered under the SLORC/SPDC rule. Many of these groups continue to operate with the direct knowledge of local authorities or relevant ministries (Kramer 2011: 18–20). A founder of a prominent NGO explains:

> The government, especially the local authority is not always unreasonable. From their perspective, as long as our organization informs them about what we are doing, and how it benefits the community, we are able to implement our projects without too much trouble.
>
> (Interview with Co-Founder and Chair of a NGO, Yangon, 22, July 8, 2011).

Outside of political organizations, different types of organizations are permitted to exist. These include formal, registered NGOs, as well as informal unregistered groups such as community-based organizations (CBOs), local charities, self-help groups, capacity-building schools, development and social welfare organizations, and even cultural and religious associations. Although NGOs have a degree of autonomy and freedom to conduct their activities, they do not have any political bargaining power and thus are unable to take on an advocacy or lobbying role, "a task which is normally attributed to civil society in democratic contexts" (Lorch 2006: 30).

Myanmar's disciplined civil society thus adopts a non-confrontational, submissive approach and does not engage in adversarial politicking. Those that have taken a political position or engaged in overtly political acts challenging the state have been silenced, driven underground, or pushed into exile. Under these conditions, assertive, political organizations simply cannot develop. Instead, a pragmatic civil society emerged inside Myanmar that functioned as a buffer against the realities of an unequal economy and an unresponsive state.

While the first "wave" of NGOs were predominately faith-based and participated primarily in developmental work and welfare relief, especially in the ethnic peripheral borders, by the early 2000s, "peace-building" as well as "capacity building" projects became popular in the development field, with the state permitting selective groups to engage in institution-building activities. The Shalom (Nyein) Foundation was founded in 2000 and works on the highly volatile issue of peace building in the ethnic peripheries (Smith 2007b: 72). They were allowed to participate in this sensitive issue primarily since they serve the interests of the *tatmadaw*'s goal: to impose a nationwide ceasefire and peace agreement with insurgent groups. In short, these groups worked closely with the government and shared the military's agenda of "peace-building." Furthermore, the leadership of Shalom is trusted by the regime and has thus been allowed greater autonomy to conduct activities that would otherwise have been considered off-limits for other groups (US Embassy 2006).

The case of Cyclone Nargis

The inadequacy of the state to respond to human security concerns is best demonstrated by the events of Cyclone Nargis in 2008. Cyclone Nargis was a Category 3 tropical storm that hit the Ayeyarwady Delta, as well as Yangon and other parts of Lower Myanmar on May 2–3, 2008. It is considered to be the largest natural disaster in Myanmar's recorded history, with more than 140,000 people killed or unaccounted for and with more than 2.4 million people affected in the aftermath of the cyclone (ASEAN 2010: 9). In the early stages, the international media portrayed the SPDC junta as merely being unresponsive toward the plights of its populace (Albright 2008). It did not help that Than Shwe stated publicly that things were already "returning to normal" just days after the cyclone had landed, unilaterally declaring just three weeks after the cyclone that relief work had ended and reconstruction of the area has begun, while "bloated bodies were lying in ditches and tens of thousands of victims were still waiting for assistance" (Selth 2008b: 388). It would later become clear that the appearance of indifference from Than Shwe did not necessarily match the actions of his subordinates, and that the state's inability to immediately respond to the crisis was not solely an act of state unresponsiveness but also reflected the weak capacity of the military regime to respond to the crisis accordingly.

In the beginning, the SPDC government made it clear that it "was not ready" for the presence of foreign journalists or international relief workers (ASEAN 2010: 14). After intense international pressure, the SPDC government began to accept foreign aid on a bilateral basis and only in the form of supplies and cash, while it also cautiously rejected offers from the US, British, and France – as the Myanmar government likely felt uneasy that their naval ships were anchored just off the coast (Seekins 2009: 727).[3]

In any case, the actions of the SPDC clearly reflected the military regime's prime concern – that is its focus on state security and political development, even above humanitarian concerns. Ever since the establishment of military rule in Myanmar, there has always been a tight restriction on the movement of people – especially for foreigners inside the country. The sudden arrival of a large number of foreign aid workers, journalists, and diplomats into the disaster hit areas would make it difficult for the state to monitor and control local interaction with these foreigners, which could, from the military's calculation, lead to a potential renewal of "political unrest along the lines of the 2007 Saffron Revolution" (Selth 2008b: 391–392).

Further, the cyclone hit the country just a week before the military's scheduled constitutional referendum set on May 10. Indicative of the military's priority, and reflective of its SOP, the military did not diverge from its original plan and pushed forward with holding the referendum, although in areas that were the worst hit the referendum was postponed until May 24 (*ibid*: 387). In a typical authoritarian fashion, and demonstrating the regime's fixated commitment to its democracy roadmap, the state media dedicated more time to covering news of the referendum rather than the cyclone and relief efforts, including public announcements for citizens to vote "with sincerity" for the sake of the country (Seekins 2009: 726). The late deployment of military personnel to disaster-hit areas to provide assistance was also likely due to the SPDC having focused its resources to ensure that the constitutional referendum was carried out to the regime's satisfaction (Selth 2008b: 387).

Cyclone Nargis however clearly effected the thinking of some of the senior leadership. According to Tin Maung Thann, President of Myanmar Egress and Vice President of the Myanmar Fisheries Federation, Cyclone Nargis must have prompted President Thein Sein to realize the "limitations of the old regime" (Fuller 2012). This is a view that is supported by many of my research informants, including ex-military officers, who believe that the aftermath of Nargis was demoralizing for the *tatmadaw* (Interview with a former major of the air force, Yangon, January 17 2014; Interview with a retired colonel, Yangon, January 20, 2014).

A cable from the US embassy in Yangon reveals that the government ordered regime cronies to coordinate and finance the relief efforts in the aftermath of

Cyclone Nargis, which led to an emerging partnership between these cronies and INGOs involved in the relief efforts (US 2008c). Although, according to a senior manager of a local NGO, the Nargis experience certainly helped to "develop more trust" between the government and civil society, if civil society had any influence over the government it was certainly very "subtle," if not negligible (Interview with the senior manager of a local NGO, Yangon, July 6 2013).

Society-driven initiatives including individuals, businesses, NGOs, and CBOs were the first to enter the Delta and preceded any action by the Myanmar state or the international community (TCG 2008: 1, 40–41). The conventional wisdom, as well as evidence documented by various organizations, indicates that civil society grew exponentially during this period, as a wide range of formal and informal citizen-led organizations were quick to provide relief and humanitarian assistance (ASEAN 2010). At the height of post-Cyclone Nargis relief, there were more than 100 INGOs operating on the ground, compared to about 40 prior to the cyclone (Saha 2011: 8).

Myanmar Egress, a prominent organization with close-ties to the government, was approached directly by the government to lead relief assistance in the disaster area (US Embassy 2008c). Top cronies were also ordered to help finance the reconstruction effort. The state was "more than inept," as it had to completely rely on its citizens, including "the monks, the very people [the military] was shooting at only a few months ago, and the international community" to respond to the massive humanitarian crisis (Interviewee 17, Senior UN affiliated International Staff, Yangon January 16, 2014). According to a former head of an INGO involved with post-Nargis relief, experiences with two senior generals proved to be a "wow" moment for him when he realized that these "two guys in uniforms, both [from] senior echelons [of] the regime, [were] both flaunting orders from Naypyidaw, and both finding local solutions to make it happen" (*ibid*).

He described how the two senior generals in charge of different disaster areas had proposed very different *ad hoc* approaches on how his organization could help in the early days of the relief work. One of the generals, a minister in the SPDC government, told the informant's Yangon-based staff to "forget what you have been told in Yangon ... no [name of the organization] t-shirts, and pretend you are a local, I will help you" [*ibid*]. Although he wanted the INGO to keep a low profile, the general was said to be very helpful with the whole process, even helping to locate functioning boats and coordinating between the organization and another INGO that had also arrived in the disaster zone in order to avoid any overlapping in the areas covered. The other senior general while showing the same eagerness to help, adopted an entirely opposite approach, and wanted the INGO to "keep a really high profile," such as putting on banners with the name of the organization on the transport going into the disaster area, as "that will get them through the roadblock from [name of town] to Yangon" (*Ibid*).

While the Cyclone Nargis disaster response suggests civil society has the ability to react autonomously and mobilize without the permission of the state, it also demonstrates the practicality of those in authority. In the face of disaster, the state leadership was more than willing to bend the official rules in order to address immediate human security concerns. However, this support was not entirely unconditional, the generals only permitted these activities as long as the relief effort did not jeopardize their own political security (thus the different approach by the two cases discussed earlier) or threaten the authority of the state.

This explains why on the one hand, most citizens were able to freely participate in post-Nargis relief work, while the high profile comedian-cum-activist Zagnar was arrested and given a long prison sentence when he politicized his post-Nargis relief efforts by criticizing the regime during interviews with the foreign press (HRW 2009a). Although Nargis demonstrated the willingness of individual agency within the SPDC to assist with relief work, the military regime and its praetorian logic continued to value state security and its political agenda over human security concerns.

"Third Force" and constitutional Myanmar

Most civic associations under the junta were service providers, but by the latter half of 2000, many new non-state groups began to participate in sensitive issues of a political nature testing the limits of the SLORC/SPDC regime. Some of those within more elite circles begin to introduce the idea of forming a "Third Force" in order to explore an alternative to the traditional political opposition and the apolitical NGOs (Prasse-Freeman 2012: 392). Groups frustrated with the political impasse between the state and the country's main opposition the NLD and various armed ethnic groups began to create this "Third Force" with the stated goal of helping to deliver gradual reconciliation and democratization.

Members of the "Third Force" essentially adopt a moderate position, where they believe that political change can only take place by working within the constitutional framework created by the *tatmadaw*. Those that are considered part of this "Third Force" are mostly elite actors that share "upper-class connections," speaking a "similar upper-class language" with close ties to those in the government (*ibid*: 392–393). Some of the most active civil society leaders, in fact, were previously members of the *tatmadaw* or former civil servants (Mark 2012). Given that many of these actors are educated, and often use well-spoken English, these elite civil society actors also enjoy support from international donors and the diplomatic community (Lidauer 2012: 101).

Perhaps the most prominent group commonly referred to as part of this "Third Force" is Myanmar Egress, a nonprofit organization founded by a group of influential businessmen, scholars, and social workers that have close ties with the state. Working within the legal parameters of the SLORC/SPDC regime, this prominent group presents itself as moderate nationalist and pro-liberalization reformers and has also demonstrated its willingness to work with all stakeholders in Myanmar from across the political divide. Myanmar Egress was also the first major group out of the so-called "Third Force" that forged, actively and publicly, a close relationship with those within the government, a strategy that has been criticized in some civil society circles (Lidauer 2012: 101).

Myanmar Egress and its allies were vocal supporters of the 2010 elections, and leading up to the election, the group played an active role in providing civic and voter education throughout the country. Many Myanmar Egress staff also crossed over and became the core staff of the quasi-governmental Myanmar Peace Center (MPC) under the Thein Sein administration between 2012 and 2016.[4] Other organizations, including informal reading groups, were also willing to utilize the platform allowed by the 2010 elections to provide capacity-building programs, which included basic civic education on issues that were considered politically sensitive such as political theory, democracy, and human rights issues, but they avoided criticizing the military government (Buzzi et al. 2012).

Although the "Third Force" approach has allowed the government to develop a new sense of trust and confidence in the benefits of an active NGO, these groups do not have an independent source of power, and their comparative advantage lies in their ability to navigate relatively successfully across different sectors of society, as they have allies which span the political spectrum and the support of the broader international community. It is unlikely that the "Third Force" has any credible influence on the regime's decision to liberalize; nevertheless, their existence and relationships with some of the top leadership of the military government (some individuals affiliated with Myanmar Egress became government advisors during the Thein Sein administration) suggests that this type of moderating politics is precisely the type of politics that is preferred and tolerated by the *tatmadaw* (Lall 2016, however, offers an alternative view and credits the agency of members of Myanmar Egress and the Thein Sein administration as being critical to the regime transition).

The development of a moderate "Third Force" and a disciplined civil society share some similarities with what Jessica Teets refers to as "consultative authoritarianism," which serves as a "social management" mechanism to deflect popular dissatisfactions with the state (Teets 2013: 2–3). Under this system, non-state groups have some channels of communication to the authoritarian state, though civil society is unable to conduct unapproved advocacy activities and does not carry the same weight as a pressure/lobby group more familiar in the context of a liberal democracy.

Myanmar's expanded pluralism during military rule never became a political threat to the government, but it appears to have helped manage societal dissatisfaction with the regime. The willingness of Myanmar's civil society to focus on humanitarian assistance and welfare work, and the growth of moderate sociopolitical actors willing to work within the political framework designed by the government, assured the military that its core interests would remain unchallenged. With a subdued, disciplined civil society, the conditions were prime for the military to introduce its version of a "genuine," disciplined multiparty democratic system.

Conclusion: vibrant but disciplined society does not lead to "democratization"

Since 1962, the military was able to dominate its society, and prior to 2011, it only made superficial attempts to reconcile with its political opposition. The authoritarian nature of successive regimes in Myanmar played a dominant role in shaping the nature, goal orientation, and types of activities engaged in by civil society. When the SLORC/SPDC regime decided to purge its autarkic-socialist ideology and began to re-legitimate societal (and market) forces, these informal networks were able to emerge as NGOs that contested public space in areas and on agendas seen as non-threatening and non-political by the state. Although the regime routinely suppress societal challengers, the junta was more than willing to "tolerate" and accept the positive supplementary role that a disciplined civil society may play in areas that the state was unable or unwilling to engage in.

Myanmar's transition from a military authoritarian regime to a hybrid regime in 2011 was initiated by a strong military in lieu of a robust, politicized civil society. The military regime had low tolerance for opposition politics and pushed forward with its two-decade long transition plan based entirely on the regime's own terms and timing without making any political concession to its detractors. Contrary to the general expectation that a strong opposition force could pressure authoritarian states to liberalize, in the case of Myanmar's voluntary regime change, a weak political opposition, and a disciplined society were the preconditions that allowed the military regime to confidently introduce its version of a disciplined democracy. Although there was evident societal discontent and frustration with military rule, oppositional forces and civil society were unable to mobilize enough support to force regime change. Even at the height of popular protests in 1988 and 2007, the military was able to close ranks and crush all opposition to its rule.

Contrary to the normative assumptions about the "democratizing" effects civic associations may have on governments, the case of Myanmar suggests a more complex picture of state-society relations. Non-state actors, through their years of working within the authoritarian framework of the junta, have demonstrated that the existence of associational life does not automatically lead to a civil society that challenges the power of the authoritarian state. Myanmar's post-2011 regime change was not determined by the actions of its civil society nor a response to social movements and popular protests. In every instance of popular mobilization against the regime, the junta had consistently suppressed alternative political views. It is when the opposition was at its weakest – and the disciplined society largely depoliticized – that the incentive structures were created for the military to enact its regime change. The ability of the opposition to deny the junta from achieving popular and international legitimacy however was a critical issue that the military had to address as part of its transition plan.

Notes

1 In contrast, since 2011, President Thein Sein and Commander-in-Chief Min Aung Hlaing have both stated publicly on the record of the importance of "human security" which included improving social, political, and economic conditions for the people (*NLM* 2011b; RFA 2015).

2 Deregistration of the NLD was however short-lived, as the party was allowed to reregister in time for the April 2012 by-elections.

3 Andrew Selth argues that this was because of the enduring perception by the upper echelon of the military command, that the US and their allies could potentially lead an invasion of Myanmar under the pretext of humanitarian aid (Selth 2008b: 388–392).

4 In May 2016, the NLD government reconfigured the MPC into a government organization, now renamed the National Reconciliation and Peace Centre (NRPC), directly under the State Counsellor's office.

5 Myanmar's regime change and the limits of international linkage

Introduction

On November 19, 2012, Barack Obama became the first (and thus far only) serving president of the United States (US) to visit Myanmar on a diplomatic call. At the University of Yangon, the US President delivered a landmark speech discussing about the positive changes taking place in Myanmar. He pledged US support for the country's ongoing economic and political reforms, including the restoration of full diplomatic relations and the easing of US sanctions. Reflective of a common "Western"-centric mainstream narrative, the *Myanmar Times* (2012) dedicated a special issue titled "Sanctioned to Success" to commemorate Obama's whirlwind daytrip. In the words of a former US official who worked on US sanctions programs, Myanmar's post-2011 political liberalization was an "unambiguous victory" for the "global sanctions regime" against Myanmar (Kucik 2016: 5).

Contrary to the celebratory narrative within pro-sanctions policy circles, Myanmar's military government was never genuinely isolated from the broader international community. Despite its "pariah" reputation, the *tatmadaw*-led government maintained several important diplomatic and commercial relations throughout its 23-year rule. In particular, the member states of the Association of Southeast Asian Nations (ASEAN), as well as China, were quick to take the lead in strengthening their diplomatic and commercial ties with the State Law and Restoration Council (SLORC) after its assumption of power in 1988. Supporters of ASEAN believed that their "constructive engagement" approach could moderate the most authoritarian instincts of the *tatmadaw*, and socialize the junta into adopting "ASEAN norms"[1] (Chow and Easley 2016: 532–535). In the opinion of the former Thai Foreign Minister Kasit Piromya, ASEAN diplomacy must have helped to convince the junta to "speed up" its transition to a "disciplined democracy" (Author's interview with Kasit Piromya, Bangkok, November 21, 2015). China also had immense geostrategic interests to ensure Myanmar remains politically stable and Beijing friendly (Steinberg and Fan 2012: 355–356). After the founding of SLORC, China actively revived its *paukphaw*[2] bilateral ties with Myanmar, especially as both countries were ostracized by the US-friendly states after the two authoritarian regimes violently cracked down against anti-government protests in Yangon in 1988, and in Beijing in 1989 (Steinberg and Fan 2012: 7–9).

These distinctively contradictory external approaches to Myanmar were simultaneously at work throughout the SLORC/SPDC's 23-year rule, yet neither sanctions nor engagement triggered the junta's decision to implement regime change in 2011. US-led sanctions may have encouraged the continuation of anti-junta struggles, which diminished the military's legitimacy, yet opposition groups did not have the capacity to force a regime change and implement an alternative political order (Jones 2015: 100–101). Although transnational activism and "Western" sanctions isolated the military regime from the broader US-centric international community, it was unable to prevent Myanmar from diversifying its trade, cultural, and political ties with other states, as well as private capital.

Similarly, the broad claims that ASEAN played a socializing role and encouraged Myanmar's domestic reforms are overstated. Since becoming an ASEAN member in 1997, there has been little evidence that the *tatmadaw* had adjusted its timeline, or the way it proceeded with its implementation of the seven-step roadmap to a disciplined democracy. Even on rare occasions when ASEAN publicly criticized Myanmar, such as after the violent crackdown of the monk-led "Saffron Revolution" protests in 2007, the junta offered minor concessions but did not change how the regime governed its society. If ASEAN indeed played a role, it would have been at best minimal. When the junta voluntarily imposed a regime change, it was four years after the 2007 crackdown. The "disciplined democratic" hybrid regime that emerged post-2011, was implemented based on the unilateral decision of the military, and the basic principles of the Constitution had remained the same since 1992. Therefore, the post-junta political arrangements did not incorporate the views of regime challengers, and Myanmar's way to democracy remains under the military's rules of the game. International factors created the structural conditions that the junta had to address, yet they were not the determinants of the post-2011 regime change.

This chapter explores the international conditions that confronted the military regime from when the SLORC assumed power in 1988 until its voluntary regime change in 2011. The chapter situates the regime in its post-Cold War context, and revisits the two opposing claims of sanctions versus engagement, and their respective impact on the regime. The chapter then assesses the role of China, which clearly has become Myanmar's most important foreign relationship since 1988. The chapter concludes that although external international conditions created obstacles and opportunities for the regime, their impact on the regime's political agenda were limited, and did not significantly influence the regime's decision to enact regime change in 2011.

Crisis and opportunities in the post-Cold War order

Post-colonial Myanmar's neutralism had largely avoided global spotlight, but when the *tatmadaw* returned to the forefront of national politics in 1988, military regimes had become an outdated antithesis in the emerging neoliberal order

(Levitsky and Way 2010: 17–18). The unravelling of the BSPP state in the late 1980s, coincided with the end of the Cold War and the rise of "people power movements" in Asia. Nationwide protests during the summer of 1988 saw the sudden ascent of Aung San Suu Kyi as a popular opposition leader who quickly captured the imagination of the general populace, as well as a legion of foreign politicians, journalists, and activists (Kyaw Yin Hlaing 2007a; Steinberg 2010b). The triumph narrative of a US-dominated neoliberal order in the 1990s, and the emergence of a transnational activist networks, encouraged US policy-makers to embrace democracy promotion as a key component in its foreign policy agenda (Poppe 2019: 530–531). Myanmar's pro-democracy movement, personified by Aung San Suu Kyi, would soon come into the orbit of US policy circles as a "boutique issue" (Steinberg 2010a). The highly authoritarian character of SLORC and an active global activist movement kept the junta in the international headlines. Myanmar may have remained a low foreign policy priority, but it received heightened attention from US politicians as a "small, specialized, and fashionable" diplomatic concern (*ibid*: 175). This emerging anti-junta sanctions regime was a critical obstacle that the military regime had to mitigate during its 23-year rule.

However, the evolving neoliberal order also presented new opportunities for Myanmar to address its pressing economic crisis. Preceding the emergent of the US-led sanctions regime, Myanmar's political establishment had already implemented gradual economic liberalization in the agricultural sector, a year before the collapse of the BSPP state. When the *tatmadaw* returned to direct gov-ernance in 1988, the junta had the immediate task of keeping the bankrupted state afloat. Just as Marxist-inspired socialism may have been a convenient ide-ology to unite and justify military rule in the 1960s, the generals' turn toward a reformist direction broadly along the neoliberal zeitgeist of "democracy" and "capitalism" provided the *tatmadaw* with a pragmatic opportunity to address its past socialist failures. In the post-Cold War context, command economy has been largely discredited, and even many communist states have abandoned autarky. By 1988, China for example, had already adopted economic liberaliza-tion for a decade, while Vietnam was in the second year of its *Doi Moi* policy to "renovate" its economy. Similarly, the small communist state of Laos had also begun to decentralize its economy since 1986 under the "New Economic Mech-anism" (Stuart-Fox 1989: 81).

Therefore, without irony, the *tatmadaw* appointed itself as an "interim"[3] gov-ernment, with the aim of reviving the dire state by transforming the Burmese way to socialism into Myanmar's way to democracy. In the initial years, SLORC's speedy decision to implement uneven, political and economic liberalization was therefore an unoriginal, pragmatic solution aimed at renewing the military's state building responsibilities, while filling the state's empty coffers.

Once the decision was made to embrace market-oriented reforms and shift toward political liberalization, the junta quickly passed several decrees that allowed expanded social, political, and economic pluralism. To avoid the finan-cial collapse of the state, the junta legalized existing underground businesses, encouraged foreign investments, and liberalized multiple sectors of the economy, including sanctioning private, domestic commercial banks (McCarthy 2019: 13). As part of its broader plan to co-opt ethnic armed organizations, after the collapse of the Burmese Community Party, insurgent groups that had agreed to a ceasefire were given concessions to participate in the formal economy.

In the emerging neoliberal order, Myanmar was an ideal source for the fast growing Asian economies to access energy, raw materials, and a new market. Then Thai Prime Minister Chatichai Choonhavan perfectly captured the zeitgeist and foreshadowed the fortunes of the Myanmar junta when he famously pledged in 1988, to turn the "battlefields" of Southeast Asia into a "marketplace" (Murray 1994). Despite some initial disagreement[4] within ASEAN, Thailand helped articulated a collective "constructive engagement" policy for ASEAN to integrate the junta, adding Myanmar to its expanded membership in 1997 (Buszynski 1998: 293). After decades of intense regional conflicts, post-Cold War Southeast Asian leaders no longer had any appetite for regional hostilities or for revolutionary changes. Advocates for ASEAN were keen to promote expanded regionalism through multilateral diplomacy and commercial ties as a strategy to minimize regional disputes, and to also serve as an effective bloc to mitigate China's growing influence in Southeast Asia (Emmerson 2008: 73–74).

The growing uneasiness of Western capital to enter or maintain their operations in Myanmar was an opportunity for Asian investors, who seized the economic openings with China and Thailand as early backers. China preceded the efforts of all others and was the first country to sign formal trade agreements with Myanmar, in the final days of the BSPP government in August 1988 (Mya Than 2005: 38). Beijing would soon become Myanmar's most important foreign patron, as it became the prime source of the junta's diplomatic, military, and financial support. By the time of the Myanmar's regime change in 2011, China would become Myanmar's largest donor, the largest source of foreign direct investments, the *tatmadaw*'s main arms supplier, and an active investor in a variety of infrastructural and energy related projects in Myanmar (Malik 2018: 363). Critically, China has protected Myanmar in the United Nations Security Council (UNSC) by using its veto powers, for example, to reject a UNSC draft resolution targeting Myanmar in 2007, alongside Russia (Maung Aung Myoe 2011: 126–128).

However SLORC's first major source of foreign income came from Thailand, when the acting supreme commander of the Thai military Chavalit Yongchaiyut became the first foreign official to visit Myanmar after the 1988 crackdown (Lang 2002: 143). Thailand's changing security priorities led to the end of its official "buffer zone policy" of supporting EAOs in the borders, which allowed the two neighbors to strengthen their bilateral relations (Beehner 2018: 19).[5] During his one-day visit on December 14, 1988, Chavalit, along with a large entourage of Thai business leaders, met with SLORC Chairman Saw Maung and brokered several concessions, giving Thailand early access to Myanmar's commodities (Aung-Thwin 1989: 160).

Beyond the ASEAN states and China, other countries, such as India, as well as traditional US allies' Japan and South Korea ultimately did not adopt the US's isolationist approach and expanded their commercial and diplomatic relations with Myanmar. India, originally a champion of Myanmar's pro-democracy movement would by the early 1990s, adopt a "Look East" policy, rekindling its diplomatic relations with the junta (Egreteau 2008). India's abandonment of its earlier idealism-inspired, anti-junta policy is best demonstrated by then Indian Minister of Petroleum and Natural Gas Murli Deora's visit to Yangon during the 2007 "Saffron Revolution" crackdown, in order to attend the signing of an oil and gas exploration contract (Lee Chan and Chan 2009: 108). By 2012, India had become Myanmar's second largest export market (Lee 2014: 294).

Similarly, the US's closest Asian ally, Japan, was quick to re-connect with the upper echelon of the *tatmadaw* hierarchy after relations between the two countries normalized in February 1989. As part of its "sunshine diplomacy," Japan continued to provide economic assistance and humanitarian aid to Myanmar, while quietly persuading Myanmar to embrace political reforms (Seekin 2007: 94).[6] For some observers, Japan appeared keen to continue to provide aid to the junta unconditionally, even after particularly violent episodes of state repression (Howe and Jang 2013: 136). By the early 2000s, Japanese assistance have provided funding and technical support for a wide range of projects that covered health, agricultural, sanitation, and other grassroots developmental work. Japan's humanitarian assistance however, also helped funded big infrastructural projects including the financing of Yangon International Airport, the construction and operation of a hydroelectric plant, and the development of an information and communications complex in Yangon, giving the junta much needed governance support (James 2005: 31).

Although the transnational advocacy network and strong US pressure prevented Japan from developing fuller economic relations with Myanmar, Japan was able to maintain a "low-risk economic presence" (Seekins 1999: 4). Japanese firms remained involved in big industrial projects and were the first foreign investors granted a 50-year long-term leasehold for their role in helping develop the Mingaladon Industrial Park (Strefford 2005: 125). Nevertheless, despite its relatively supportive relationship of the junta, Japan appeared to have little leverage over the domestic politics of the military regime. This is best demonstrated by an incident during the "Saffron Revolution" protests, when Japanese photojournalist Kenji Nagai was shot and killed by Myanmar soldiers. In an interview, a former diplomat familiar with the case pointed out that the junta had grave misgivings about the deceased journalist, who had applied for a Myanmar visa based on affiliation with a bogus company. The journalist's death led to Myanmar's deliberate, albeit informal, cooling of relations with Japan, and for a time Myanmar made it particularly difficult for Japanese nationals to apply for Myanmar visas (Interview with a former diplomat, Yangon, November 13, 2015).[7] Nevertheless, as the events of the Saffron Revolution have faded, Japanese-Myanmar ties have returned to their original path, and deepened further since the post-2011 reforms (Hartley 2018).

In other words, despite their efforts, global anti-junta activism and the US-led sanctions regime were never successful in their endeavors to effectively isolate

Myanmar from the broader international political economy. By the early 1990s, modest economic development began to pay dividends for the military regime. Even with a limited pool of trading partners, the opening up of Myanmar's under-developed economy provided plenty of business opportunities, which handsomely rewarded regime insiders and co-opted groups with great wealth (Callahan 2007a). This concentration of wealth within an elite group of the *tatmadaw* estab-lishment further reinforced the military's capacity, incentivizing its dominance of the political economy (Pedersen 2008: 161–164).

Throughout the junta's uninterrupted 23 years of direct rule, however, the military never formally abandoned plans to proceed with its long-promised power transition to an elected government. As discussed in detail in Chapter 3, SLORC followed through with its promised elections in 1990. In the lead-up to and in the aftermath of the elections, however, the junta changed its tone and amended the purpose of the elections. The uneven but significant economic growth during the early years of reforms boosted the junta's confidence in its ability to govern without including the country's political opponents (Brown 2013: 182). International criticisms may have denied the junta from attaining broader regime legitimacy, yet the *tatmadaw*'s coercive powers and capacity to discipline its society strengthened during SLORC/SPDC rule.

In any case, it was not repression alone that kept the military in power. In addition to the junta's highly authoritarian practices, their ability to provide a basic socio-political order meant that *tatmadaw* enjoyed "pockets of support and social acceptance," especially in the rural communities of Myanmar's low-lands (Thawnghmung 2004: 7). Although US-led sanctions hurt the financial interests of the regime and its associates and limited Myanmar's developmental potentials, the *tatmadaw* government was able to make some progress in improv-ing the general economic conditions and provide enough materialist improve-ments to its state and society.

Overview of US sanctions regime and the transnational advocacy networks

Until 2012, the US and a number of its European allies intended to delegitimize military rule by imposing a myriad of embargoes. The rationale behind the US-led sanctions policy was to isolate the SLORC/SPDC government from the inter-national community and global market (Pedersen 2008: 63). Besides the moral argument, sanction advocates assume that punitive embargoes would force the regime to succumb to pressure, face regime collapse, or embrace political reforms. In emerging transnational activist circles, Myanmar quickly became the "South Africa of the 1990s" (Pedersen 2008: 1).

US sanctions began initially on an *ad hoc* basis, just days following the forma-tion of the SLORC junta. In this post-Cold War context, all US presidents since Ronald Reagan, until Barack Obama, maintained a downgraded diplomatic pres-ence in Myanmar. The US, along with its Anglophone allies, refused to recognize Myanmar's official name change in 1989, and continued to refer to the country as

Burma. Successive US administrations starting with George H.W. Bush, begin to impose increasingly punitive and complicated sanctions, with the explicit aim of pressuring the junta into adopting political reforms, if not an outright regime change (Ewing-Chow 2007: 178). The US-led sanctions gained momentum with an active anti-junta transnational activist network, backed primarily by several European allies. For over two decades, this sanctions-centric approach systematically locked-in the foreign policy options available to "Western" policymakers, therefore limiting potential negotiations and direct dialogues with the junta.

After the 1988 crackdown, both houses of Congress passed separate resolutions condemning the junta, and calling on President Ronald Reagan to review ongoing ties with Myanmar (Martin 2013c: 6). This led to the suspension of US aid programs to Myanmar on September 23, 1988, including the International Military Education and Training Program to *tatmadaw* officers, which had been operating since 1980, and was soon followed by arms embargoes (Riley and Balaram 2013: 118). Against the advice of the US Drug Enforcement Administration, the US government also suspended the anti-narcotics assistance program indefinitely (Branigin 1990). The newly elected George H.W. Bush carried on his predecessor's anti-junta policy and issued Proclamation 5955, which effectively removed Myanmar's preferred trading status, ostensibly due to the country's violation of labor rights (Kaufmann 2007: 177). The executive branch was further empowered by Congress through the Customs and Trade Act of 1990, which allowed the president to enact "economic sanctions upon Burma as the President determined to be appropriate" (Martin 2013c: 7).

Formal sanctions intensified under the successive administrations of President Bill Clinton and President George W. Bush. The first major presidential proclamation, the 1996 Visa Ban, specifically targeted the SLORC senior leadership and their families, prohibiting their entry to the US (Clinton 1996). On May 20 1997, President Clinton signed Executive Order 13047, the first formal investment ban, which prohibited any new investments in Myanmar by US citizens. Following the Depayin massacre in 2003, where Aung San Suu Kyi and her supporters were attacked by government-sponsored mobs, the Bush administration responded with even more comprehensive sanctions. Among the many punitive measures, the 2003 Burmese Freedom and Democracy Act stipulated a total embargo on all Myanmar imports to the US (Seekins 2005a: 439–440). A major component of the Act effectively made it illegal for Myanmar entities to transact legally in US dollars.

During George W. Bush's second term in office, monk-led "Saffron Revolution" protests ended in another decisive crackdown by the *tatmadaw*. Unsurprisingly, President Bush introduced another round of sanctions in October 2007 and April 2008, with the intention of targeting specific individuals and their business associates in an attempt to damage the financial interests of regime cronies (Holliday 2011: 115). The last major Bush-era sanction, the 2008 Tom Lantos Block Burmese Jade Act, barred all imports of jadeite and rubies from Myanmar to the US. When Barack Obama came into office, the US had passed five federal laws, issued four presidential executive orders, and a series of presidential documents, which produced a comprehensive "web of overlapping sanctions" specifically targeting Myanmar (Martin 2013c: 1–2).

The emergence of a global transnational activist networks in the 1990s played a critical role in isolating Myanmar from "Western" capital, and their lobbying efforts also helped "lock-in" US policy positions on Myanmar. Global anti-junta campaigns, consumer-led boycott movements, and lobbying by exiled Myanmar dissidents and the diaspora community. including the peripheral borders of Myanmar, contrasted sharply with the lack of robust political agency inside the country (Williams 2012; Simpson 2013). The emergent politicized Myanmar diaspora, composed primarily of recently exiled dissidents and students that had escaped the country after the 1988 crackdown, was able to capture the attention and support of emerging transnational activist circles, creating a "boomerang effect" (Keck and Sikkink 1998: 12–13). From London to Bangkok, high profile activist groups were particularly successful in recruiting foreign supporters, leading consumer boycotts against (primarily "Western") companies that held investments in Myanmar as well as lobbying their governments to take increasingly punishing actions against the SLORC/SPDC (Duell 2014). However, given the relatively low geostrategic interest of Myanmar for the US, the imposition of sanctions was a low-cost "symbolic" policy that could appease activists while also bolstering domestic support for politicians (Whang 2011).

By the mid-1990s, several university towns in the US, as well as municipal and state governments had embraced an anti-junta boycott campaign (Cleveland 2001: 12). Just as the Myanmar government was overturning decades of self-imposed isolation policy, the disinvestment movement pushed many multinational companies to freeze their investments in Myanmar, or leave the country completely. Therefore, by the time formal trade sanctions were actually put in place against Myanmar by foreign governments, this "served mainly to confirm individual and corporate decisions taken years previously" (Holliday 2011: 68). While many foreign businesses left Myanmar, those with significant financial stakes, especially in the energy sector such as Unocal and Total, continued to operate inside the country (Jones 2015: 112). The revenues generated by the exportation of natural gas were especially lucrative, and by 2002, the government's financial standing had significantly improved, with Myanmar's balance of payments in the positive for the first time in decades (Taylor 2009: 454–455).

In addition to trade embargoes, a key strategy adopted by sanctions advocates was to limit the scope of international organizations' activities in Myanmar. The US, with support coming primarily from its European allies, consistently voted against all requests by Myanmar for multilateral loans and technical assistance from international financial institutions, such as the World Bank and the IMF (Pedersen 2008: 44–45, 58–60). Under these harsh conditions imposed by the West, international organizations endured a restricted mandate in supporting Myanmar's socio-economic development, including provisions for humanitarian assistance (Fletcher et al. 2014: 299). UN agencies and INGOs operated in Myanmar, but Western pressure and sanctions legislations meant that there were strict regulations, which limited the scope and range of activities that these organizations could carry out in Myanmar.

The limits of sanctions

Contemporary economic sanctions, especially against authoritarian and totalitarian regimes, rarely achieve the intended objective of their advocates (Allen 2005). In the contemporary international political economy, effective sanctions regimes are difficult to implement both formally and informally. A total blockade of any regime is difficult to enforce, and in any case, those regimes targeted may be able to seek alliance and support from sympathetic states, or overcome official sanctions through back channels and underground networks. Strong authoritarian or totalitarian regimes generally do not require popular support or votes for their political survival, thus any economic burden incurred by the country could be directed to the general populace or diverted to regime opponents and other marginalized groups, with diminished costs for regime supporters and the elites (Pape 1997: 107). In the event of a socio-economic crisis, the regime leadership may also deflect pressure and ignore its own mismanagement, by shifting the blame to externally imposed sanctions (ICG 2004: 17). If faced with a significant reduction of material wealth, authoritarian regimes, especially single-party and military governments, can still manage societal frustration by increasing their tax revenue, and continuing to patronage the regime's core loyalists and the security apparatus (Escriba-Folch and Wright 2010).

Further, authoritarian or totalitarian regimes are apt at utilizing ideologies and symbols to justify their rule, and thus external pressure can often be translated as foreign hostility, and in post-colonial states, viewed as neo-imperialistic aggression, which could actually bolster the nationalist credentials of the regime leadership (Pape 1997: 106–107). Especially in Myanmar, where nationalists have largely perceived British colonial rule as discriminatory and exploitative, external pressure has only served to reinforce nationalistic and xenophobic attitudes among the *tatmadaw* leadership, further convincing them that foreign intervention is aimed at undermining Myanmar's national interests (Gravers 1999).

Years of self-imposed isolation from 1962 to 1988 meant foreign pressure and sanctions were always going to have limited impact as foreign trade had only accounted for roughly 3.5 percent of Myanmar's GDP in the 1980s (Taylor 2009: 466). Critically, the majority of sanction-imposing states had relatively weak trade, political, and cultural linkages to Myanmar.[8] Therefore, these predominantly "Western" democracies could not translate their sanctions policies into credible leverage that could punctuate the authoritarian equilibrium, which sustained military rule.[9] Two decades of US-led economic sanctions and consumer boycott campaigns further limited the leverage and influence that "Western" democracies had over the junta's control of its domestic political developments.

The new sanctions legislation introduced by the US in 2003 had the biggest impact on Myanmar's economic development. On top of the government's mismanaged and uneven economic policy, the 2003 legislation made it difficult for Myanmar-based businesses to use US dollars in their financial transactions and banned Myanmar exports to the US. To mitigate against the 2003 US dollar ban, the junta and Myanmar companies adopted multiple tactics to continue their business operations. The old *hundi*[10] underground banking system, which allowed transnational monetary transfers without going through the international banking system, had always been an option. Cash-based transactions, especially in the borders were also common (Jones 2015: 113). Other currencies, particularly the euro became the official currency for many financial transactions, including for example, the government's annual gem auctions. Finally, entrepreneurs with the means have registered their companies in oversea jurisdictions, many through proxies, thereby circumventing sanctions and allowing these firms access to international banking services. As one interviewee, an editor of a Myanmar newspaper, explained, Singapore in particular would become Asia's "Switzerland" for Myanmar's elites to keep their assets (Interview with the editor of a Myanmar newspaper, July 8, 2013, Yangon; also see US Embassy 2007c).[11]

Therefore, although the 2003 sanctions made it difficult for the Myanmar state and companies to conduct businesses, the economic cost was largely passed on to small and medium enterprises (SME), while regime cronies and high ranking officials were able to tolerate the additional economic burden and still amass greater wealth, even after the implementation of comprehensive sanctions. SMEs and those who did not have the right connections to the regime were therefore unable to compete with their regional counterparts and many businesses were forced to shut down (Kudo 2008: 998). Myanmar's light manufacturing sector, especially the garment industry was particularly hard hit, as prior to the 2003 ban the US was one of Myanmar's largest export destinations (Alamgir 2008: 987).

The impact of undercutting Myanmar's commercial relations from the "Western" market has led the development of an "illiberal" trade pattern, whereby Myanmar's trade is reliant on a small group of regional partners (*ibid*). Although the 2003 ban was especially damaging for small businesses, the denial of US markets only further strengthened Myanmar's commercial ties with its Asian partners. Suspended investments from the "West" were replaced by Chinese and Thai interests, which were primarily involved in the extractive and power sector (Bissinger 2012). A year after the investment ban, in 2004, Myanmar was able to increase total exports by 18 percent, rising to 24 percent in 2005 (Alamgir 2008: 987). By 2005, 82 percent of all Myanmar trade was with Asian trading partners (*ibid*). However, these deepened commercial links with Asia strengthened capital-intensive sectors that limited wealth and benefits to the military state and a small group of investors, and they did not create an environment conducive to independent entrepreneurship. The oil and natural gas sector was exploitive in nature and sold off to power the economies of China and Thailand, with little direct linkages to Myanmar's domestic economy (Brown 2013: 196–197).

Given the continued legacy of state-dominated industrialization policy, the liberalization of Myanmar's economy was quickly captured by the material interests of the military (Alamgir 2008: 991–993). The government's control of trading licenses led to the monopolization of the most profitable economic sectors at the hands of military conglomerates and a very selective group of "nationalist entrepreneurs"; while in the peripheral borders, a small group of primarily Chinese traders, and a few ethnic business and political elites that had signed ceasefire agreements with the government also benefited (Lintner 2000: 170; McCarthy 2019: 12–19).[12] The result of Myanmar's partial transition to a market economy was rent-seeking and primitive capital accumulation (Kubo 2012; Woods 2011: 751). No independent, trading class therefore emerged, and regime outsiders were unable to amass the "material bases for sustained opposition to the regime" (Alamgir 2008: 979).

Apart from limiting Myanmar's economic development options, the dogmatic position of some of the Western-based activists groups also led to suspension of critical humanitarian assistance for the underdeveloped country. The most critical foreign-based pro-democracy campaign groups adopted a zero sum binary position vis-à-vis the military government. From their perspective, Myanmar-based organizations that were not explicitly anti-military should be considered junta collaborators, which aided in the perpetuation of military rule (James 2005: 145–148). As a result, whether through genuine belief or merely as a strategic propaganda offensive against the military regime, many foreign-based pressure groups and exiled activists regularly criticized individuals and Myanmar-based civic associations, including UN agencies and INGOs that failed to explicitly challenge the legitimacy of the military regime (Personal correspondence with a senior foreign activist, February 17, 2007).

Many veteran domestic civil society activists who actively worked to develop Myanmar's civil society from within the country often complained about some of the more radical actions of those outside of the country, which were perceived to be counter-productive toward Myanmar's socio-political developments (Interviews with NGO, INGO, and UN staff July 4–12, 2011, Yangon). On August 17, 2005, pressure from the US government as well as transnational activists groups led to the termination of the Global Fund's Myanmar program on HIV/AIDS, tuberculosis, and malaria (Perry 2007: 179–180). A veteran staff affiliated with the UN indicated that this decision eventually led to serious splits within the diaspora community:

> The hardcore lobby just went too far. These were lifesaving programs. People were put on ART [antiretroviral therapy], if you withdraw that, people die. This shows that for certain organizations and people, they were willing to let people die, in order to make a point. For some of them [former anti-junta critics], they say that is the trigger [to work with the Thein Sein government]. Whose interests are we really serving?
>
> (Author's interview with UN affiliated International
> Staff, January 16, 2014)

Regional engagements and deepened commercial links also failed to persuade the junta to pursue genuine reconciliation with its political opposition. Countries that have elected to develop closer ties with Myanmar come from diverse political traditions, normative values, and have different materialist interests determined by realpolitik calculations (Jones 2009). Liberal democratic methods were never a particularly strong aspect of politics and governance in Southeast Asia (and China), and the main commonality shared by those that have developed bilateral ties with Myanmar has been adherence to the regional norm of "non-interference" in Myanmar's internal affairs (Lee et al. 2009: 113). The availability of Myanmar's resources for the energy demands of neighboring China, Thailand, and India has also meant that there has been little incentive for these countries to alter their relationship with the military junta.

Despite growing denunciations against the regime even among its traditional diplomatic partners following the 2007 "Saffron Revolution" crackdown, international action and opposition movements failed to redirect the military's political agenda. The junta remained defiant, and according to a US internal cable, was confident that it could "survive any sanctions" because of its natural resources (US Embassy 2007b). The US-enforced sanctions regime had serious economic repercussions; however, it was unable to meaningful alter the political behavior of the military regime. In an internal assessment, Yangon-based US diplomats admitted that international sanctions appeared to have made no difference, as "Than Shwe appears determined to proceed with the roadmap on his terms only" (US Embassy 2008a). Indeed, this was how Myanmar's regime transition and change unfolded when Than Shwe voluntarily retired following the dissolution of the SPDC on March 30, 2011, when Myanmar's way to democracy was formally realized.

US Asian Pivot and returning to a balance of relationship

Although Myanmar's post-2011 regime change was not a direct consideration of external influences, the changing US rhetoric certainly provided the opportunity for the post-junta hybrid regime to improve its relations with the US and other sanctions-enforcing countries *after* the regime change. The decision for the US to normalize its relations with Myanmar indicates more about the US's own strategic interests and change of foreign policy direction, rather than any changes in Myanmar's foreign policy behaviors. Despite the US's public hostility against the SLORC/SPDC, the *tatmadaw* leadership have not completely dismissed opportunities to improve relations with the US and the "West." In the early 1990s, other than opening the doors for multinational companies to invest in Myanmar, the junta has also tried to communicate directly with the US government. A SLORC delegation headed by senior foreign ministry official Ohn Gyaw visited Washington in February 1990, appealing for US support to restart its anti-narcotics assistance, although the US State Department refused to meet the delegation (Lintner 1999: 377). In 2002, the junta passed the "Law to Control Money and Property Obtained by Illegal Means," which, at least, "on paper, met many of the objections regarding money-laundering noted by the US Treasury" (Turnell 2009: 277). Upon the re-election of George W. Bush, Senior General Than Shwe sent a congratulatory letter to the US President via the US embassy in Yangon, and the letter was also published on the front page of the state-run newspaper, the *New Light of Myanmar* (*NLM* 2004). Than Shwe would repeat this diplomatic gesture, similarly congratulating Barack Obama on his inauguration as US President on the front page of the same newspaper (*NLM* 2009).

The election of Barack Obama as US President, and his administration's declaration of the US Asian Pivot[13] policy, created the optimal conditions just as Myanmar was on its way to finalizing plans for its transition to a disciplined democracy. Détente between Myanmar and the US and the broader international community after the regime change in Myanmar, reflected the US's changing foreign policy direction and agenda and not an indication of a change in Myanmar's foreign policy behavior. President Barack Obama clearly had a different approach and vision for the US's role in the broader international community, and in this sense normalization of US-Myanmar relations had more to do with the shift in US foreign policy direction rather than the changing domestic circumstances in Myanmar.[14] The Obama administration's decision to re-prioritize Asia was reflected in the US's policy transition from its outright sanction policy on Myanmar toward a policy of engagement with Myanmar (Martin 2010: 13–17). The perceived shift of the post-junta government's relations with China while Myanmar improves its relations with the "West," however, is in line with Myanmar's long-term "balance of relationship" approach (Huang 2015). That is, Myanmar has returned to its old policy roots of neutralism as its main foreign policy consideration in order to avoid becoming overtly aligned or dependent on any one external actor (*ibid*: 204–205).

The ASEAN Way

Contrary to the US-led sanctions regime, the majority of Myanmar's neighbors were keen to strengthen ties with the junta from the very beginning. After decades of regional conflicts, the ASEAN member states sought to promote regional stability and prosperity through expanded multilateralism.[15] The "ASEAN Way" emphasizes conflict avoidance as a key rule for ASEAN member states to address regional concerns (Masilamani and Peterson 2014: 11). Based on this informal process of quiet diplomacy, collective decisions are to be made through a regional consensus, and adhere to the fundamental rule of non-interference, at least publicly, with one another's domestic affairs. Advocates for indigenous-led regionalism believe that regular interactions through a formal regional organization could help socialize pariah regimes to conform to international norms and standards, which, in time, would lead to greater respect for human rights and democratic principles (Pevehouse 2005: 16).[16] Strategically, both Myanmar and ASEAN shared a mutual interest in counter-balancing China's growing influence in Myanmar, as well as more broadly in Southeast Asia.

As previously discussed, Myanmar has long adhered to a neutralist position and has strategically embrace a "balance of relationship" to ensure that it was not beholden and dependent on any one external actor (Huang 2015). Myanmar, although a founding member of the non-aligned movement (NAM), withdrew its membership in 1979 after it had deemed that the movement had become too involved in Cold War politics (Aung Kin 1980: 112–114). For similar reasons, Myanmar had maintained its distance from ASEAN. Although Myanmar was invited to join ASEAN as a founding member, the junta rejected the opportunity, in part because ASEAN was considered part of the anti-communist bloc and the association did not afford diplomatic recognition of the People's Republic of China (McCarthy 2008b: 915).[17] The decision by SLORC to join ASEAN and to actively revive and expand its external relationship with the regional body in the 1990s demonstrated the *tatmadaw* leadership's reevaluation of how to tackle its immediate political and economic crisis, as well as the address the US-led attempt to isolate the regime. In 1992, for example, Myanmar would also rejoin the NAM, in line with its strategic decision to sought external support for the regime. ASEAN membership provided Myanmar with new diplomatic and economic channels and afforded the junta a degree of international legitimacy. By re-engaging with global networks and regional multilateralism, Myanmar sought to mitigate the impact of sanctions and move away from an overtly dependent relationship with China, a strategic objective shared by ASEAN member states.

Myanmar–ASEAN relations have however not been without problems. The junta's weak governance has cross-national implications as a major source of narcotics production, as well as the influx of political exiles and economic migrants, which have caused tensions with its ASEAN partners. Myanmar's abysmal human right record, its ongoing civil war with various ethnic rebels, and the unwillingness of the military to reconcile with its political opposition would also routinely attract international condemnation and prove to be a major source of contention between the "West" and the ASEAN bloc. ASEAN's Myanmar policy therefore went through various phases, from "constructive engagement" to "critical disengagement," with growing frustration, which led to occasional public criticisms of the junta by ASEAN, contrary to its general practice of non-interference (Jones 2008).

ASEAN's limitations

ASEAN may have allowed greater political representation and a platform for Myanmar to engage in international diplomacy; however, their collective attempt to "socialize" Myanmar appeared to have made little impact in Myanmar's domestic politics (Chow and Easley 2016: 532–533). In part, ASEAN has long publicly advocated a policy of non-interference in the sovereignty of other states, at least when it suited their national interests. The majority of ASEAN's political establishment were also skeptical about expanded socio-political pluralism within their own regimes, which did not have the best track records in affording their citizens greater civil and political rights. ASEAN's "ideological conservatism" emphasizes on regional cohesion and stability, with little interest in changing the status quo (Jones 2008: 288). ASEAN states therefore have consistently rejected sanctions as an option to pressure Myanmar. Despite misgivings about Myanmar, ASEAN has continued to back the country in the face of international criticisms. For example, all ten ASEAN members boycotted the 2005 economic ministers' Asia-Europe Meeting in Rotterdam after the Netherlands refused to issue visas to the Myanmar delegation (Egreteau and Jagan 2013: 179). Even on rare occasions where ASEAN has moved away from its general adherence to non-interference in individual states' domestic affairs, the public outcry has not been followed-up with any concrete actions. ASEAN has instead pushed consistently for the UN to take the lead by backing UN appointed special envoys to facilitate talks (Jones 2008: 285).

However, as a way of deflecting international criticism against ASEAN's unwillingness to confront Myanmar's worst behaviors, ASEAN has repeatedly appealed to the junta to embrace political reforms. These efforts have, however, generally revolved around national reconciliation in relation to the role of Aung San Suu Kyi – either calling for her release during different bouts of her house arrest or for political dialogues. The junta has rarely made any meaningful concessions to these demands, and more critically, since the introduction of its seven-step roadmap, it has not diverged from the political direction nor accelerated the pace of its implementation.

During the junta's 23-year rule, three critical events – the 2003 Depayin Massacre, the "Saffron Revolution" in 2007, and the 2008 Cyclone Nargis – have led to intensified responses from the international community. In each case, ASEAN has taken a much more visible and assertive approach in addressing the perceived failings of the junta. Nevertheless, despite the public rhetoric, these were in effect moderate reactions to extraordinary events. In none of these cases, was there any evidence that the junta felt sufficiently threatened to amend its policies. Even after the near universal condemnation of its actions, the junta remain united and made no changes to the way the regime governed its disciplined society.

In May 2002, the junta released Aung San Suu Kyi from her second bout of house arrest, ostensibly as a response to the visits of UN Special Envoy Razali Ismail, a top Malaysian diplomat. However, if this was a response to appease ASEAN and other international actors, the alleged overture was soon reversed by the junta. A year after her release, a state-mobilized mob attacked Aung San Suu Kyi's convoy near the town of Depayin, killing several NLD supporters. In the aftermath of the Depayin Massacre, the junta re-incarcerated Suu Kyi and amplified its assault against the opposition, leading to the arrest of hundreds of NLD supporters nationwide and the closing down of all remaining NLD offices (McCarthy 2008b: 919–920).

In response to the Depayin incident, ASEAN would, for the first time since its founding, collectively criticize one of its own members (*ibid*). ASEAN's response, however, was relatively moderate, with its prime objective being securing Aung San Suu Kyi's release. Although this initial demand may have facilitated Razil Ismail's return visit to Myanmar and allowed for a meeting with the re-incarcerated Suu Kyi, the opposition leader remained imprisoned for the next seven years. Further, the junta would once again revise its attitude toward the UN and ASEAN, consistently rejecting the Special Envoy's visa applications in subsequent years. This effectively made the Malaysian diplomat's work in Myanmar untenable, forcing his resignation by the end of 2005. The junta also did not relax its societal control and continued to suppress open dissent. On the one-year anniversary of the Depayin violence, the junta beefed up its security and quickly suppressed a few isolated incidents of opposition activism, leading to the arrests of a number of activists (US Embassy 2004b).

Some observers have suggested that the military's seven-step roadmap unveiled in August 2003 was a direct response to international pressures after the Depayin killings (Chow and Easley 2016: 533). A month before the unveiling of the *tatmadaw*'s roadmap, Bangkok attempted to broker Myanmar's reconciliation with its domestic and international challengers by proposing a five-step plan.[18] The Thai version was motivated by the need to ensure a smooth transition to Myanmar's scheduled tenure as ASEAN Chair in 2006. According to a retired SPDC official, if any considerations were given to external pressure, it was certainly not a concession to the West but, ostensibly, a platitude to satisfy its ASEAN neighbors in order for the bloc to "continue to defend us" (Kyaw Yin Hlaing 2014b: 181–182). However, even if this were true, when Khin Nyunt unveiled the military's seven-step roadmap the content did not reflect any of the critical suggestions made by the Thais and offered no timeline (McCarthy 2008b: 921). The roadmap reflected the military's considerations of its own praetorian interests more so than any genuine response to outside influences. Given the junta's unwillingness to revise its transition plan, the most tangible outcome was merely Myanmar's forfeit of the ASEAN Chair in 2006.

Although the government unveiled its seven-step roadmap to a disciplined flourishing democracy, which included the restarting of the NC only a few months after the Depayin killings, the roadmap was not an *ad hoc* response to external pressure. First, the foundations of the NC, and its constitutional drafting responsibilities, were formally endorsed by the SLORC back in 1992. The purpose, function, and the procedures of the NC, largely mirrored the failed attempt of the 1990s. Although the government extended an invitation to the previously expelled NLD, it was under the condition that all delegates must follow the government's rules and procedures, and any contribution to the constitution must reflect the political vision of the *tatmadaw*. That is, the military-determined "basic principles" of the Union are non-negotiable and must be included in the final version of the Constitution. The junta was unwilling to change its rules of the game, while the NLD also could not acquiesce to the military's preconditions, which predictably led to its boycott of the NC.

If the introduction of its roadmap and the reconvening of the NC was to address intensified international condemnations, then the junta clearly was not making any genuine efforts to appease the critics with its political proposal. Rather, as discussed in Chapter 3, the imposition of the roadmap clearly reflected the regime's coordinated efforts to implement its own political vision, based on its praetorian ethos and own self-rationalizing belief that it was their praetorian duty to implement gradual socio-political changes, reflecting the military regime's political vision and material interests.

By far, the biggest challenge for the Myanmar–ASEAN relationship was the junta's decision to violently suppress the monks-led protest in 2007. Dubbed the "Saffron Revolution" by the Anglophone press, the protests were widely covered globally, which was particularly embarrassing for ASEAN, as it was in the midst of celebrating its fortieth anniversary (Emmerson 2008: 71). Singapore, then ASEAN Chair and host of the celebrations, switched from "quiet to loud diplomacy," and the association would collectively release its strongest-ever public criticism, expressing its "revulsion" at the junta's actions (*ibid*: 72). Even after ASEAN's unusual outcry, other than some minor concessions, the junta made no efforts to reconcile with oppositional forces nor loosen its socio-political controls, or diverge from its roadmap. Myanmar initially allowed the new UN Special Envoy Ibrahim Gambari to visit Myanmar and meet with the regime leadership as well as opposition leader Aung San Suu Kyi. However, these meetings produced no concrete outcomes. More embarrassingly for ASEAN and its chair Singapore, Prime Minister Thein Sein blocked Gambari from presenting his findings to delegates at the East Asia Summit held in Singapore in November 2007, even as Gambari was on his way to the city-state by invitation of the Singaporean government. Ironically, this episode suggests that rather than having ASEAN moderate Myanmar's behaviour, the junta, using the non-interference and regional consensus principles, was able to censor the Singaporean government in Singapore (Emmerson 2008: 75).

ASEAN had greater success in its dealings with Myanmar the following year during the aftermath of the devastating Cyclone Nargis of May 2008. The junta had refused initially to allow foreign humanitarian teams to help with emergency relief work, despite the scale of death and destruction brought by the cyclone. The renewed international focus on Myanmar and the global pressure for action meant that ASEAN could no longer remain on the sidelines without taking any concrete actions. Following successful negotiation, a Tripartite Core Group (TCG) was formed comprising ASEAN, alongside the UN and the Myanmar government to coordinate disaster relief efforts (ASEAN 2010). However even with the *tatmadaw*'s greater acceptance of multilateral efforts in addressing a critical human security crisis, the military regime, as discussed in Chapter 4, continued to carry on with its roadmap as planned and made no significant changes to its dealings with regime challengers. Significantly, after the mandate of the TCG had concluded in July 2010, the ASEAN Special Envoy to Post-Nargis Recovery Willy Sabandar made it clear that ASEAN would play no role in Myanmar's planned 2010 general elections (US Embassy 2010).

Growing international pressure following the Depayin violence and the "Saffron" crisis, as well as after expanded international engagement during Cyclone Nargis, neither forced the regime to collapse nor socialized the regime to liberalize. In the aftermath of the 2008 Cyclone, the Myanmar government's critically inadequate response was exposed, but it also simultaneously demonstrated the devastating cost brought about by Western disengagement, with the international community's efforts to provide relief assistance challenged by past misgivings and inexperience of bilateral cooperation between Myanmar and Western states (ICG 2008: 15).

Several ASEAN leaders have expressed their frustration both publicly and privately about Myanmar's leaders and their unwillingness to tolerate any divergent views. In a private meeting with US officials, Singapore's Minister Mentor Lee Kuan Yew conceded that it was a mistake to allow Myanmar's entry to ASEAN (US Embassy 2007b). Lee claimed that by the late 1990s, he had given up hope that the *tatmadaw* would be open to foreign advice, called the Myanmar generals "dense" and "stupid," and dialogues with the regime akin to "taking to dead people" (*ibid*). Former Thai Foreign Minister Kasit Piromya took a more positive view of the role ASEAN had played in pressuring Myanmar to embrace greater political liberalization, suggesting that ASEAN may have played a role in speeding up the final stages of the seven-step roadmap to democracy. Nevertheless, he concedes that there were "many arguments," sometimes very "heated," in closed-door meetings with their Myanmar counterparts (Interview with the author, Kasit Piromya, *op. cit.*). Kasit also recognized that although the civilian diplomats were more accommodating in their discussions, their military superiors were aloof, "entrenched in their position," with the upper echelon of the *tatmadaw* difficult to access.

The China quandary

Despite the importance of ASEAN in the junta's foreign policy direction, it is Myanmar's relationship with China that would become the most important and impactful post-1988. Historically, the two countries have a complicated and uneasy relationship, although "Western" hostility pushed Myanmar to develop a mutually beneficial relationship with China based on reciprocal, albeit asymmetrical arrangements (Steinberg and Fan 2012).[19] Myanmar has long been considered a geostrategic interest, which could help China's developmental plans in the landlocked Yunnan province, while providing a potential access point to the Indian Ocean (Li and Zheng 2009: 627–633). Since the mid-1980s, Chinese policymakers have explored plans to integrate Myanmar as part of its strategic interest to expand its influence in Southeast Asia (Malik 2018: 364). In Myanmar's search for international security, China therefore became a natural ally, albeit an asymmetrical one, where China clearly was the dominant partner (James 2004: 534–536). In return for China's diplomatic protection, Myanmar has often repaid China's patronage with further access to the country's natural resources. Shwe Gas Movement reported that three days after the China's veto of a UNSC draft resolution against Myanmar in January 2007, the SPDC signed a "Production Sharing Contract" with the China National Petroleum Company (CNPC) for further "exploration, drilling and production rights" in the Andaman Sea (2009: 9). Months later, in 2008, the junta awarded CNPC exclusive rights to buy gas from the Shwe gas field for below market price (*ibid*; also see: Aung Shin 2015).

The Sino-Myanmar *pauk-phaw* relationship would become a major lifeline that counter-balanced "Western" sanctions, while the *tatmadaw* also used the "China Card" to convince ASEAN of Myanmar's strategic importance in counter-balancing Chinese influence over the region (Seekins 1997: 526). China replaced Thailand as the country's largest foreign investor in 2009, and by 2010, officially accounted for more than a third of all Myanmar's trade (Min Zin and Joseph 2012: 107). Chinese capital, whether in the form of direct investments, economic assistance, or loans, would also fund many of Myanmar's infrastructural projects and businesses (Malik 2018: 363). China is also Myanmar's main external arms supplier, providing technical expertise and a wide range of military hardware from fighter jets to radar systems and ammunition (ICG 2009: 21).

Despite Myanmar's great economic and geopolitical significance for Chinese interests, Myanmar's nationalistic military regime have always felt troubled by the country's growing dependency on China for international support. There is also a general perception that China's behavior is akin to a neo-colonial power, exploiting Myanmar's natural resources for its own economic development without consideration of the local communities (EarthRights International 2008: 1). The influx of Chinese traders and migrant workers to Myanmar has led to escalating local resentment against the Chinese (ICG 2009: 24–25). The increasingly visible expansion of Chinese economic, social, and diplomatic presence in Myanmar has led to the painful awareness that Myanmar has a "partial, uncomfortable dependency" on China (Steinberg and Fan 2012: 262). The wariness of growing Chinese influence over Myanmar is a common thread that is reflected in the thinking of many of Myanmar's elites from different sides of the political spectrum. One interviewee, a well-known veteran activist argues that China is the most important external actor, with the potential to influence the domestic political outcome in Myanmar (Interview with the author, prominent activist, Yangon, January 13, 2014). Similarly, another interviewee, a retired colonel, was also of the opinion that decades of bilateral ties with Myanmar were leading the country dangerously to "becoming a slave to China" (Interview with a retired colonel, *op. cit*). The role of China was also considered by other interviewees, with an elite Myanmar activist explaining:

Burma has [a] long [and] bitter history of China interfering in Burmese politics and security. They are the ones which supported the BCP [Burma Communist Party] which is one of the key [problems] for the government for many years. [The Chinese] also provided Kokang and Wa support, and also the Kachin which is very much a security issue. The mindset of the Burmese military towards the Chinese is anti-China, but the former senior general [Than Shwe] rewarded China's UN veto by giving away the Kyaukpyu [pipeline] project to China. People see this as a give and take relationship. People in the military also noticed the over-dependence and over giving to the Chinese. [The] only way out of this over-influence is quick democratic reform. The government is using the citizens' voices as excuses to re-negotiate with China. That is why they allow the media and public debates on Chinese investments. One of President Thein Sein's advisors ... has openly argued against the Kyaukpyu project. He used to be in the military, he is the one who [is] very much against the Chinese project. So to cut it short, [the] government can use civil society and media and Daw Suu as a reason to re-negotiate the terms with the Chinese and their investments.

(Interview with a veteran activist, June 22, 2012, Yangon)

Many scholars appeared to have subscribed to this view, linking Myanmar's decision to enact a regime transition in 2011 as a means of distancing the country from its over-dependence on China (Chow and Easley 2016: 541). Since the 1990s, analysts have written about the "sinonization" of upper Myanmar, the fear of Myanmar becoming China's "strategic pawn" and the possibility of Myanmar turning into a Chinese satellite state (Malik 1997; Mya Maung 1994; Singh 1997). In the ethnic minority borderlands, many EAO controlled areas have been *de facto* satellite Chinese states years before the implementation of Myanmar's post-2011 regime change. In much of the EAO-controlled areas in the Myanmar-China borderlands, the *lingua franca* is Chinese and the preferred currency of trade is the Chinese *renminbi*. The United Wa State Party (UWSP), which commands Myanmar's largest insurgent group, also has a Wa State Constitution, entirely written in simplified Chinese. Local businesses and the few prosperous casino towns, such as the National Democratic Alliance Army-controlled Mong La, have long been financed by Chinese capital, with the EAO leadership often receiving informal Chinese political (and weapons) support, at least from the Yunnan provincial level (Keenan 2012: 81–108; Tharaphi Than 2016). In the mid to late 2000s, armed Chinese units occasionally carried out raids across the border into official Myanmar territory under EAO control, to shutdown casinos, arrest gamblers and operators, and close off borders (ICG 2009: 16).

Even in the so-called Myanmar "heartland" of Mandalay, which was the last capital of the Konbaung dynasty, as well as in Yangon, Myanmar's commercial capital, the prevalence of Chinese influence is undeniable. Chinese businesses and migrants from Yunnan province have outpaced all other ethnic groups for example in Mandalay (Guo 2010: 96). As early as 2002, the late Ludu Daw Amar referred to Mandalay as "an undeclared colony of Yunnan" (Min Zin 2002). Ten years after the well-known writer's comment, the singer Lin Lin would write the song "Death of Mandalay" lamenting the influx of Chinese immigrants overtaking the city (Miller 2017: 140). This wariness of Chinese influence has been in the public consciousness for at least the past two decades. The junta has, for example, diversified its arms purchases to buy arms from other countries, including India, Pakistan, North Korea, Singapore, Ukraine, and Russia (Li and Lye 2009: 267; Egreteau 2008: 952–953). Since 2003, Myanmar has also conducted a series of joint naval exercises with India.

In any case, the *tatmadaw* has consistently positioned it state building project and national security priorities above all other considerations. With the *tatmadaw*'s growing confidence following its military upgrade, it has renewed fighting against some EAOs in the lead-up to the next stages of its disciplined democracy roadmap. When the Kokang-based Myanmar National Democratic Alliance Army (MNDAA) refused to transform into a *tatmadaw*-approved Border Guard Force, the junta launched an offensive in August 2009, and successfully defeated the Chinese-speaking insurgents within days. The Chinese had previously cautioned the *tatmadaw* against attacking the Kokang militia; however, the SPDC launched its offensive anyway, without giving the Chinese advanced warnings (ICG 2009: 26). The *tatmadaw* installed MNDAA defectors in Kokang to support the Naypyidaw government, while an estimated 37,000 refugees fled into Yunnan after the 2009 raid (Song 2017: 468).[20]

Undeniably, Myanmar's uncomfortable, critical (but not absolute) dependency on Chinese diplomatic and economic support is a real concern for Myanmar. However, Sino-Myanmar relations have gone through a routine ebb-and-flow of mistrust, followed by occasional warming ties (Steinberg and Fan 2012). Even with the occasional escalated tension, there is no identifiable urgency for the military regime to embark on a regime change as a strategy to address international considerations. Thein Sein for example visited China and met with his Chinese counterpart Hu Jintao just two weeks after his presidential inauguration and signed a "comprehensive strategic cooperative partnership" to reaffirm China's importance to Myanmar's "disciplined democratic" government (Chan 2018: 1). In the same month, after two years of negotiations, the two countries signed a memorandum of understanding (MOU) for plans to develop a China-Myanmar High-Speed Railway, also known as the Kunming–Kyaukpyu railway project (*ibid*: 11). Although the post-junta government under Thein Sein would later unilaterally suspend or cancel several Chinese-backed infrastructural projects, these decisions were made *after* the regime change and reflected the continuity of Myanmar's preferred "balance of relations" strategy – that is to maintain its sovereignty and independence (Huang 2015: 199). The normalization of relations with the US and its allies provided the opportunity for Myanmar to strategically re-balancing its relations with China, but these decisions were not made as a rebuke of Sino-Myanmar relations. In the 2016 Defense White Paper for example, the military noted its concern with the rising Chinese-Indian rivalries in their attempts to dominate the Asia-Pacific region, and implicitly referred to Chinese involvement with EAOs in the borders, which were in line with the *tatmadaw*'s national security concerns (Maung Aung Myoe 2019). The military however took a positive view of Chinese diplomacy, noting China's role in managing regional and international tensions, while working to promote regional stability through improving bilateral relations. As a clear indication that Myanmar is keen to return to its traditional neutralist position, one of the key military objectives rejects the possibility for Myanmar to enter into any military alliances and opposes foreign troops' deployment inside Myanmar (*ibid*).

In any case, with the exception of the Myitsone Dam, which remains suspended, the post-junta government has since renegotiated and restarted other previously disrupted projects, such as the Letpaduang Copper Mine, and the China-Myanmar oil pipeline after renegotiating new terms that are more favorable to Myanmar's interests (Chan 2018: 2). Since the advent of the NLD-led government, Myanmar has also agreed to revive the Kunming–Kyaukpyu railway project, especially as "Western" capital did not match popular anticipations after the US lifted remaining trade sanctions (Amara Thiha 2018). In other words, the China quandary may be necessary, but it is certainly not a sufficient condition to explain the junta's long considered process of regime change.

Conclusion

When the *tatmadaw* returned to direct governance in 1988, the military leadership recognized that its two-decade old socialist revolution was a failure. Immediately, the junta had the objective of addressing its failing economy and turned to foreign investments and trade. However the gradual expansion and institutionalization of a comprehensive US-led sanctions regime prevented the normalization of relations between Myanmar and the wider "Western"-centric international community until 2011. Nevertheless, a hostile US-centric international environment toward the SLORC/SPDC regime did not weaken the *tatmadaw*'s control of Myanmar politics, as the military regime was able to push forward consistently with its agenda with little regard for societal demands or international pressure.

International agency was not a key determinant of Myanmar's internal regime evolution, but the sanctions policy created the structural conditions, which limited Myanmar's foreign policy strategies in a global capitalist system. In the face of Western hostilities to the *tatmadaw*'s continued rule, the SLORC/SPDC government had to adapt to the changing international environment by soliciting and strengthening closer ties with neighboring states such as China that did not follow the US-led isolationist strategy. Inadvertently, the sanctions regime effectively pushed Myanmar to become increasingly dependent on its neighbors for economic and diplomatic support. In the context of a rising China as a regional hegemon, and the re-calibration of US foreign policy interests in the Asia-Pacific, the changing international dynamics allowed Myanmar to return to its earlier foreign policy roots, that is, to ensure that the country did not become overly dependent on or aligned with any particular country or political bloc. This is in line with military's decision to implement its Myanmar's way to democracy, and not as a direct reaction toward any changes in the international environment.

Sanctions never delivered the promised regime collapse, or change, as envisioned by anti-junta advocates. Similarly, ASEAN's greater linkage with Myanmar and its constructive engagement diplomacy did not change the content, manner, and timing of the *tatmadaw*'s political reform plans. Instead, during its 23-year direct rule, the junta remained steadfast in their authoritarian approach to silence all political contenders and made no efforts to reconcile, compromise, or share power with regime outsiders.

Notes

1 This is generally referred to as the "ASEAN way": commitment to individual member states' sovereignty, non-interference with each other's domestic affairs, and a consensus among all members to come up with regional decisions.

2 *Pauk-phaw*, which is often translated as fraternity or brotherhood, was coined in the mid-1950s to encourage cordial Sino-Myanmar relations. The term disappeared from official discourse after the anti-Chinese riots in Myanmar in 1967, and would only reappear in public narratives years during Than Shwe's visit to Beijing in 2010 (Steinberg and Fan 2012: 9).

3 Although the junta lasted for over two decades, at the time of its founding in 1988, the then SLORC Chairman Saw Maung had publicly announced that the junta would allow elections and eventually transfer power to a new government. See Chapter 3 for more on this point.

4 Malaysia and to a lesser extent Indonesia initially opposed Myanmar's membership due to the SLORC government's persecution of the Rohingya populace in the early 1990s. Malaysia would later change its position and become a key supporter, enabling Myanmar's membership into the regional association (McCarthy 2008b: 917–918).

5 According to former Thai Foreign Minister Kasit Piromya, that despite the improving Thai–Myanmar relations, the Myanmar side appeared to have an underlying distrust of Thailand and believes that Thailand continues to support and arm minority groups in the border (Interview with Kasit Piromya, November 21, 2015, in Bangkok).

6 Japan has been providing war reparations and other forms of economic assistance to Myanmar since 1955, and had, for several decades, been the leading donor to Myanmar (Steinberg 1990: 69–72).

7 The Myanmar government has always maintained that the journalist was killed because he was in an area declared off-limits by soldiers and refused to obey the army's orders. The actual negotiation to return Kenji Nagai's body, as well as his belongings, back to Japan turned into a long, drawn-out, bureaucratic process, while some belongings, such as the deceased's camera, were never returned (Interview with a former diplomat, Yangon, November 13, 2015).

8 Although Myanmar was a British colony until 1948, independent Myanmar maintained limited relations with the UK. Myanmar is one of the former colonies that never joined the Commonwealth.

9 For a discussion about "Western" linkages and leverages and their role in regime change, see: (Levitsky and Way 2006).

10 For a brief history of how *hundi* became a regular financial service in Myanmar see: (Turnell 2009: 29–31).

11 The city-state not only provided Myanmar's elites access to financial services and products but also provided opportunities for them to spend their wealth on luxuries, education, and access to high quality medical services. Further, the city-state is considered an attractive destination for Myanmar expatriates, providing job opportunities to Myanmar professionals, as well as migrant workers.

12 Notorious drug warlords such as Khun Sa and Lo Hsing Han, both deceased, were given amnesty from their past activities in the 1990s and allowed to develop their businesses inside Myanmar (ICG 2019: 4). Lo's son, Steven Law, is one of Myanmar's richest tycoons, and his Asia World is the largest conglomerate in Myanmar. Asia World is also a key contractor in the building of the country's capital, Naypyidaw (Wai Moe 2011).

13 The "pivot to Asia" was a key policy platform during Hillary Clinton's tenure as secretary of state, which aimed to restore the US's influence and attention in the Asia-Pacific region, with the implicit goal of countering China's expanding influence in the Asia-Pacific region (Campbell and Andrews 2013; Clinton 2014: Chapters 3, 4, and 6; Campbell and Andrews 2013). According to some analysts, a key defining

moment of the "pivot" was when Secretary Clinton asserted the US's interest to ensure the "freedom of navigation" in the South China Sea (as a snub to China's claims) and strengthened security relationships with its Asian-Pacific allies at the ASEAN Regional Forum in July 23 2010, Hanoi (Ba 2011: 283).

14 For example, under Obama, the US restored its diplomatic relations with Cuba in December 2014, and reached a multilateral "nuclear deal" with Iran in 2015, demonstrating the different type of international politics that the Obama administration embraced. Ironically, since the advent of the Trump presidency, US–Cuba relations has deteriorated significantly, and the US has also officially abandoned the Iran nuclear deal.

15 ASEAN was founded in 1967 by the governments of Indonesia, Malaysia, Philippines, Singapore, and Thailand. Brunei joined in 1984. ASEAN's embracement of socialist or former socialist economies took an active turn in the 1990s, with Vietnam joining in 1995, followed by Myanmar and Laos in 1997, and Cambodia in 1999. There are ongoing discussions about Timor-Leste's ASEAN application, applied back in 2011.

16 These assumptions are linked to the broader neoliberal beliefs that through greater commercial and diplomatic relations, states would be more willing to work with each other, and that greater economic development could foster and facilitate the growth of a politicized middle class (Teorell 2010: Chapter 4).

17 Many of the founding ASEAN member states also did not have bilateral diplomatic relations with China in 1967.

18 For the Thai proposal, see: (McCarthy 2008b: 921).

19 Myanmar is the first non-socialist country to recognize the People's Republic of China (PRC) by establishing diplomatic ties on June 9, 1950, although this is based on Myanmar's attempt to prevent China from threatening Myanmar's national security (Steinberg and Fan 2012: 15–20). There were several reasons for Myanmar to be concerned about China's interests in Myanmar in the early years of the founding of the PRC, such as the presence of Kuomintang (KMT) remnant soldiers in northern Myanmar, suspicion of the loyalties of overseas Chinese residing in Myanmar, and later China's support of Myanmar's communist insurgency. At the height of China's Cultural Revolution, China advocated openly for a turn towards "Revolutionary Diplomacy," which included China's public support of the Burma Communist Party's (BCP) insurgency against the Yangon government. This was a major source of contention that troubled Sino-Myanmar relations until the collapse of the BCP in April of 1989 (Lintner 1990).

20 The MNDAA leadership has since used China as a base to launch a series of failed counter-offensives in 2015 and 2017, leading to an even larger influx of refugees into Yunnan. The Chinese however refused to recognize the displaced Kokangs as refugees and refer to them as "border residents" (*bianmin*), providing the displacement camps with very limited support (Song 2017: 470).

6 Myanmar's way to democracy

Constructing a hybrid regime in the Thein Sein years

Introduction

Two decades of pro-market reforms under the State Peace and Development Council (SPDC) have built-up the scope, capacity, and reach of the military dominated state significantly. The restive society has largely been subdued and "disciplined," and the *tatmadaw* has expanded its presence into long contested ethnic-minority dominated areas in the borderlands. Despite the US-centric sanctions regime, the SPDC was not politically isolated, and had several meaningful diplomatic and trading partners. After more than two decades of direct military rule, the junta was at the apex of the political economy, having overcome various obstacles to its disciplined democratic blueprint, when it voluntarily dissolved the SPDC on March 30, 2011. This transition to the military's long planned seven-step roadmap to a disciplined democracy is the military's solution to the failure of the Burmese Socialist Program Party (BSPP) single-party state apparatus. Much akin to the yesteryears of the discredited Burmese way to socialism, the advent of the new USDP-led administration marked the beginnings of the military-orchestrated "Myanmar's way to democracy" (Huang 2017).

As a partially civilianized, diminished authoritarian regime, the most consequential change is that the military no longer monopolizes all avenues of formal politics. As a self-proclaimed "democratic" system, the military's Constitution has diffused formal power into several new political institutions. Recognizing the BSPP's disastrous single-party rule, the military was committed to constructing its version of a multiparty "democratic" hybrid regime. As part of their transitional plan, the SPDC managed the 2010 general elections carefully to ensure that the military's preferred party, the Union Solidarity and Development Party (USDP), would form the first post-junta government (Lall 2016: 54–55). As a military-endorsed, notionally elected and partially civilianized administration, the USDP-led government, under Thein Sein's presidency, had a wide breadth to introduce far-reaching reform that did not conflict with the military's corporate interests (Jones 2014b: 785).

Under the reformist direction of the Thein Sein administration, there has been a significant relaxation of state control over society, and the emergence of expanded, albeit conditional pluralism. Critically, President Thein Sein reached out and convinced the opposition leader Aung San Suu Kyi to participate in Myanmar's way to democracy. With evidence of nascent partisan politics, Myanmar's relations with the Western-centric international community significantly improved, leading to an influx of international organizations and a new wave of foreign investments. These meaningful socio-political changes however remain conditional. By design, disciplined democracy is premised on a hybrid regime – with power shared between elected civilians and the *tatmadaw*. In the Thein Sein years (2011–2016), many of the top public officials were former senior SPDC officials. Therefore, there was a high degree of coordination between the civilian branches of the government, and the military, particularly in the early post-junta years. The expanded socio-political pluralism however has at times conflicted with the military-backed government, and in the lead-up to the 2015 general elections, the military-backed Thein Sein administration found itself frequently resorting to the old strategies of repression to correct any perceived errors. This included, for example, the purge of Shwe Mann and some of the older regime insiders, when they began to advance a political agenda that diverged from the interests of the pro-military establishment.

This chapter revisits this critical juncture in Myanmar's regime transition from military authoritarianism into an emerging hybrid regime of the Thein Sein years (2011–2016). It begins by first outlining the new constitutional-determined rules of the game, and the distribution of power underpinning the military's disciplined democracy. The chapter then re-examines the reconciliatory politics during the Thein Sein years and the opening up of socio-political space. It argues that the renegotiation of state-societal relations and the emergence of partisan politics cannot be sufficiently explained as the product of political "pacts." Critical actors have instead become co-opted to ensure the legitimation and realization of the military's disciplined democracy (Morgenbesser 2016). Despite dramatic policy reversals in the state's relaxation of societal controls, these broad USDP-led reforms were steered by the pro-military establishment through a process of trial and error, to implement its disciplined, democratic constitutional system. The chapter concludes with a discussion about the implications of the 2015 general elections.

The authoritarian constitution: rules of the game in a disciplined democracy

As a top-down, carefully planned process, Myanmar's regime change is only possible with the promulgation of the country's third constitution. The detailed constitutional framework took 16 years to draft, and contains several clauses that define the basic structure, purpose, principles, and procedures governing the state. Unlike the ideologically inspired arrangements of the BSPP's 1974 Constitution, the 2008 Constitution is the military's proposed political solution to address the major problems that the country has faced since independence, such as political autonomy for ethnic states, separation of powers between the various political institutions, and, critically, the role of the military (Taylor

2009: 496). Recognizing and rejecting its failed BSPP one-party socialist system, the 2008 Constitution allows for competitive multiparty politics and recognizes a market-oriented economy but retains broad powers, allowing the military to operate with impunity. By design, the military's post-junta political system is a hybrid regime. While allowing for democratic politics within the civilian realm of influence, the Constitution enforces a coalition government where, irrespective of the electoral outcome, the military holds an active political role and retains control over the national security agenda. This is not only reflected by the military's self-appointed role as praetorian guards of the Myanmar nation but also by the military's understanding of diverse representation in government. Regime authority is therefore pluralistic, although the military maintains the *de facto* authority to veto any fundamental structural changes to its disciplined democratic system. In addition to the army's traditional role as a defensive force protecting the nation-state, the military-drafted charter also instructs the army to safeguard the 2008 Constitution. As a prerequisite for Myanmar's transition to a disciplined democracy, the Constitution provides immunity to all former SLORC/SPDC officials, prohibiting their prosecution for carrying out official duties during the junta years. In short, the constitutional framework is a result of the cumulative efforts of the military to address the legacy of political struggles that have plagued Myanmar ever since its independence with the "promise of sharing power with those who currently monopolize state authority," without dismantling the military's lion's share of control over the political economy (Taylor 2014: 132–148). The authoritarian constitution underpins the rules of the game of the military's disciplined democracy.

At the Union level, state power is distributed into four main institutions: the executive branch, the bicameral parliament (*Pyidaungsu Hluttaw*), the judiciary, and the commanding military.[1] Of these, the judiciary has consistently played a subordinate role to other state institutions, largely delivering procedural justice to maintain "law and order" as determined by the executive office or the military (Cheesman 2015: 276).[2] Subsequent laws passed during the Thein Sein administration would further "subordinate the courts to executive and parliamentary control" (Crouch 2016: 227). Nevertheless, formal political power is no longer concentrated solely in the hands of the *tatmadaw*. The genuine reconfiguration of state authority has vastly diminished the authoritarian powers of the emerging hybrid regime.

In part due to its long-held skepticism of partisan politics, the military's Constitution affords a number of special military prerogatives, which limit the powers of civilian officials. Irrespective of the electoral results, the Constitution mandates a strong military presence that reflects the military's enduring corporate interests. At the heart of this new political arrangement is the segregation of powers between elected civilians and the military. The un-elected military retains enough formal powers to determine the terms of any critical structural changes in Myanmar's way to democracy. The President, elected by an electorate college composed of all MPs in the bicameral National Parliament, must form a cabinet with active military personnel in the three security-related portfolios of

Defence, Home Affairs, and Border Affairs. The President however has the authority to appoint the remaining cabinet positions and the civilian officials are tasked with everyday governing responsibilities.[3] Partisan politics is limited within the civilian's sphere of influence, and politicians only have limited authority to check and balance the military's discretionary powers.

Contrary to liberal-democratic norms, the President, who is the head of state and government, is not the supreme commander of the armed forces. It is the Commander-in-Chief of the *tatmadaw* who commands the armed forces, which includes the police force and paramilitary organizations. Attempts to establish a parliamentary security unit that answers directly to the legislature have thus far failed (Egreteau 2017: 10). Evidently, the military intends to retain their monopoly over all legitimate use of violence. With a distinct parallel chain of command, the army is guaranteed institutional autonomy, allowing the military independent control of its own bureaucratic and financial affairs. Although elected officials have a range of legislative and executive powers, they are prevented from making unilateral decisions on a number of contentious issues related to national security including sovereignty, national defense, and, critically, the ongoing intrastate conflicts, particularly in the ethnic peripheries and borderlands.

This *de jure* separation of powers ensures that the army has plenty of "reserve domains" (Linz and Stepan 1996: 67), which are not accountable to any elected body. While civilians are excluded from the military's sphere of influence, the *tatmadaw*, in addition to being a part of the executive branch, are also represented in parliamentary politics. The Commander-in-Chief appoints 25 percent of the seats in the country's bicameral National Parliament.[4] The reserved military seats in parliament give the *tatmadaw* just enough *de facto* veto votes to block any critical changes to the Constitution.[5] Military MPs can and have been removed at will by the Commander-in-Chief (Egreteau 2015: 339).

Finally, a constitutional body, the National Defence and Security Council (NDSC), is the highest governing authority on all defensive and security matters. The membership of the NDSC is exclusive, and designed in a way that the pro-military establishment will always have a simple majority. Of the NSDC's 11 executive members, at least five are serving military officers. The president and both vice presidents are also included in the NDSC. Given that at least one vice president is directly elected by military MPs, this essentially gives the military a *de facto* majority of at least six pro-military members in the NDSC. The NSDC has the power to grant the Commander-in-Chief the right to take over the government during times of national emergency. Therefore, the Council can be used as the last legal resort for the *tatmadaw* to restore temporary direct military rule during times of crises without the need to overhaul the Constitution.[6] The first NDSC's membership was exclusively composed of military veterans and active officers.[7]

Even with genuine openings for partisan politics, the Constitution perpetuates and institutionalizes the military's role in politics, and its ultimate authority over elected politicians on critical issues related to national security, as well as any vital decisions related to the fundamental structure and principles of the constitutional system. In short, the authoritarian constitution sets out the basic rules of the game to "help control and discipline ... and co-opt or pacify rival political groups" (Frankenberg 2019: 30).

Diffusion of power within the ruling establishment

With the civilian authorities afforded executive and legislative powers, the military ensured, through a highly manipulated 2010 electoral process, that its USDP allies would lead the first post-junta government. Senior SPDC officials resigned from their military positions in order to run in the 2010 elections, and effectively became the key civilianized leadership of the "new" ruling party. The pro-military establishment clearly continued to dominate the halls of power, with much of Thein Sein's cabinet staffed with active or retired military veterans. Of the 35 cabinet ministers, 28 were recently retired military officers (Arakan Oil Watch 2012: 16). Leading members of the *ancien régime* therefore continued to hold different levers of political power during the transition into a disciplined democracy under the Thein Sein presidency.

The redistribution of political power in the different institutions meant that the new batch of civilianized leaders – former SPDC leaders such as Thein Sein and Shwe Mann – could no longer promote their interests through the *tatmadaw* directly, now headed by a younger cohort of officers, under the command of a new Commander-in-Chief, Min Aung Hlaing. The new rules of the game, however, opened up a new agency for these elite USDP officials to shape the post-junta institutions. The delineation of civilian/military spheres of influence meant that these retired military veterans could only advance their post-military careers within the realm of civilian politics. These elites have therefore fashioned themselves as reformist politicians and made genuine efforts to strengthen the institutional powers of the executive and legislative branches of the state (Kyaw Yin Hlaing 2012: 210). Shwe Mann for example, is often cited as an important figure who has utilized his position as lower house speaker and USDP chair to strengthen the independence of the legislature and its oversight powers, albeit in order to advance his post-military political career (Kean 2014: 55–57). Thein Sein on the other hand, effectively utilized the executive powers of the civilian authority to foster a more tolerant political environment. By actively reaching out to regime outsiders, including critical opposition leaders and exiled dissidents, Thein Sein was able to gain greater legitimacy and momentum to push forward with his reformist agenda.

A reincarnation of the SPDC-sponsored Union Solidarity and Development Association (USDA), the USDP was the military's response to the failure of the BSPP single party state apparatus. As the military has always claimed to be a non-partisan institution, they have imposed rules that forbid agents of the state, including military personnel, from affiliation with any political party. In order for the military to cultivate an "organic link" between the military state and its populace without breaking its own rules, they established the USDA, a state-sponsored association in 1993 as the *de facto* civilian arm of the *tatmadaw*

(Taylor 2009: 446).[8] This decidedly military creation shared similar structures to the military's previous mass civilian organizations, with obvious parallels to the BSPP (1962–1988) and its earlier predecessor, the National Solidarity Association founded during Ne Win's Caretaker government in 1958–1960. During the SLORC/SPDC years, the USDA was the military's attempt to create a catchall organization to broaden its coalition partners. In addition to all civil servants and military personnel, the USDA co-opted strategic actors including prominent businesspeople, and anyone "who sought to do business with or receive services from the state" (*ibid*).

This trend is reflected in the composition of the first post-junta parliament. Contrary to some observers' suggestion, the USDP was not merely a "political extension of the military" (David and Holliday 2018: 78) but also represents the interests of the *tatmadaw*'s civilian and civilianized allies. Given the previous experience of internal disunity when the military was involved actively in BSPP factional politics, the *tatmadaw* leadership appeared to be serious about the formal segregation of military personnel and their affiliation with political parties. That is, the USDP would function as an alternative route for career advancement for retiring *tatmadaw* officers following the end of their active services in the military, with the assumption that these officers would remain loyal and promote the military's interests in the civilian realm of politics. The majority of elected MPs, including USDP legislators, were civilians with no direct military background, primarily coming from business circles, followed by educators and professionals such as former civil servants and public administrators (Egreteau 2017: 23).[9] By design and in practice, politics in disciplined democracy did not function simply as a continuation of direct military rule. In the first post-junta parliamentary sessions, voting behavior was often unpredictable, and MPs did not always follow party lines (Kean 2014: 44, 54–55). The *tatmadaw*, now under the leadership of Commander-in-Chief Min Aung Hlaing generally respects the parliamentary procedures. Apart from issues related to the Constitution, or sensitive issues that the military perceives could undermine political stability, military parliamentarians have otherwise voted freely on a number of issues (*ibid*: 63).

Although it was certainly not a "rubber stamp" legislature (ICG 2013c), the first post-junta parliament was broadly supportive of the government's legislative agenda and reform programs, and a high number of laws passed during the Thein Sein presidency (Egreteau 2017: 30–32). In a move that would have been unthinkable just months earlier, on August 26, 2011 an opposition MP proposed a general amnesty of political prisoners, which was endorsed by the majority of the parliamentarians, including MPs from both the USDP and the military (Egreteau 2016: 45).

Especially in the early Thein Sein years, there was a concerted effort by the major political actors to work together to open up socio-political space and realize the legitimacy and viability of the new post-junta constitutional system (Kyaw Yin Hlaing 2014a: 48–49). Under a proactive Thein Sein presidency, the executive branch pushed forward several laws covering everything from everyday issues to amending and repealing some of the most repressive laws from its authoritarian past. As Egreteau has observed, the same key personalities of the SPDC, who had long defended and benefited from the old authoritarian regime, now actively distinguished their USDP-led government as distinctively different from its junta days, and indicated that they would not revert to the "old days of direct military rule" (2016: 41). These laws have also directly shaped the new political institution, at times exacerbating tensions within the ruling clique (Crouch 2016: 224–228). The increasingly divergent interests within the USDP, for the most part, did not derail the high degree of coordination between the major political stakeholders in consolidating the budding disciplined democratic hybrid regime. Throughout the Thein Sein presidency, the important NDSC met regularly, which allowed the *tatmadaw's* high command to communicate directly with the heads of the executive and legislative branches of government. Reportedly, all the major political appointees in the first post-junta government required the approval of the NDSC (Egreteau 2016: 27).

The new structure of governance and the multiple centers of power have led to institutional rivalries within the ruling coalition. This soft-liner within the government triumphing over their most conservative colleagues may offer a partial explanation of post-junta reforms, yet it does not sufficiently account for the broad unity of the pro-*tatmadaw* establishment. For example, the eventual resignation of the first Vice President Tin Aung Myint Oo in July 2012, and the purge of Shwe Mann and his allies from the USDP leadership in August 2015, demonstrate that the corporate interests of the *tatmadaw*, and its institutional cohesion, continued to guide the collective actions of the pro-military establishment. Tin Aung Myint Oo represented the more conservative faction, and likely wanted the post-junta administration to govern in a similar manner to its SPDC predecessors, contrary to the reformist direction pushed forward by the majority of the parliamentarians and the military-backed President Thein Sein administration (Kyaw Yin Hlaing 2012: 209). Speaker of the Lower House Shwe Mann on the other hand has generally been portrayed as a liberal soft-line reformist. Often credited by observers as a key elite personality that aided the strengthening of the autonomous powers of the legislature, in the lead-up to the 2015 general elections, Shwe Mann began to take positions drastically different to those of the Thein Sein government.

Given the military's general acceptance to abide by its own constitutional rules, Thein Sein was pressured to handover his position as USDP Chair in May 2013, allowing Shwe Mann to become the new party boss. In his position as USDP Chair, Shwe Mann derailed the military's electoral plans, by rejecting 100 out of 159 recently retired military veterans from running under the USDP banner in the 2015 general elections (Crispin 2015). Just months earlier, Shwe Mann had also tacitly aligned himself with Aung San Suu Kyi and the opposition, allowing for a parliamentary debate and vote on critical amendments of the Constitution. Although there was never any real possibility that the amendments would succeed, Shwe Mann's actions would have been viewed as a betrayal by the *tatmadaw*. The elite infighting within the ruling USDP ended with the military-backed Thein Sein faction prevailing, and Shwe Mann and his allies were expelled from their USDP positions. Shwe Mann was allowed to keep his position as lower house speaker for the remainder of his electoral mandate, as his removal from parliament would likely have caused greater ramifications on the viability of the military's disciplined democracy.

Elite agency and internal rivalries therefore provide some context on how reforms unfolded, but power struggles and factionalism are "more the rule than the exception" and have been a common feature of all post-colonial Myanmar governments (Kyaw Yin Hlaing 2008: 149). Since the *tatmadaw* came into direct power in 1962, factional and elite rivalries have not undermined the military's institutional cohesion nor derailed the *tatmadaw's* unified political agenda. In fact, as Kyaw Yin Hlaing has long observed, after internal purges, especially with the removal of senior officials, the *tatmadaw* has always ended up even more "unified" and "coordinated" (*ibid*: 173–173). Therefore, the political liberalization undertaken by the post-junta government does not signify a democratic transition. Rather the same pro-*tatmadaw* establishment that long supported a repressive authoritarian regime, were now the driving force diminishing and removing some of its most authoritarian structures, as a genuine implementation of its disciplined democratic system.

Realizing and legitimizing disciplined democracy

From the very beginning of the partially civilianized administration, President Thein Sein indicated that politics would be different in the new disciplined democracy. His inaugural speech was considered a dramatic departure from the opaque style of the SPDC government, as the new president indicated a willingness to work with a variety of political actors, including former foes (Callahan 2012: 120). In contrast to the SLORC/SPDC years, President Thein Sein would also public discuss about the importance of improving "human security," that is the social, political, and economic conditions for Myanmar citizens (NLM 2011b).[10] The President's new reputation as a more receptive leader was further reinforced by his unilateral suspension of the Myitsone Dam project in September 30, 2011 (Kyaw Yin Hlaing 2012: 207). Although many observers have argued that the suspension of the controversial China-backed project may have been motivated by the regime's shifting foreign policy, Thein Sein nevertheless justified his decision publicly as a direct response to public demand (Chan 2017: 684–685; also see Chapter 5). When parliament reconvened after a long recess[11] for its second legislative session (August–November 2011), the executive branch actively drafted several legal reforms, recognizing basic civil and political rights that have long been absent in Myanmar. Before the end of Thein Sein's first year in office, the USDP controlled legislature endorsed a series of laws that gave citizens new legal rights to participate in public demonstrations, form labor unions, and engage in labor strikes (Egreteau 2016: 44). Under the instruction of the president, Myanmar's National Human Rights Commission (MNHRC) was also established. Despite not being a constitutionally mandated institution, the MNHRC openly advocated for the government to become a state party to a number of international human right treaties, including the International Covenant on Economic, Social and Cultural Rights (ICESCR), which was signed by the end of Thein Sein's tenure.[12]

In August 2012, one of the state's oldest authoritarian tools – the prepublication censorship program that had endured since the Revolutionary Council (RC) years over half a century ago – formally ended. Further, in early 2013, the government abolished its official censorship division. The government also introduced new laws, which eased the state's control over citizen's right to information and dissent. The News Media Law, for example, openly recognizes the media's role as the "fourth estate with full freedoms and rights," including the right to criticize state institutions (Venkiteswaran et al. 2019: 66).

Myanmar's online environment also changed seemingly overnight. Just a few months after the changeover of government, Myanmar's tight internet control was dropped, transforming its reputation as one of the world's most restricted and underdeveloped (Warf 2011: 10), into one of the world's freest and fastest growing cyberspaces (Yan Naung Oak and Brooten 2019: 327–360). This dramatic transformation of Myanmar's digital environment was facilitated by the liberalization of the telecommunications sector. The contentious 2013 Telecommunications Law[13] formally ended the state's monopoly of the telecommunications sector, allowing a handful of foreign operators to enter the nascent market by 2014. The transformation of this critically underdeveloped sector was immediate. The cost of SIM cards, which had cost up to thousands of US dollars in the past, plunged to as little as US$ 1.50 by 2014 (Leong 2017: 140). By the end of Thein Sein's tenure, there were more than 43 million SIM cards sold, in a country with an estimated 55 million citizens (Aung Kyaw Nyunt 2016).

This dramatically changing media and digital landscape also changed how the government communicates with the public. Facebook has practically become a synonym for the internet, which an estimated 20 million registered Myanmar "netizens" regularly access as their primary source for news and information (Wong 2019). As a result, even government officials have turned to Facebook to disseminate official announcements. One of the most notable examples is that of Ye Htut, the presidential spokesperson during Thein Sein's reign. A prolific Facebook user, he was dubbed the "Facebook Minister" for his frequent use of social media to engage with citizens online and to announce government policies (Yan Naung Oak and Brooten 2019: 341). The notoriously opaque *tatmadaw* also maintained a visible online presence. Even Commander-in-Chief Min Aung Hlaing had an official Facebook page, which amassed 1.35 million followers, before it was shut down by the social media company in August 2018, for inciting violence against the Rohingya populace (David and Holliday 2018: 82).[14] Nevertheless, the *tatmadaw* head continues to maintain an official online presence with a website that regularly promotes the military's messages.

An indicator that there was a genuine expansion of pluralism is the creative industry's ability to openly engage with a wider range of sensitive subjects, producing works that would have been banned in the pre-2011 years. By June 2013, a group of filmmakers were able to establish the annual "Human Rights, Human Dignity Film Festival." The ambitious festival included screening human right documentaries in different parts of the country, and allowed audiences an avenue to discuss about their individual rights (Mon Mon Myat 2019: 307–314).

The greater tolerance for socio-political pluralism has allowed the normalization of contentious politics, in the forms of cyclical protest movements, boycott campaigns, and labor strikes – all strategies of social activism that the *tatmadaw* had long distrusted. By 2014, there were a recorded 185 protests since the post-junta government came into power, suggestive of a mobilized society that had gained greater confidence in utilizing the expanded public space (Buschmann 2018: 129). The surge of social mobilization has also led to the emergence an ultra-nationalist "969" Buddhist movement in 2012. The illiberal movement that originated as a boycott campaign targeting Muslim owned businesses was quickly capitalized by radical nationalist monks, and transformed into the Organization for the Protection of Race and Religion (referred to in Burmese colloquially as *MaBaTha*)[15] in June 2013. Within a couple of years, *MaBaTha* became the leading ultra-nationalist force that had coordinated socio-political campaigns that were decidedly anti-Islam with misogynous and chauvinistic undertones (Schonthal and Walton 2016: 84–85). Working with both the ruling USDP and opposition parties, including the National League for Democracy (NLD)-splinter political party, the National Democratic Force (NDF), *MaBaTha* was successful in advocating the passage of a package of "race and religion" laws in 2015, ostensibly to defend the Myanmar nation and protect the Buddhist faith (Barrow 2015; Walton et al. 2015: 37).

Beyond the fast-changing socio-political landscape, the government also actively sought to liberalize and develop Myanmar's primitive economy. A new foreign investment law was passed in 2012, which was followed by a larger number of government-approved foreign investments compared to previous years (Bissinger 2014: 246–247). These early economic reform efforts however were introduced in a piecemeal manner, until the government finally released a series of strategic policy papers, such as the "Framework for Economic and Social Reforms" (FESR) and a 20-year National Comprehensive Development Plan (Findlay et al. 2016: 43). The intention of the FESR is to link existing economic programs with the government's short-term agenda, and with the intention of attracting new sources of foreign investments in the longer term. With the US no longer objecting to working with the Myanmar government, international organizations and a myriad of other foreign states pursued new diplomatic and trade opportunities with Naypyidaw. The changing international narrative on Myanmar was further aided by numerous reports from influential organizations from McKinsey & Company to the IMF, touting the economic potential of the country (for example see: Chhor et al. 2013; IMF 2012). A 2013 report suggested that Myanmar was by far the most popular overseas posting for a large majority of World Bank (WB) employees surveyed (Rieffel and Fox 2013: 3). Myanmar's GDP growth increased by 8.5 percent in 2013 and 2014, making it one of the fastest growing economies in the world during that period (Rab et al. 2016: 1).

The relatively high rate of economic growth was in part facilitated by the return of technical assistance and funding from international financial institutions such as the WB and Asian Development Bank (ADB) (Mieno 2013: 114). For example, the ADB provided a total of US$ 2.1 billion in loans and grants to Myanmar between 2013–2018 (ADB 2019).

Of all these broad, liberalizing changes, the most indicative signal, at least for several "Western" states as well as the domestic populace, that a multiparty "democratic" system was attainable was the government's outreach to include former foes, especially Aung San Suu Kyi and the NLD, into the disciplined democratic system. In the ethnic peripheries, a myriad of ethnic minority communities formed political parties and participated in the military's disciplined democracy, with mixed electoral results (David and Holliday 2018: 89–90). Critically, the Thein Sein-led administration resolutely pursued a new peace process with the myriad of ethnic armed organizations (EAOs). By 2015, a new, formal multilateral Nationwide Ceasefire Agreement (NCA), a first in the country long plagued by civil war, replaced the various *de facto* bilateral ceasefire agreements of the 1990s (Thawnghmung 2017: 381). Despite the participation of 16 EAOs in the drafting of the document, several of the best-armed insurgent groups either refused or were blocked by the *tatmadaw* from being a party to the agreement (*ibid*: 382).

Nevertheless, the broad social, political, and economic reforms were significant enough that many observers believed that Myanmar's disciplined democracy was on a trajectory toward liberal democracy. President Thein Sein was invited to a number of high-level visits in various prominent capitals, including a visit to the White House, a first for a Myanmar President since Ne Win's visit in 1966 (Hartley 2018: 384). In return, prominent heads of government, including US President Barack Obama and Japanese Prime Minister Shinzo Abe visited Myanmar. Obama famously delivered a public speech celebrating Myanmar's reforms at the University of Yangon in 2012. With its reputation rehabilitated, Myanmar also played host to several prominent international events, including taking over the ASEAN Chairmanship in 2014.

Despite this optimistic outlook, the post-2011 regime change is decidedly a non-democratic transition enforced by the military. The reforms may have been adopted quickly and gone further than originally planned, yet this fits the pattern of the trial and error process of top-down regime construction guided by the coordinated efforts and corporate interests of the *tatmadaw* establishment. "Former" authoritarians collaborated with all the co-opted major stakeholders to push forward a liberalization agenda, and reforms were largely rolled out in an *ad hoc* manner while sticking within the remits of the constitutional framework. Further, the emerging pluralism is tolerated only when it does not present a direct threat to the vested interests of the *tatmadaw*. Crucially, part of the success story of this transformation from a highly authoritarian military rule into a diminished, partially civilianized authoritarianism is due to the entry of strategic outsiders and their begrudging consent to abide by the rules of disciplined democracy.

Co-opting strategic actors in a disciplined democracy

Contrary to earlier interpretations (for example: Callahan 2012; Egreteau 2016; Kipgen 2016), the reconciliatory politics of the Thein Sein years was not, and did not lead to, an elite-pacted democratic transition. Rather, as part of the broader *tatmadaw*-enforced trial and error regime change, the much-touted landmark meeting between Thein Sein and Aung San Suu Kyi on August 19, 2011 for example, concluded with the co-optation of the critical opposition into supporting Myanmar's way to democracy. If any agreements were made, they were lopsided, and favorable asymmetrically to the government's regime construction agenda. The NLD's decision to compete in the 2012 by-elections was a reversal of the opposition's two-decade old policy of rejecting the *tatmadaw*'s legitimacy to govern. Throughout the SLORC/SPDC years, the NLD refused to participate in the military-led reforms and the *tatmadaw*'s transitions plan. It was the party leadership's decision to spurn the opportunity to participate in the 2010 general elections that led the NLD to become outlawed.[16] Therefore, when the military-backed USDP government went out of its way to facilitate the NLD's return to the legal fold, the ruling establishment had effectively rectified one of the longstanding obstacles to the military's transition into a disciplined democracy. Beyond the state's acceptance of partisan politics, which is already a feature of the new constitutional system, even before the NLD's entry to parliament, the pro-military establishment appeared to have made no concession to their fundamental position. The endgame from the military's perspective remains the same, which is the conditional liberalization of its political economy, while the fundamental *de jure* division of civilian/military powers remains intact. By deciding to participate in the military's democracy, the NLD and other co-opted "strategically-relevant actors" have gained greater access to political power and resources (Gerschewski 2013: 22), however, their newfound agency is restricted to the game set forth by the *tatmadaw*. As newly invested players in Myanmar's way to democracy, these co-opted regime outsiders are "persuaded not to exercise [their] power to obstruct" (Shleifer and Treisman 2000: 8) the regime transition, as they now have a stake in the emerging political system in their new roles as lawmakers, government advisors, or consultants. This strategy of co-optation parallels the *tatmadaw*'s consistent policy throughout its long-rule. Regime outsiders can partake in formal politics, only if they submit to the rules of the game as determined by the *tatmadaw* – whether it is supporting the socialist cause of the BSPP, drafting the military's constitution during the SPDC years, or partaking multiparty politics in a disciplined democracy. In other words, partisan power remain bounded to the basic rules of the game as set out by the Constitution.

For most of the Thein Sein tenure, the NLD functioned less as a genuine opposition party, but as more of a bystander. NLD lawmakers were largely passive in parliament and were apparently instructed by the party leadership "not to antagonize their counterparts in the USDP or the military" (Kean 2014: 54). Several unpopular and publicly protested laws were passed by parliament, often without any input or participation from NLD parliamentarians (Venkiteswaran et al. 2019: 66; Egreteau 2017: 33). Two of the most contentious issues that have resulted in violent state repression include the Letpaduang Copper mine project and the National Education Law, which the Aung San Suu Kyi-led NLD effectively backed and was relatively silent about the state's use of violence (AP in Rangoon 2013; Wa Lone 2014). Since entering parliamentary politics, the NLD has abandoned its longstanding rejectionist policy and have acquiesced to advocating political reform as "loyal opposition" within the parameters of the 2008 Constitution (David and Holliday 2018: 81).

This is best illustrated by two widely reported public confrontations during the Thein Sein presidency. After initial rumblings, Suu Kyi and her NLD parliamentary colleagues begrudgingly conceded and took the parliamentary oath on April 30, 2012, legally pledging to "safeguard the constitution" as new MPs in Myanmar's disciplined democracy. Although the NLD has long declared its intention to amend the constitution and dismantle many of the military's constitutional privileges, the NLD only began to take its role as an opposition party more vigorously in the lead-up to the 2015 elections. Working with Shwe Mann, the NLD introduced changes that would have lowered the parliamentary threshold required to approve critical constitutional amendments, as well as changed eligibility requirements for the presidency (Fuller 2015). As expected, despite three days of parliamentary debates, there was never a realistic chance of passing these constitutional amendments, with the *tatmadaw* delegates voting *en masse* to reject the proposed constitutional changes. Constitutional debates may have been legalized, yet there is no indication that the *tatmadaw* were prepared to compromise on their fundamental constitutional powers. Even if significant and frank dialogue among former foes is now a reality, any significant gains for the opposition have been confined to "issues that do not seriously challenge USDP/military interests" (Kean 2014: 44). Like all opposition parties, the NLD is playing the military's game.

Outside of the Bamar-centric national politics of Naypyidaw, the Thein Sein-led government also attempted to co-opt ethnic armed organizations (EAOs) through a "nationwide" ceasefire agreement (NCA) (South 2018: 55–56). Significantly, the NCA replaced the state's 1990 bilateral ceasefire agreements with a myriad of EAOs to enhance multilateral peace building efforts, with an expansion of previous non-ceasefire groups such as the Karen National Union (KNU). However, despite its claim, the "nation-wide" ceasefire agreement excludes the best-equipped armed insurgent groups such as the United Wa State Army, the Kachin Independence Army (KIA) and the Arakan Army. Further, the NCA fell "between a ceasefire agreement and a more comprehensive and ambitious political text," which contained "a lot of political provisions; however, as a political agreement it lacked substance" (*ibid*: 56). Therefore, the NCA did not provide a genuine change of the military's positions from their previous attempts to negotiate with the various EAOs. The number of EAOs incorporated as part of the border guard force (BGF) has not expanded, while the SPDC-imposed "ceasefire capitalism" continues to structure the state's relationship with NCA signatories (Woods 2018: 28).

Most importantly, the touted peace building achievements supported by growing international attention and multilateral funding did not match realities in the conflict areas – intrastate violence actually increased and intensified under disciplined democracy (Macgregor 2016). According to veteran journalist Bertil Lintner, the renewed fighting during the Thein Sein years, especially against the Kachin and the Kokang forces has elevated to a scale not seen since the *tatmadaw* offensives against Karen and communist insurgents in the late 1980s (Lintner 2015). Critically, the ongoing fighting in the ethnic peripheries also demonstrated the limited powers of civilian officials, and even retired general and head of state President Thein Sein, had over the *tatmadaw*. Repeated public and private orders by Thein Sein for the military to halt its operations against the KIA were effectively ignored, and even declarations of ceasefires have not stopped ongoing clashes (Sun 2014: 5). Evidently, the segregation of civilian and military spheres of influence is taken seriously by the *tatmadaw*, and the control of military operations remained firmly under the command of the Commander-in-Chief.

Reform adjustment and error correction

The vastly liberalized environment and the upsurge of socio-political pluralism has at times crossed the *tatmadaw*'s redlines, leading to pushback by the state. Although the military-backed state no longer suppresses all dissident activities indiscriminately, they also considered activities that undermine the *tatmadaw* establishment's critical interests as unacceptable errors and have not hesitated to resort to state-directed violence in the form of physical coercion or imprisonment. This shifting pattern of state repression mirrors the tactics of the SLORC/SPDC years. The oscillation between greater tolerance for dissent and the use of hard repression is dependent on the political agenda of the regime, and the level of state violence is dependent on the credibility of the threat posed by regime outsiders to the stability of the *tatmadaw* establishment (Kyaw Yin Hlaing 2013: 252). Especially in the lead-up to the 2015 elections, the pro-military establishment became far more cautious, often resorting to authoritarian tactics on selected targets, leading to the creation of a new generation of political prisoners (AI 2015).

In particular, activists and journalists that worked in insurgent areas or on sensitive topics related to the military's image or operations remain at a high risk of retribution by the *tatmadaw* (Huang 2017: 32). Even under the improved media environment, existing and newly introduced draconian laws and state violence have led to a number of journalists' imprisonment, harassment, and even murder (For example see MNHRC 2014; Regan and Stout 2014; Zarni Mann 2014; Zarni Mann and Kyaw Phyo Tha 2015).[17] The Thein Sein-led government also sees the value of the symbiotic relationship it has with the populist Buddhist-nationalist movement and have defended and promoted ultra-nationalist narratives repeatedly (Schonthal and Walton 2016: 96). Seemingly minor offenses were highlighted by ultra-nationalists as serious religious offences and have resulted in a number of high profile prosecutions of individuals for insulting Buddhism.[18] This included the fall from grace of NLD information officer Htin Lin Oo for his public speech at a literary event that promoted religious tolerance and discouraged the exploitation of Buddhism as a tool for extremism and discrimination (Zarni Mann 2015). Htin Lin Oo was convicted for insulting Buddhism with a two-year prison sentence with hard labor, and the NLD expelled him from the party.

This resurgence of state repression however remained selective, and the pro-military establishment generally respected the legally sanctioned space available for partisan politics to function. There are reasons, besides the silencing of critics and the constitutional designs in place, that the military establishment is comfortable with the expanded but conditional socio-political pluralism. Not dissimilar to the past practices of rewarding retired military personnel with positions in the civil bureaucracy, the USDP-led government has also appointed several military veterans in senior civil service positions. Htun Htun Oo, an ex-military officer who has worked in the judiciary since the 1990s, was promoted to Chief Justice by President Thein Sein, a critical position that he will hold until his mandatory retirement when he reaches 70 years old in 2026 (Htet Khaung Linn 2018). In the lead-up to the 2015 general elections, there is also a concerted effort to accelerate the quasi-militarization of various government ministries (Wade 2015). The appointment of several military officers to managerial positions in the Ministry of Health provoked a significant backlash from healthcare professionals, which led to the "black ribbon movement" in August 2015. Other sectors soon followed with a variety of "color ribbon" campaigns in a bid to reject the continued appointments of military officials in the civil bureaucracy (Kyaw Hsu Mon 2015). Although the Health Minister conceded to stop further appointments of military officials into the ministry, military appointees that have already transferred to the ministry were able to keep their new positions as health ministry staffers (Shwe Yee Saw Myint 2015).

The 2015 general elections and the ascent of the NLD

Even with the military establishment's return to more repressive practices in the latter Thein Sein years, the liberalized socio-political environment allowed the NLD and its supporters to compete with, and comfortably defeat, the military-preferred political parties in the 2015 elections. By most accounts, although there were some noticeable irregularities, the general election was largely successful and relatively fair (The Carter Centre 2015; Interviews in November 2015, Naypyidaw, Yangon, Mandalay). Retired Lieutenant General Tin Aye, a Thein Sein-appointee to chair the Union Election Commission (UEC), had previously organized the April 2012 by-elections and supported the importance of electoral integrity publicly (*The Irrawaddy* 2015b). However, the elections were not entirely free. The UEC had singled out Muslim candidates for exclusion in the electoral process. The large majority of aspiring Muslim politicians, including at least one incumbent USDP MP, were disqualified by the UEC on citizenship grounds, leading to the dissolution of two Muslim parties (Carter

Center 2015: 10). Several ethnic minority groups, including the majority of the Rohingya populace who had been allowed to vote in the 2010 elections, were denied the right to vote. None of the major political parties ran any Muslim candidates. When the USDP government disenfranchised the right to vote of those holding Temporary Registration Certificates, or "white cards," of which the majority are Rohingyas, the NLD also complied with the "legislative mandate" and expelled more than 20,000 white-card holders from its party membership (Yen Snaing 2015). Nevertheless, the structural disenfranchisement of a significant minority of the population did not prevent much of the international and domestic community from celebrating the success of the NLD electoral victory, marking a new milestone in Myanmar's political development.

Under Aung San Suu Kyi, the NLD won a majority in the bicameral national parliament, and with the exception of Rakhine and Shan states dominated the regional/state legislatures (ICG 2015: 4). Of the 578 contestable seats in the national legislature, the NLD won 135 seats in the upper house and 255 seats in the lower house, giving the NLD control over the bicameral parliament. The USDP was effectively wiped out as a legislative force, with a vastly diminished representation at all levels of the legislature. Few candidates with a military background were elected, and even in areas presumed to be military strongholds, USDP candidates lost to the NLD, including many senior USDP veterans such as acting USDP Chairman Htay Oo and the disgraced former Chairman Shwe Mann (Egreteau 2016: 55). This resulted in the military taking on the new role as the *de facto* opposition party with its 25 percent reserved seats. However, other than its continued power to veto any critical amendments to the Constitution, the *tatmadaw* does not have the legislative capacity to block bills, as general legislations only require the endorsement of a simple parliamentary majority.

The triumphant and decisive victory for the NLD demonstrated that the *tatmadaw* establishment had implemented its constitutional system faithfully. The top *tatmadaw* leadership and leading USDP officials quickly endorsed the electoral results and pledged their support for an NLD-led government. The incumbent president Thein Sein and the Commander-in-chief Min Aung Hlaing both met with Aung San Suu Kyi on December 2, 2015, to discuss the forthcoming power transfer. A few days later, on December 5, 2015, Aung San Suu Kyi also met with former SPDC Chairman Than Shwe. According to a public Facebook post by Than Shwe's grandson, the former dictator pledged at the meeting to help his erstwhile nemesis Aung San Suu Kyi in any way he can as the "future leader of Myanmar" (Lun Min Mang 2015). Although the former dictator's endorsement is highly symbolic, Presidential Spokesperson Ye Htut downplayed the significance of the meeting publicly, declaring that Than Shwe did "not have any influence on the power transition" (Kyaw Phyo Tha 2015). This is consistent with the *tatmadaw*'s culture – while the retired leader may continue to be respected by his former subordinates, without an official position in the military or government, Than Shwe no longer has any direct influence over the pro-*tatmadaw* establishment.

When the new parliament convened in February of 2016, the partial transferal of civilian power to the opposition party demonstrated that Myanmar's disciplined democracy was not merely a façade for continued military rule. The NLD was able to use its parliamentary majority to install party members in key positions of power in both the executive and legislative branches of government. For the first time since 1962, Myanmar's head of state was not a *tatmadaw* loyalist. For their part, the *tatmadaw* did not play the role of spoilers to the emerging hybrid regime of its own design and did not prevent the relatively smooth transferal of power to the NLD-led administration. This reflected clearly the *tatmadaw*'s attitudes toward partisan politics and its regime-building agenda. The USDP may be the *tatmadaw*'s preferred party, but it was not a mere extension of the military institution, and disciplined democracy is not designed as a hegemonic party regime. The military's praetorian principles clearly differentiates the military's "national" interests to the "partisan" interests of political parties.[19]

The military made no extrajudicial attempts to interfere with parliamentary operations, even when the NLD-controlled parliament deliberately circumvented article 59f of the Constitution[20] by installing Aung San Suu Kyi as the *de facto* head of government through the quick passage of the State Counsellor Bill. The contentious State Counsellor Bill demonstrated the newfound legislative prowess of the NLD, but it also signaled the *tatmadaw*'s commitment to its disciplined democracy. Further, the bill did not alter the fundamental rules of the game – the civilian/military segregation of powers, and the constitutional autonomy and powers of the *tatmadaw*, remain intact.

Conclusion

After two decades of fostering the socio-political conditions conducive to prolonged military domination over the political economy, the *tatmadaw* evidently felt confident enough to enforce its transition to Myanmar's way to democracy. With a new set of rules in place, the ruling establishment was determined to implement its disciplined democracy – effectively a hybrid regime – to become the only acceptable game in town. Former autocrats of the *ancien régime* rebranded themselves as reformist civilians and guided a controlled regime transition toward consolidating disciplined democracy. The liberalizing reforms, which had dramatically expanded socio-political pluralism, and the emergence of genuine but conditional partisan politics, continue to follow the military's determined trial and error path to impose its new constitutional system. The Thein Sein years was not a façade to disguise continued military rule, yet it was also not the beginning of a democratic transition. The number of political participants, including regime outsiders, may have expanded, yet the rules of the game remains rooted firmly in the *tatmadaw*'s Constitution.

With the development of two parallel spheres of politics, state authority has vastly diffused and the authoritarian powers of the regime, greatly reduced. Nevertheless, the *tatmadaw* remains favorably entrenched in the political economy, and continues to monopolize the legal use of state violence, a power that has not been transferred to elected civilian offices. The greater tolerance for public dissent and partisan politics, and the expansion of conditional pluralism, has allowed the new regime to gain greater legitimacy and support from a significant majority of domestic and international stakeholders. This post-junta reconciliatory politics and the broad socio-economic reforms reflect a genuine implementation of the military's constitutional plans, which have the additional benefit of co-opting potential spoilers to support and legitimize disciplined democracy. Therefore, the government's active courting of strategic actors such as the NLD, critical dissident groups, and EAOs have only further strengthened, not diminished, the foundations of the emerging disciplined democracy. With the Myanmar government's reputation largely rehabilitated during the Thein Sein administration, the increased diplomatic and economic opportunities have created additional incentives for the *tatmadaw* establishment to stay its course in support of their disciplined democracy.

The growth of associational life and the reactivated social movements have found the military-backed state resorting to a new pattern of targeted repression against detractors to the constitutional system. Particularly in the lead-up to the 2015 general elections, the so-called "reformist" Thein Sein-government, alongside the *tatmadaw*, routinely enlisted the use of state violence and draconian laws to silence critics that sought to undermine government policies or interfere with the military's sphere of influence. Nevertheless, by the end of Thein Sein's tenure, the concerted efforts of the old establishment to construct a "disciplined democratic" hybrid regime was realized. The military-preferred USDP may have lost the election, nevertheless, with the rules of the game clearly established, the *tatmadaw*'s institutionalized role protected, and in the near future unlikely seeing Myanmar returning to the *status quo ante*.

Notes

1 The Constitution originally conceives a separation of executive and legislative powers under a semi-presidential system, although the NLD would later bypass this arrangement by passing the State Counsellor Bill after they formed a government in 2016. Formally, these two institutions remain separate.

2 However, the role of the Constitutional Tribunal, another new institution established by the 2008 Constitution, may in the long-run become a new source of independent power, which may potentially play a role in subsequent political developments (see: Marti 2015).

3 The President also has the power to appoint the Chief Ministers of all 14 state/regional governments directly. Similar to its national counterpart, military officers also hold security-related portfolios in the state/regional governments.

4 Similar to its national makeup, the military is allocated one-third of seats in the 14 region/state unicameral assemblies.

5 Amending the most critical principles of the charter is a difficult two-step process. The recommended amendments must first receive the approval of more than 75 percent of the bicameral national parliamentary. Finally, these parliamentary approved amendments must receive more than half of the total eligible votes in a national referendum.

6 At the time of writing this book, the NLD-led administration (2016–present) has refused repeatedly to call for a formal NDSC meeting, likely as a strategy to diminish military involvement in state affairs.

7 After Tin Aung Myint Oo resigned as the First Vice President in July 2012, he was replaced by Sai Mauk Kham, a physician, which meant ten out of the 11 NDSC members had a background in military services.

8 When the USDA converted into the USDP, all civil servants and military personnel had to resign their USDA membership.

9 According to Renaud Egreteau's study, retired military officers formed a minority of the elected MPs, at 12.4 percent, which is still a significant bloc (2017: 23).

10 Commander-in-Chief Min Aung Hlaing would later also echo the "human security" rhetoric in an interview in 2015 (RFA 2015).

11 The first regular session of the USDP-led parliament met for the first time in January, and no legislation was passed. Instead, the first session was dedicated to selecting the speaker and deputy speakers of the two houses, as well as the election of the president and two vice presidents. Constitution-mandated standing committees were also formed during the first parliamentary session (Egreteau 2017: 14–15).

12 The NLD-led government would later ratify the ICESCR in 2017.

13 The government-drafted 2013 Telecommunications Law received little input from the professional community and retains a number of problematic clauses, and it has been widely used by public officials, politicians, and military personnel to silence critics and journalists.

14 The senior general's profile, alongside a number of other military-managed accounts were banned by Facebook in August 2018 for their role in promoting hate speech, particularly against the Rohingya populace.

15 Since the NLD-led government came into power, both religious and political authorities have outlawed *MaBaTha*. However, the organization remains active by rebranding as a charity organization – the Buddha Dhamma Prahita Foundation.

16 Throughout the repressive SLORC/SPDC years, the junta employed a variety of tactics to weaken and discredit the NLD. However, they have never banned the party formally. The NLD only became an illegal organization for the first time in May 2010, ironically, just as the SPDC was heading toward a voluntarily end. A splinter National Democratic Force was founded by former NLD members who disagreed with the leadership's boycott decision and managed to win a few seats in the 2010 elections.

17 According to the government, Aung Kyaw Naing was an information officer with the Klo Htoo Baw Karen Organization (KKO), the political wing of the DKBA. Aung Kyaw Naing's family, the DKBA, as well as some other journalists, refute this. His family has also claimed that there is evidence that Aung Kyaw Naing may have been tortured during his detention prior to being killed (Regan and Stout 2014). According to a December report released by the Myanmar National Human Rights Commission (MNHRC), the military claimed that they were not aware that Aung Kyaw Naing was a journalist and that he was shot only because he tried to seize a gun from his guard. In the same report, the commission writes that there is no evidence to either support or refute Aung Kyaw Naing's alleged membership and role with the KKO (MNHRC 2014).

18 In one particularly notorious case, the boss and staff of a bar, including both Myanmar and foreign nationals, were sentenced to two years in prison for posting an image of the Buddha wearing headphones on the bar's Facebook page to promote a bar event, and separately an additional six months sentence for operating a bar illegally after 10 p.m. The bar quickly removed the image and apologized for their insensitivity, although it was not enough to get these individuals' convictions revoked, which, according to Phil Robertson, the deputy director of the Asian Division of the HRW, is likely due to the authority's intention to win over the populist sentiment as the 2015 election

approaches (Wai Moe and Ramzy 2015). President Thein Sein pardoned the foreign national just prior to leaving office.

19 The uneasy military-political party relationship is a recurring theme in Myanmar's post-independence history. Except for the BSPP years, pro-military parties, including ones that observers have labeled as military proxies, were never a direct extension of the *tatmadaw*. They are at best considered allies but are separate entities from the military institution.

20 As Aung San Suu Kyi's children have foreign citizenship, 59f of the Constitution disqualifies her from the office of the presidency and vice presidency.

7 Consolidating a disciplined democracy

A preliminary analysis of the early Aung San Suu Kyi years (2016–2019)

Introduction

Excluding Myanmar's flawed 2010 general elections, the changeover of administration in March 30, 2016, under the Htin Kyaw presidency, is the first time a popularly elected civilian party was able to form a government since the 1962 coup d'état. Just days into the new administration, the NLD-controlled bicameral National Parliament passed the State Counsellor Bill swiftly and installed Aung San Suu Kyi as the inaugural State Counsellor. Despite *en bloc* protest by the military MPs, the evidently disgruntled *tatmadaw* did not have the parliamentary numbers to stop the bill in Parliament and had no desire to undermine the disciplined democratic system of its own design. This early legislative showdown demonstrates that a new era for competitive, multiparty electoral politics has materialized. With Suu Kyi as the *de facto* head of the new government, and the longtime opposition now in control of the legislative and executive branches of government, many observers believe that Myanmar is transforming into "Southeast Asia's next democratic country" (Ganesan 2017: 212).

As this book has argued, the NLD's victory is not the beginning of transitologist's "democratization," nor has the military lost their power. At the heart of the *tatmadaw*'s disciplined democracy is the division of power between elected civilians and the military. While the Constitution bestows the military extensive powers and a permanent role in government, it also promises formal legislative and executive powers to elected political parties. Under this civilian–military hybrid regime, elected politicians and their military counterpart hold parallel powers, with separate responsibilities, in the form of a coalition government. The peaceful changeover of government has allowed the NLD to push through new legislation and govern, in line with the rules of the game underpinning the military's disciplined democracy. Partisan attempts by the NLD-driven agenda to roll back the military's power and privileges, however, have failed. Even with the popular Aung San Suu Kyi at the helm, and with a parliamentary majority, the innate power sharing arrangement as designed by the military remains intact.

This chapter begins by unpacking how the Constitution has "locked-in" the fundamental rules of the game, which continue to dictate the composition and powers of the new government. By establishing clear rules that the *tatmadaw* will tolerate, it has the effect of molding the behavior of the various institutional actors that participate in Myanmar's way to democracy. It will then examine how the military's disciplined democracy has endured even with a non-military endorsed party in government. The chapter will examine three key areas of the country's political economy to scrutinize how civilian–military relations have operated in practice: central-peripheral relations, considering the implications of renewed fighting and the stalled peace process; regression of socio-political pluralism; and, finally, the continuation of crony military capitalism. The chapter concludes that more than three years after the advent of the NLD-led government, the institutionalized role of the military remains unchanged, while the civilian leadership finds itself increasingly aligned with the position of the *tatmadaw*. Despite the uneasy, tense relationship, thus far the civilians and the military have an uneasy *modus vivendi*, with no indication that the foundations of the military's disciplined democracy is at risk.

An implicit modus vivendi: the State Counsellor and a coalition government

It was evident in the last months of Thein Sein's lame duck presidency, that the *ancien régime* would not obstruct a government change. In spite of Aung San Suu Kyi's well-known intentions that she plans to reign "above the president" and "make all the decisions" (*SCMP* 2015), all the major bigwigs from the *tatmadaw*, including the retired Than Shwe, signaled their support for Aung San Suu Kyi after the NLD's electoral victory (Lun Min Mang 2015). Given that Section 59f of the Constitution disqualifies Suu Kyi from the presidency, the NLD-dominated parliament passed the State Counsellor Bill, which allowed Suu Kyi to serve as *de facto* head of government, while avoiding the herculean task of amending the Constitution. Despite their strong reservations, the military made only a token attempt to block Suu Kyi from being crowned State Counsellor. The military tacitly accepted the legislative process with a symbolic, but restrained, protest during the parliamentary vote. After several years of planning and investing in its own disciplined democratic system, the military appears to be confident that its Constitution remains a failsafe institution that will protect their position indefinitely.

Using the president's constitutional purview, the NLD further strengthened the credibility of the State Counsellor's powers by establishing a new Ministry of State Counsellor's Office. Additionally, Suu Kyi was co-currently appointed as the Minister of Foreign Affairs and the Minister of the President's Office, the latter role giving her full access to the executive office (ICG 2018: 9). Suu Kyi's position as Foreign Minister also gives her a seat in the exclusive 11-member National Defence and Security Council (NDSC), constitutionally defined as the highest authority on issues of national security. The State Counsellor Bill, and the NLD's active consolidation of power in a single individual, has critical implications: Suu Kyi now has access to both legislative and executive powers, which had direct implications for the separation of power as outlined in the Constitution. The hollowing out of the powers of the presidency meant that during Htin Kyaw's two-year service, he served merely as a place-holder for the Suu Kyi government to fulfill a constitutional requirement. Days after his resignation in March 2016, Htin Kyaw's wife, MP Su Su Lwin claimed that the original plan was for him to serve only for a period of three to six months, which suggests that the NLD overestimated their ability to amend the constitution for a Suu Kyi presidency (ICG 2018: 8).

The establishment and centralization of power in the office of the State Coun-sellor is creative and bold, yet even with a non-military endorsed executive in place, these divergences do not alter the fundamental power relations between the civilian and military representation in government. Whatever agreement may have taken place between Suu Kyi and the *ancien régime* leading up to the gov-ernment change, it was not an elite pact, as it clearly did not extend to changing the basic rules of the game, that is, critical, meaningful amendments to the military's Constitution. As a constitutionally enforced coalition government, the NLD-led administration has no direct authority to command the autonomous *tatmadaw* nor control over the appointment of the three security-focused portfo-lios of Defense, Home Affairs, and Border Affairs. Apart from the constitution-ally required military cabinet members and the handful of old military retirees, the majority of the new cabinet ministers are civilians with limited links to the *tatmadaw* (Thawnghmung and Robinson 2017: 240–241). In other words, the long legacy of military-dominated rule, with policy decisions made by a small group of officers, was no longer true in 2016.

The composition of the civilian cabinet ministers is unimaginative and largely staffed with NLD faithful, technocrats, former civil servants, and purged USDP veterans, mostly selected based on their ties to Suu Kyi (Lun Min Mang et al. 2016). Two NLD members exposed to have dubious academic qualifications during the nomination process both kept their portfolios as Minister of Finance and Commerce Minister (Wai Moe and Ramzy 2016). Those that carried over from the Thein Sein administration were mostly allies of the deposed USDP Chair Shwe Mann, and the former Speaker of the Lower House was known to have formed a close working relationship with Suu Kyi. The NLD also took advantage of the constitutional powers granted to the presidency by appointing party loyalists as Chief Ministers in all 14 states and regions. Even after a change of presidency from Htin Kyaw to Win Myint in March 2018, with a few minor exceptions, the cabinet faced no major reshuffling. Even after two years of civilian-led administration, the legacy of the quasi-militarization of the bureaucracy has not been altered significantly. Several USDP veterans, as well as many ex-military officials and SPDC era officials, remained in the new cabinet, while only 11 out of the 56 cabinet positions were NLD members (Htet Khaung Linn 2018). In December 2018, the important General Administra-tions Department (GAD), which was under the military-controlled Ministry of Home Affairs, was transferred to the recently established Ministry of the Office of the Union Government (Arnold 2019). Although this is a critical step for the further expansion of civilian control over state administration, this important reform is broadly reflective of the military's vision of a civilian/military divide over their respective political responsibilities. The Minister responsible for overseeing GAD operations is Min Thu, a retired Air Force colonel who appears to have close ties with the State Counsellor (*ibid*). Min Thu has been serving the NLD-led government since May 2016 as deputy minister of the Office of the President during the Htin Kyaw administration. There is evidence that the NLD has sought to work with these former military men, utilizing their old networks and understanding of the *tatmadaw* to serve as a bridge between the NLD government and the military establishment. It is unclear, however, whether these are the right military connections, given that the NLD has initially collaborated with the USDP-purged Shwe Mann, who is considered a turncoat by many in the military establishment (Aung Zaw 2019a).[1]

The NLD-led government has utilized its legislative and executive powers in a perceptive manner without directly confronting their remit under the military's disciplined democracy. Thus far, the NLD has purposefully avoided convening an official NDSC meeting, in a bid to prevent further military participation in government operations. The centralization of powers within the position of State Counsellor may have diverged from the constitutional separation of powers between the executive and the legislature, yet this power reconfiguration is limited within the realm of electoral politics and civilian governance, with limited implications for the military's constitutional role. The military, for their part, largely abided by its own rules of the game, and beyond protecting its spheres of influence, "made no overt, systematic attempt to interfere with politics and policy" (David and Holliday 2018: 82).

Apart from the dispute over the position of State Counsellor, the NLD did not initially push forward with any legislation directly challenging the Constitution and the military's political role, until halfway through their five-year tenure. In January 2019, on the second anniversary of the assassination of NLD legal advisor and key advocate for constitutional reforms, Ko Ni, the NLD-controlled parliament established a parliamentary committee on constitutional reforms. The military's boycott against the parliamentary committee was once again ineffective. However, outside of parliament, Senior General Ming Aung Hlaing and his subordinates have reiterated the importance of the reserved military seats in the parliament to "ensure national stability," and opposed any amendments to the national charter that could change the "essence of the constitution" (Min Aung Hlaing 2019; also see *The Irrawaddy* 2019). As Sai Wansai and many others have observed, what this means in practice is that the *tatmadaw* can tolerate minor changes to its disciplined democracy, as long as it does not challenge the institutionalized "leading role" of the military in national politics (Sai Wansai 2018: 10).

When the Union Parliament's Charter Amendment Committee submitted its recommendations in July 2019, the military MPs refused to participate in the debate and challenged the constitutionality of the process (Htet Naing Zaw 2019a). In any case, amendments to the country's Constitution is difficult to achieve. First, proposed constitutional changes must pass the high threshold of 75 percent approval in the National Parliament. Next, if the proposed amendments survive the parliamentary vote, it then goes through a referendum, where at least 50 percent of the registered electorates must approve these changes. Therefore, even with its comfortable parliamentary majority, the NLD cannot break through the first stage of the process for constitutional change, given the *tatmadaw*'s *de facto* veto, with its constitutionally guaranteed 25 percent of the parliamentary seats.

There is no doubt that the NLD aspires to push back, ultimately, against the military's political role; however, Aung San Suu Kyi has studiously avoided undermining the military openly. Instead, Suu Kyi has routinely praised the *tatmadaw*. On August 21, 2018, at a widely reported event in Singapore, Suu Kyi freely commended the military officers in "her" cabinet as "rather sweet" and suggested the relationship between her administration and the *tatmadaw* as "not that bad" (Paddock 2018). According to the editor-in-chief of *The Irrawaddy* Aung Zaw, Suu Kyi, whose father Aung San is considered the founding father of independent Myanmar and the *tatmadaw*, must see herself as part of the "establishment . . . entitled to govern the country" (Aung Zaw 2019b). In her bid to reconcile with the military, she has often reached out to her former enemies, including a personally written letter of condolence to former junta leader Than Shwe, following the death of the former dictator's son-in-law (*ibid*).

In short, neither the NLD nor the military have deviated fundamentally from their constitutionally determined roles, and there is thus far, a *modus vivendi*. Even with mounting NLD attempts to amend the Constitution, the civilian administration has carefully operated within the parameters of the disciplined democracy. The civilian authority is also finding itself increasingly converging with the military's position in multiple issues. As the next section will explore, when it comes to the ongoing peace process, the NLD and the military have kept a largely united front vis-à-vis the EAOs. Given constitutional limitations of civilian's authority over the *tatmadaw*, the NLD-led government have given the *tatmadaw* largely free rein in its military operations in the ethnic peripheries and have seldom questioned the military's actions publicly.

Elusive national reconciliation, 21st-century Panglong, and the stalled peace process

In her first *Thingyan* New Year speech as State Counsellor, Suu Kyi publicly declared that national reconciliation and peace building are top priorities for her administration (Aung San Suu Kyi 2016). There were some immediate, visible changes made at the beginning of the new administration intended to improve the decades-long multi-ethnic tensions. The NLD appointed Naing Thet Lwin, an ethnic Mon and non-NLD member as the inaugural minister for the newly established Ministry of Ethnic Affairs (Thawnghmung and Robinson 2017: 245). The NLD also backed a little-known Christian, ethnic Chin, Henry Van Thio, as the second vice president.

Despite these appointments, the NLD also set the tone of an uneasy relationship with ethnic minority parties, including the successful Shan Nationalities League for Democracy (SNLD) and the Arakan National Party (ANP). Although the NLD did not win a plurality of seats in the states of Shan and Rakhine, they nevertheless utilized the president's constitutional powers to appoint NLD members as the Chief Ministers in the respective states. As a result, both the SNLD and ANP, who had gained the most seats respectively, in the states of Shan and Rakhine, refused to serve in any position under the NLD-led administration (ICG 2016: 9).

The NLD also set an early precedence in their support of the military, against ethnic minority interests, in order to diffuse a potential constitutional crisis. Just weeks into the first parliamentary session, the NLD-dominated parliament effectively stopped an ANP motion that called for a ceasefire in the Rakhine State and for the government to engage the Arakan Army (AA) in peace talks. As the motion has implications to the institutional autonomy and interests of the military, the NLD blocked the ANP proposal by introducing and swiftly passing a different motion (Sithu Aung Myint 2016). Kyaw Ying Hlaing has suggested that there is prior precedence in Suu Kyi's track record as oppositional leader to suggest that the NLD's attitude toward ethnic minority concerns are broadly similar to those of the military leadership (2007a: 363). Even with its reputation as an anti-junta, pro-democracy party, Bamar leadership dominates the NLD, and the party generally represents Bamar-centric interests (Walton 2013: 17–19).

Aung San Suu Kyi has also taken a personal interest in peace building work by taking over the role as Chair of the National Reconciliation Peace Centre (NRPC), a scaled-down reincarnation of the disbanded Myanmar Peace Centre (MPC) (Saw Yan Naing 2017). The State Counsellor's longtime doctor Tin Myo Win was appointed lead negotiator and Vice Chair of the NRPC, a job that an ICG report suggested that he "performed part-time and never seemed to relish," especially as he is undermined routinely by the State Counsellor and other senior ministers during meetings (ICG 2018: 5). Other observers have also commented on Tin Myo Win's inexperience and lack of connection with the military and EAOs as being problematic (Thawnghmung 2017: 384). Tin Myo Win may be tasked with the responsibilities of facilitating talks, but he does not have the authority to made decisions without the permission of the NRPC Chair, Suu Kyi. This meant that the NLD-led negotiation team are often in confusion and lacked a coherent policy on the EAOs (*ibid*).

Despite the initial rhetoric, the main difference from the Thein Sein administration's peace work is the changeover of personnel, as only a handful of MPC staff were retained by the NRPC. The inexperienced and understaffed NRPC team appeared to lack knowledge about the complexities of the EAOs grievances, and the much better prepared and informed *tatmadaw* has therefore taken "greater authority to lead and shape the agenda" (Thawnghmung 2017: 385). In terms of policy program, the NRPC has adopted most of her predecessor's position vis-à-vis the EAOs and the broader peace process (Thawnghmung and Robinson 2017: 245).

The two main institutions put together by Thein Sein's team prior to the government change – the so-called Nationwide Ceasefire Agreement (NCA) and the Union Peace Conference – have both been retained by the NLD administration. The NLD accepted the NCA, signed on October 15, 2015, as the only acceptable framework for rebel groups to engage in formal peace talks with the state. The NLD also did not deviate from the military's policy to exclude some EAOs from the NCA, especially with intensified fighting between the *tatmadaw* and the AA and other members of the Northern Alliance[2] (ICG 2017: 6, 15). The NCA was initially celebrated as a milestone in the country's divisive politics, especially as the country's oldest armed rebel group, the Karen National Union (KNU), is among the original signatories. Despite the positive rhetoric, the reality is that the best armed EAOs, including the powerful United Wa State Army (UWSA) and the Kachin Independence Army (KIA), have declined repeatedly to sign the agreement (Buchanan 2016: 22; Lintner 2019: 20).

Just prior to leaving office, the Thein Sein government also quickly put together the Union Peace Conference in January 2016, which allowed NCA signatories to begin formal peace negotiations with the government. Instead of reinventing the wheel, the NLD-led government also inherited this platform, but rebranded the peace talks as the 21st-Century Panglong (21UPC), playing on the founding myth of independent Myanmar. The original Panglong Agreement, signed in the small Shan town of Panglong between Myanmar's "founding" father Aung San (who was also Suu Kyi's father) and a handful of non-Bamar leaders on February 12, 1947, was meant to be the founding basis for a new political arrangement for the different ethnic groups following Myanmar's decolonization. The significance of this "Union Day" in the national imagination cannot be understated, and February 12 continues to be celebrated as a public holiday.

As the mainstream Bamar-centric narrative goes, this critical event demonstrated ethnic solidarity against British colonialism, and later the Japanese occupation. Further, the "spirit" of Panglong – that is, a united Myanmar – was, according to this myth, only possible due to the dedicated efforts of the government and the *tatmadaw* to preserve the country's independence and unity (Walton, 2008: 904). However, as Matthew Walton suggests, that is just one of the three prevailing, divergent "myths" about the Panglong Agreement (*ibid*: 903). What was or was not agreed to in the agreement, and what the so-called "spirit" actually means remains disputed between the various stakeholders. Despite the contested interpretation, Walton argues that Panglong "is likely the only event in Burmese history that retains some degree of legitimacy with regard to ethnic unity" (2008: 908).

The 21st-Century Panglong is no longer held in the Shan town, but as Michael Dunford (2019: 59) observes, in the military-designated capital of Naypyidaw, suggesting that the NLD, like its military predecessors, has utilized this critical event as "a metaphor for state engagement with ethnic minorities." The inaugural 21UPC, held in August 2016, was highly symbolic and included non-NCA signatories, but the event lacked any real substance and was marred with poor planning and logistic issues, leading to the powerful USWP to walk out of the conference (Thawnghmung and Robinson 2017: 246–247).

Since the inaugural meeting, the NLD has not detracted from its predecessor's policy of excluding non-NCA signatories from participating in formal peace talks (*ibid*: 246). The NLD's original plan to routinize the conference did not materialize, with constant delays and irregular schedules. The second session of the 21UPC was held in May 2017, and the third session took place more than a year later in July 2018. The NLD-led peace talks have been much more rigid than the approach under Thein Sein, with non-elected political parties excluded from participation, and civic organizations are kept at arm's length (Thawnghmung 2017: 384–385). In the latter part of 2018, just months after the third conference took place, two of the best-armed NCA signatories – the KNU and the Restoration Council of Shan State (RCSS) – decided to defer further formal participation in the peace process, therefore, putting on hold any future 21UPCs. For most experts, these peace conferences have exposed the divergent positions of the different stakeholders, especially the irreconcilable views between the EAOs, the *tatmadaw*, and the NLD-led team (Callahan and Myo Zaw Oo 2019: 18).

The most critical issues, such as concerns over the sharing of the resource economy, security reforms, federalism, and the decentralization of power, were kept off the table in the UPC21 talks (*ibid*). With the backing of the NLD leadership, the *tatmadaw* insisted that the NCA signatories must also accept a non-secession clause as a package of agreements for a "Union Accord" (*ibid*, ICG 2017: 12). This is a particularly contentious issue, as some EAO leaders argue that this clause runs contrary to the spirit of the original Panglong Agreements, as it ignores the right of self-determination (and secession rights for the Shan and Kayah/Karenni) that was included in the country's founding 1947 Constitution (ICG 2017: 12; Sai Wansai 2018: 11). Attempts by the government and other NCA signatories to revive the peace process has so far been unsuccessful, with the KNU refusing to attend an informal meeting in June of 2019, chaired by Aung San Suu Kyi at the NRPC (*The Myanmar Times* 2019). This new "low point" for the peace process has now put into doubt whether the NCA or the UPC21, both institutions inherited from the previous Thein Sein administration, could still have any value in the promotion of peace building in Myanmar (Sai Wansai 2018: 13).

Intrastate conflict in a disciplined democracy

The most evident failings of the peace building process has been the surge in internal conflicts since the transition to a disciplined democracy. The Constitution ensures the military high command has independent decision-making powers on all national security issues, therefore intrastate conflicts falls directly in the purview of the *tatmadaw*. The issue of center-peripheral relations, particularly the challenges of a myriad of civil wars, often perceived through the lens of ethnic cleavages, has always been a key driver of Myanmar's post-colonial politics. Since the advent of the NLD-led administration, part of the Kachin, Shan, and Rakhine states are witnessing some of the most brutal resurgence of political violence. Increasingly, the NLD administration is finding itself publicly defending, if not supporting the *tatmadaw*'s operations in the ethnic peripheries.

By far, much of international attention and criticism has focused on the systematic violence against the Rohingya in Rakhine. The plight of the Rohingya is particularly gloomy. In addition to facing systematic, physical violence perpetuated by the state, the community has long been under decades of state-led structural and cultural violence. The Myanmar state has denied their right to self-identify as Rohingya repeatedly, while stringent citizenship requirements have made the community *de facto* stateless (Hein 2018: 379). Ostensibly, as a response to an attack carried out by the little-known militant group, the Arakan Rohingya Salvation Army (ARSA), the *tatmadaw* began "clearance operations" on August 25, 2017, in northern Rakhine state. The military's actions have led to the exodus of more than 700,000 Rohingya Muslims. The Independent International Fact-Finding Mission on Myanmar (FFM), established by the United Nations Human Rights Council (UNHRC), found that at least 10,000 individuals died as a result of the military's actions (UNHRC 2018: 353). Satellite images also suggest the destruction of 392 villages, with many of the destroyed homes replaced with military installations (*ibid*: 221). The FFM finds that the *tatmadaw* has likely committed war crimes, crimes against humanity, and genocide (*ibid*: 1). Since the violent ethnic cleansing campaign, only an estimated 600,000 Rohingya remain in isolated townships and internal displaced people (IDP) camps in northern and central Rakhine (*ibid*: 99; Ware and Laoutides 2019: 63). Despite the mounting evidence of military-sponsored violence against the Rohingya community, the State Counsellor has rejected allegations of ethnic cleansing and has refuted the mandate, findings, and recommendations of the FFM. In response to genocide charges brought to the International Court of Justice by The Gambia in November 2019, the NLD-led government announced that Aung San Suu Kyi would personally lead a delegation to The Hague to defend Myanmar against the charges (Safi 2019). The decision was made after direct discussions between the *tatmadaw* and the civilian administration, with two military officers to form part of the State Counsellor's defense team (Htet Naing Zaw 2019b).

Understandably, much of international focus has been on the humanitarian crisis of the Rohingya populace; yet, in the Rakhine state, it is the actions of another group, the AA, that has proven to be a greater challenge to the Myanmar state. With a long history of civil wars and a diversity of armed rebel groups, the AA is a relative newcomer, founded in 2009 in the Kachin State by a group of KIA-trained ethnic Rakhine migrants working in the Hpakant mines (UNHRC 2018: 100). By late 2015, the AA, who is a member of the Northern Alliance, established a presence in their home state, and attacks against military and police posts in Rakhine became increasingly frequent, resulting in far more substantial loss for the *tatmadaw* compared to clashes with the ARSA (*ibid*). The escalation of AA insurgency has had a significant impact on the region, with the conflict spilling over to the Chin state. Civilians accused by the AA of collaborating or affiliated with the *tatmadaw* have been held hostage, including the November

2019 kidnapping of Chin lawmaker Whei Tin from the ruling NLD party (Nyein 2019).

There is evidence of growing support for the AA within the broader ethnic Rakhine community, especially as relations between the Rakhine community and the Union government have deteriorated significantly, especially after the arrest and sentencing of two high profile Rakhine leaders for "high treason" and defamation against the state (Min Aung Khine 2019). The AA has grown bolder with its political agenda and is now advocating openly for the "Arakan Dream 2020," which aspires for the Rakhine State to achieve self-determination by 2020, akin to the autonomy enjoyed by the UWSA (Ye Mon 2019).

Not unlike the government's defense of the military's actions against the Rohingya, Aung San Suu Kyi has also supported the *tatmadaw*'s actions against the AA publicly. In one of the most evident convergences of positions between the civilian and military leaderships, the State Counsellor publicly ordered the military to crack down against the AA as retaliation following a well-coordinated AA attack on a number of security posts on Independence Day, 2019 (Htoo Thant and Nyan Lynn Aung 2019). As the State Counsellor does not have the constitutional authority to command the *tatmadaw*, the message is largely symbolic. Beyond tokenism, the civilian authorities have also actively offered strategic help to the military's campaign against the AA. With the backing of the President's Office, the Minister of Transport and Communications, Thant Zin Maung, ordered on June 21, 2019, the shutdown of all mobile internet access in parts of Rakhine, leading to a total internet blackout for an estimated 1.1 million people (Naw Betty Han 2019a). Ostensibly, the information shutdown is to prevent the spread of hate speech and the passing on of information to AA rebels, but this indiscriminate internet shutdown has led to criticisms from a diversity of voices, including Rakhine State lawmakers concerned that human rights violations may be taking place (Ye Ni 2019). In a surprising move, two months after the internet shutdown and following a series of setbacks for the AA and other members of the Northern Alliance, the Northern Alliance launched a coordinated attack in several government facilities on August 15, 2019 (Myat Thura 2019). The targets included the highly symbolic Defence Services Technological Academy, an elite army college located in Pyin Oo Lwin, Mandalay Division. The Northern Alliance clearly aimed to embarrass the *tatmadaw* in this unprecedented bold attack, bringing the fight into government-controlled Bamar-centric areas.

In addition to the escalation of violence between the *tatmadaw* and members of the Northern Alliance, intrastate conflict has also flared up elsewhere, including clashes against NCA signatories such as the RCSS in the Shan state (Chit Min Tun 2019). Although many of these are minor, military engagements, a fight against the Mon National Liberation Army (MNLA) on November 27, 2019, ended up with the *tatmadaw* temporary taking over several of the MNLA bases and outposts, in violation of the NCA (Lawi Weng 2019).

Ultimately, one of the country's most salient challenges, that of ethnic relations, have not seen any genuine reconciliation under the NLD-led government.

The civilian authority, on multiple occasions, finds itself constitutionally power-less to command the military, and instead of acting as a balancing act to check against the military's interests and instincts, has found itself increasingly in a united front with the *tatmadaw*. The NLD administration has also shown that when it comes to engaging the broader society, it is turning to the old strategies of fear to silence critiques and dissent through several legal instruments.

Resurgence of illiberalism under a consolidated democracy

There is no indication that under the NLD, a party that campaigned on a platform for "democracy" has made any efforts in developing democratic institutions and promoting best practices to cultivate a culture acquiescent to liberal democratic values. The NLD-led administration generally appears to be aloof and unrecep-tive to the opinion of non-state actors. Protests against unpopular decisions of naming local bridges after the State Counsellor's father or the erection of Aung San statues have demonstrated the NLD's tone deafness, often at the expense of ethnic minority voices. Further, despite public outcry and opposition by civic organizations, the NLD administration passed the amended Vacant, Fallow and Virgin Land Management Law in September 2018, which analysts have warned could further drive intrastate conflicts and mass landlessness (Gelbort 2018). Activists, especially elite leaders from the younger generation, have now largely abandoned the NLD and see the country's disciplined democ-racy as a failed system (Dunant 2018).

Just as the NLD finds itself broadly sharing the military's intrinsic policies vis-à-vis the stalled peace process, the new civilian government has also demon-strated similar instincts to their military counterparts when facing public criti-cisms. The nascent, greater civic space that begin to regress by the later Thein Sein years continue to backslide, in part, fostered by the NLD administration. Not unlike the selective pattern of repression prominent during Thein Sein's "transitional" years, anti-military protests and criticisms of government policies continue to be routinely shut down by the state (Huang 2017: 31–32). Since coming into government, the NLD, which had campaigned heavily on the theme of accountability and transparency, has found itself resorting to using the same legal instruments to punish government detractors and critics. Activists and journalists, especially those investigating or criticizing the military, often face harassment and prosecution, while the surging Buddhist-nationalist senti-ments have also threatened minority voices (AI 2018: 271). Notably, a nation-wide campaign advocating for peace in the Kachin State in May of 2018 ended with the state-led prosecution of at least 47 participants in different parts of the country (HRW 2019: 62).

Prior to coming into office, there is already a hint of an authoritarian streak when the NLD leadership banned its MP candidates, which later extended to all MP-elects, from talking to the media freely (Shwe Yee Saw Myint 2016). The initial wave of optimism by media outlets, which has been overwhelmingly positive about the NLD, quickly reversed, as the expectation that the NLD-led government would usher in a new era of greater liberty and civil rights has been widely off the mark. In the opinion of Tha Lun Zaung Htet, a member of the Protection Committee for Myanmar Journalists, the Thein Sein government was in fact much more responsive than NLD ministers, who in his opinion "don't care about the media" (HRW 2019: 70). The NLD leadership in actuality is wary of the media's influence, as it has actively hardened its stance vis-à-vis the media, as well as the broader civic community since coming into office – both President Win Myint and State Counsellor Aung San Suu Kyi have expressed their distrust with traditional media openly (Nyi Nyi Kyaw 2019).

The policing of the online space has further tightened, with social media users who have criticized the military, Aung San Suu Kyi, and public officials, increasingly prosecuted for online defamation. NLD officials and their supporters, parallel to their military counterpart, have continued to rely on repressive laws, in particular Section 66 (d) of the Telecommunications Act, to silence social media users, including a substantial number of journalists and government detractors (Venkiteswaran et al. 2019: 80). In an ironic twist of fate, the firebrand Wirathu, who has led a populist anti-Muslim movement for years, became a refugee after a court issued a warrant for his arrest. The charges however are unrelated to his violent anti-Muslim rhetoric but rather for sedition charges after he gave a public speech that included explicit remarks about Aung San Suu Kyi (Khin Myat Wai 2019).

Although the NLD-controlled parliament have made efforts to change or revoke some repressive laws, their efforts to foster a more liberal environment is inadequate, if not insincere. Amendments made in August 2017 to the notorious 2013 Telecommunications Act fall short of decriminalizing defamation. State-led criminal prosecutions against journalists and critics have surged, with at least 246 individuals charged under this controversial law by June 2019 (San Yamin Aung 2019). For example, the *tatmadaw* sued Min Htin Ko Ko Gyi for defamation based on a series of Facebook posts the filmmaker posted that mocked the military. Despite being diagnosed with liver cancer, he was given a one-year hard labor jail sentence in 2019 under 505(a) of the Penal Code, while a separate charge under the notorious section 66 (d) of the Telecommunications Law remains pending (Naw Betty Han 2019b). These prosecutions of citizens' online activities have led to a new generation of activists who are increasingly censoring themselves out of fear of reprisal by the state (HRW 2019: 3).

The high profile prosecution of Kyaw Soe Oo and Wa Lone is illustrative of the NLD's uneasy relationship with the press. In a case reminiscent of the days of direct, military rule, the State detained the two Reuter journalists under the colonial-era 1924 Official Secrets Act, in retaliation against the duos' exposé of the Inn Din Village massacre. Their report led to the jailing of seven soldiers and embarrassed the military. Despite credible testimonies that the duo were framed, Suu Kyi not only defended their prosecution but also prejudiced their case by announcing the journalists' guilt even before a court ruling was made (Venkiteswaran et al. 2019: 82). Sustained public outcry after the Supreme Court upheld the duo's seven-year custodial sentence likely pressured the

NLD government to finally intervene in the case. In a mass presidential pardon, the journalists were finally released along with several thousand inmates after spending more than 500 days in prison. It was later reported that the soldiers jailed for the Inn Din massacres were released months earlier after having served less than a year of their ten-year prison sentence – emblematic of the military impunity for human right violations and continued influence over the various organs of the state.

As Nyi Nyi Kyaw observes, NLD officials and their supporters have revived the legacy of state hostility against independent and foreign journalism, engaging in a "soft repression" of the country's nascent media by driving a new "anti-media populist narrative" that is "more nuanced" than previous "cruder" forms of anti-media sentiments (2019). By the halfway point of the NLD's five-year tenure, the number of journalists and activists prosecuted for political offences has far surpassed the arrests made in the entire tenure of the Thein Sein administration (ICG 2018: 6). Under these circumstances, a report by Human Rights Watch (HRW) argue that a "new climate of fear" has taken hold of the country, threatening a new generation of journalists, human rights defenders, and government and military critics (HRW 2019: 3). In short, the NLD has sustained the state's continued assault against the nascent socio-political pluralism. With both the civilian and military leadership distrustful and intolerant of critical and dissenting voices, Myanmar's disciplined democracy continue to operate within an illiberal environment, with society subjecting to more discipline and less democracy.

The disciplined democracy, under the NLD administration, is also finding itself increasingly attracted to the orbits of illiberalism in the international setting. While in Hungary, for example, Suu Kyi met with Viktor Orban, the far-right prime minister of Hungary, and jointly released a statement warning against the issue of "coexistence with continuously growing Muslim populations" in their respective countries (Ellis-Petersen 2019). Further, alongside a number of non-democratic countries with abysmal human rights records, the Myanmar Ambassador to the UN signed a public letter not only defending China's "counter-terrorism" policy in Xinjiang but also praised the Chinese single-party state's human rights records (Miles 2019).

Military capitalism in a disciplined democracy

The "gold rush" narrative following the Thein Sein reforms did not materialize into a sustained high growth following the government change. Growth slumped significantly during the NLD's first year in office; however, it has since rebounded, with more than 6 percent GDP growth per year (Beck et al. 2019: 52). Despite the relatively robust economy, there is a lingering, popular perception that the NLD administration has woefully mismanaged the economy (ICG 2018: 8). In part, this is due to the government's slow start to put together a coherent economic plan, which disappointed many potential investors and business leaders (Thawnghmung and Robinson 2017: 250–251). Despite greater attempts to improve the business, the country continues to face systematic resistance and bureaucratic inertia. Land grabs, rising costs, and inflation have significantly hurt the poor, while the uneven distribution of rents, and a drop in foreign investments, have led to a slower growth pace, which simply did not match the predictions and anticipations of economists, urbanites, and business elites (*ibid*, Htoo Thant 2019).

The much-anticipated dismantlement of the US economic sanctions regime, announced by President Barack Obama in September 2016, did not translate to a significant influx of Western investments to the country. In part, this is due to the increased international awareness of the political violence in the northern Rakhine state; however, the steady FDI decline has been ongoing since 2015 (Nan Lwin 2018; Beck et al. 2019: 25–26, 37). Further, the NLD is perceived as incompetent economic managers who have failed to facilitate an attractive investment environment for foreign capital (ICG 2018: 5). Myanmar has thus turned back to its Asian neighbors for support, with Singapore and China as the country's two largest investors (Htoo Thant 2019). Broadly reflective of the changing regional dynamics, Myanmar has responded positively to China's determined push to realize its "Belt and Road Initiative" and is cooperating with China to develop the China-Myanmar Economic Corridor (CMEC). The CMEC is part of a massive infrastructure-intensive project that is also a major component of China's planned Bangladesh-China-India-Myanmar Economic Corridor, which will give China strategic access to the Indian Ocean (Li and Song 2018: 319–321; Tourangbam and Amin 2019). For example, in 2018, the NLD-led government revived the controversial Kunming–Kyaukpyu railway that was suspended by Thein Sein in 2014 (Amara Thiha 2018). In January 2019, the Central Bank of Myanmar relaxed foreign currency controls by adding Chinese *renminbi* and Japanese yen to its list of approved foreign currencies that can be used to settle international payments and trade deals, with the aim of cutting down transaction costs and strengthening Myanmar's economic ties with China and Japan (Becks et al. 2019: 28).

Ultimately, it is the long legacy of "military capitalism" that continues to shape the structure and direction of the country's economy (McCarthy 2019: 19–25). In addition to a special fund reserved at the discretion of the military, and a consistent generous allocation of the government's budget, the *tatmadaw* is embedded deeply in the formal and informal economy (Bünte 2017a: 116). Their most notable possessions – Union Myanmar Economic Holding Limited (UMEHL) and the Myanmar Economic Corporation (MEC) – remain actively invested in nearly every sector of the economy, generating massive revenues that far surpass all other Myanmar-based companies (UNHRC 2019: 4). Contrary to earlier predictions, the opening up of the economy and the several rounds of privatization campaigns have not hurt these military conglomerates, and they remain well placed to access rent (Bünte 2017a: 117). As the Defense Ministry is directly responsible for these enterprises, the *tatmadaw* is the best-funded organization in Myanmar, with no signs that their economic role has subsided under the NLD administration.

With their established networks, the military and established elites continue to be the preferred local partners for international businesses entering the Myanmar market (Miklian 2019: 55–56). The entry of a new wave of foreign investors and international organizations have introduced "new corruption dynamics," where "the 'Big Boys' of politics, military and industry" benefit disproportionately from these new business and development projects, often at the expense of local communities (*ibid*: 61). Further, the inbound of these international aid agencies and foreign businesses have produced an "anti-politics machinery" that inadvertently strengthens the "gradual reform and stability" mantra of the military's disciplined democracy while excluding non-institutionalized actors from participating in the political process of development and peace building (Bächtold 2015: 1969).

Renewed intrastate conflicts continue to drive the underground economy, particularly with the resurgence of the extensive illicit drug industry. The Shan state is now a major global production center of crystal methamphetamines, while heroin found in the Asia-Pacific region almost exclusively originates from the Shan and Kachin states (UNODC 2019: 1–3). The methamphetamine trade has become the most lucrative business for transnational criminal organizations in the Asia-Pacific region, with its market value estimated to be between US$ 30.3 and US$ 61.4 billion annually (*ibid*: 42). To put into context, World Bank estimates Myanmar's official nominal GDP in 2018 as US$ 71.2148 billion (World Bank 2019). An ICG report suggests that the size and profitability of the narcotics trade surpasses legitimate businesses in the Shan state (ICG 2019: 18). Further, the NLD government has renewed the "ceasefire capitalism" in the ethnic peripheries that emerged in the 1990s and re-brokered by the Thein Sein administration (Woods 2018: 28). The NLD government has now repackaged its arrangements with the EAOs by adopting the language of the UN-endorsed "Business for Peace" (B4P) (*ibid*). Not unlike past practices, the B4P plan offers lucrative financial incentives for leaders of NCA signatories to participate in the formal economy, without any clear provision that these "peace dividends" will benefit the local communities (*ibid*). Nevertheless, under the endorsement of representatives from both the state and the NCA signatories, the Myanmar Ethnic Entrepreneurs Association was established in March 2018 as a platform to help EAOs establish public companies to finance its activities.

In short, three years into the NLD-led administration, there has been little genuine structural change in Myanmar's political economy. The military's vast business interests and networks ensure the *tatmadaw*, individual officers, and their civilian "crony" partners continue to accumulate the lion's share of the country's wealth. The high degree of off-budget financial security also means that the military is not beholden to the government's formal budget allocation. This financial independence further reinforces the military's institutional autonomy and serves as a major pillar, sustaining the *tatmadaw*'s role as praetorian guards of Myanmar's disciplined democracy. Similar to the ceasefire arrangements of the recent past powerful EAOs remain embedded in the "conflict resource economy" through the updated B4P initiative, or continue to profit from the intrastate conflicts and the large underground economy (Woods 2018: 6).

The NLD authorities are not only powerless to investigate the military's vast business interests, but have also found themselves following the "same rationales and mechanisms" supportive of "military capitalism" (McCarthy 2019: 38). In a complete reversal of Suu Kyi's past position on targeted sanctions, the Ministry of Foreign Affairs and the Union Enterprise for Humanitarian Assistance, Resettlement and Development in Rakhine (UEHRD), both headed by the State Counsellor, released public rebuttals of the 2019 FFM report, which advocates for the economic isolation of the *tatmadaw*. It is as if the NLD has come full circle, submitted to the interests of the *tatmadaw*, and co-opted by the disciplined democracy

Conclusion

This chapter argues that the NLD's ascent to government signaled not the beginning of a democratic transition but rather the consolidation of the military's "disciplined" democracy. The electoral victory and the installment of an Aung San Suu Kyi-led government has allowed Myanmar's transitions from a diminished authoritarian regime under Thein Sein into a hybrid regime, as designed by the military establishment. Although the longtime opposition now holds genuine, albeit conditional, powers in government, they have thus far diverged little from the practices of its predecessors when confronting non-state actors and alternative voices. Those that were optimistic that the NLD-led government would be able to reconcile the contentious ethnic politics and manage intrastate conflicts fail to appreciate neither the limits of parliamentary politics in Myanmar's disciplined democracy nor NLD's own illiberal, Bamar-chauvinist streak. NLD's successes in the realm of electoral politics have not diminished the military's constitutionally proscribed powers and roles nor rolled back the military's deep engagement in the country's economy.

In the most divisive of issues – that of the ethnic-peripheral relations – the Bamar-centric NLD appears to have lost tremendous support from many ethnic minority communities, especially in areas of significant fighting. The seven-decade long intrastate conflicts remain far from resolved, while political violence has further escalated under the NLD-led administration. National reconciliation and peace building remain elusive, while the NLD leadership finds itself backing the *tatmadaw*'s policy and operations against the various EAOs and minority communities repeatedly. The violent campaigns have also led to the re-emergence of a limited, US-led sanctions regime, with growing support in the Western-centric international community.

On the socio-political front, the civilian government, in parallel with the *tatmadaw*, has resorted to illiberal and repressive tactics to silence critics and activists. Both the civilian and military authorities have utilized judicial means to punish those that challenged or "defamed" state officials. After the initial expansions of social-political pluralism in the early years of the Thein Sein reforms, civic space continues to dwindle and have faced further assault under the NLD-led administration.

Aung San Suu Kyi remains, by far, the most popular politician in the country and will likely carry the NLD again in the 2020 general elections. However, if the by-elections in April 2017 and November 2018 are any indicator, the NLD will likely win smaller margins, as they no longer hold the same electoral appeal, especially outside of Bamar-dominated constituencies. Fundamentally, civilian governance was always going to be restricted. The Constitution-determined separation of civilian–military powers, and, critically, the enduring legacy of a highly militarized political economy, meant that the civilian administration has limited agency. Even as the NLD becomes bolder with its constitutional challenges in the lead-up to the 2020 elections, there is no suggestion that the military has the slightest interest in participating in these constitutional debates, let alone allowing any fundamental restructuring of the Constitutional system. The military remains involved intimately in all aspects of the country's political economy, and irrespective of the 2020 electoral results, it appears that Myanmar will likely remain more disciplined and less democratic.

Notes

1 The NLD-controlled parliament has initially appointed Shwe Mann as Chair of the Legal Affairs and Special Cases Assessment Commission in the parliament but refused to renew the Commission's mandate in February 2019 (Hammond 2019).
2 The Northern Alliance is composed of four EAOs: the AA, KIA, MNDAA, and the Ta'ang National Liberation Army (TNLA).

8   Conclusion

On November 20, 2019, the National League for Democracy (NLD)-led government announced that State Counselor Aung San Suu Kyi would personally lead a delegation to contest genocide charges brought by The Gambian government at the International Court of Justice (ICJ) in The Hague. The uninitiated observer may not have predicted Aung San Suu Kyi's dramatic fall from grace from that of democracy icon to an apologist of the *tatmadaw*. However, as this book has argued, the post-2011 regime change, which allowed the popularly elected NLD to co-govern alongside the military, has followed the military's vision toward Myanmar's way to democracy. Myanmar's transition into a disciplined democracy is by no means democratization. The military not only remains embedded intimately in the political economy, but its praetorian views also continue to shape the political discourse in post-junta Myanmar. The steady rise of ultra-Buddhist nationalism in recent years, and the increasingly illiberal and authoritarian practices of the NLD-led government do not bode well for the prospects of Myanmar's transformation into a genuine "liberal" democracy (David and Holliday 2018: 201; also see Thant Myint-U 2019).

This book has proposed a regime-centric explanation for Myanmar's seemingly paradoxical regime change. It has argued that since 2011, Myanmar's regime change has been a carefully considered and controlled process in line with the political vision of the *tatmadaw*. There was no guarantee at the beginning of the transition in 2011 that the new hybrid regime would necessarily allow for what turned out to be a relatively fair electoral process in 2015. Certainly few if any observers could have predicted that at the end of the SPDC years the Aung San Suu Kyi-led NLD would have become part of the state within one term of Myanmar's "disciplined democracy," and that the NLD would increasingly defend the actions of the military that it has long opposed. While neither the NLD nor the *tatmadaw* may be particularly satisfied with how political developments have unfolded since the 2016 government change, thus far, both sides have continued to operate within the constitutional parameters of their prescribed powers. Much like the military's attempt to build its version of the Burmese way to socialism, the post-2011 regime is the military's version of Myanmar's way to democracy.

The central argument of this book is that Myanmar's regime transformation is a top-down, *voluntary* liberalization that is neither a direct response to domestic challenges nor a submission to external influences. Since reforms began in 2011, Myanmar has seen greater social, political, and economic liberty, but as discussed throughout the book, this meticulously planned regime change does not represent a push by so-called liberal reformers inside the *tatmadaw* to introduce Western-style democracy in Myanmar. Further, the narrative that Myanmar is currently undergoing a regime transition oscillating between democratization and a regression toward authoritarianism ignores the empirical realities of the new hybrid regime equilibrium, as designed by the military. The *tatmadaw* may no longer monopolize political power, but the 2008 constitutional framework assures the military of near absolute-control of core issues such as national and border security, institutional autonomy, and military representation at all levels of the legislature as well as the power to veto any critical structural changes to its political institutions. In other words, Myanmar "disciplined democracy" as conceived of by the *tatmadaw* codifies the military's role in a hybrid regime.

This conclusion begins by revisiting the limitations of the popular democratization paradigm in contextualizing Myanmar's regime change and explains the rationale behind Myanmar's non-democratic regime change. It reiterates that post-junta Myanmar is not a regime in transition; rather it has already changed into a hybrid regime, in line with the political vision of the *tatmadaw*. The constitutional segregation of the civilian–military spheres of political influence are therefore institutionalized and likely to remain as such in the near future. The chapter concludes with a discussion about the possible scenarios arising from this self-initiated regime change and any implications for Myanmar's disciplined democracy.

A trial and error regime change: Myanmar's way to democracy as a hybrid regime

This book has developed a regime-centric, trial and error approach, providing an alternative interpretation to help understand Myanmar's endogenous regime change. As discussed in Chapter 2, regime logic can be explained by the attributes and the institutions that make up the regime. In the case of Myanmar, the regime change enacted in 2011 demonstrates a continuity of the praetorian mindset. Although political liberalization may have accelerated since the regime change, this gradual process was one designed by the military and was not an abrupt departure brought about by institutional failures or sudden regime collapse. Myanmar's military regime is led by politicized praetorian warfighters that are inspired by a Bamar-centric nationalist ideology and committed to the preservation of the country's territorial boundaries that were assembled broadly by the British colonial state. The regime leadership may be indoctrinated politically, yet they are not ideologues but rather trained soldiers that resolve conflicts through military tactics and not political means.

Prior to 2011, the military leadership made no real attempt to take the role of partisan politics seriously, and thus they have never been able to master the art of politics. Despite the resources and influence that the military holds, they were unable to transform their despotic power into a constructive infrastructural power or vertical solidarity with the populace it sought to govern. This is best demonstrated by the fact that whenever the military has allowed fair elections to be held under its watch, the military's patronage networks have been unable to garner popular support for the party of its preference (that is the "stable" AFPFL faction in 1960, the NUP in 1990 and the USDP in 2012 and 2015).[1] Despite efforts to create a mass network of grassroots support through their control of GONGOs, the military was never able to create an organic bond with its populace. The reason is that the stability of the regime was based on the coherence and strength of the *tatmadaw*, and the support of a small group of co-opted crony capitalists, and thus it was important for society to be weak and depoliticized vis-à-vis the regime, but unimportant for the regime to gain the support of its populace.

Why, then, has the military allowed this transition? The roots of this question go back to events leading up to 1988. The *tatmadaw* strongly self-identifies as a praetorian ruler, and although socialism was initially an important ideology that motivated the political establishment; it never developed into a fixated totalitarian-like ideology. Once the discredited socialist ideology was thrown out and Ne Win voluntarily retired from all positions of power, the SLORC/SPDC junta had the opportunity and a high degree of flexibility to reorganize the power dynamics of its institution, as well as adjust its policies in order to adapt to the changing circumstances of the day. The dissolution of the SPDC in March 30, 2011, shares certain parallels with the civilizing efforts of the 1974 BSPP single-party state system. Not unlike the transition from direct military rule under the RC (1962–1974) to the single-party military-backed and staffed state under the 1974 constitutional system (1974–1988), Myanmar's disciplined democracy is a military-led project that has no intention of divorcing the formal (and informal) role of the military from national politics. Yet, unlike 1974, there has been a genuine attempt to liberalize the regime, with new legal provisions that allow limited pluralism in the country. This is, however, not the result of an *ad hoc*, spontaneous "democratization" of its regime but rather a well-calculated strategy of gradual liberalization.

In 1988, the self-identifying praetorians finally admitted that its single-party state-initiated socialism had failed. Nationwide anti-government protests underpinned by a failing economy forced the military to address this exogenous shock. The military realized its socialist project was untenable, and the BSPP ideology had become a liability for the military. Once the upper echelon of the *tatmadaw* had authorized an internal coup to dismantle the 26-year-old socialist state apparatus, it sought to develop immediate policy options to save the failed state. Given the post-Cold War context where even the most revolutionary communist regimes such as China and Vietnam, for example, were embracing economic (but not political) liberalization, the military's shift toward economic liberalization was a pragmatic decision. Further, the BSPP regime never genuinely developed into a party-state but served as an adjunct to the military. With the return of direct military rule in 1988, there was therefore no incentive for the *tatmadaw* to offer continue support to the failed party. The "military-economic" complex that developed under the SLORC/SPDC government privileged the military with material benefits, thus creating the incentives for the military to perpetuate its unrelenting dominance over the state apparatus, which delayed its long promise to transfer power to an elected authority (Prager-Nyein 2009: 641–642). The modest post-1988 economic growth placed a new source of wealth in the hands of the military and its affiliates and provided the *tatmadaw* with funds to rebuild the military both as the state and as a coercive institution. The promise of "rebalancing" its foreign relations or the potential financial incentives generated by expanding trading partners beyond its Asian neighbors do not adequately explain the long-term and consistent logic of Myanmar's *tatmadaw* in advancing its political transition roadmap.

External influences, such as the role of international sanctions, are necessary conditions that offer some insight into the military regime's behavior, but they are not the determinant of how and why the authoritarian military regime enacted its eventual transition into a "disciplined democratic" hybrid regime. Despite the regime's inability to cultivate an organic state-societal connection, it has provided a basic social-political order and subdued a disciplined society, which ensured a durable authoritarian equilibrium throughout the SLORC/SPDC years. Critical events, including, for example, the 2007 "Saffron Revolution" and the 2008 Cyclone Nargis, arguably particular low points of its rule, failed to punctuate the authoritarian equilibrium. In both events, heightened international focus neither dislodged regime unity nor led to changes in the junta's political agenda. Throughout the military's authoritarian rule, the regime has maintained unity in its basic political positioning and has not altered the content of its seven-step roadmap nor changed the way it implemented the political transition plan. It did not make any effort to incorporate divergent political views or share power with regime outsiders prior to implementing a "disciplined" democracy in 2011.

In implementing its long, drawn-out roadmap toward a disciplined democracy, the military has remained consistent. Tellingly, the main objectives and principles of the Constitutional "disciplined" democratic system that were first unveiled in 1992, remain unchanged and have been realized after 16 years of constitutional "development." Since 2016, regime outsiders have gained access to genuine power in the civilian spheres of politics under the condition that all political stakeholders continue to operate within the rules of the game as determined by the original *tatmadaw* designers of the Constitution. The military's historic distrust of partisan politics and its self-rationalized role as an objective representative of the national interests meant that the *tatmadaw* eventually came up with its disciplined democratic diarchy to allow genuine sharing of power with military outsiders. At the same time, the military reserved a praetorian arbitrator role to ensure that the foundations of its "disciplined democracy" remain unchanged, unless it has received the military's approval. The carefully designed hybrid governance structure dividing civilian and military spheres of influence is therefore the equilibrium the military sought to maintain.

Rethinking the democratization narrative

Thirty years earlier, veteran journalist Bertil Lintner observed that, "the general consensus in Burma in the spring of 1989 is that the movement towards democracy which began exactly a year ago is irreversible" (Lintner 1989: 239). Lintner was of course right about the popular sentiments, as the large majority of the electorates voted for the NLD in a landslide victory at the 1990 general election. Since the 1990s, democratization theory has captured the imagination of academics, policymakers, and the broader society. From people's power in the Philippines to the fall of the Berlin Wall, and finally the collapse of the Soviet Union, many were optimistic of what Francis Fukuyama (1992) referred to as the "end of history," that is humanity had finally reached its ultimate ideal form of political arrangement. However, as events unfolded, the military was not only able to deflect popular rejection of its rule, but it also proceeded to further build, strengthen, and consolidate the powers of the military regime. Myanmar's democratization potential has never materialized thus far. This is an important point to remember when understanding the political context of the military's "disciplined democracy." Aung San Suu Kyi and the NLD may have maintained their 1990s electoral appeal and finally ascended to a position of power a generation later in 2016; however, this is not the result of an "elite pact" nor of a "democratic transition."

The accelerated reform process in the early years of the Thein Sein government, and later, the successful changeover of government to a non-military endorsed, National League for Democracy (NLD) administration, gave the impression that Myanmar was on a track to a genuine democratization. Especially during the height of his international popularity, Thein Sein was lauded in international capitals from Washington, D.C. to London for his apparent contribution to promoting Myanmar's so-called "democratization." The partial transferal of power to the NLD is only possible politically because the military had decided that it was satisfied with its hybrid regime political arrangements, following the institutionalization of the military's political role within the Constitution. Although disciplined democracy has sanctioned far greater pluralism compared to pre-2011 years, the expanded public space for socio-political actors remains conditional. The military (and the new NLD-led government) continues to limit the extent of this pluralism. Those who are perceived to have interfered with the military's sphere of politics, which include criticism of the military or insults to their reputation, continue to be disciplined. With a new set of rules governing the disciplined democratic game, the military was confident that it had the institutions and resources in place to ensure that its role as self-appointed praetorian guards is entrenched. The first post-junta government, therefore, reflected the military's tentative experimentation with its disciplined democratic system. The handover of civilian powers to its long-time opposition following the 2015 elections demonstrated the willingness of the *tatmadaw* to remain committed to the hybrid regime of its own design.

Although the popular "pacted" transition arguments provide some explanation for how post-junta politics are unfolding, these elite agency explanations do not sufficiently explain the long-term logic behind the military-led regime change. The retirement of the junta's top leadership, Than Shwe and Maung Aye, and their decision to play no formal role in post-junta politics, while important, did not provide the sufficient conditions for Myanmar's post-2011 regime change. The post-junta leadership's willingness to reconcile and co-opt key opposition groups, especially the figure of Aung San Suu Kyi, became possible only after the regime change. By focusing on the role of elite agency, it may offer an explanation on how subsequent political developments in "disciplined" democracy unfolds but does not consider the longer structural process behind Myanmar's regime change sufficiently. Myanmar's regime transition has been designed deliberately with the aim of reaffirming the praetorian role of the *tatmadaw* as a critical actor within the state apparatus yet without the duties associated with everyday governance. Even if there has been a more liberal and genuine acceptance of partisan politics, the foundational powers of the military are not affected directly by the expanded pluralism.

The popular game theatrical model of liberals versus hardliners may help to explain the pace and the general direction of the reforms, as well as why some of the more conservative officials were dismissed following the regime transition, yet this model insufficiently explains why the military regime, as an institution, is committed to the current regime change. The democratic transitions explanation suggests that military regimes generally civilianize or democratize as an exit strategy from politics or governance. Part of the problem with this explanation is that transitions theory is more concerned about explaining regime change outcome rather than understanding the triggers of political liberalization, especially in the absence of any failures or conflicts (McFaul 2010: 10).

As this book emphasizes, the collective unity of the military, and its self-initiated actions, remains key to explaining the motivations and actions of the *tatmadaw* as an institutional actor. Despite occasional purges and competing internal interests, the *tatmadaw* has maintained remarkable unity as a collective. Throughout its 23-year direct rule, the military did not distinguish between its corporate interests and those of the nation-state. Therefore, without the military regime's voluntary decision to diminish its powers and enact institutional changes, the subsequent liberalizing reforms and political openings would not have been possible. The way Myanmar's regime change unfolded, along with subsequent political developments, has remained within the political parameters of the military's rules of the game.

With trusted members of the dissolved SPDC leadership in the civilian spheres of "disciplined" democratic politics, the Thein Sein-led administration provided a period of tentative experimentation for the military establishment to demonstrate how Myanmar's way to democracy could function. Perceived errors were fixed, for example, through the removal and purge of Shwe Mann when he begin to detract from the political vision of the *tatmadaw* with his actions. Similarly, despite the significantly liberalized socio-political environment, in critical areas of national security concerns – broadly interpreted by the *tatmadaw*

as including all things related to the military, including its image and reputation –
the pro-military establishment has resorted to authoritarian tactics.

Disciplined democracy may have features of parliamentary politics, yet the military retains expansive powers, and national security, broadly defined by the *tatmadaw*, remains exclusively the purview of the military, unaccountable to civilian politicians. Myanmar's disciplined democracy is not simply what Samuel Huntington referred to as "halfway houses" that would inevitably "democratize" (1991: 174–175). Nor is Myanmar's disciplined democracy simply a case of electoral authoritarian regime or a defective democracy (Bogaards 2009). Unlike the 1988 regime change, which was a response to an exogenous shock, the 2011 transformation had undergone 23 years of trial and error before the military was confident enough to impose its controlled endogenous-led regime change. The hybrid regime structure is based on the strategic interests and political vision of the military.

Constitutional Myanmar, may offer genuine partisan politics and greater pluralism, as demonstrated by the agency of the NLD-led government since 2016; however when it comes to constitutional issues such as the military's political role and control over national security, which includes the critical center-peripheral relations and the ongoing intrastate violence, the military retains its dominance. Therefore, it is necessary to understand the logic of this seemingly paradoxical regime change, the consideration of the praetorian identity, and its corporate interests beyond the materialist concerns of the *tatmadaw*.

Prospects and challenges to Myanmar's way to democracy

Not unlike the Burmese way to socialism of a bygone era, the *tatmadaw* continues to see itself as being responsible for leading the country toward Myanmar's way to democracy. Even with the emergence of partisan politics and the opening up of public spaces, the basic rules of the game underpinning the civilian–military divide remained unchanged throughout the Thein Sein years. To this day, the military is committed to preserving the disciplined democratic system of its design, with no concessions to expand the powers of the civilian authority. The so-called reformists such as Thein Sein have repeatedly credited the actions of the SPDC, of which he served as the last prime minister, as being instrumental in creating the necessary conditions for Myanmar to "implement a democratic system" in Myanmar (Weymouth 2012). Without irony, the senior military leadership are convinced of their role in promoting the military's understanding and version of "democracy." It would be imprudent to suggest that the military will exit from official politics soon.

Yet after nearly 50 years of depoliticizing its society, the new multiparty political system has allowed the re-emergence of limited political pluralism, as political parties are now allowed to participate in official "partisan" politics, and the former opposition NLD is now formally the ruling party in Myanmar. Significant legal spaces have opened up for civil society groups. NGOs are now able to engage in political advocacy, with observable expanded pluralism on a wide range of issues such as women's rights, ethnic minority rights,

LGBT rights, environmental protection, investment laws, media protection, education reform, and grassroots activism (For example see: Barrow 2015; Chua 2019; Kramer 2011; Morgan 2014; Paung Ku 2013; Venkiteswaran et al. 2019). However, despite the newly opened up spaces, the actual influence of these civil society groups remains limited and is subject to contestation with increasingly illiberal attitudes defining mainstream societal mood. A four-year study by Roman David and Ian Holliday concluded that in Myanmar's hybrid regime, a political culture of "limited liberalism" appears to be taking shape (2018: Chapter 6).[2] This "limited liberal" attitude is displayed at the very top, as suggested in the beginning of this chapter – Aung San Suu Kyi's increasing defense of state-sanctioned political violence against large groups of ethnic minority populations particularly against the Rohingya populace has been framed as counter-terrorism strategies.

Despite increasing international criticisms of Aung San Suu Kyi, she remains, undisputedly, the most popular individual in Myanmar. While civilian–military relations remain strained and tense, publicly, other than the critical issue of the military's constitutional powers, the NLD appears to have largely backed the military's national security policies. Unless an extraordinary development takes place before the 2020 elections, Aung San Suu Kyi is set to carry the NLD to another victory, albeit one that is likely to result in a reduced mandate, with increasingly dissatisfied constituents, especially in the ethnic peripheries. If things remain largely the same, it appears that the military's hybrid regime structure will remain in equilibrium in the near future. However, two critical issues – the rejuvenated, intensified intrastate violence between the *tatmadaw* and the EAOs and the rise of Bamar-Buddhist chauvinism – could still punctuate the disciplined democratic equilibrium, if mismanaged.

Resurgence of intrastate violence and the failing peace process

Perhaps the most challenging aspect since the regime change is the continued inability of the state to resolve its differences with armed ethnic groups, many of which continue to have *de facto* control over their respective territories. Since the beginning of reforms, a massive increase in Western aid and assistance has led to the growth of a peace-making *industry* in Myanmar (Lintner 2015). The signing of the nationwide ceasefire agreement (NCA) in 2015 appears to have delivered little in terms of establishing any momentum for a real peace settlement. Fighting has also occasionally broken out not only between the *tatmadaw* and some NCA signatories but also between NCA signatories. Fighting between the Northern Alliance and government troops has intensified in recent years, most surprisingly when the EAOs were able to bring the fight into government-controlled areas, and most notably with the brazen attack on the prestigious military academy in Pyin Oo Lwin.

Further, the drug trade, which has been a major source of funding for several armed ethnic groups, has grown exponentially in recent years. Myanmar's opium poppy cultivation has expanded, and Myanmar has become the largest exporter of heroin in the region, as well as one of the main producers of methamphetamine (UNODC 2019: 1–3). The narcotics trade is further fueling intrastate violence. Despite State Counsellor Aung San Suu Kyi's self-declared priority of achieving peace and reconciliation, intrastate violence has only intensified since the NLD came into government. Given the military's control over operations and issues of national security, it remains to be seen whether further deterioration could potentially disturb the disciplined democratic equilibrium, therefore provoking a response by the *tatmadaw* to take more drastic actions that could have implications for the viability of its "disciplined democracy."

Bamar-Buddhist chauvinism and its implications

Although the NLD-led government has outlawed the Buddhist-chauvinist *MaBaTha* since coming into power, the organization has remained active by rebranding itself as a charity. Its titular leader Wirathu is currently a fugitive, not because of his anti-Islam hate speech but rather because of his public insults of Aung San Suu Kyi. Although the NLD-led government has not openly courted the ultra-Buddhist movement in the same way that the Thein Sein government did, especially in the lead up to the 2015 elections, neither has Aung San Suu Kyi and her subordinates actively opposed the ultra-Buddhist nationalism that is becoming widely normalized in mainstream narratives. Aung San Suu Kyi's personal interest in presenting Myanmar's case in response to allegations of genocide in part suggests that the NLD leader is turning toward more populist strategies in order to ensure continued support of her base supporters. Depending on how the international community responds to legal developments in the ICJ case, as well as how the civilian and military authorities manage the rising xenophobia, further outbreaks of communal violence could occur. However, there is evidence that the ICJ case has mobilized supporters publicly praising both Aung San Suu Kyi and the *tatmadaw* (*The Straits Time*: 2019).

Myanmar's non-democratic regime transition in the broader international context

If we relate Myanmar's regime change to the broader international context, although most states have allowed greater civil, political, and economic pluralism since the end of the Cold War, recent reports suggest that these earlier gains for "global freedom" have been in steady decline (Freedom House 2019: 1). The findings of the Freedom House's 2019 report indicate that, globally, democracy has been in retreat for 13 consecutive years, with civil and political rights deteriorating even in older, consolidated democracies such as the US. The Arab Spring, initially lauded by democratic activists and supporters as a possible "Fourth wave" of democratization, has failed to materialize (Santini and Hassan 2012). In Southeast Asia, countries that were once considered to be on the path to democratic consolidation have seen prolonged illiberal politics deteriorate their nascent democratic institutions, leading to the resurgence of authoritarian forces. Cambodia under Hun Sen is now, effectively, a single-party state, with the country's main opposition leaders imprisoned or exiled (Kheang Un 2011). Thailand, despite returning nominally to "democracy" after a flawed electoral process in 2019, is increasingly illiberal and authoritarian. In the other "democracies," such as Indonesia under Joko Widodo, illiberalism has been on the rise, with a more conservative and less tolerant Islam becoming increasingly normalized. The Philippines under Roderigo Duterte has seen a large-scale "War on Drugs" campaign that has led to systematic extrajudicial killings and a further erosion of its democratic institutions (Curato 2017). Singapore, on the other hand, has been recognized as a successful electoral authoritarian regime, and following the death of the nation's founder Lee Kuan Yew, popular support for the country's ruling party has resurged, with the success of the Singaporean authoritarian "meritocratic" model capturing China's "infatuation" and "obsession" as a model to emulate (Ortmann and Thompson 2016). Taking into consideration this regional context, Aung San Suu Kyi's turn to "limited liberalism" and utilize populist strategies are not particularly unique, as she appears to be in good company among her ASEAN neighbors.

Conclusion

This book has argued that a regime-centric explanation, identifying the motivations of the regime and the environment in which it operates within, provides the rationale for Myanmar's endogenous-led, voluntary regime change. Through a process of trial and error, the contours of the regime's transition plan are shaped by its self-initiated actions, which may sometimes result in errors. Reacting to adversaries, opposition and obstacles, the military aims to correct any perceived errors in its transition plan. By cementing its role and powers through the 2008 Constitution, the military seeks to retain its role as a key political actor in Myanmar's governance and is evidently confident enough to have allowed the NLD to ascend into government following the 2015 general elections. Contestations over the constitutional role of the military will undoubtedly persist; however, with Aung San Suu Kyi's decision to defend Myanmar personally at the ICJ against charges of genocide, it appears that the NLD and its supporters are now united behind Myanmar's way to democracy.

Notes

1 This does not account for the elections during the BSPP era, as they were non-competitive; nor does this include the 2008 referendum or the 2010 general elections, as those elections were held in dubious, flawed conditions.
2 For David and Holliday, limited liberalism is "a set of inconsistent beliefs in the tenets of liberalism" (2018: 189). That is, an individual may hold contradictory liberal and illiberal beliefs simultaneously. For example, in their study, they found the Bamar Buddhist majority as having a largely positive and tolerant relationship with ethnic minorities, but they express particular xenophobic and Islamophobia attitudes – with the Rohingya being the most disliked group by the large majority of their interviewees (*ibid*: 200–201).

Bibliography

Acemoglu, Daron, and Robinson, James A. (2012) *Why Nations Fail: The Origins of Power, Prosperity, and Poverty*. New York: Crown Business.

Alagappa, Muthiah (ed.) (2001) *Military Professionalism in Asia: Conceptual and Empirical Perspectives*. Honolulu: East West Center.

Alamgir, Jalal (2008) "Myanmar's Foreign Trade and Its Political Consequences." *Asian Survey*, vol. 48, no. 6, pp. 977–996.

Albrecht, Holger, and Schlumberger, Olivier (2004) "Waiting for Godot: Regime Change without Democratization in the Middle East." *International Political Science Review*, vol. 25, no. 4.

Albright, Madeleine (2008) "The End of Intervention." *The New York Times*, June 11.

Allen, Susan Hannah (2005) "The Determinants of Economic Sanctions Success and Failure." *International Interactions*, vol. 31, no. 2, pp. 117–138.

Amara Thiha (2018) "Myanmar Speeds up Progress on China's Belt and Road." *The Diplomat*. <https://thediplomat.com/2018/12/myanmar-speeds-up-progress-on-chinas-belt-and-road>, last accessed December 3, 2019.

Amnesty International (AI) (2015) *Going Back to the Old Ways: A new Generation of Prisoners of Conscience in Myanmar*. London: Amnesty International.

Amnesty International (AI) (2018) *Amnesty International Report 2017/2018*. London: Amnesty International.

Arakan Oil Watch (2012) *Burma's Resource Curse: The Case for Revenue Transparency in the Oil and Gas Sector*. <http://burmalibrary.org/docs13/Burmas_Resource_Curse%28en%29-red.pdf>, last accessed February 15, 2020.

Arnold, Matthew (2019) "Why GAD Reform Matters to Myanmar." *East Asian Forum*, August 24. <www.eastasiaforum.org/2019/08/24/why-gad-reform-matters-to-myanmar/>, last accessed December 5, 2019.

Asian Development Bank (ADB) (2019) *Asian Development Bank and Myanmar: Fact Sheet*. <www.adb.org/publications/myanmar-fact-sheet>, last accessed October 16, 2019.

Aspinall, Edward (2015) "Money Politics: Patronage and Clientelism in Southeast Asia." In William Case (ed.), *Routledge Handbook of Southeast Asian Democratization*. Abingdon: Routledge.

Aspinall, Edward, and Farrelly, Nicholas (2014) "Myanmar's Democratization: Comparative and South East Asian Perspectives: Introduction." *South East Asia Research*, vol. 22, no. 2, pp. 163–169.

Assistance Association for Political Prisoners (Burma) (AAPP) (2004) *Burma: A Land Where Buddhist Monks Are Disrobed and Detained in Dungeon*. Mae Sot, Thailand: Assistance Association for Political Prisoners (Burma), November.

Assistance Association for Political Prisoners (Burma) (AAPP) (2014) *A Briefing Paper on the Shrinking Space for Civil Society in Burma/Myanmar*. Mae Sot, Thailand: Assistance Association for Political Prisoners (Burma), October 1.

Association of South East Asian Nations (ASEAN) (2010) *A Humanitarian Call: The ASEAN Response to Cyclone Nargis*. Jakarta: ASEAN Secretariat, July.

Aung Aung (2019) *Emerging Political Configurations in the Run-up to the 2020 Myanmar Elections*. Singapore: ISEAS-Yusof Ishak Institute.

Aung Kin (1980) "Burma in 1979: Socialism with Foreign Aid and Strict Neutrality." *Southeast Asian Studies*, pp. 93–117.

Aung Kyaw Nyunt (2016) "Ministry Puts Mobile Penetration at 90 Percent." *Myanmar Times*, July 19. <https://www.mmtimes.com/business/technology/21466-ministry-puts-mobile-penetration-at-90-percent.html>, last accessed February 15, 2020.

Aung San Suu Kyi (2016) "Amendment Essential: State Counsellor Offers New Year Message." *The Global New Light of Myanmar*, April 18.

Aung Shin (2015) "Shwe Gas Cost to be Covered within Four Years." *Myanmar Times*, August 3. <www.mmtimes.com/business/15798-shwe-gas-cost-to-be-covered-within-four-years.html>, last accessed December 3, 2019.

Aung-Thwin, Maureen (1989) "Burmese Days." *Foreign Affairs*, vol. 68, no. 2, pp. 143–161.

Aung-Thwin, Maureen, and Thant Myint-U (1992) "The Burmese Ways to Socialism." *Third World Quarterly*, vol. 13, no. 1, pp. 67–75.

Aung Zaw (2019a) "For U Shwe Mann, Enemies Lurk Everywhere." *The Irrawaddy*, March 5. <www.irrawaddy.com/opinion/commentary/u-shwe-mann-enemies-lurk-everywhere.html>, last accessed December 5, 2019.

Aung Zaw (2019b) "The State Counselor Keeps Her Former Enemies Close." *The Irrawaddy*, June 17. <www.irrawaddy.com/opinion/commentary/the-state-counselor-keeps-her-former-enemies-close.html>, last accessed December 5, 2019.

Ba, Alice (2011) "Staking Claims and Making Waves in the South China Sea: How Troubled Are the Waters?." *Contemporary Southeast Asia*, vol. 33, no. 3, pp. 269–291.

Bächtold, Stefan (2015) "The Rise of Anti-Politics Machinery: Peace, Civil Society and the Focus on Results in Myanmar." *Third World Quarterly*, vol. 36, no. 10, pp. 1968–1983.

Badgley, John H. (1965) "Burma's Zealot Wungyis: Maoists or St. Simonists." *Asian Survey*, vol. 5, no. 1, pp. 55–62.

Barany, Zoltan (2015) "Exits from Military Rule: Lessons for Burma." *Journal of Democracy*, vol. 26, no. 2, pp. 86–100.

Barany, Zoltan (2018) "Suu Kyi's Missteps." *Journal of Democracy*, vol. 29, no. 1, pp. 5–19.

Barrow, Amy (2015) "Contested Spaces during Transition: Regime Change in Myanmar and Its Implications for Women." *The Cardozo Journal of Law and Gender*, vol. 22, no. 1, pp. 75–108.

Beck, Hans Anand et al. (2019) *Building Reform Momentum: Myanmar Economic Monitor*. Washington, DC: World Bank Group.

Beehner, Lionel (2018) "State-Building, Military Modernization and Cross-Border Ethnic Violence in Myanmar." *Journal of Asian Security and International Affairs*, vol. 5, no. 1, pp. 1–30.

Béland, Daniel, and Cox, Robert H. (2010) "Introduction: Ideas and Politics." In Daniel Béland and Robert H. Cox (eds.), *Ideas and Politics in Social Science Research*. New York: Oxford University Press.

Berman, Sheri (1997) "Civil Society and the Collapse of the Weimar Republic." *World Politics*, vol. 49, no. 3, April, pp. 401–429.

Bermeo, Nancy (1990) "Rethinking Regime Change." *Comparative Politics*, vol. 22, no. 3, pp. 359–377.

Bernhard, Michael et al. (2004) "The Legacy of Western Overseas Colonialism on Democratic Survival." *International Studies Quarterly*, vol. 48, no. 1, pp. 225–250.

Bertrand, Jacques (2013) *Political Change in Southeast Asia*. Cambridge: Cambridge University Press.

Bissinger, Jared (2012) "Foreign Investment in Myanmar: A Resource Boom but a Development Bust?" *Contemporary Southeast Asia*, vol. 34, no. 1, pp. 23–52.

Bissinger, Jared (2014) "Myanmar's Economic Institutions in Transition." *Journal of Southeast Asian Economies*, vol. 31, no. 2, pp. 241–255.

Bogaards, Matthijs (2009) "How to Classify Hybrid Regimes? Defective Democracy and Electoral Authoritarianism." *Democratization*, vol. 16, no. 2, pp. 399–423.

Boudreau, Vincent (2004) *Resisting Dictatorship: Repression and Protest in Southeast Asia*. Cambridge: Cambridge University Press.

Branigin, William (1990) "As Burmese Opium Production Rises, U.S. Debates Resuming Anti-Drug Aid." *New York Times*, Nov. 5.

Bratton, Michael, and van de Walle, Nicholas (1997) *Democratic Experiments in Africa: Regime Transitions in Comparative Perspective*. Cambridge, UK: Cambridge University.

Brooker, Paul (2009) *Non-Democratic Regimes: Theory, Government and Politics*. Basingstoke: Palgrave Macmillan Press.

Brooten, Lisa (2004) "Human Rights Discourse and the Development of Democracy in a Multi-Ethnic State." *Asian Journal of Communication*, vol. 14, no. 2, pp. 174–191.

Brooten, Lisa (2016) "Burmese Media in Transition." *International Journal of Communication*, vol. 10, pp. 182–199.

Brown, Ian (2013) *Burma's Economy in the Twentieth Century*. Cambridge: Cambridge University Press.

Brownlee, Jason (2007) *Authoritarianism in an Age of Democratization*. Cambridge: Cambridge University Press.

Brownlee, Jason (2009) "Portents of Pluralism: How Hybrid Regimes Affect Democratic Transitions." *American Journal of Political Science*, vol. 53, no. 3, pp. 515–532.

Buchanan, John (2016) *Militias in Myanmar*. Yangon: The Asia Foundation.

Bunce, Valerie (1995) "Should Transitologists Be Grounded?" *Slavic Review*, vol. 52, no. 1, pp. 111–127.

Bunce, Valerie (2000) "Comparative Democratization: Big and Bound Generalization." *Comparative Political Studies*, vol. 33, no. 6/7, pp. 703–734.

Bunce, Valerie (2004) "Comparative Democratization: Lessons from Russia and the Post-communist World." In Michael McFaul and Kathryn Stoner-Weiss (eds.), *After the Collapse of Communism: Comparative Lessons of Transition*. Cambridge: Cambridge University Press.

Bünte, Marco (2014) "Burma's Transition to Quasi-Military Rule: From Rulers to Guardians?" *Armed Forces & Society*, vol. 40, no. 4, pp. 742–764.

Bünte, Marco (2016) "Myanmar's Protracted Transition: Arenas, Actors and Outcomes." *Asian Survey*, vol. 56, no. 2, pp. 369–391.

Bünte, Marco (2017a) "The NLD-Military Coalition in Myanmar." In Paul Chambers and Napisa Waitoolkiat (eds.), *Khaki Capital*. Copenhagen: NIAS Press.

Bünte, Marco (2017b) "Policing Politics: Myanmar's Military Regime and Protest Spaces in Transition." In Eva Hansson and Meredith Weiss (eds.), *Political Participation in Asia: Defining & Deploying Political Space*. London: Routledge.

Bünte, Marco, and Dosch, Jörn (2015) "Myanmar: Political Reforms and the Recalibration of External Relations." *Journal of Current Southeast Asian Affairs*, vol. 34, no. 2, pp. 3–19.

Buschmann, Andy (2018) "Introducing the Myanmar Protest Event Dataset: Motivation, Methodology, and Research Prospects," *Journal of Current Southeast Asian Affairs*, Vol. 37, no. 2, pp. 125–142.

Buszynski, Leszek (1998) "Thailand and Myanmar: The Perils of 'Constructive Engagement'." *The Pacific Review*, vol. 11, no. 2, pp. 290–305.

Butwell, Richard (1961) "Civilian and Soldiers in Burma." In Robert K. Sakai (ed.), *Studies in Asia*. Lincoln: University of Nebraska Press.

Buzzi, Camilla, Hayes, Mike, and Mullen, Matthew (2012) *Education in Transition: A Preliminary Study of Capacity Development for Civil Society Actors in Burma/Myanmar*. Bangkok: Institute for Human Rights and Peace Studies, Mahidol University.

Callahan, Mary P. (2003) *Making Enemies: War and State Building in Burma*. Ithaca & London: Cornell University Press.

Callahan, Mary P. (2007a) "Of Kyay-zu and Kyet-su: The Burma/Myanmar Military in 2006." In Trevor Wilson and Monique Skidmore (eds.), *Myanmar: The State, Community and the Environment*. Canberra: ANU E-Press and Asia Pacific Press.

Callahan, Mary P. (2007b) "Political Authority in Burma's Ethnic Minority States: Devolution, Occupation, and Coexistence." *Policy Studies 31 (Southeast Asia)*. Washington, DC: East-West Center.

Callahan, Mary P. (2009) "Myanmar's Perpetual Junta: Solving the Riddle of the Tatmadaw's Long Reign." *New Left Review*, vol. 60, pp. 27–63.

Callahan, Mary P. (2012) "The Generals Loosen Their Grip." *Journal of Democracy*, vol. 23, no. 4, pp. 120–131.

Callahan, Mary P., and Myo Zaw Oo (2019) "Myanmar's 2020 Elections and Conflict Dynamics." In *Peaceworks*, no. 146. Washington, DC: United States Institute of Peace.

Callahan, Mary P., and Steinberg, David (2012) "Drivers of Change in Post-Junta, Constitutional Burma." Washington, DC: *US Agency for International Development*.

Calvert, Peter (ed.) (1987) *The Process of Political Succession*. London: Macmillan.

Calvert, Peter, and Burnell, Peter J. (eds.) (2004) *Civil Society in Democratization*. Portland: Frank Cass.

Campbell, Kurt, and Andrews, Brian (2013) "Explaining the US 'Pivot' to Asia." Programme Paper, London: Chatham House.

Capoccia, Giovanni, and Kelemen, R. Daniel (2007) "The Study of Critical Junctures: Theory, Narrative, and Counterfactuals in Historical Institutionalism." *World Politics*, vol. 59, no. 3, pp. 341–369.

Carlson, Melissa (2016) "Painting as Cipher: Censorship of the Visual Arts in Post-1988 Myanmar." *SOJOURN: Journal of Social Issues in Southeast Asia*, vol. 31, no. 1, pp. 117–172.

Carothers, Thomas (1994) "Democracy and Human Rights: Policy Allies or Rivals?" *The Washington Quarterly*, vol. 17, no. 3, pp. 109–120.

Carothers, Thomas (2002) "The End of the Transition Paradigm." *Journal of Democracy*, vol. 13, no. 1, pp. 5–21.

The Carter Center (2015) "Election Observation Mission, Myanmar General Elections, Preliminary Statement." November 10.

Casper, Gretchen, and Taylor, Michelle M. (1996) *Negotiating Democracy: Transitions from Authoritarian Rule*. Pittsburg, PA: University of Pittsburgh Press.

Cavatorta, Francesco (2013) "Civil Society Activism under Authoritarian Constraints." In Francesco Cavatorta (ed.), *Civil Society Activism under Authoritarian Rule: A Comparative Perspective*. London & New York: Routledge.

Centre for Peace and Conflict Studies (CPCS) (2009) *Listening to Voices from the Inside: Myanmar Civil Society's Response to Cyclone Nargis*. Phnom Penh: Centre for Peace and Conflict Studies.

Centre for Peace and Conflict Studies (CPCS) (2010) *Listening to Voices from the Inside: Ethnic People Speak*. Phnom Penh: Centre for Peace and Conflict Studies.

Chambers, Paul (2014) "Constitutional Change and Security Forces in Southeast Asia: Lessons from Thailand and Myanmar." *Contemporary Southeast Asia*, vol. 26, no. 1, pp. 101–127.

Chan, Debby Sze Wan (2017) "Asymmetric Bargaining between Myanmar and China in the Myitsone Dam Controversy: Social Opposition Akin to David's Stone against Goliath." *The Pacific Review*, vol. 30, no. 5, pp. 674–691.

Chan, Debby Sze Wan (2018) "China's Diplomatic Strategies in Response to Economic Disputes in Myanmar." *International Relations of the Asia-Pacific*, pp. 1–30.

Chang Wen-Chin (2013) "The Everyday Politics of the Underground Trade in Burma by the Yunnanese Chinese since the Burmese Socialist Era." *Journal of Southeast Asian Studies*, vol. 44, no. 2, pp. 292–314.

Charities Aid Foundation (2017) *World Giving Index 2014: A Global View of Giving Trends*.

Charney, Michael W. (2009) *A History of Modern Burma*. Cambridge: Cambridge University Press.

Cheesman, Nick (2002) "Seeing 'Karen' in the Union of Myanmar." *Asian Ethnicity*, vol. 3, no. 2, pp. 199–220.

Cheesman, Nick (2015) "That Signifier of Desire, the Rule of Law." *Social Research*, vol. 82, no. 2, pp. 267–290.

Cheesman, Nick, Farrelly, Nicholas, and Wilson, Trevor (eds.) (2014) *Debating Democratization in Myanmar*. Singapore: Institute of Southeast Asian Studies.

Chhor, Heang et al. (2013) *Myanmar's Moment: Unique Opportunities, Major Challenges*. McKinsey Global Institute.

Chit Min Tun (2019) "Tatmadaw Has Engagement with RCSS in Namtu." *Mizzima*, November 30. <http://mizzima.com/article/tatmadaw-has-engagement-rcss-namtu>, last accessed December 4, 2019.

Chow, Jonathan T., and Easley, Leif-Eric (2016) "Persuading Pariahs: Myanmar's Strategic Decision to Pursue Reform and Opening." *Pacific Affairs*, vol. 89, no. 3, pp. 521–542.

Chua, Lynette J. (2019) *The Politics of Love in Myanmar*. Stanford: Stanford University Press.

Chua, Lynette J., and Gilbert, David (2015) "Sexual Orientation and Gender Identity Minorities in Transition: LGBT Rights and Activism in Myanmar." *Human Rights Quarterly*, vol. 37, no. 1, pp. 1–28.

Cleveland, Sarah H. (2001) "Norm Internalization and US Economic Sanctions." *The Yale Journal of International Law*, vol. 26, no. 1, pp. 1–102.

Clinton, Hillary (2014) *Hard Choices*. New York: Simon & Schuster.

Clinton, William (1996) "Executive Order 6925-Suspension of Entry as Immigrants and Nonimmigrants of Persons who Formulate or Implement Policies That Are Impeding the Transition to Democracy in Burma or Who Benefit from Such Policies." *Federal Register*, vol. 61, October 7.

Clinton, William (1997) "Executive Order 13047-Prohibiting New Investment in Burma." *Federal Register*, vol. 62, no. 99, May 22.

Cooper, Frederick (2014) *Citizenship Between Empire and Nation: Remaking France and French Africa, 1945–1960*. Princeton: Princeton University Press.

Crispin, Shawn (2015) "What Does Myanmar's Purge Mean for Its Election?" *The Diplomat*, August 14. <https://thediplomat.com/2015/08/what-does-myanmars-purge-mean-for-its-election>, last accessed December 4, 2019.

Croissant, Aurel, and Kamerling, Jil (2013) "Why Do Military Regimes Institutionalize? Constitution-Making and Elections as Political Survival Strategy in Myanmar." *Asian Journal of Political Science*, vol. 21, no. 2, pp. 105–125.

Croissant, Aurel, and Kuehn, David (2009) "Patterns of Civilian Control of the Military in East Asia's New Democracies." *Journal of East Asian Studies*, vol. 9, no. 2, pp. 187–217.

Crouch, Melissa (2016) "Legislating Reform? Law and Conflict in Myanmar." In Nick Cheesman Cheesman and Nicholas Farrelly Farrelly (eds.), *Conflict in Myanmar: War, Politics, Religion*. Singapore: ISEAS Publications.

Crouch, Melissa (2019) "Renewed Calls for Constitutional Change in Myanmar's 'Military-State'." *East Asia Forum*. <www.eastasiaforum.org/2019/03/13/renewed-calls-for-constitutional-change-in-myanmars-military-state/>, last accessed May 15, 2019.

Curato, Nicole (2017) "Flirting with Authoritarian Fantasies? Rodrigo Duterte and the New Terms of Philippine Populism." *Journal of Contemporary Asia*, vol. 47, no. 1, pp. 142–153.

Dahl, Robert A. (1957) "The Concept of Power." *Behavioral Science*, vol. 2, no. 3, pp. 201–215.

David, Roman, and Holliday, Ian (2012) "International Sanctions or International Justice? Shaping Political Development in Myanmar." *Australian Journal of International Affairs*, vol. 66, no. 2, pp. 121–138.

David, Roman, and Holliday, Ian (2018) *Liberalism ad Democracy in Myanmar*. Oxford: Oxford University Press.

Department of Information (1962) *The Policy Declaration of the Revolutionary Council: The Burmese Way to Socialism*. Rangoon: Department of Information, April 30.

Dequech, David (2001) "Bounded Rationality, Institutions, and Uncertainty." *Journal of Economic Issues*, vol. 35, no. 4, pp. 911–929.

Desaine, Lois (2011) *The Politics of Silence: Myanmar's NGOs, Ethnic, Religious and Political Agenda*. IRASEC Occasional Paper 17. Bangkok: IRASEC.

Diamond, Larry (1999) *Developing Democracy: Toward Consolidation*. Baltimore: John Hopkins University Press.

Diamond, Larry (2002) "Election without Democracy: Thinking about Hybrid Regimes." *Journal of Democracy*, vol. 13, no. 2, pp. 21–35.

Diamond, Larry (2012) "The Need for a Political Pact." *Journal of Democracy*, vol. 23, no. 4, pp. 138–149.

Diller, Janelle M. (1997) "The National Convention and Impediment to the Restoration of Democracy." In Peter Carey (ed.), *Burma: The Challenge of Change in a Divided Society*. Basingstoke: Macmillan Press Ltd.

DiMaggio, Paul J., and Powell, Walter W. (1983) "The Iron Cage Revisited: Institutional Isomorphism and Collective Rationality in Organizational Fields." *American Sociological Review*, vol. 48, no. 2, pp. 147–160.

Di Palma, Giuseppe (1990) *To Craft Democracies: An Essay on Democratic Transitions*. Berkeley, CA: University of California Press.

Dorning, Karl (2006) "Creating an Environment for Participation: International NGOs and the Growth of Civil Society in Burma/Myanmar." In Trevor Wilson (ed.), *Myanmar's Long Road to National Reconciliation*. Singapore: ISEAS Publications.

Dosch, Jorn (2012) "The Role of Civil Society in Cambodia's Peace-Building Process: Have Foreign Donors Made a Difference?" *Asian Survey*, vol. 52, no. 6, pp. 1067–1088.

Duell, Kerstin (2014) "Sidelined or Reinventing Themselves? Exiled Activists in Myanmar's Political Reforms." In Nick Cheesman, Nicholas Farrelly, and Trevor Wilson (eds.), *Debating Democratization in Myanmar*. Singapore: Institute of Southeast Asian Studies.

Dukalskis, Alexander and Raymond, Christopher D. (2018) "Failure of Authoritarian Learning: Explaining Burma/Myanmar's Electoral System." *Democratization*, vol. 25, no. 3, pp. 545–563.

Dunant, Ben (2018) "Myanmar Democracy Activists Break Ranks with NLD Party." *Voice of America*, June 29.

Dunford, Michael R. (2019) "Indigeneity, Ethnopolitics, and *Taingyinthar*: Myanmar and the Global Indigenous Peoples' Movement." *Journal of Southeast Asian Studies*, vol. 50, no. 1, pp. 51–67.

EarthRights International (2008) *China in Burma: The Increasing Investment of Chinese Multinational Corporations in Burma's Hydropower, Oil and Natural Gas, and Mining Sectors*. Chiang Mai: EarthRights International.

Egreteau, Renaud (2008) "India's Ambitions in Burma: More Frustration Than Success?" *Asian Survey*, vol. 48, no. 6, pp. 936–957.

Egreteau, Renaud (2011) "Burmese Indians in Contemporary Burma: Heritage, Influence, and Perceptions since 1988." *Asian Ethnicity*, vol. 12, no. 1, pp. 33–54.

Egreteau, Renaud (2015) "Who Are the Military Delegates in Myanmar's 2010–2015 Union Legislature?" *Sojourn: Journal of Social Issues in Southeast Asia*, vol. 30, no. 2, pp. 338–370.

Egreteau, Renaud (2016) *Caretaking Democratization: The Military and Political Change in Myanmar*. London: Hurst & Co.

Egreteau, Renaud (2017) *Parliamentary Development in Myanmar: An Overview of the Union Parliament 2011–2016*. Yangon: The Asia Foundation.

Egreteau, Renaud, and Jagan, Larry (2008) *Back to the Old Habits: Isolationism or the Self-Preservation of Burma's Military Regime*. Bangkok: Research Institute on Contemporary Southeast Asia.

Egreteau, Renaud, and Jagan, Larry (2013) *Soldiers and Diplomacy in Burma: Understanding the Foreign Relations of the Burmese Praetorian State*. Singapore: NUS Press.

Ei Ei Toe Lwin (2015) "Consider the Party and the Candidate." *U Htay Oo*, September 2. <www.mmtimes.com/national-news/16276-consider-the-party-and-the-candidate-q-a-with-u-htay-oo.html>, last accessed December 5, 2019.

Ellis-Petersen, Hannah (2019) "Aung San Suu Kyi Finds Common Ground with Orbán over Islam." *The Guardian*, June 6. <www.theguardian.com/world/2019/jun/06/aung-san-suu-kyi-finds-common-ground-with-viktor-orban-over-islam>, last accessed December 5, 2019.

Emmerson, D. K. (2008) "ASEAN's Black Swans." *Journal of Democracy*, vol. 19, no. 3, pp. 70–84.

Encarnacion, Omar G. (2006) "Civil Society Reconsidered." *Comparative Politics*, vol. 38, no. 3, pp. 357–376.

Englehart, Neil A. (2005) "Is Regime Change Enough for Burma? The Problem of State Capacity." *Asian Survey*, vol. 45, no. 4, pp. 622–644.

Englehart, Neil A. (2012) "Two Cheers for Burma's Rigged Election." *Asian Survey*, vol. 52, no. 4, pp. 666–686.

Escriba-Folch, Abel, and Wright, Joseph (2010) "Dealing with Tyranny: International Sanctions and the Survival of Authoritarian Ruler." *International Studies Quarterly*, vol. 54, no. 2, pp. 335–359.

Ewing-Chow, Michael (2007) "First Do No Harm: Myanmar Trade Sanctions and Human Rights." *Northwestern Journal of International Human Rights*, vol. 5, no. 2, pp. 153–180.

Fan, Hongwei (2012) "ASEAN's 'Constructive Engagement' Policy toward Myanmar." *China International Studies*, March/April, pp. 54–70.

Farrelly, Nicholas (2013) "Discipline without Democracy: Military Dominance in Post-Colonial Burma." *Australian Journal of International Affairs*, vol. 67, no. 3, pp. 312–326.

Farrelly, Nicholas (2015) "Beyond Electoral Authoritarianism in Transitional Myanmar." *European Journal of East Asian Studies*, vol. 14, no. 1, pp. 15–31.

Farrelly, Nicholas, and Chit Win (2016) "Inside Myanmar's Turbulent Transformation." *Asia & the Pacific Policy Studies*, vol. 3, no. 1, pp. 35–44.

Feit, Edward (1972) *The Armed Bureaucrats: Military-Administrative Regimes and Political Development*. New York: Houghton Mifflin.

Ferrara, Federico (2003) "Why Regimes Create Disorder: Hobbes's Dilemma During a Rangoon Summer." *Journal of Conflict Resolution*, vol. 47, no. 3, pp. 302–325.

Findlay, Ronald, Park, Cyn-Young, and Verbiest, Jean-Pierre A. (2016) "Myanmar: Building Economic Foundations." *Asian-Pacific Economic Literature*, vol. 30, no. 1, pp. 42–64.

Finer, Samuel E. (1985) "The Retreat to the Barracks: Notes on the Practice and the Theory of Military Withdrawal from the Seats of Power." *Third World Quarterly*, vol. 7, no. 1, pp. 16–30.

Finer, Samuel E. (2002) [1962] *The Man on Horseback: The Role of the Military in Politics*. New Brunswick, NJ: Transaction Publishers.

Fink, Christina (2001) *Living Silence: Burma under Military Rule*. London & New York: Zed Books.

Fisher, Max (2017) "Myanmar, Once a Hope for Democracy, Is Now a Study in How It Fails." *The New York Times*, October 19. <www.nytimes.com/2017/10/19/world/asia/myanmar-democracy-rohingya.html>, last accessed December 4, 2019.

Fletcher, Gillian et al. (2014) "The Paung Ku Model: Encouraging Change through Learning." *Development in Practice*, vol. 24, no. 2, pp. 298–306.

Foley, Michael W., and Edwards, Bob (1996) "The Paradox of Civil Society." *Journal of Democracy*, vol. 7, no. 3, pp. 38–52.

Ford, Michele, Gillan, Michael, and Htwe Htwe Thein (2016) "From Cronyism to Oligarchy? Privatisation and Business Elites in Myanmar." *Journal of Contemporary Asia*, vol. 46, no. 1, pp. 18–41.

Frankenberg, Günter (2019) "Authoritarian Constitutionalism: Coming to Terms Withmodernity's Nightmares." In Helena Alviar García and Günter Frankenberg (eds.), *Authoritarian Constitutionalism: Critique and Appraisal*. Cheltenham: Edward Elgar Publishing.

Freedom House (2019) "Democracy in Retreat." In *Freedom in the World 2019*. Washington, DC & New York: Freedom House.

Freeman, Nick, Sorpong, Peou, and Tin Maung Maung Than (1997) "Political Outlook 1997–1998: Indochina and Myanmar." In *Regional Outlook: Southeast Asia, 1997–98*. Singapore: Institute of Southeast Asian Studies.

Fukuyama, Francis (1992) *The End of History and the Last Man*. New York: Free Press.

Fuller, Thomas (2012) "As Myanmar Changes, So Does Its Leader." *The New York Times*, April 4. <www.nytimes.com/2012/04/04/world/asia/myanmar-president-praises-weekend-elections.html>, last accessed December 4, 2019.

Fuller, Thomas (2015) "Myanmar's Military Uses Political Force to Block Constitutional Changes." *The New York Times*, June 26. <www.nytimes.com/2015/06/26/world/asia/myanmar-parliament-constitution-vote.html>, last accessed December 5, 2019.

Gandhi, Jennifer, and Przeworski, Adam (2006) "Cooperation, Cooptation, and Rebellion under Dictatorships." *Economics and Politics*, vol. 18, no. 1, pp. 1–26.

Ganesan, N. (2017) "Appraising Myanmar's Democratic Transition and Evolving Challenges." *Japanese Journal of Political Science*, vol. 18, no. 1, pp. 196–215.

Gans-Morse, Jordan (2004) "Searching for Transitologists: Contemporary Theories of Post-Communist Transitions and the Myth of a Dominant Paradigm." *Post-Soviet Affairs*, vol. 20, no. 4, pp. 320–349.

Geddes, Barbara, Frantz, Erica, and Wright, Joseph G. (2014) "Military Rule." *Annual Review of Political Science*, vol. 17, pp. 147–162.

Gelbort, Jason (2018) "Implementation of Burma's Vacant, Fallow and Virigin Land Management Law: At Odds with the Nationwide Ceasefire Agreement and Peace Negotiations." *Transnational Institute*. <www.tni.org/en/article/implementation-of-burmas-vacant-fallow-and-virgin-land-management-law>, last accessed July 29, 2019.

Gerschewski, Johannes (2013) "The Three Pillars of Stability: Legitimation, Repression, and Co-Optation in Autocratic Regimes." *Democratization*, vol. 20, no. 1, pp. 13–38.

Girke, Felix, and Beyer, Judith (2018) "'Transition' as a Migratory Model in Myanmar." *Journal of Burma Studies*, vol. 22, no. 2, pp. 215–241.

Gleeson, Sean (2015) "Still Not Sorry: Neither Modesty Nor Mea Culpa in Khin Nyunt Memoir." *The Irrawaddy*, March 3. <www.irrawaddy.com/news/burma/still-not-sorry-neither-modesty-nor-mea-culpa-in-khin-nyunt-memoir.html>, last accessed December 5, 2019.

Goldstone, Jack A. (1998) "Initial Conditions, General Laws, Path Dependence, and Explanation in Historical Sociology." *American Journal of Sociology*, vol. 104, no. 3, pp. 829–845.

Gravers, Mikael (1999) *Nationalism as Political Paranoia in Burma: An Essay on the History Practice of Power*. Richmond, Surrey: Curzon.

Guilmartin, John F., Jr. (1997) "Light Troops in Classical Armies: An Overview of Roles, Functions, and Factors Affecting Combat Effectiveness." In James C. Bradford (ed.), *The Military and Conflict between Cultures: Soldiers at the Interface*. College Station: Texas A&M University Press.

Guo, Xiaolin (2010) "Boom on the Way from Ruili to Mandalay." In Lex Rieffel (ed.), *Myanmar/Burma: Inside Challenges, Outside Interests*. Washington, DC: Konrad Adenauer Foundation and Brookings Institution Press.

Guyot, Dorothy (1966) "The Burma Independence Army: A Political Movement in Military Garb." In Josef Silverstein (ed.), *Southeast Asia in World War II: Four Essays*. New Haven: Yale University, Southeast Asia Studies.

Haacke, Jürgen (2006) *Myanmar's Foreign Policy: Domestic Influences and International Implications*. New York: Routledge.

Haacke, Jurgen (2008) "ASEAN and Political Change in Myanmar: Towards a Regional Initiative?" *Contemporary Southeast Asia*, vol. 30, no. 3, pp. 351–378.

Haccke, Jürgen (2010) "China's Role in the Pursuit of Security by Myanmar's State Peace and Development Council: Boon or Bane?" *Pacific Review*, vol. 23, no. 1, pp. 113–137.

Haacke, Jürgen (2011) "The Nature and Management of Myanmar's Alignment with China: The SLORC/SPDC Years." *Journal of Current Southeast Asian Affairs*, vol. 30, no. 2, pp. 105–140.

Haggard, Stephan, and Kaufman, Robert R. (1997) "The Political Economy of Democratic Transitions." *Comparative Politics*, vol. 29, no. 3, pp. 263–283.

Hall, Peter (1986) *Governing the Economy: The Politics of State Intervention in Britain and France.* Oxford: Oxford University Press.

Hammond, Clare (2019) "Is Shwe Mann Out in the Cold?" *Frontier Myanmar*, March 25. <https://frontiermyanmar.net/en/is-shwe-mann-out-in-the-cold>, last accessed December 5, 2019.

Hartley, Ryan (2018) "Japan's Rush to Rejuvenate Burma Relations: A Critical Reading of Post-2011 Efforts to Create 'New Old Friends'." *South East Asia Research*, vol. 26, no. 4, pp. 367–415.

Heidel, Brian (2006) *The Growth of Civil Society in Myanmar.* Bangalore: Books for Change.

Hein, Patrick (2018) "The Re-Ethnicisation of Politics in Myanmar and the Making of the Rohingya Ethnicity Paradox." *India Quarterly*, vol. 74, no. 4, pp. 361–382.

Henderson, Sarah L. (2002) "Selling Civil Society: Western Aid and the Nongovernmental Organization Sector in Russia." *Comparative Political Studies*, vol. 35, no. 2, pp. 139–167.

Holliday, Ian (2011) *Burma Redux: Global Justice and the Quest for Political Reform in Myanmar.* Hong Kong: Hong Kong University Press.

Holliday, Ian (2013) "Myanmar in 2012: Toward a Normal State." *Asian Survey*, vol. 53, no. 1, pp. 93–100.

Hollyer, James R., Peter, Rosendorff B., and Vreeland, James Raymond (2011) "Democracy and Transparency." *The Journal of Politics*, vol. 73, no. 4, pp. 1191–1205.

Horsey, Richard (2008) "The Dramatic Events of 2007 in Myanmar: Domestic and International Implications." In Monique Skidmore and Trevor Wilson (eds.), *Dictatorship, Disorder, and Decline in Myanmar.* Canberra: Australian National University E Press.

Howard, Marc Morjé (2003) *The Weakness of Civil Society in Post-Communist Europe.* Cambridge & New York: Cambridge University Press.

Howard, Marc Morjé, and Walters, Meir R. (2014) "Explaining the Unexpected: Political Science and the Surprises of 1989 and 2011." *Perspectives on Politics*, vol. 12, no. 2, pp. 394–408.

Howe, Brendan M., and Jang, Suyoun (2013) "Human Security and Development: Divergent Approaches to Burma/Myanmar." *Pacific Focus*, vol. 28, no. 1, pp. 120–143.

Htaike Htaike Aung, and Wai Myo Htut (2019) "From Blogging to Digital Rights: Telecommunications Reform in Myanmar." In Lisa Brooten, Jane McElhone, and Gayathry Venkiteswaran (eds.), *Myanmar Media in Transition: Legacies, Challenges and Change.* Singapore: Singapore: ISEAS-Yusof Ishak Institute.

Htet Khaung Linn (2018) "The Outsiders: Who Are the NLD's Military-Linked Leaders?" *Myanmar Now*, December 10. <https://myanmar-now.org/en/news/the-outsiders-who-are-the-nlds-military-linked-leaders>, last accessed December 5, 2019.

Htet Naing Zaw (2019a) "Charter Amendments Won't Pass without Military Support: U Shwe Mann." *The Irrawaddy*, August 5. <www.irrawaddy.com/news/burma/charter-amendments-wont-pass-without-military-support-u-shwe-mann.html>, last accessed December 5, 2019.

Htet Naing Zaw (2019b) "Myanmar Military Chief Defends Political Power." *The Irrawaddy*, December 2. <www.irrawaddy.com/news/burma/myanmar-military-chief-defends-political-power.html>, last accessed December 5, 2019.

Htoo Thant (2019) "Singapore Surpasses China as Myanmar's Biggest Investor." *Myanmar Times*, May 13. <www.mmtimes.com/news/singapore-surpasses-china-myanmars-biggest-investor.html>, last accessed December 5, 2019.

Htoo Thant, and Nyan Lynn Aung (2019) "Govt Orders Crackdown on Arakan Army." *Myanmar Times*, January 21. <www.mmtimes.com/news/govt-orders-crackdown-arakan-army.html>, last accessed December 5, 2019.

Htoo Thant, and Swan Ye Htut (2016) "Ex-President Purges Rivals from USDP." *Myanmar Times*, April 25. <www.mmtimes.com/national-news/19934-ex-president-purges-rivals-from-usdp.html>, last accessed December 5, 2019.

Huang, Chiung-Chiu (2015) "Balance of Relationship: The Essence of Myanmar's China Policy." *The Pacific Review*, vol. 28, no. 2, pp. 189–210.

Huang, Roger Lee (2013) "Re-Thinking Myanmar's Political Regime: Military Rule in Myanmar and Implications for Current Reforms." *Contemporary Politics*, vol. 19, no. 3, pp. 247–261.

Huang, Roger Lee (2017) "Myanmar's Way to Democracy and the Limits of the 2015 Elections." *Asian Journal of Political Science*, vol. 25, no. 1, pp. 25–44.

Human Rights Watch (HRW) (2009a) *Burma: One Year after Cyclone, Repression Continues*. <www.hrw.org/news/2009/04/30/burma-one-year-after-cyclone-repression-continues>, last accessed July 18, 2014.

Human Rights Watch (HRW) (2009b) *Burma's Forgotten Prisoners*. <www.hrw.org/sites/default/files/reports/burma0909_brochure_web.pdf>, last accessed July 18, 2014.

Human Rights Watch (HRW) (2016) "Burma: Growing Political Prisoner Population." January 17. <www.hrw.org/news/2016/01/17/burma-growing-political-prisoner-population>, last accessed January 19, 2016.

Human Rights Watch (HRW) (2019) "Dashed Hopes: The Criminalization of Peaceful Expression in Myanmar." January 31. <www.hrw.org/report/2019/01/31/dashed-hopes/criminalization-peaceful-expression-myanmar>, last accessed July 28, 2019.

Huntington, Samuel (1968) *Political Order in Changing Societies*. New Haven: Yale University Press.

Huntington, Samuel (1985) *The Soldier and the State: The Theory and Politics of Civil-Military Relations*. Cambridge, MA: Belknap Press of Harvard University Press.

Huntington, Samuel (1991) *The Third Wave: Democratization in the Late Twentieth Century*. Norman: University of Oklahoma Press.

Huntington, Samuel (1992) "How Countries Democratize." *Political Science Quarterly*, vol. 106, no. 4, pp. 578–616.

Ibrahim, Azeem (2018) "Democracy's False Dawn in Myanmar." *Washington Post*, August 7. <www.washingtonpost.com/news/democracy-post/wp/2018/08/07/democracys-false-dawn-in-myanmar>, last accessed December 5, 2019.

International Crisis Group (ICG) (2000) *Burma/Myanmar: How Strong Is the Military Regime?* Asia Report No. 11, December 21.

International Crisis Group (ICG) (2001) *Myanmar: The Military Regime's View of the World*. Asia Report No. 28, December 7.

International Crisis Group (ICG) (2004) *Myanmar: Sanctions, Engagement or Another Way Forward*. Asia Report No. 79, April 26.

International Crisis Group (ICG) (2006) *Myanmar: New Threats to Humanitarian Aid*. Asia Briefing No. 58, December 6.

International Crisis Group (ICG) (2008) *Burma/Myanmar after Nargis: Time to Normalise Aid Relations.* Asia Report No. 161, October 20.

International Crisis Group (ICG) (2009) *China's Myanmar Dilemma.* Asia Report No. 177, September 14.

International Crisis Group (ICG) (2011) *Myanmar's Post-Election Landscape.* Asia Briefing No. 118, March 7.

International Crisis Group (ICG) (2013a) *A Tentative Peace in Myanmar's Kachin Conflict.* Asian Briefing No. 140, June 12.

International Crisis Group (ICG) (2013b) *The Dark Side of Transition: Violence against Muslims in Myanmar.* Asia Report No. 251, October 1.

International Crisis Group (ICG) (2013c) *Not a Rubber Stamp: Myanmar's Legislature in a Time of Transition.* Asian Briefing No. 142, December 13.

International Crisis Group (ICG) (2014) *Myanmar's Military: Back to the Barracks?* Asia Briefing, No. 43, April 22.

International Crisis Group (ICG) (2015) *The Myanmar Elections: Results and Implications.* Asia Briefing, No. 147, December 9.

International Crisis Group (ICG) (2016) *Myanmar's New Government: Finding Its Feet?* Asia Report, No. 282, July 9.

International Crisis Group (ICG) (2017) *Building Critical Mass for Peace in Myanmar.* Asia Report, No. 287, June 29.

International Crisis Group (ICG) (2018) *Myanmar's Stalled Transition.* Asia Briefing, No. 151, August 28.

International Crisis Group (ICG) (2019) *Fire and Ice: Conflict and Drugs in Myanmar's Shan State.* Asia Report, No. 299, January 8.

International Monetary Fund (IMF) (2012) *Statement at the Conclusion of the 2011 Article IV Mission to Myanmar.* Press Release No. 12/25, January 25. <www.imf.org/external/np/sec/pr/2012/pr1225.htm>, last accessed February 10, 2012.

The Irrawaddy (2015a) "Ex-Spy Chief Criticizes Journalists in Rare On-Screen Interview." June 23. <www.irrawaddy.com/news/burma/ex-spy-chief-criticizes-journalists-in-rare-on-screen-interview.html>, last accessed December 5, 2019.

The Irrawaddy (2015b) "Tin Aye: I Want the USDP to Win, But to Win Fairly." June 29. <www.irrawaddy.com/election/interview/tin-aye-i-want-the-usdp-to-win-but-to-win-fairly>, last accessed December 5, 2019.

The Irrawaddy (2019) "In Their Own Words: Warnings against Constitutional Reform." February 22. <www.irrawaddy.com/news/burma/words-warnings-constitutional-reform.html>, last accessed December 5, 2019.

Jagan, Larry (2019) "Suu Kyi Gears Up for Genocide Hearing." *Bangkok Post*, December 2. <www.bangkokpost.com/opinion/opinion/1806409/suu-kyi-gears-up-for-genocide-hearing>, last accessed December 5, 2019.

James, Helen (2004) "Myanmar's International Relations Strategy: The Search for Security." *Contemporary Southeast Asia*, vol. 26, no. 3, pp. 530–553.

James, Helen (2005) *Governance and Civil Society in Myanmar: Education, Health, and Environment.* London & New York: Routledge Curzon.

James, Helen (2010) "Resources, Rent-Seeking, and Reform in Thailand and Myanmar (Burma)." *Asian Survey*, vol. 50, no. 2, pp. 426–448.

Janowitz, Morris (1964) *The Military in the Political Development of New Nations.* Chicago: Chicago University Press.

Jessop, Bob (1990) *State Theory: Putting the Capitalist State in Its Place.* Cambridge: Polity Press.

Jobert, Bruno, and Kohler-Koch, Beate (eds.) (2008) *Changing Images of Civil Society: From Protest to Governance*. New York: Routledge.

Jolliffe, Kim (2019) *Democratising Myanmar's Security Sector: Enduring Legacies and a Longroad Ahead*. London: Saferworld.

Jones, Bryan D. (2001) *Politics and the Architecture of Choice*. Chicago: Chicago University Press.

Jones, Lee (2008) "ASEAN's Albatross: ASEAN's Burma Policy, from Constructive Engagement to Critical Disengagement." *Asian Security*, vol. 4, no. 3, pp. 271–293.

Jones, Lee (2009) "Democratization and Foreign Policy in Southeast Asia the Case of the ASEAN Inter-Parliamentary Myanmar Caucus." *Cambridge Review of International Affairs*, vol. 22, no. 3, pp. 387–406.

Jones, Lee (2014a) "The Political Economy of Myanmar's Transition." *Journal of Contemporary Asia*, vol. 44, no. 1, pp. 144–170.

Jones, Lee (2014b) "Explaining Myanmar's Regime Transition: The Periphery Is Central." *Democratization*, vol. 21, no. 5, pp. 780–802.

Jones, Lee (2015) *Societies under Siege: Exploring How International Economic Sanctions (Do Not) Work*. Oxford: Oxford University Press.

Kaufmann, Christine (2007) *Globalisation and Labour Rights: The Conflict between Core Labour Rights and International Economic Law*. Oxford: Hart Publishing.

Kean, Thomas (2014) "Myanmar's Parliament: From Scorn to Significance." In Nick Cheesman, Nicholas Farrelly, and Trevor Wilson (eds.), *Debating Democratization in Myanmar*. Singapore: Institute of Southeast Asian Studies.

Keane, John (1998) *Civil Society: Old Images, New Visions*. Malden, MA: Polity Press.

Keck, Margaret E., and Sikkink, Kathryn (1998) *Activists Beyond Borders: Advocacy Networks in International Politics*. Ithaca & London: Cornell University Press.

Keenan, Paul (2012) *By Force of Arms: Armed Ethnic Groups in Burma*. Chiang Mai: The Burma Centre for Ethnic Studies.

Kenny, David A. (1994) *Interpersonal Perception: A Social Relations Analysis*. New York: The Guildford Press.

Kheang Un (2011) "Cambodia: Moving Away from Democracy?" *International Political Science Review*, vol. 32, no. 5, pp. 546–562.

Khin Myat Myat Wai (2019) "Ministry Condemns Fugitive Monk U Wirathu." *Myanmar Times*, June 17. <www.mmtimes.com/news/ministry-condemns-fugitive-monk-u-wirathu.html>, last accessed December 5, 2019.

Kim, Nam Kyu, and Kroeger, Alex M. (2018) "Regime and Leader Instability under Two Forms of Military Rule." *Comparative Political Studies*, vol. 51, no. 1, pp. 3–37.

Kipgen, Nehginpao (2016) *Democratisation of Myanmar*. New Delhi: Routledge.

Kopecký, Petr, and Muddle, Cas (eds.) (2003) *Uncivil Society? Contentious Politics in Post-Communist Europe*. London & New York: Routledge.

Kramer, Tom (2007) "The United Wa State Party: Narco-Army or Ethnic Nationalist Party?" In *Policy Studies 38 (Southeast Asia)*. Washington, DC: East-West Center.

Kramer, Tom (2011) *Civil Society Gaining Ground: Opportunities for Change and Development*. Amsterdam: Transnational Institute.

Kubo, Koji (2012) "Myanmar's Two Decades of Partial Transition to a Market Economy: A Negative Legacy for the New Government." *Institute of Developing Economies Discussion Paper*, no. 376, pp. 1–27.

Kucik, Peter (2016) *Difficulties in Easing Sanctions on Myanmar*. New York: The Center on Global Energy Policy, Columbia University.

Kudo, Toshihiro (2008) "The Impact of US Sanctions on the Myanmar Garment Industry." *Asian Survey*, vol. 48, no. 6, pp. 997–1017.

Kuhonta, Erik Martinez, and Sinpeng, Aim (2014) "Democratic Regression in Thailand: The Ambivalent Role of Civil Society and Political Institutions." *Contemporary Southeast Asia*, vol. 36, no. 3, pp. 333–355.

Kurti, Laszlo (2003) "The Uncivility of a Civil Society: Skinhead Youth in Hungary." In Petr Kopecký and Cas Muddle (eds.), *Uncivil Society? Contentious Politics in Post-Communist Europe*. London & New York: Routledge.

Kyaw Hsu Mon (2015) "Colorful Campaigns Set to Expand against Military Appointments." *The Irrawaddy*, September 16. <www.irrawaddy.com/news/burma/colorful-campaigns-set-to-expand-against-ministry-militarization.html>, last accessed December 5, 2019.

Kyaw Phyo Tha (2015) "Info Minister: Than Shwe Has No Influence over Political Transition." *The Irrawaddy*, December 11. <www.irrawaddy.com/election/news/info-minister-than-shwe-has-no-influence-over-political-transition>, last accessed December 5, 2019.

Kyaw Yin Hlaing (2003) "Reconsidering the Failure of the Burma Socialist Program Party Government to Eradicate Internal Economic Impediments." *South East Asia Research*, vol. 11, no. 1, pp. 5–58.

Kyaw Yin Hlaing (2004) "Civil Society in Burma: Skirting the Regime's Rule." In Muthiah Alagappa (ed.), *Civil Society and Political Change in Asia*. Stanford: Stanford University Press.

Kyaw Yin Hlaing (2007a) "Aung San Suu Kyi of Myanmar: A Review of the Lady's Biographies." *Contemporary Southeast Asia*, vol. 29, no. 2, pp. 359–376.

Kyaw Yin Hlaing (2007b) "Associational Life in Myanmar: Past and Present." In N. Ganesan and Kyaw Yin Hlaing (eds.), *Myanmar: State, Society and Ethnicity*. Singapore: Institute of Southeast Asian Studies, pp. 143–171.

Kyaw Yin Hlaing (2008) "Power and Factional Struggles in Post-Independence Burmese Governments." *Journal of Southeast Asian Studies*, vol. 39, no. 1, pp. 149–177.

Kyaw Yin Hlaing (2009) "Setting the Rules for Survival: Why the Burmese Military Regime Survives in an Age of Democratization." *The Pacific Review*, vol. 22, no. 3, July, pp. 271–291.

Kyaw Yin Hlaing (2010) "Problems with the Process of Reconciliation." In Lex Rieffel (ed.), *Myanmar/Burma: Inside Challenges, Outside Interests*. Washington, DC: Konrad Adenauer Foundation and Brookings Institution Press.

Kyaw Yin Hlaing (2012) "Understanding Recent Political Changes in Myanmar." *Contemporary Southeast Asia*, vol. 34, no. 2, pp. 197–216.

Kyaw Yin Hlaing (2013) "The Four-Eights Democratic Movement and Political Repression in Myanmar." In N. Ganesan and Sung Chull Kim (eds.), *State Violence in East Asia*. Lexington: The University Press of Kentucky.

Kyaw Yin Hlaing (2014a) "Political Impasse in Myanmar." In Kyaw Yin Hlaing (ed.), *Prisms on the Golden Pagoda: Perspectives on National Reconciliation in Myanmar*. Singapore: NUS Press.

Kyaw Yin Hlaing (2014b) "Reassessing the Economic Sanctions Imposed by Western Governments on Myanmar." In Kyaw Yin Hlaing (ed.), *Prisms on the Golden Pagoda: Perspectives on National Reconciliation in Myanmar*. Singapore: NUS Press.

Lall, Marie (2016) *Understanding Reform in Myanmar People and Society in the Wake of Military Rule*. London: Hurst.

Lang, Hazel J. (2002) *Fear and Sanctuary: Burmese Refugees in Thailand*. Ithaca, NY: SEAP Publications.

Lawi Weng (2019) "Myanmar Military Returns Base Near Thai Border to Mon National Liberation Army." *The Irrawaddy*, December 3. <www.irrawaddy.com/news/burma/myanmar-military-returns-base-near-thai-border-mon-national-liberation-army.html>, last accessed December 5, 2019.

Lee, Lavina (2014) "Myanmar's Transition to Democracy: New Opportunities or Obstacles for India?" *Contemporary Southeast Asia*, vol. 36, no. 2, pp. 290–316.

Lee, Pak K., Chan, Gerald, and Chan, Lai-Ha (2009) "China's 'Realpolitik' Engagement with Myanmar." *China Security*, vol. 5, no. 1, pp. 101–123.

Leong, Lorian (2017) "Mobile Myanmar: The Development of a Mobile App Culture in Yangon." *Mobile Media & Communication*, vol. 5, no. 2, pp. 139–160.

Levitsky, Steven, and Way, Lucan A. (2002) "The Rise of Competitive Authoritarianism." *Journal of Democracy*, vol. 13, no. 2, pp. 51–65.

Levitsky, Steven, and Way, Lucan A. (2006) "Linkage versus Leverage: Rethinking the International Dimension of Regime Change." *Comparative Politics*, vol. 38, no. 4, pp. 379–400.

Levitsky, Steven, and Way, Lucan A. (2010) *Competitive Authoritarianism: Hybrid Regimes after the Cold War*. New York: Cambridge University Press.

Li, Chenyang, and Lye, Liang Fook (2009) "China's Policies towards Myanmar: A Successful Model for Dealing with the Myanmar Issue?" *China: An International Journal*, vol. 7, no. 2, pp. 255–287.

Li, Chenyang, and Song, Shaojun (2018) "China's OBOR Initiative and Myanmar's Political Economy." *The Chinese Economy*, vol. 51, no. 4, pp. 318–332.

Li, Hak Yin, and Zheng, Yongnian (2009) "Re-Interpreting China's Non-Intervention Policy towards Myanmar: Leverage, Interest and Intervention." *Journal of Contemporary China*, vol. 18, no. 61, pp. 617–637.

Lidauer, Michael (2012) "Democratic Dawn? Civil Society and Elections in Myanmar 2010–2012." *Journal of Current Southeast Asian Affairs*, vol. 31, no. 2, pp. 87–114.

Liddell, Zunetta (1999) "No Room to Move: Legal Constraints on Civil Society in Burma." In *Strengthening Civil Society in Burma*. Chiang Mai: Silkworm Books, pp. 54–68.

Lieberman, Robert C. (2002) "Ideas, Institutions, and Political Order: Explaining Political Change." *American Political Science Review*, vol. 96, no. 4, pp. 697–712.

Lintner, Bertil (1989) *Outrage: Burma's Struggle for Democracy*. London: Review Publishing Company Ltd.

Lintner, Bertil (1990) *The Rise and Fall of the Communist Party of Burma*. Ithaca, NY: Southeast Asia Program, Cornell University.

Lintner, Bertil (1999) *Burma in Revolt: Opium and Insurgency since 1948* (2nd edn). Chiang Mai: Silkworm Books.

Lintner, Bertil (2000) "Drugs and Economic Growth in Burma Today." In Morten B. Pedersen, Emily C. Rudland, and Ronald May (eds.), *Burma/Myanmar: Strong Regime Weak State?* Adelaide, SA: Crawford House Publishing.

Lintner, Bertil (2015) "The Core Issues Not Addressed." *The Irrawaddy*, May 5. <www.irrawaddy.com/features/the-core-issues-not-addressed.html>, last accessed December 5, 2019.

Lintner, Bertil (2019) "The United Wa State Army and Burma's Peace Process." In *Peaceworks*, no. 147, Washington, DC: United States Institute of Peace.

Linz, Juan J., and Stepan, Alfred (1996) *Problems of Democratic Transition and Consolidation: Southern Europe, South America, and Post-Communist Europe*. Baltimore: John Hopkins University Press.

Liow, Joseph Chinyong (2017) *Ambivalent Engagement: The United States and Regional Security in Southeast Asia after the Cold War*. Washington, DC: Brookings Institution Press.

Lissak, Moshe (1976) *Military Roles in Modernization: Civil-Military Relations in Thailand and Burma*. Beverly Hills: Sage Publications.

London, Jonathan D. (2012) "Market Leninism." *Southeast Asia Research Centre Working Paper Series*, no. 124, pp. 1–57.

Lorch, Jasmin (2006) "Civil Society under Authoritarian Rule: The Case of Myanmar." *Journal of Current Southeast Asian Affairs*, vol. 25, no. 2, pp. 3–37.

Lorch, Jasmin (2008) "The (Re)emergence of Civil Society in Areas of State Weakness: The Case of Education in Burma/Myanmar." In Monique Skidmore and Trevor Wilson (eds.), *Dictatorship, Disorder and Decline in Myanmar*. Canberra: ANU E-Press.

Lovell, John, and Kim, Eugene (1967) "The Military and Political Change in Asia." *Pacific Affairs*, vol. 40, no. 1/2, pp. 113–123.

Lun Min Mang (2015) "Former Dictator Said to Accept Daw Suu as 'Future Leader'." *Myanmar Times*, December 5. <www.mmtimes.com/national-news/18002-former-dictator-said-to-accept-daw-suu-as-future-leader.html>, last accessed December 5, 2019.

Lun Min Mang et al. (2016) "Who's Who: Myanmar's New Cabinet." *Myanmar Times*, March 23. <www.mmtimes.com/national-news/nay-pyi-taw/19609-who-s-who-myanmar-s-new-cabinet.html>, last accessed December 5, 2019.

Lun Min Mang, and Htoo Thant (2016) "Shwe Mann to Hold Press Conference as Tatmadaw Takes a Swipe." *Myanmar Times*, April 27. <www.mmtimes.com/national-news/nay-pyi-taw/19977-shwe-mann-to-hold-press-conference-as-tatmadaw-takes-a-swipe.html>, last accessed December 5, 2019.

MacDonald, Adam P. (2013) "From Military Rule to Electoral Authoritarianism: The Reconfiguration of Power in Myanmar and Its Future." *Asian Affairs*, vol. 40, no. 1, pp. 20–36.

MacFarquhar, Neil (2010) "U.N. Doubts Fairness of Election in Myanmar." *The New York Times*, October 21.

Macgregor, Fiona (2016) "'Nationwide' Pact Turns into Disaster." *Myanmar Times*, February 19. <www.mmtimes.com/opinion/19086-nationwide-pact-turns-into-disaster.html>, last accessed December 5, 2019.

MacLachlan, Heather (2011) *Burma's Pop Music Industry: Creators, Distributors, Censors*. Rochester, NY: University of Rochester Press.

MacLean, Ken (2010) "The Emergence of Private Indirect Government in Burma." In Susan Levenstein (ed.), *Finding Dollars, Sense, and Legitimacy in Burma*. Washington, DC: Woodrow Wilson International Center for Scholars.

Mahoney, James (2000) "Path Dependence in Historical Sociology." *Theory and Society*, vol. 29, no. 4, pp. 507–548.

Mahoney, James, and Thelen, Kathleen (2010) "A Theory of Gradual Institutional Change." In James Mahoney and Thelen Kathleen (eds.), *Explaining Institutional Change: Ambiguity, Agency and Power*. New York & Cambridge: Cambridge University Press.

Malik, J. Mohan (1997) "Myanmar's Role in Regional Security: Pawn or Pivot?" *Contemporary Southeast Asia*, vol. 19, no. 1, pp. 52–73.

Malik, J. Mohan (2018) "Myanmar's Role in China's Maritime Silk Road Initiative." *Journal of Contemporary China*, vol. 27, no. 111, pp. 362–378.

Malik, Preet (2015) *My Myanmar Years: A Diplomat's Account of India's Relations with the Region*. New Delhi: Sage Publications India Pvt Ltd.

Malseed, Kevin (2009) "Networks of Noncompliance: Grassroots Resistance and Sovereignty in Militarised Burma." *The Journal of Peasant Studies*, vol. 36, no. 2, pp. 365–391.

Mann, Michael (1984) "The Autonomous Power of the State: Its Origins, Mechanism and Results." *European Journal of Sociology*, vol. 25, no. 2, pp. 185–213.

Manning, Frederick (1991) "Morale, Cohesion, and Esprit de Corps." In David A. Mangelsdorff and Reuven Gal (eds.), *Handbook of Military Psychology*. London: John Wiley.

March, James G. (1994) *Primer on Decision Making: How Decisions Happen*. New York: Free Press.

Mark, SiuSue (2012) "How Civil Society Can Engage with Policy Making in Myanmar's Transitional Context." *Journal of International Affairs*, July 29, <https://jia.sipa.colum bia.edu/online-articles/how-civil-society-can-engage-policy-making-myanmar%E2% 80%99s-transitional-context>, last accessed February 15, 2020.

Marston, Hunter (2013) "Myanmar's Electoral System: Reviewing the 2010 and 2012 Elections and Looking Ahead to the 2015 General Elections." *Asian Journal of Political Science*, vol. 21, no. 3, pp. 268–284.

Marti, Gabriela (2015) "The Role of the Constitutional Tribunal in Myanmar's Reform Process." *Asian Journal of Comparative Politics*, vol. 10, no. 1, pp. 153–184.

Martin, Michael F. (2010) *Burma's 2010 Elections: Implications of the New Constitution and Election Laws*. Washington, DC: Congressional Research Service.

Martin, Michael F. (2013a) *Burma's Political Prisoners and US Sanctions*. Washington, DC: Congressional Research Service.

Martin, Michael F. (2013b) *US Policy Towards Burma: Issues for the 113th Congress*. Washington, DC: Congressional Research Service.

Martin, Michael F. (2013c) *US Sanctions on Burma: Issues for the 113th Congress*. Washington, DC: Congressional Research Service.

Martson, Hunter (2013) "Myanmar's Electoral System: Reviewing the 2010 and 2012 Elections and Looking Ahead to the 2015 General Election." *Asian Journal of Political Science*, vol. 21, no. 3, pp. 268–284.

Masilamani, Logan, and Peterson, Jimmy (2014) "The 'ASEAN Way': The Structural Underpinnings of Constructive Engagement." *Foreign Policy Journal*, pp. 1–21.

Mathieson, David Scott (2015) "Myanmar Reneges on Effort to Free Political Prisoners." *Bangkok Post*, January 29.

Maung Aung Myoe (2009) *Building the Tatmadaw: Myanmar Armed Forces since 1948*. Singapore: Institute of Southeast Asian Studies.

Maung Aung Myoe (2011) *In the Name of Pauk-Phaw: Myanmar's China Policy Since 1948*. Singapore: Institute of Southeast Asian Studies.

Maung Aung Myoe (2014) "The Soldier and the State: The Tatmadaw and Political Liberalization in Myanmar since 2011." *Southeast Asia Research*, vol. 22, no. 2, pp. 233–249.

Maung Aung Myoe (2016) "Myanmar Military's White Paper Highlights Growing Openness." *Nikkei Asian Review*, March 28. <https://asia.nikkei.com/Politics/Maung-Aung-Myoe-Myanmar-military-s-white-paper-highlights-growing-openness>, last accessed December 3, 2019.

Maung Maung (1969) *Burma and General Ne Win*. London: Asia Publishing House.

Maung Maung (1999) *The 1988 Uprising in Burma*. New Haven, CT: Yale University Southeast Asia Studies.

Maung Maung (2015) [1962] *Aung San of Burma*. Yangon: Unity Publishing House.

Maung Zarni (2000) "Resistance and Cyber-Communities: The Internet and Free Burma Movement." In Anne De Vaney, Stephen Gance, and Yan Ma (eds.), *Technology and Resistance: Digital Communications and New Coalition around the World*. New York: Peter Lang International Academic Publishers.

Maung Zarni (2010) "Understanding Burma's Military Reshuffle." *The Irrawaddy*, September 6.

Maung Zarni (2012) "Orientalisation and Manufacturing of 'Civil Society' in Contemporary Burma." In Zawawi Ibrahim (ed.), *Social Science and Knowledge in a Globalising World*. Kajang: Malaysian Social Science Association and Petaling Jaya: Strategic Information and Research Development Centre, pp. 287–310.

McCarthy, Gerard (2019) *Military Capitalism in Myanmar: Examining the Origins, Continuities and Evolution of "Khaki Capital"*. Singapore: ISEAS-Yusof Ishak Institute.

McCarthy, Stephen (2006) *The Political Theory of Tyranny in Singapore and Burma: Aristotle and the Rhetoric of Benevolent Despotism*. London: Routledge.

McCarthy, Stephen (2008a) "Overturning the Alms Bowl: The Price of Survival and the Consequences for Political Legitimacy in Burma." *Australian Journal of International Affairs*, vol. 62, no. 3, pp. 298–314.

McCarthy, Stephen (2008b) "Burma and ASEAN: Estranged Bedfellows." *Asian Survey*, vol. 48, no. 6, pp. 911–935.

McCarthy, Stephen (2010) "From Coup d'Etat to 'Disciplined Democracy': The Burmese Regime's Claims to Legitimacy." In *Griffith Asia Institute, Regional Outlook*, no. 23. Brisbane: Griffith University.

McCarthy, Stephen (2012) "Civil Society in Burma: From Military Rule to 'Disciplined Democracy'." In *Griffith Asia Institute, Regional Outlook*, no. 37. Brisbane: Griffith University.

McCormick, Ty (2013) "Thein Sein Faces Ethnic Cleansing Charge, Accepts Peace Prize on Same Day." *Foreign Policy*, April 22. <https://foreignpolicy.com/2013/04/22/thein-sein-faces-ethnic-cleansing-charge-accepts-peace-prize-on-same-day/>, last accessed December 5, 2019.

McFaul, Michael (2010) "This Missing Variable: The 'International System' as the Link between Third and Fourth Wave Models of Democratization." In Valerie Bunce, Michael McFaul, and Kathryn Stoner-Weiss (eds.), *Democracy and Authoritarianism in the Postcommunist World*. Cambridge: Cambridge University Press.

Meehan, Patrick (2011) "Drugs, Insurgency and State-Building in Burma: Why the Drugs Trade Is Central to Burma's Changing Political Order." *Journal of Southeast Asian Studies*, vol. 42, no. 3, pp. 376–404.

Melvin, Jess (2017) "Mechanics of Mass Murder: A Case for Understanding the Indonesian Killings as Genocide." *Journal of Genocide Research*, vol. 19, no. 4, pp. 487–511.

Mercer, Claire (2002) "NGOs, Civil Society and Democratization: A Critical Review of the Literature." *Progress in Development Studies*, vol. 2, no. 1, pp. 5–22.

Mieno, Fumiharu (2013) "Toward Myanmar's New Stage of Development." *Asian Economic Policy Review*, no. 8, pp. 94–117.

Migdal, Joel (1988) *Strong Societies and Weak States: State-Society Relations and State Capabilities in the Third World*. Princeton, NJ: Princeton University Press.

Miklian, Jason (2019) "Contextualising and Theorising Economic Development, Local Business and Ethnic Cleansing in Myanmar." *Conflict, Security & Development*, vol. 19, no. 1, pp. 55–78.

Miles, Tom (2019) "Saudi Arabia and Russia among 37 States Backing China's Xinjiang Policy." *Reuters*, July 13. <www.reuters.com/article/us-china-xinjiang-rights/saudi-arabia-

and-russia-among-37-states-backing-chinas-xinjiang-policy-idUSKCN1U 721X>, last accessed December 5, 2019.

Miller, Michael K. (2012) "Electoral Authoritarianism and Democracy: A Formal Model of Regime Transitions." *Journal of Theoretical Politics*, vol. 25, no. 2, pp. 153–181.

Miller, Tom (2017) *China's Asian Dream: Empire Building Along the New Silk Road*. London: Zed Books.

Min Aung Hlaing (2019) "Senior General Min Aung Hlaing Receives Asahi Shimbun of Japan, Answers the Questions." February 17. <www.seniorgeneralminaunghlaing.com.mm/en/11912/senior-general-min-aung-hlaing-receives-asahi-shimbun-japan-answers-questions>, last accessed June 12, 2019.

Min Aung Khine (2019) "Arakanese Politician, Author Sentenced to 20 Years in Rakhine State." *The Irrawaddy*, March 19. <www.irrawaddy.com/news/burma/arakanese-politician-author-sentenced-20-years-rakhine-state.html>, last accessed December 5, 2019.

Ministry of Defense (1960) *The National Ideology and the Role of the Defence Services* (3rd edn). Yangon: Ministry of Defense.

Ministry of Information (1989) *The Conspiracy of Treasonous Minions within the Myanmar Naing-Ngan and Traitorous Cohort Abroad*. Yangon: Union of Myanmar Government.

Ministry of Information (2008) *Constitution of the Republic of the Union of Myanmar*. Naypyidaw: Union of Myanmar Government.

Min Zin (2002) "Ludu Daw Amar: Speaking Truth to Power." *The Irrawaddy*, vol. 10, no. 8.

Min Zin, and Joseph, Brian (2012) "The Opening in Burma: The Democrats' Opportunity." *Journal of Democracy*, vol. 23, no. 4, pp. 104–119.

Moe Thuzar (2012) "Myanmar: No Turning Back." In Daljit Singh and Pushpa Thambipillai (eds.), *Southeast Asian Affairs 2012*. Singapore: Institute of Southeast Asian Studies.

Mon Mon Myat (2019) "Films for Dignity." In Lisa Brooten, Jane McElhone, and Gayathry Venkiteswaran (eds.), *Myanmar Media in Transition: Legacies, Challenges and Change*. Singapore: Singapore: ISEAS-Yusof Ishak Institute.

Morgan, Andrew J. (2014) "Introduction: A Remarkable Occurrence: Progress for Civil Society in an 'Open' Myanmar." *Pacific Rim Law & Policy Journal Association*, vol. 23, no. 3, pp. 495–509.

Morgenbesser, Lee (2016) *Behind the Façade: Elections under Authoritarianism in Southeast Asia*. Albany: States University of New York Press.

Munck, Gerardo L., and Leff, Carol Skalnik (1997) "Modes of Transition and Democratization: South America and Eastern Europe in Comparative Perspective." *Comparative Politics*, vol. 29, no. 3, pp. 342–362.

Murray, David (1994) "From Battlefield to Market Place: Regional Economic Co-Operation in the Mekong Zone." *Geography*, vol. 79, no. 4, pp. 350–353.

Mutebi, Alex (2006) "Changing Governance and Governance Culture in Myanmar." In *Active Citizen under Wraps: Experiences from Myanmar/Burma and Vietnam*. Chiang Mai: Henrich Boll Foundation.

Mya Maung (1992) *Totalitarianism in Burma: Prospects for Economic Development*. New York: Paragon House.

Mya Maung (1994) "On the Road to Mandalay: A Case Study of the Sinonization of Upper Burma." *Asian Survey*, vol. 34, no. 5, pp. 447–459.

Myanmar National Human Rights Commission (MNHRC) (2014) "The Inquiry Report of the Myanmar National Human Rights Commission into the Death of Ko Aung Naing (a) Ko Aung Kyaw Naing (a) Ko Par Gyi." December 2. <www.mnhrc.org.mm/en/2014/12/

the-inquiry-report-of-the-myanmar-national-human-rights-commission-into-the-death-of-ko-aung-naing-a-ko-aung-kyaw-naing-a-ko-par-gyi/>, last accessed August 29, 2015.

Myanmar Times (2012) "Sanctions to Success: United States President Barak Obama's Historic Visit to Myanmar." November 19. <www.mmtimes.com/special-features/3175-sanctions-to-sucess.html>, last accessed December 5, 2019.

Myanmar Times (2019) "KNU Says It Had No Time for Peace Meeting." June 19. <www.mmtimes.com/news/knu-says-it-had-no-time-peace-meeting.html>, last accessed December 5, 2019.

Mya Than (1990) "Agriculture in Myanmar: What Has Happened to Asia's Rice Bowl?" *Southeast Asian Affairs*, pp. 240–254.

Mya Than (1992) *Myanmar's External Trade: An Overview in the Southeast Asian Context*. Singapore: Institute of Southeast Asian Studies.

Mya Than (2005) "Myanmar's Cross Border Economic Relations and Cooperation with the People's Republic of China and Thailand in the Greater Mekong Sub Region." *Journal of Greater Mekong Subregion Development Studies*, vol. 2, no. 1, pp. 37–54.

Myat Thein (2004) *Economic Development of Myanmar*. Singapore: Institute of Southeast Asian Studies.

Myat Thura (2019) "Ethnic Armed Alliance Launches Coordinated Attacks in Six Places." *Myanmar Times*, August 16. <www.mmtimes.com/news/ethnic-armed-alliance-launches-coordinated-attacks-six-places.html>, last accessed December 5, 2019.

Naing Ko Ko (2018) "Democratisation in Myanmar: Glue or Gloss?" In *Panorama: Insights Into Asian and European Affairs*. Singapore: Konrad-Adenauer-Stiftung Ltd.

Nakanishi, Yoshihiro (2013) *Strong Soldiers, Failed Revolution: The State and Military in Burma, 1962–1988*. Singapore: NUS Press & Kyoto University Press.

Nan Lwin (2018) "Major Reforms Around the Corner, Says Key Economic Adviser to Suu Kyi." *The Irrawaddy*, August 21. <www.irrawaddy.com/news/burma/major-reforms-around-the-corner-says-key-economic-adviser-to-suu-kyi.html>, last accessed December 5, 2019.

Nasir, Kamaludeen Mohamed, and Turner, Byran S. (2013) "Governing as Gardening: Reflections on Soft Authoritarianism in Singapore." *Citizenship Studies*, vol. 17, no. 3/4, pp. 339–352.

Naw Betty Han (2019a) "Rakhine in the Dark: Life after the Internet Blackout." *Frontier Myanmar*, July 16. <https://frontiermyanmar.net/en/rakhine-in-the-dark-life-after-the-internet-blackout>, last accessed July 16, 2019.

Naw Betty Han (2019b) "Filmmaker Min Htin Ko Ko Gyi Sentenced to One Year's Hard Labour." *Frontier Myanmar*, August 29. <https://frontiermyanmar.net/en/filmmaker-min-htin-ko-ko-gyi-sentenced-to-one-years-hard-labour>, last accessed December 4, 2019.

New Light of Myanmar (NLM) (2004) "Senior General Than Shwe Sends Felicitations to US President." November 6.

New Light of Myanmar (NLM) (2006) "The Plenary Meeting of National Convention Concluded." February 1.

New Light of Myanmar (NLM) (2008) "92.48 Percent Approve Constitution." May 27.

New Light of Myanmar (NLM) (2009) "Senior General Than Shwe Congratulates President of USA." January 23.

New Light of Myanmar (NLM) (2011a) "President U Thein Sein Delivers Inaugural Address to Pyidaungsu Hluttaw." March 31.

New Light of Myanmar (NLM) (2011b) "The Government Is Elected by the People and It Has to Respect People's Will." October 1.

Newton, Kenneth (2001) "Trust, Social Capital, Civil Society, and Democracy." *International Political Science Review*, vol. 22, no. 2, pp. 201–214.

The New York Times (2010) "Myanmar's Ruling Junta Is Selling State's Assets." March 7. <www.nytimes.com/2010/03/08/world/asia/08myanmar.html>, last accessed December 5, 2019.

Nordlinger, Eric A. (1970) "Soldiers in Mufti: The Impact of Military Rule Upon Economic and Social Change in the Non-Western States." *The American Political Science Review*, vol. 64, no. 4, pp. 1131–1148.

Nordlinger, Eric A. (1977) *Soldiers in Politics: Military Coups and Governments*. Englewoods Cliffs, NJ: Prentice-Hall.

Nyein Nyein (2019) "Indian Man Dies, Lawmaker still Held after AA Abduction in Myanmar's Rakhine State." *The Irrawaddy*, November 4. <www.irrawaddy.com/news/burma/indian-man-dies-lawmaker-still-held-after-aa-abduction-in-myanmars-rakhine-state.html>, last accessed December 5, 2019.

Nyi Nyi Kyaw (2019) "The Hardening Grip of Myanmar's Soft Media Repression." *East Asian Forum*. <www.eastasiaforum.org/2019/02/02/the-hardening-grip-of-myanmars-soft-media-repression>, last accessed July 26, 2019.

O'Donnell, Guillermo, and Schmitter, Philippe (eds.) (1986) *Transitions from Authoritarian Rule: Tentative Conclusions about Uncertain Democracies*. Baltimore: Johns Hopkins University Press.

O'Donnell, Guillermo, Schmitter, Philippe, and Whitehead, Laurence (eds.) (1986) *Transitions from Authoritarian Rule: Comparative Perspectives*. Baltimore: The Johns Hopkins University Press.

Okamoto, Ikuko (2008) *Economic Disparity in Rural Myanmar: Transformation under Market Liberalization*. Singapore: NUS Press.

Organization for Economic Cooperation and Development (OECD) (2015) *Geographical Distribution of Financial Flows to Developing Countries: Disbursements, Commitments, Country Indicators*. Paris: OECD Publishing.

Ortmann, Stephan, and Thompson, Mark R. (2016) "China and the 'Singapore Model'." *Journal of Democracy*, vol. 27, no. 1, pp. 39–48.

Osnos, Evan (2012) "Letter from Rangoon: The Burmese Spring." *The New York*, August 6. <www.newyorker.com/magazine/2012/08/06/the-burmese-spring>, last accessed December 5, 2019.

Paddock, Richard C. (2018) "From Hero to Pariah, Aung San Suu Kyi Dashes Hopes about Myanmar." *New York Times*, September 29. <www.nytimes.com/2018/09/29/world/asia/myanmar-aung-san-suu-kyi-rohingya.html>, last accessed December 5, 2019.

Pape, Robert A. (1997) "Why Economic Sanctions Do Not Work." *International Security*, vol. 22, no. 2, pp. 90–136.

Park, Cyn-Young, Khan, Muhamma Ehsan, and Vandenberg, Paul (2012) *Myanmar in Transition: Opportunities and Challenges*. Mandaluyong City, Philippines: Asian Development Bank.

Paung Ku (2010) *Strengthening Civil Society in Myanmar*. Yangon: Paung Ku.

Paung Ku (2013) *Growing Networks? Supporting Networks in Myanmar: A Case Study of Paung Ku and Village Networks in the Ayeyawaddy Delta*. Yangon: Paung Ku.

Pedersen, Morten B. (2008) *Promoting Human Rights in Burma: A Critique of Western Sanctions Policy*. Lanham, MD: Rowman & Littlefield.

Pedersen, Morten B. (2010) "Burma, the International Community, and Human Rights (with Particular Attention to the Role of Foreign Aid)." In Susan Levenstein (ed.),

Finding Dollars, Sense, and Legitimacy in Burma. Washington, DC: Woodrow Wilson International Center for Scholars.

Pedersen, Morten B. (2011) "The Politics of Burma's 'Democratic' Transition: Prospects for Change and Options for Democrats." *Critical Asian Studies*, vol. 43, no. 1, pp. 49–68.

Pedersen, Morten B. (2014) "Myanmar's Democratic Opening: The Process and Prospect of Reform." In: Nicholas Cheesman, Nicholas Farrelly, and Trevor Wilson (eds.), *Debating Democratization in Myanmar*. Singapore: ISEAS Publications, pp. 19–42.

Pedersen, Morten B. (2019) "Myanmar in 2018: New Democracy Hangs in the Balance." *Southeast Asian Affairs*, pp. 224–241.

Pe Myint (2012) "The Emergence of Myanmar Weekly New Journals and Their Development in Recent Years." In Nick Cheesman, Monique Skidmore, and Trevor Wilson (eds.), *Myanmar's Transition: Openings, Obstacles, and Opportunities*. Singapore: Institute of Southeast Asian Studies, pp. 204–213.

Perlmutter, Amos (1969) "The Praetorian State and the Praetorian Army: Toward a Taxonomy of Civil-Military Relations in Developing Countries." *Comparative Politics*, vol. 1, no. 3, pp. 382–404.

Perlmutter, Amos (1974) *Egypt: The Praetorian State*. New Brunswick, NJ: Transaction Publishers.

Perry, Peter J. (2007) *Myanmar (Burma) since 1962: The Failure of Development*. Aldershot: Ashgate.

Peters, Guy B., Pierre, Jon, and King, Desmond S. (2005) "The Politics of Path Dependency: Political Conflict in Historical Institutionalism." *The Journal of Politics*, vol. 67, no. 4, pp. 1275–1300.

Pevehouse, Jon (2005) *Democracy from Above: Regional Organizations and Democratization*. Cambridge: Cambridge University Press.

Pfeffer, Jeffery, and Salancik, Gerald (1978) *The External Control of Organizations: A Resource Dependence Perspective*. New York: Harper & Row.

Pick, David, and Htwe Htwe Thein (2010) "Development Failure and the Resource Curse: The Case of Myanmar." *International Journal of Sociology and Social Policy*, vol. 30, no. 5/6, pp. 267–279.

Pierson, Paul (2004) *Politics in Time: History, Institutions, and Social Analysis*. Princeton & Oxford: Princeton University Press.

Pishchikova, Kateryna (2007) "What Happened after the 'End of History'? Foreign Aid and Civic Organizations in Ukraine." In Derrick Purdue (ed.), *Civil Societies and Social Movements: Potentials and Problems*. London & New York: Routledge.

Poppe, Annika E. (2019) "Harmony and Resilience: US Democracy Promotion's Basic Premises." *Foreign Policy Analysis*, vol. 15, no. 4, pp. 530–547.

Posner, Daniel N. (2004) "Civil Society and the Reconstruction of Failed States." In Robert Rotberg (ed.), *When States Fail: Causes and Consequences*. Princeton, NJ: Princeton University Press.

Prager-Nyein, Susanne (2009) "Expanding Military, Shrinking Citizenry and the New Constitution in Burma." *Journal of Contemporary Asia*, vol. 39, no. 4, pp. 638–648.

Prager-Nyein, Susanne (2013) "Aung San Suu Kyi between Biographical Myth and Hard Realities." *Journal of Contemporary Affairs*, vol. 43, no. 3, pp. 546–554.

Prasse-Freeman, Elliott (2012) "Power, Civil Society, and an Inchoate Politics of the Daily in Burma/Myanmar." *The Journal of Asian Studies*, vol. 71, no. 2, pp. 371–397.

Przeworski, Adam (1991) *Democracy and Markets: Political and Economic Reforms in Latin America and Eastern Europe*. Cambridge: Cambridge University Press.

Przeworski, Adam et al. (2000) *Democracy and Development: Political Institutions and Well-Being in the World, 1950–1990.* Cambridge: Cambridge University Press.

Putnam, Robert D. (1993) *Making Democracy Work: Civic Traditions in Modern Italy.* Princeton: Princeton University Press.

Putnam, Robert D. (2007) "E Pluribus Unum: Diversity and Community in the Twenty-First Century." *Scandinavian Political Studies*, vol. 20, no. 2, pp. 137–174.

Rab, Habib Nasser et al. (2016) *Myanmar Economic Monitor: Growing Economic Vulnerabilities.* Myanmar Economic Monitor 2016. Washington, DC: World Bank Group.

Radio Free Asia (RFA) (2013) "Myanmar's Speaker Says Junta Constitution Written to 'Transfer Power'." September 9. <www.rfa.org/english/news/myanmar/constitution-09092013175352.html>, last accessed September 10, 2013.

Radio Free Asia (RFA) (2015) "Interview: Retiree Than Shwe Exerts 'No Influence Whatsoever' on Myanmar Politics." August 20. <www.rfa.org/english/news/myanmar/influence-08202015151523.html>, last accessed August 24, 2015.

Regan, Helen, and Stout, David (2014) "A Reporter's Death Shows Just How Little Burma Has Changed." *Time*, November 4. <https://time.com/3550460/burma-myanmar-military-journalist-killing-aung-kyaw-naing>, last accessed December 5, 2019.

Renshaw, Catherine S. (2013) "Democratic Transformation and Regional Institutions: The Case of Myanmar and ASEAN." *Journal of Current Southeast Asian Affairs*, vol. 32, no. 1, pp. 29–54.

Reynolds, Andrew, Stepan, Alfred C., Zaw Oo, and Levine, Stephen I. (2001) "How Burma Could Democratize." *Journal of Democracy*, vol. 12, no. 4, pp. 95–108.

Rieffel, Lex (2015) "Policy Options for Improving the Performance of the State Economic Enterprise Sector in Myanmar." *The ISEAS Working Paper Series*, no. 1. Singapore: Yusof Ishak Institute.

Rieffel, Lex, and Fox, James W. (2013) *Too Much, Too Soon? The Dilemma of Foreign Aid to Myanmar/Burma?* Arlington, VA: Nathan Associates Inc.

Riley, Mark S., and Balaram, Ravi A. (2013) "The United States International Military Education and Training (IMET) Program with Burma/Myanmar: A Review of the 1980–1988 Programming and Prospects for the Future." *Asian Affairs: An American Review*, vol. 40, no. 3, pp. 109–132.

Risse, Thomas, and Babayan, Nelli (2015) "Democracy Promotion and the Challenges of Illiberal Regional Powers: Introduction to the Special Issue." *Democratization*, vol. 22, no. 3, pp. 381–399.

Risse, Thomas, Ropp, Stephen C., and Sikkink, Kathryn (1999) *The Power of Human Rights: International Norms and Domestic Change.* Cambridge: Cambridge University Press.

Roberts, Christopher (2010) *ASEAN's Myanmar Crisis: Challenges to the Pursuit of a Security Community.* Singapore: Institute of Southeast Asian Studies.

Robinson, Gwen (2012) "Transcript of Interview with Thein Sein." *Financial Times*, July 12. <www.ft.com/cms/s/0/98722032-cba8-11e1-911e-0144feabdc0.html#axzz3aByZTgI3>, last accessed May 10, 2015.

Robinson, Gwen (2013) "The Listener-in-Chief: On the Road with Burma's Reformist President." *Foreign Policy*, November 19.

Rodan, Garry, Hewison, Kevin, and Robison, Richard (2006) "Theorising Markets in South-East Asia: Power and Contestation." In Gary Rodan, Kevin Hewison, and Richard Robison (eds.), *The Political Economu of South-East Asia: Markets, Power and Contestation* (3rd edn). Oxford & New York: Oxford University Press.

Rosenblum, Nancy L., and Lesch, Charles H. T. (2011) "Civil Society and Government." In Michael Edwards (ed.), *The Oxford Handbook of Civil Society*. Oxford: Oxford University Press.

Rotberg, Robert I. (2004) "Failed States, Collapsed States, Weak States: Causes and Indicators." In Robert I. Rotberg (ed.), *When States Fail, Causes and Consequences*. Princeton: Princeton University Press, pp. 1–25.

Rouquié, Alain (1986) "Demilitarization and the Institutionalization of Military-Dominated Polities in Latin America." In Guillermo O'Donnell, Philippe C. Schmitter, and Laurence Whitehead (eds.), *Transitions from Authoritarian Rule: Comparative Perspectives*. Baltimore, MD: John Hopkins University Press.

Safi, Michael (2019) "Aung San Suu Kyi to Defend Myanmar against Genocide Charge at The Hague." *The Guardian*, November 21.

Saha, Soubhik Ronnie (2011) *Working through Ambiguity: International NGOs in Myanmar*. The Hauser Center for Nonprofit Organizations, Harvard University.

Sai Wansai (2018) "Constitution-Making and Peace Process Stagnation in Myanmar: Will a Conditional Clause Help Restore Confidence in the 21st Century Panglong Conference?" In: *Myanmar Commentary*. Amsterdam: The Transnational Institute.

Sakhing, Lian H. (2014) "Burma at a Crossroad." In Kyaw Yin Hlaing (ed.), *Prisms on the Golden Pagoda: Perspectives on National Reconciliation in Myanmar*. Singapore: National University of Singapore Press.

Santini, Ruth Hanau, and Hassan, Oz (2012) "Transatlantic Democracy Promotion and the Arab Spring." *The International Spectator: Italian Journal of International Affairs*, vol. 47, no. 3, pp. 65–82.

San Yamin Aung (2019) "Total Number of Defamation Cases under Telecommunications Law Hits 200." *The Irrawaddy*, June 24. <www.irrawaddy.com/news/burma/total-number-defamation-cases-telecommunications-law-hits-200.html>, last accessed December 5, 2019.

Sardamov, Ivelin (2005) "Civil Society and the Limits of Democratic Assistance." *Government and Opposition*, vol. 40, no. 3, pp. 379–402.

Saw Yan Naing (2017) "The UNFC Will Continue to Exist as Long as It Continues to Be Useful to Its Members." *The Irrawaddy*, April 4. <www.irrawaddy.com/in-person/127767.html>, last accessed December 5, 2019.

Schedler, Andreas (2002) "Elections without Democracy: The Menu of Manipulation." *Journal of Democracy*, vol. 13, no. 2, pp. 36–50.

Schedler, Andreas (2006) "The Logic of Electoral Authoritarianism." In Andreas Schedler (ed.), *Electoral Authoritarianism: The Dynamics of Unfree Competition*. Boulder & London: Lynne Rienner Publishers.

Schedler, Andreas (2010) "Authoritarianism's Last Line of Defense." *Journal of Democracy*, vol. 21, no. 1, pp. 69–80.

Schmitter, Philippe, and Karl, Terry Lynn (1991) "What Democracy Is … and Is Not." *Journal of Democracy*, vol. 2, no. 3, pp. 75–88.

Schonthal, Benjamin, and Walton, Matthew J. (2016) "The (New) Buddhist Nationalisms? Symmetries and Specificities in Sri Lanka and Myanmar." *Contemporary Buddhism*, vol. 17, no. 1, pp. 81–115.

Seekins, Donald M. (1997) "Burma-China Relations: Playing with Fire." *Asian Survey*, vol. 37, no. 6, pp. 525–539.

Seekins, Donald M. (1999) "The North Wind and the Sun: Japan's Response to the Political Crisis in Burma, 1988–1998." *The Journal of Burma Studies*, vol. 4, pp. 1–33.

Seekins, Donald M. (2005a) "Burma and US Sanctions: Punishing an Authoritarian Regime." *Asian Survey*, vol. 45, no. 3, pp. 437–452.

Seekins, Donald M. (2005b) "The State and the City: 1988 and the Transformation of Rangoon." *Pacific Affairs*, vol. 78, no. 2, pp. 257–275.

Seekins, Donald M. (2007) *Burma and Japan since 1940: From "Co-Prosperity" to "Quiet Dialogue".* Copenhagen: NIAS Press.

Seekins, Donald M. (2009) "State, Society and Natural Disaster: Cyclone Nargis in Myanmar (Burma)." *Asian Journal of Social Science*, vol. 37, no. 5, pp. 717–737.

Seekins, Donald M. (2010) *State and Society in Modern Rangoon.* London & New York: Routledge.

Selth, Andrew (1986) "Race and Resistance in Burma, 1942–1945." *Modern Asian Studies*, vol. 20, no. 3, pp. 483–507.

Selth, Andrew (2002) *Burma's Armed Forces: Power without Glory.* Norwalk: EastBridge.

Selth, Andrew (2008a) "Burma's 'Saffron Revolution' and the Limits of International Influence." *Australian Journal of International Affairs*, vol. 62, no. 3, pp. 281–297.

Selth, Andrew (2008b) "Even Paranoids Have Enemies: Cyclone Nargis and Myanmar's Fears of Invasion." *Contemporary Southeast Asia*, vol. 30, no. 3, pp. 379–402.

Selth, Andrew (2010) "Burma and North Korea: Conventional Allies or Nuclear Partners?" *Australian Journal of International Affairs*, vol. 64, no. 2, pp. 141–165.

Selth, Andrew (2019) "Myanmar's Intelligence Apparatus and the Fall of General Khin Nyunt." *Intelligence and National Security*, vol. 34, no. 5, pp. 619–636.

Shen, Simon, and Chan, Paul Chi-yuen (2010) "Failure of the Saffron Revolution and Aftermath: Revisiting the Transitologist Assumption." *The Journal of Comparative Asian Development*, vol. 9, no. 1, pp. 31–57.

Shils, Edward A., and Janowitz, Morris (1948) "Cohesion and Disintegration in the Wehrmacht in World War II." *Public Opinion Quarterly*, vol. 12, no. 2, pp. 280–315.

Shleifer, Andrei, and Treisman, Daniel (2000) *Without a Map: Political Tactics and Economic Reform in Russia.* Cambridge: Cambridge University Press.

Shwe Aung (2014) "Amending Constitution Will 'Hurt the People', Says Thein Sein." *Democratic Voice of Burma*, May 17. <www.dvb.no/news/amending-constitution-will-hurt-the-people-says-thein-sein-burma-myanmar/40799>, last accessed May 17, 2014.

Shwe Gas Movement (2009) *Corridor of Power: China's Trans-Burma Oil and Gas Pipelines.* Chiang Mai: Shwe Gas Movement.

Shwe Lu Maung (1989) *Burma, Nationalism and Ideology: An Analysis of Society, Culture, and Politics.* Dhaka: University Press.

Shwe Yee Saw Myint (2015) "Black Ribbons Fail to Deter Militarisation of Health Ministry." *Myanmar Times*, August 31. <www.mmtimes.com/national-news/16219-black-ribbons-fail-to-deter-militarisation-of-health-ministry.html>, last accessed December 5, 2019.

Shwe Yee Saw Myint (2016) "Lost in Non-Communication: NLD Media Ban Frustrates." *Myanmar Times*, January 8. <www.mmtimes.com/national-news/18393-lost-in-non-communication-nld-media-ban-frustrates.html>, last accessed December 5, 2019.

Silverman, David (1994) *Interpreting Qualitative Data Methods for Analysing Talk, Text and Interaction.* London: Sage Publications.

Silverstein, Josef (1977) *Burma, Military Rule and the Politics of Stagnation.* Ithaca: Cornell University Press.

Silverstein, Josef (1997) "Fifty Years of Failure in Burma." In Michael E. Brown and Sumit Ganguly (eds.), *Government Policies and Ethnic Relations in Asia and the Pacific.* Cambridge: MIT Press.

Silverstein, Josef (2001) "Burma and the World: A Decade of Foreign Policy under the State Law and Order Restoration Council." In Robert H. Taylor (ed.), *Burma: Political Economy under Military Rule*. London: Hurst & Company.

Silverstein, Josef, and Wohl, Julian (1964) "University Students and Politics in Burma." *Pacific Affairs*, vol. 37, no. 1, pp. 50–65.

Simpson, Adam (2013) "An 'Activist Diaspora' as a Response to Authoritarianism in Myanmar: The Role of Transnational Activism in Promoting Political Reform." In Francesco Cavatorta (ed.), *Civil Society Activism under Authoritarian Rule: A Comparative Perspective*. London & New York: Routledge.

Simpson, Adam, and Park, Susan (2013) "The Asian Development Bank as a Global Risk Regulator in Myanmar." *Third World Quarterly*, vol. 34, no. 10, pp. 1858–1871.

Singh, Swaran (1997) "The Sinicization of Myanmar and Its Implications for India." *Issues & Studies*, vol. 33, no. 1, pp. 116–133.

Sithu Aung Myint (2016) "A Lesson in Defusing Tensions." *Frontier Myanmar*, May 22. <https://frontiermyanmar.net/en/lesson-defusing-tensions>, last accessed May 14, 2019.

Skidmore, Monique (2004) *Karaoke Fascism: Burma and the Politics of Fear*. Philadelphia, PA: University of Pennsylvania Press.

Slater, Dan (2010a) "Altering Authoritarianism: Institutional Complexity and Autocratic Agency in Indonesia." In James Mahoney and Kathleen Thelen (eds.), *Explaining Institutional Change: Ambiguity, Agency, and Power*. Cambridge: Cambridge University Press.

Slater, Dan (2010b) *Ordering Power: Contentious Politics and Authoritarian Leviathans in Southeast Asia*. Cambridge & New York: Cambridge University Press.

Slater, Dan (2014) "The Elements of Surprise, Assessing Burma's Double-Edged Détente." *South East Asia Research*, vol. 22, no. 2, pp. 171–182.

Smith, Martin (1999) *Burma: Insurgency and the Politics of Ethnicity*. London: Zed Books.

Smith, Martin (2007a) *State of Strife: The Dynamics of Ethnic Conflict in Burma*. Washington, DC: East-West Center.

Smith, Martin (2007b) "Ethnic Politics and Regional Development in Myanmar: The Need for New Approaches." In Kyaw Yin Hlaing, Robert H. Taylor, and Tin Maung Maung Than (eds.), *Myanmar: Beyond Politics to Societal Imperatives*. Singapore: Institute of Southeast Asian Studies.

Smith, Martin, and Allsebrook, Annie (1994) *Ethnic Groups in Burma: Development, Democracy and Human Rights*. London: Anti-Slavery International.

Soe Thane (2018) *Myanmar's Transformation & U Thein Sein*. Yangon: Tun Foundation Literature Committee.

Song, Lili (2017) "Refugees or Border Residents from Myanmar? The Status of Displaced Ethnic Kachins and Kokangs in Yunnan Province, China." *International Journal of Refugee Law*, vol. 29, no. 3, pp. 466–487.

South, Ashley (2003) *Mon Nationalism and Civil War in Burma: The Golden Sheldrake*. London: RoutledgeCurzon.

South, Ashely (2004) "Political Transition in Myanmar: A New Model for Democratization." *Contemporary Southeast Asia*, vol. 26, no. 4, pp. 233–255.

South, Ashely (2007) "Ceasefires and Civil Society: The Case of the Mon." In Mikael Graver (ed.), *Exploring Ethnic Diversity in Burma*. Copenhagen: Nordic Institute of Asian Studies Press.

South, Ashley (2008) *Ethnic Politics in Burma: States of Conflict*. New York: Routledge.

South, Ashley (2011) *Burma's Longest War: Anatomy of the Karen Conflict*. Amsterdam: Burma Center Netherlands.

South, Ashley (2018) "'Hybrid Governance' and the Politics of Legitimacy in the Myanmar Peace Process." *Journal of Contemporary Asia*, vol. 48, no. 1, pp. 50–66.

South China Morning Post (2015) "'I'll Be above the President ...': Aung San Suu Kyi Determined to Lead Despite the Constitutional Block on Leading Myanmar." November 14. <www.scmp.com/news/asia/southeast-asia/article/1878700/whos-charge-after-myanmars-elections-aung-san-suu-kyi>, last accessed July 22, 2019.

Spetalnick, Matt (2014) "Obama Optimistic on Change in Burma, More Work to Be Done." *Reuters*, November 13.

Springer, Simon (2010) *Cambodia's Neoliberal Order: Violence, Authoritarianism, and the Contestation of Public Space*. New York & London: Routledge.

Steinberg, David I. (1982) "Economic Growth with Equity? The Burmese Experience." *Contemporary Southeast Asia*, vol. 4, no. 2, pp. 124–152.

Steinberg, David I. (1990) "Japanese Economic Assistance to Burma: Aid in the 'Tarenagashi' Manner?" *Crossroad: An Interdisciplinary Journal of Southeast Asian Studies*, vol. 5, no. 2, pp. 51–107.

Steinberg, David I. (1999) "A Void in Myanmar: Civil Society in Burma." In David Steinberg (ed.), *Strengthening Civil Society in Burma*. Burma Center Netherlands & Transnational Institute. Chiang Mai: Silkworm Books.

Steinberg, David I. (2001) *Burma, the State of Myanmar*. Washington, DC: Georgetown University Press.

Steinberg, David I. (2006) "Civil Society and Legitimacy: The Basis for National Reconciliation in Burma/Myanmar." In Trevor Wilson (ed.), *Myanmar's Long Road to National Reconciliation*. Singapore: ISEAS Publications.

Steinberg, David I. (2010a) "The United States and Myanmar: A 'Boutique Issue'?" *International Affairs*, vol. 86, no. 1, pp. 175–194.

Steinberg, David I. (2010b) "Aung San Suu Kyi and US Policy toward Burma/Myanmar." *Journal of Current Southeast Asian Affairs*, vol. 29, no. 3, pp. 35–59.

Steinberg, David I., and Fan, Hongwei (2012) *Modern China-Myanmar Relations: Dilemmas of Mutual Dependence*. Copenhagen: Nordic Institute of Asian Studies Press.

Stepan, Alfred (1988) *Rethinking Military Politics: Brazil and the Southern Cone*. Princeton: Princeton University Press.

Stokke, Kristian, Khine Win, and Soe Myint Aung (2015) "Political Parties and Popular Representation in Myanmar's Democratization Process." *Journal of Current Southeast Asian Affairs*, vol. 34, no. 3, pp. 3–35.

Stokke, Kristian, and Soe Myint Aung (2019) "Transition to Democracy or Hybrid Regime? The Dynamics and Outcomes of Democratization in Myanmar." *European Journal of Development Research*.

Strefford, Patrick (2005) "Japanese ODA to Myanmar: Resulting from the Mutual Dependence It Created." *Journal of International Cooperation Studies*, vol. 13, no. 2, pp. 109–133.

Stuart-Fox, Martin (1989) "Laos in 1988: In Pursuit of New Directions." *Asian Survey*, vol. 29, no. 1, pp. 81–88.

Steinmo, Sven (2008) "What Is Historical Institutionalism?" In Donatella Della Porta and Michael Keating (eds.), *Approaches and Methodologies in the Social Sciences: A Pluralist Perspective*. Cambridge: Cambridge University Press.

Steinmo, Sven, Thelen, Kathleen, and Longstreth, Frank (eds.) (1992) *Structuring Politics: Historical Institutionalism in Comparative Analysis*. Cambridge: Cambridge University Press.

Sun, Yun (2014) "China, the United States and the Kachin Conflict." *Issue Brief.* Washington, DC: Stimson Center.

Sundhaussen, Ulf (1984) "Military Withdrawal from Government Responsibility." *Armed Forces & Society*, vol. 10, no. 4, pp. 543–562.

Svolik, Milan W. (2009) "Power Sharing and Leadership Dynamics in Authoritarian Regimes." *American Journal of Political Science*, vol. 53, no. 2, pp. 477–494.

Svolik, Milan W. (2012) *The Politics of Authoritarian Rule.* New York: Cambridge University Press.

Szep, Jason, and Marshall, Andrew R. C. (2012) "Special Report: An Image Makeover for Myanmar Inc." *Reuters*, April 13.

Takahashi, Nobuo (2015) "Where Is Bounded Rationality From?" *Annals of Business Administrative Science*, vol. 14, pp. 67–82.

Tanneberg, Dag, Stefes, Christoph, and Merkel, Wolfgang (2013) "Hard Times and Regime Failure: Autocratic Responses to Economic Downturns." *Contemporary Politics*, vol. 19, no. 1, pp. 115–129.

Taylor, Robert H. (1974) *The Relationship between Burmese Social Classes and British-Indian Policy on the Behaviour of the Burmese Political Elite, 1937–1942.* PhD Thesis. Ithaca: Cornell University.

Taylor, Robert H. (1979) "Burma's National Unity Problem and the 1974 Constitution." *Contemporary Southeast Asia*, vol. 1, no. 3, pp. 232–248.

Taylor, Robert H. (1986) "Burmese Concepts of Revolution." In Mark Hobart and Robert H. Taylor (eds.), *Context, Meaning, and Power in Southeast Asia*. Ithaca: Cornell University Southeast Asia Program.

Taylor, Robert H. (1989) "Burma: Political Leadership, Security Perceptions and Policies." In Mohammed Ayoob and Chai-Anan Samudavanija (eds.), *Leadership Perceptions and National Security: The Southeast Asian Experience*. Singapore: Institute of Southeast Asian Studies.

Taylor, Robert H. (1991) "Myanmar in 1990: New Era or Old?" In *Southeast Asian Affairs 1991*. Singapore: Institute of Southeast Asian Studies, pp. 199–219.

Taylor, Robert H. (1995) "Disaster or Release? J.S. Furnivall and the Bankruptcy of Burma." *Modern Asian Studies*, vol. 29, no. 1, pp. 45–64.

Taylor, Robert H. (1996) "Elections in Burma/Myanmar: For Whom and Why?" In Robert H. Taylor (ed.), *The Politics of Elections in Southeast Asia*. Cambridge: Woodrow Wilson Center Press & Cambridge University Press.

Taylor, Robert H. (ed.) (2001) *Burma: Political Economy under Military Rule.* New York: Palgrave Macmillan.

Taylor, Robert H. (2005) "Do States Make Nations? The Politics of Identity in Myanmar Revisited." *South East Asia Research*, vol. 13, no. 2, pp. 261–286.

Taylor, Robert H. (2006) "Colonial Forces in British Burma: A National Army Postponed." In Karl Hack and T. Rettig (eds.), *Colonial Armies in Southeast Asia*. London: Routledge.

Taylor, Robert H. (2008) *Dr Maung Maung: Gentleman, Scholar, Patriot.* Singapore: ISEAS Publications.

Taylor, Robert H. (2009) *The State in Myanmar.* Honolulu: The University of Hawaii Press.

Taylor, Robert H. (2012a) "Myanmar: From Army Rule to Constitutional Rule?" *Asian Affairs*, vol. 43, no. 2, pp. 221–236.

Taylor, Robert H. (2012b) "Obama in Myanmar: A Visit with Limited Significance." *ISEAS Perspective*, November 19.

Taylor, Robert H. (2013) "Myanmar's 'Pivot' toward the Shibboleth of 'Democracy'." *Asian Affairs*, vol. 44, no. 3, pp. 392–400.

Taylor, Robert H. (2014) "The Third Constitution of the Union of Myanmar." In Kyaw Yin Hlaing (ed.), *Prisms on the Golden Pagoda: Perspectives on National Reconciliation in Myanmar*. Singapore: NUS Press.

Taylor, Robert H. (2015a) *The Armed Forces in Myanmar Politics: A Terminating Role?* Singapore: Institute of Southeast Asian Studies Publishing.

Taylor, Robert H. (2015b) *General Ne Win: A Political Biography*. Singapore: ISEAS Publications.

Teets, Jessica C. (2009) "Post-Earthquake Relief and Reconstruction Efforts: The Emergence of Civil Society in China?" *China Quarterly*, vol. 198, pp. 330–347.

Teets, Jessica C. (2013) "Let Many Civil Societies Bloom: The Rise of Consultative Authoritarianism in China." *China Quarterly*, vol. 213, pp. 19–38.

Teivainen, Teivo (2002) *Enter Economism, Exit Politics: Experts, Economic Policy and the Damage to Democracy*. London & New York: Zed Books.

Teorell, Jan (2010) *Determinants of Democratization Explaining Regime Change in the World, 1972–2006*. Cambridge: Cambridge University Press.

Thalemann, Andrea (1997) "Laos: Between Battlefield and Marketplace." *Journal of Contemporary Asia*, vol. 27, no. 1, pp. 85–105.

Thant Myint-U (2007) *The River of Lost Footsteps: A Personal History of Burma*. London: Faber and Faber.

Thant Myint-U (2019) *The Hidden History of Burma: Race, Capitalism, and the Crisis of Democracy in the 21st Century*. New York: W. W. Norton & Company.

Tharaphi Than (2016) "Mongla and the Borderland Politics of Myanmar." *Asian Anthropology*, vol. 15, no. 2, pp. 152–168.

Thawnghmung, Ardeth Maung (2003) "Preconditions and Prospects for Democratic Transition in Burma/Myanmar." *Asian Survey*, vol. 43, no. 3, pp. 443–460.

Thawnghmung, Ardeth Maung (2004) *Behind the Teak Curtain: Authoritarianism, Agricultural Policies and Political Legitimacy in Rural Burma/Myanmar*. London: Kegan Paul.

Thawnghmung, Ardeth Maung (2011) "The Politics of Everyday Life in Twenty-First Century Myanmar." *The Journal of Asian Studies*, vol. 70, no. 3, August, pp. 641–656.

Thawnghmung, Ardeth Maung (2014) "Contending Approaches to Communal Violence in Rakhine State." In Mikael Gravers and Felmming Ytzen (eds.), *Burma/Myanmar: Where Now?* Copenhagen: NIAS Press.

Thawnghmung, Ardeth Maung (2016) "The Myanmar Elections 2015: Why the National League for Democracy Won a Landslide Victory." *Critical Asian Studies*, vol. 48, no. 1, pp. 132–142.

Thawnghmung, Ardeth Maung (2017) Signs of Life in Myanmar's Nationwide Ceasefire Agreement? Finding a Way Forward." *Critical Asian Studies*, vol. 49, no. 3, pp. 379–395.

Thawnghmung, Ardeth Maung, and Maung Aung Myoe (2008) "Myanmar in 2007: A Turning Point in the Roadmap?" *Asian Survey*, vol. 48, no. 1, pp. 13–19.

Thawnghmung, Ardeth Maung, and Robinson, Gwen (2017) "Myanmar's New Era: A Break from the Past, or Too Much of the Same?" *Southeast Asian Affairs*, pp. 238–257.

Thelen, Kathleen (1999) "Historical Institutionalism in Comparative Politics." *Annual Review of Political Science*, vol. 2, pp. 369–404.

Thelen, Kathleen, and Steinmo, Sven (1992) "Historical Institutionalism in Comparative Politics." In Sven Steinmo, Kathleen Thelen, and Frank Longstreth (eds.), *Structuring*

Politics: Historical Institutionalism in Comparative Analysis. Cambridge: Cambridge University Press.

Thompson, Mark R. (2004) *Democratic Revolutions: Asia and Eastern Europe.* London: Routledge.

Thompson, Mark R. (2008) "People Power Sours: Uncivil Society in Thailand and the Philippines." *Current History*, vol. 107, no. 712, pp. 381–387.

Tin Maung Maung Than (2001) "The 'New Professionalism' of the Tatmadaw." In Muthiah Alagappa (ed.), *Military Professionalism in Asia: Conceptual and Empirical Perspectives.* Honolulu: East West Center, pp. 163–179.

Tin Maung Maung Than (2004) "The Essential Tension: Democratization and the Unitary State in Myanmar (Burma)." *South East Asia Research*, vol. 12, no. 2, pp. 187–212.

Tin Maung Maung Than (2007) *State Dominance in Myanmar: The Political Economy of Industrialization.* Singapore: Institute of Southeast Asian Studies.

Tin Maung Maung Than (2012) "Burma/Myanmar's By-Elections: Will Personalities Trump Institutions?" *Asia Pacific Bulletin*, no. 161, April 20.

Tin Maung Maung Than (2013) "The 1988 Uprising in Myanmar: Historical Conjuncture or Praetorian Redux?" In N. Ganesan (ed.), *Conjunctures and Continuities in Southeast Asian Politics.* Singapore: ISEAS Publications.

Tin Maung Maung Than (2014) "Introductory Overview: Myanmar's Economic Reforms." *Journal of Southeast Asian Economies*, vol. 31, no. 2, pp. 165–172.

Tin Maung Maung Than (2015a) "Myanmar's Economic Reforms: Hard Choices Ahead." *Social Research*, vol. 82, no. 2, pp. 453–480.

Tin Maung Maung Than (2015b) "Myanmar in 2014: Great Expectations Unfulfilled." *Asian Survey*, vol. 55, no. 1, pp. 184–191.

Transnational Institute (2015) "Ethnic Politics and the 2015 Elections in Myanmar." *Myanmar Policy Briefing*, September 16.

Tripartite Core Group (TCG) (2008) *Post-Nargis Joint Assessment*, July.

Tonkin, Derek (2007) "The 1990 Elections in Myanmar: Broken Promises or a Failure of Communication?" *Contemporary Southeast Asia*, vol. 29, no. 1, pp. 33–54.

Tonkin, Derek (2014) "The Burmese Exile Community and the National Reconciliation Process." In Kyaw Yin Hlaing (ed.), *Prisms on the Golden Pagoda: Perspectives on National Reconciliation in Myanmar.* Singapore: NUS Press.

Tourangbam, Monish, and Amin, Pawan (2019) "China's Dynamic Grip on Myanmar." *The Diplomat.* <https://thediplomat.com/2019/05/chinas-dynamic-grip-on-myanmar>, last accessed June 29, 2019.

Trager, Frank N. (1963) "The Failure of U Nu and the Return of the Armed Forces in Burma." *The Review of Politics*, vol. 25, no. 3, pp. 309–328.

The Transnational Institute (TNI) (2015) "The 2015 General Election in Myanmar: What Now for Ethnic Politics?" *Myanmar Policy Briefing*, no. 17, December.

Trubowitz, Peter (1998) *Defining the National Interest: Conflict and Change in American Foreign Policy.* Chicago: Chicago University Press.

Turnell, Sean (2008) "Burma's Insatiable State." *Asian Survey*, vol. 48, no. 6, pp. 958–976.

Turnell, Sean (2009) *Fiery Dragons: Banks, Moneylenders and Microfinance in Burma.* Copenhagen: NIAS Press.

Turnell, Sean, Bradford, Wylie, and Vicary, Alison (2009) "Burma's Economy 2009: Disaster, Recovery … and Reform." *Asian Politics and Policy*, vol. 1, no. 4, pp. 631–659.

Turnell, Sean, Vicary, Alison, and Bradford, Wylie (2008) "Migrant Worker Remittances and Burma: An Economic Analysis of Survey Results." *Burma Economic Watch Working Paper.*

Tushnet, Mark (2015) "Authoritarian Constitutionalism." *Cornell Law Review*, vol. 100, no. 2, pp. 391–462.

United Nations Human Rights Council (UNHRC) (2018) *Report of the detailed findings of the Independent International Fact-Finding Mission on Myanmar, A/HRC/39/CRP.2,* September 18). <https://www.ohchr.org/Documents/HRBodies/HRCouncil/FFM-Myanmar/A_HRC_39_CRP.2.pdf>, last accessed February 15, 2020.

UNHRC (2019) *The Economic Interests of the Myanmar Military, Independent International Fact-Finding Mission on Myanmar, A/HRC/42/CRP.3,* September 12. <https://www.ohchr.org/Documents/HRBodies/HRCouncil/FFM-Myanmar/EconomicInter estsMyanmarMilitary/A_HRC_42_CRP_3.pdf>, last accessed February 15, 2020.

United Nations Office on Drugs and Crime (UNODC) (2014) *World Drug Report 2014.* New York: United Nations Publication.

United Nations Security Council (UNSC) (2007) *Security Council Fails to Adopt Draft Resolution on Myanmar Owing to Negative Votes by China, Russia Federation.* Press Release No. SC/8939, January 12. <www.un.org/press/en/2007/sc8939.doc.htm>, last accessed February 12, 2012.

UNODC (2019) *Transnational Organized Crime in Southeast Asia: Evolution, Growth and Impact.* Bangkok: UNODC Regional Office for Southeast Asia and the Pacific.

U Nu (1975) *Saturday's Son.* New Haven: Yale University Press.

US Department of State (n.d.) "Derek J. Mitchell." *Biography.* <www.state.gov/r/pa/ei/biog/170595.htm>, last accessed August 14, 2014.

US Department of State (2010) *Comments by Secretary Clinton in Hanoi, Vietnam.* <http://iipdigital.usembassy.gov/st/english/texttras/2010/07/20100723164658su0.4912989.html>, last accessed June 3, 2015.

US Department of the Treasury (2013) "Treasury Designates Burmese LT. General Thein Htay, Chief of Directorate of Defense Industries." Press Release, July 2. <www.treasury.gov/press-center/press-releases/Pages/jl1998.aspx>, last accessed March 11, 2014.

US Department of the Treasury (2014) "Announcement of Treasury Sanctions against Aung Thaung." Press Release, October 31. <www.treasury.gov/press-center/press-releases/Pages/JL2680.aspx>, last accessed November 3, 2014.

US Embassy (2004a) "Than Shwe and Khin Nyunt: A Contrast in Style." Yangon, January 5, last accessed October 10, 2014.

US Embassy (2004b) "Activists Arrested on Anniversary of Depayin." Yangon, June 1, last accessed December 2, 2019.

US Embassy (2006) "NLD's Flexible Offer to the Burmese Regime." Yangon, February 22, last accessed May 1, 2015.

US Embassy (2007a) "GOB Tried to Defend Its Actions against Protestors." Yangon, September 27, last accessed May 1, 2015.

US Embassy (2007b) "Lee Kuan Yew on Burma's 'Stupid' Generals and the 'Gambler' Chen Shui-Bian." Singapore, October 19, last accessed November 30, 2019.

US Embassy (2007c) "Burma: Pavo Trading's Financial Activities." Singapore, November 1, last accessed September 13, 2015.

US Embassy (2008a) "Burma: No Love for Than Shwe." Yangon, January 28, last accessed November 30, 2019.

US Embassy (2008b) "Exiles See Opportunity for Political Change in Nargis." Chiang Mai, May 15, last accessed August 5, 2013.

US Embassy (2008c) "Burma: Cronies Told to Rebuild the Delta." Yangon, May 20, last accessed August 5, 2013.

US Embassy (2009) "Burma's Generals: Starting the Conversation." Yangon, April 2, last accessed March 12, 2014.

US Embassy (2010) "Burma: ASEAN Presence Winding Down: No Role Envisioned in Elections." Yangon, February 5, last accessed March 12, 2014.

Venkiteswaran, Gayathry, Yin Yadanar Thein, and Myint Kyaw (2019) "Legal Changes for Media and Expression: New Reforms, Old Controls." In Lisa Brooten, Jane McElhone, and Gayathry Venkiteswaran (eds.), *Myanmar Media in Transition: Legacies, Challenges and Change*. Singapore: Singapore: ISEAS-Yusof Ishak Institute.

Wade, Francis (2015) "Burma's Militarized Ministries." *Foreign Policy*, November 15. <https://foreignpolicy.com/2015/11/15/burmas-militarized-ministries>, last accessed September 30, 2019.

Wai Moe (2011) "Steven Law's Rising Empire." *The Irrawaddy*, July 22.

Wai Moe, and Ramzy, Austin (2015) "Myanmar Sentences 3 to Prison for Depicting Buddha Wearing Headphones." *The New York Times*, March 17.

Wai Moe, and Ramzy, Austin (2016) "Myanmar Approves Cabinet Nominees, But Some Face Questions over Credentials." *The New York Times*, March 24.

Wa Lone (2014) "Behind the Student Protests." *Myanmar Times*, November 24.

Walton, Matthew J. (2008) "Ethnicity, Conflict, and History in Burma: The Myths of Panglong." *Asian Survey*, vol. 48, no. 6, pp. 889–910.

Walton, Matthew J. (2013) "The 'Wages of Burman-Nes': Ethnicity and Burman Privilege in Contemporary Myanmar." *Journal of Contemporary Asia*, vol. 43, no. 1, pp. 1–27.

Walton, Matthew J. (2015) "Buddhism, Politics, and Political Change." In David I. Steinberg (ed.), *Myanmar: The Dynamics of an Evolving Polity*. Boulder, CO: Lynne Rienner.

Walton, Matthew J., and Hayward, Susan (2014) *Contesting Buddhist Narratives: Democratization, Nationalism, and Communal Violence in Myanmar*. Policy Studies No. 71. Honolulu: East West Center.

Walton, Matthew J., McKay, Melyn, and Daw Khin Mar Mar Kyi (2015) "Women and Myanmar's 'Religious Protection Laws'." *The Review of Faith & International Affairs*, vol. 13, no. 4, pp. 36–49.

Walzer, Michael (1995) "Introduction." In Michael Walzer (ed.), *Toward a Global Civil Society*. Providence: Bergham Books.

Wang, Zichang (2014) "Myanmar Political Development in 2013." *Southeast Asian Studies*, no. 2, pp. 28–34.

Ware, Anthony, and Laoutides, Costas (2019) "Myanmar's 'Rohingya' Conflict: Misconceptions and Complexity." *Asian Affairs*, vol. 50, no. 1, pp. 60–79.

Warf, Barney (2011) "Geographies of Global Internet Censorship." *GeoJournal*, vol. 76, no. 1, pp. 1–23.

Wells, Tamas (2018) "Democratic 'freedom' in Myanmar." *Asian Journal of Political Affairs,* vol. 26, no. 1, pp. 1–15.

Weyland, Kurt (2008) "Toward a New Theory of Institutional Change." *World Politics*, vol. 60, no. 2, pp. 281–314.

Weymouth, Lally (2012) "Burma President Thein Sein: Country Is on 'Right Track to Democracy'." *Washington Post*, January 19. <www.washingtonpost.com/opinions/burma-president-thein-sein-country-is-on-right-track-to-democracy/2012/01/19/gIQA NeM5BQ_story.html>, last accessed December 5, 2019.

Whang, Taehee (2011) "Playing to the Home Crowd? Symbolic Use of Economic Sanctions in the United States." *International Studies Quarterly*, vol. 55, no. 3, pp. 787–801.

Williams, David C. (2011) "Cracks in the Firmament of Burma's Military Government: From Unity through Coercion to Buying Support." *Third World Quarterly*, vol. 32, no. 7, pp. 1199–1215.

Williams, David C. (2012) "Changing Burma from without: Political Activism among the Burmese Diaspora." *Indiana Journal of Global Legal Studies*, vol. 19, no. 1, pp. 121–142.

Wilson, Trevor (2014) "Debating Democratization in Myanmar." In Nick Cheesman, Nicholas Farrelly, and Trevor Wilson (eds.), *Debating Democratization in Myanmar*. Singapore: Institute of Southeast Asian Studies.

Win Min (2008a) "Internal Dynamics of the Burmese Military: Before, during and after the 2007 Demonstrations." In Monique Skidmore and Trevor Wilson (eds.), *Dictatorship, Disorder, and Decline in Myanmar*. Canberra: Australian National University E Press.

Win Min (2008b) "Looking Inside the Burmese Military." *Asian Survey*, vol. 48, no. 6, pp. 1018–1037.

Win Min (2010) "Under an Iron Heel: Civil-Military Relations in Burma/Myanmar." In Paul Chambers and Aurel Croissant (eds.), *Democracy under Stress: Civil-Military Relations in South and Southeast Asia*. Bangkok: Institute of Security and International Studies, Chulalongkorn University.

Wiseman, John A. (1988) "Militarism, Militarisation and Praetorianism in South Africa." *Africa*, vol. 58, no. 2, pp. 230–233.

Wong, Julia Carrie (2019) "'Overreacting to Failure': Facebook's New Myanmar Strategy Baffles Local Activists." *The Guardian*, February 8. <www.theguardian.com/technology/2019/feb/07/facebook-myanmar-genocide-violence-hate-speech>, last accessed December 5, 2019.

Woods, Kevin (2011) "Ceasefire Capitalism: Military Private Partnerships, Resource Concessions, and Military Style Building in the Burma-China Borderland." *Journal of Peasant Studies*, vol. 38, no. 4, pp. 747–770.

Woods, Kevin (2018) "The Conflict Resource Economy and Pathways to Peace in Burma." *Peaceworks*, no. 144. Washington, DC: United States Institute of Peace.

World Bank (2019) "World Development Indicators Database." *World Bank*. <https://data.worldbank.org/indicator/NY.GDP.MKTP.CD?locations=MM>, last accessed December 3, 2019.

Yan Naung Oak, and Brooten, Lisa (2019) "The Tea Shop Meets the 8 O'Clock News: Facebook, Convergence and Online Public Spaces." In Lisa Brooten, Jane McElhone, and Gayathry Venkiteswaran (eds.), *Myanmar Media in Transition: Legacies, Challenges and Change*. Singapore: Singapore: ISEAS-Yusof Ishak Institute.

Ye Mon (2019) "The Arakan Army and the 'Storm of the Revolution'." *Frontier Myanmar*, March 29. <https://frontiermyanmar.net/en/the-arakan-army-and-the-storm-of-the-revolution>, last accessed July 18, 2019.

Ye Ni (2019) "Federal Union Won't Be Built with Guns: Rakhine Parliament Speaker." *The Irrawaddy*, July 19. <www.irrawaddy.com/in-person/interview/federal-union-wont-built-guns-rakhine-parliament-speaker.html>, last accessed December 5, 2019.

Yen Snaing (2015) "NLD Expels 20,000 White Card Holders from Party." *The Irrawaddy*, March 17. <www.irrawaddy.com/news/burma/nld-expels-20000-white-card-holders-from-party.html>, last accessed December 5, 2019.

Zakaria, Fareed (1997) "The Rise of Illiberal Democracy." *Foreign Affairs*, vol. 76, no. 6, pp. 22–43.

Zarni Mann (2014) "Journalists Detained for Reporting Alleged Burmese Chemical Weapons Factory." *The Irrawaddy*, February 2. <www.irrawaddy.com/news/burma/journalists-detained-reporting-alleged-burmese-chemical-weapons-factory.html>, last accessed December 5, 2019.

Zarni Mann (2015) "Htin Lin Oo's Appeal Rejected in Religious Offense Case." *The Irrawaddy*, July 2. <www.irrawaddy.com/news/burma/htin-lin-oos-appeal-rejected-in-religious-offense-case.html>, last accessed December 5, 2019.

Zarni Mann, and Kyaw Phyo Tha (2015) "Freelance Photographer Detained over Facebook Post Mocking Authorities." *The Irrawaddy*, February 27. <www.irrawaddy.com/news/burma/photographer-detained-kokang-facebook-post.html>, last accessed December 5, 2019.

Zöllner, Hans-Bernd (2009) "Neither Saffron Nor Revolution: A Commentated and Documented Chronology of the Monks' Demonstrations in Myanmar in 2007 and Their Background." *Südostasien Working Papers*, no. 36.

Index

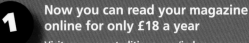

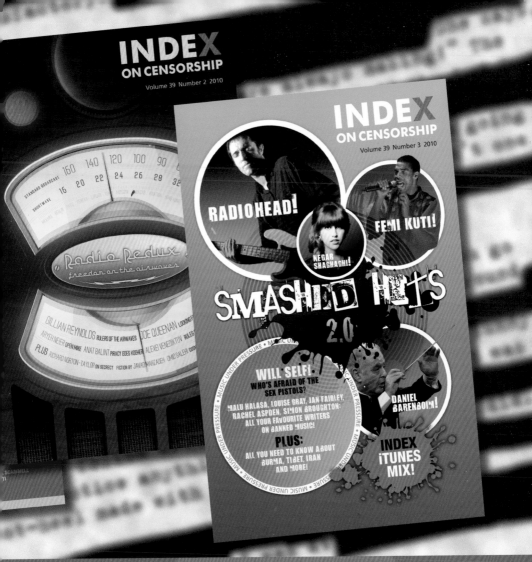

access **Index on Censorship**

purchasing options for libraries and individuals, accessing **Index on**

Index in 2010...

Brave New Words: Is Technology the Saviour of Free Speech?
Volume 39, Issue 1, March

New technology has revolutionised freedom of expression, but it has also transformed the business of censorship. In this issue writers, bloggers, journalists, activists and technology experts assess the new challenges for free speech.

Radio Redux:
Freedom on the Airwaves
Volume 39, Issue 2, June

Despite the explosion in new forms of communication, radio remains on the front line in free speech. From the shock jocks of the US to community radio in Mexico, **Index on Censorship** takes a close listen to battles on the airwaves.

Smashed Hits 2.0
Volume 39, Issue 3, September

Read about the songs they tried to ban, the musicians stopped from playing live and the singers who are put on trial in the bumper smashed hits issue of Index.

Writers in Prison
Volume 39, Issue 4, December

From Russia to Burma to Mexico, writers are silenced for expressing their views. To mark 50 years of solidarity with imprisoned and persecuted writers around the world, English PEN and Index on Censorship are collaborating on a special issue of the magazine assessing what unique role writers can play in supporting their colleagues around the world.

Index on Censorship

Free Word Centre, 60 Farringdon Road, London, ECIR 3GA

Volume 39 No 4 2010

If you are interested in republishing any article featured in this issue, please contact us at permissions@indexoncensorship.org

Supported by
ARTS COUNCIL ENGLAND

STRENGTH IN NUMBERS

Natasha Schmidt

This issue brings together some of the world's finest writers to look back at one of the longest running campaigns for freedom of expression: PEN's Writers in Prison Committee (WiPC). Run mostly by writers, for writers, it marks its fiftieth anniversary this year, and while its case histories and supporters read like a hall of literary fame, including Wole Soyinka, Václav Havel, Breyten Breytenbach, Alexander Solzhenitsyn and Anna Politkovskaya, the continuing necessity of its existence can never be a cause for celebration.

Sometimes, the committee's campaigns have caused outrage, as in the case of Arthur Miller and Harold Pinter's visit to Turkey in 1985, when they confronted the US ambassador to Ankara about torture and were thrown out of his residence. At others, they have been part of a sustained international outcry that ends with the prisoner's release, as in the cases of Jack Mapanje from Malawi and Irina Ratushinskaya from Russia. At the very least, the committee provides support to the writer who fears that the world has forgotten them: attending trials, visiting countries, writing letters and always bearing witness.

'It helps to remember that we are not alone, nor forgotten, as our captors would like us to think,' writes Léster Luis González Pentón, one of the Black Spring writers released from a Cuban jail last July (pp. 115-119). Faraj Sarkoohi, imprisoned in Iran in the 1990s, told novelist and PEN campaigner Moris Farhi: 'Though I was held incommunicado in prison, news of your activities somehow reached me. That gave me the strength to keep going' (pp. 24-26).

Even though the world has changed dramatically since the WiPC was founded, writers remain as vulnerable to dictators and bullies as ever. As Ron Deibert points out, the freedom so happily anticipated online has not quite come to fruition. Bloggers are the most recent to join the front line, exposed to the surveillance and intimidation of regimes wanting to control information (pp. 88-92).

The contributors to this issue also explore the moral dilemmas and pitfalls that face all human rights campaigners. Maureen Freely points out

the dangers of being seen as a human rights tourist, blundering into countries without adequate knowledge of the complexities of the politics at play (pp. 27-40). There's a danger, too, in expecting writers to have a political function or focus, as Margaret Atwood points out. 'Many is the revolution that has ended by eating its writerly young, as their once-acceptable productions are pronounced heretical by the victors in the inevitable power struggles,' she writes (pp. 58-63).

There are also difficulties facing any writer who makes their name for taking a stand. 'Becoming the news is a doubled-edged sword,' writes celebrated Mexican journalist Lydia Cacho, joint winner of the PEN/Pinter prize. Thrust into the limelight after exposing an international paedophile ring in her book *The Demons of Eden*, she has faced death threats, abduction and imprisonment to bring both the crimes against children and her own experiences into the public eye. 'This dilemma dominates the rest of our lives,' she says, 'because for us to come through safely we need to be out there, in public, and never be silenced' (pp. 72-81).

And at the heart of this issue is the difference that any writer makes in society. For some, it's a difference that can rob them of their freedom and even their life. 'It's debatable,' Tom Stoppard writes, 'whether the writing exerts any leverage on the fate of nations, but when it comes to the fate of individuals no one, not even a writer, needs to be useless. Political prisoners are less vulnerable when they are kept in our view and known to be so' (pp. 14-16). We're still living in a world where writing can be a dangerous business. Writers are locked up for exercising their right to free speech; torture, intimidation and legal recourse are still among the tactics used to silence them. It is essential that writers are cherished and valued as documenters and yarn-spinners; they also need to be challenged, engaged with and invited into debate. Open exchange and imagination must be allowed to flourish – it's vital to protecting our own democracies, and to fostering democracies elsewhere. Defending our writers is as important now as it has ever been. ❏

©Natasha Schmidt
39(4): 1/5
DOI: 10.1177/0306422010390302
www.indexoncensorship.org

CONTENTS

Naar Napout

Guzel

Zarpana

Giles Ji Ungpakorn

Philo Ikonya

José Gallardo Rocha

Tran Khai Thanh Thuy

Aung Myint

Akbar Ganji

Yousef Azizi

...imov

Faraj Bayrakdar

Mohamed Nasheed

BEYOND BARS

The freedom to write is still under threat.
Index and PEN look back at the challenges
to journalists, poets, playwrights and
novelists since 1960 – and assess
the battles still to be won

Editor: Natasha Schmidt
Deputy Editor: Cat Lucas Assistant Editor: Robert Sharp

*Journalist detained during a protest against media curbs in
Hyderabad, Pakistan, November 2007
Credit: Akram Shahid/Reuters*

LETTER FROM THE OUTSIDE

Playwright **Tom Stoppard** on why he would never have been a writer in prison – and the importance of communicating with those who are

To begin with, I've always liked the name of the committee: the Writers in Prison Committee. I like the way it simply describes a concrete reality, and doesn't lay claim to superior abstractions about the sanctity of the spoken or written word. It deals with the immediate fact: there's a writer in prison and the committee is on the case. I also like the name because it reminds me that I'm not in prison. This is quite an important fact about me, and normally I don't give it any thought. Why would I? I live in a country where not being in prison is the state of rest. I don't even catch myself thinking, 'There but for the grace of God …'. I don't think it's true.

A very small part of what I've written would have got me into trouble in a dictatorship, but in a dictatorship I probably wouldn't have written it.

I'm not a confrontational kind of writer. The words 'writer in prison' evoke a stark, dangerous, head-on, stand-up-and-be-counted sort of world, which makes me conscious of the displacement between harsh reality and the way I write about harsh reality. I come at it from an angle; an ironic angle, or an absurdist angle, or even a farcical angle. This is not a plan, it's the way the writing writes itself. In Russia in Soviet times, a word one heard was 'Aesopian', which referred to a way of writing dangerous things more or less safely – by concealing the true subject matter beneath an ostensible 'Aesopian' subject matter. But I don't know if that's a trick I could have learned. My trick is different, especially because it's not a trick.

On the few occasions I have approached a truly unfunny 'harsh reality', I found I couldn't change my tone of voice to fit the occasion. The main character in *Every Good Boy Deserves Favour* shapes up as what you might call a tragic hero, I suppose, but inevitably (in my case) he has to compete with a punning madman and a ludicrous doctor, and the device which ultimately frees him from his prison hospital is a verbal joke, by which time the play has departed from any kind of totalitarian reality. I should make it clear that I'm not apologising, and anyway funny writers go to prison, too, if they're in the wrong place at the wrong time. But when I think about the Writers in Prison Committee (WiPC), when I simply see those words on paper, I am made aware again that whatever my subject matter, my life is life on a bouncy castle.

In 1960, when the WiPC was established, I wrote a play about a writer in prison. At least, I think he was a writer. I can't really remember, and I hope no one else can. What I do remember is that the play wasn't much like prison. Its main intention was to feed off, and hopefully into, the current fashion for absurdist theatre. Then and later I had no urge to be an 'engaged' playwright. When my 1967 play *Rosencrantz and Guildenstern Are Dead* was banned from performance (although published) behind the Iron Curtain, I was surprised and bemused. In the end (in 1977, which was officially Prisoners of Conscience Year), I did write two plays which would have earned banning, but I never did, and still have not, could not, write a play from 'the inside'. My thoughts while writing this piece are closer to an awareness of the inside than while writing fiction, and all the closer on the occasions when I have met imprisoned writers or writers in the firing line.

In my own life, Václav Havel was the most inspiring, partly from love of his plays, which significantly include very funny satires of life under an unfunny regime. I never for a moment questioned his oblique, absurd, ironical angle on harsh reality, because writing from the inside earns the right to any tone you can call your own. Getting to know someone like Havel, or even meeting someone like Wole Soyinka just once (I shared a prize with him about 40 years ago), brings you up against the idea of the writer who is not oneself, and, from the perspective of WiPC, the writer who is oneself is not that interesting, in the way that good fortune is not that interesting.

When you're safe and sound, you think that being a writer is the most interesting thing about you, and a kind of protection. The simple statement which is the name of the Writers in Prison Committee cuts right through that to a world where it's sometimes safer not to be one. Out here, it's debatable whether the writing exerts any leverage on the fate of nations, but when it comes to the fate of individuals, no one, not even a writer, needs to be useless. Political prisoners are less vulnerable when they are kept in our view and known to be so. Write to the writers in prison. The committee has their addresses. ❒ writersinprison@englishpen.org

© Tom Stoppard
39(4): 14/16
DOI: 10.1177/0306422010388577
www.indexoncensorship.org

Sir Tom Stoppard has been honorary vice president of English PEN since 1983. His plays include *Rosencrantz and Guildenstern Are Dead*, *Professional Foul* and *Rock n Roll*, all published by Faber

POWER OF THE PEN

Carole Seymour-Jones celebrates the achievements of 50 years of fighting for authors' freedoms and explains why there is so much more work to be done

The birch trees shiver in the wind. Cardiologist Galina Bandazhevskaya, wife of imprisoned medical scientist Professor Yury Bandazhevsky, beckons us to follow her into the clearing behind her office. Her room is bugged, so there is no point in talking inside. Instead, she upturns three logs, and we squat awkwardly under the trees, on the edge of the grey Minsk suburb.

'How is Yury?' I ask.

'The government has offered him a deal. He can be freed, if …'. She pauses. The fear is evident in her eyes as she pulls her beige jacket closer, and whispers, 'Lukashenko has promised an amnesty and that Yury will be released if he withdraws what he has written about Chernobyl.' She lifts her head defiantly. 'My husband will never withdraw his books. We know that people are dying.'

Professor Bandazhevsky, rector of the Gomel State Medical Institute, had been arrested in July 1999 on a trumped-up charge of accepting bribes from his students. By then he was well known as the Chernobyl whistleblower. After the explosion of the nuclear reactor in 1986, the prize-winning scientist had left his post as director of the Central Laboratory for Scientific Research at Grodno, in the safe western area of the country, to work in the irradiated region near the Ukraine border, in order to research the links between radioactive fallout and the appearance of leukaemia and other serious illnesses in the contaminated population.

'I had been able to examine the children in maternity hospitals in the Gomel area, and I reported the results in an official document,' writes Bandazhevsky in his prison diary. 'The reaction of the government was extremely negative; they tried to muzzle me by every possible means.'

Sitting in the clearing behind Galina's office, Trevor Mostyn and I, fellow members of the Writers in Prison Committee (WiPC), can feel the despair in her voice. It is July 2004, a cold, overcast day. Trevor and I have travelled to Belarus to do what we can for Yury Bandazhevsky, an honorary member of PEN. If we can secure his release, all well and good, but the odds are against us.

'Can we see him in prison?'

Galina shrugs. 'You can try. But it will be very difficult. He has been moved to a settlement far away. Eleven European Union ambassadors drove down last week to see Yury, and the president is very angry.'

'How can we help you?'

'We are short of money. I have been asked to leave my job at the hospital. My daughter has been blacklisted too, even though she is a pathologist like her father. She can't get work.' A nervous glance. 'You must go now. Go!'

Bandazhevsky had become a thorn in President Alexander Lukashenko's flesh because of his research, published in a series of books and papers, which showed that radiation damaged embryos as well as causing cardiac irregularities. In July 1999, PEN was told, the scientist was kidnapped on the streets of Minsk in broad daylight and driven to the Ukrainian border. As the KGB's car slowed at the barrier, Yury, convinced that he would be killed in Ukraine, shouted out to the border guards: 'Help me! I'm Professor Yury Bandazhevsky.' Recognising the famous scientist, the guards refused to allow the car through. Instead, Yury was thrown into solitary confinement in Moguilev detention centre. A few months later the position of chair of pathology at Gomel Medical Institute was abolished and his unique collection of embryos exhibiting congenital malformation was destroyed.

In 2001 he was given an eight-year sentence and detained in Minsk prison, where his health deteriorated and he was operated on for peritonitis. As he struggled to continue thinking and writing, his mood alternated between despair and defiance. 'I suffer terribly waiting for my lawyer', he wrote in his prison diary on 26 October 2001, 'because it's impossible for me to prove my innocence ... sometimes I no longer have faith in the future.'

I follow his case with growing concern and, early in 2004, PEN decides to send a mission to Belarus to appeal directly to the government on his behalf. Months are spent trying to obtain visas, but finally an invitation from the Belarus PEN centre to make a cultural visit breaks the deadlock.

In Minsk our interpreter calls the authorities every morning to ask if we can visit but, as the British ambassador confirms, Lukashenko is infuriated by the pressure from the international community to release the imprisoned scientist. Every day the answer is no. Meanwhile, we meet Galina again and, thanks to a grant from the Prisoners of Conscience Appeal Fund, give her the roubles she desperately needs.

In Grodno the dingy, green-painted newsroom of a Belarussian paper closed down by the government smells of fear. The editor has just come out of prison and the dispirited journalists sit at empty desks: their computers have been taken by the KGB. In Gomel, another journalist who has published articles on Bandazhevsky's case tells us of death threats she has received. Her office, too, has been ransacked, her computer smashed up, and she is preparing to go into exile. On the edge of the Chernobyl exclusion zone, Trevor and I walk through ghost villages and past the dark, poisoned forest; in the local hospital the doctors confirm Bandazhevsky's findings.

On our last day, the phone rings. It is Bandazhevsky himself, calling from prison. He speaks in French and thanks us for our support. 'I have my PEN library here,' he says, referring to books sent by members, which serve as a reminder that he is part of an international community of writers working for his release. 'Thank you for helping Galina, thank you for helping my family.'

Months later, in October, Lukashenko wins a controversial referendum that will allow him to stand for a third term. Opposition politicians face further repression, and dissident journalist Veronika Cherkasova is found dead in her apartment in Minsk, her body covered in stab wounds. The following January, the WiPC launches a petition calling for Bandazhevsky's release, and more than 400 British writers sign. On 5 August 2005, Lukashenko unexpectedly frees the scientist.

As Orhan Pamuk, the Turkish novelist and Nobel laureate, says: 'If another writer in another house is not free, then no writer is free.' That trip taught me the meaning of the word 'solidarity'. Returning from Chernobyl, I ask myself how writers in the comfortable West can ignore the suffering of fellow writers prepared to die for their belief in free speech. How can we not become *ecrivains engagés*?

In 1937, Arthur Koestler, in Spain for the *News Chronicle*, was arrested and condemned to death. Forty PEN members, with the addition of EM

Forster and Aldous Huxley, sent a cable to General Francisco Franco appealing for Koestler's release. This first, vigorous campaign proved an outstanding success. Arriving in London, Koestler thanked PEN members for their expression of solidarity, given not for any personal merit of his own, but 'in the deeper interests of freedom of expression of opinion, which is the life-blood of democracy and humanity'.

For Storm Jameson, the first woman president of English PEN and founder member of the WiPC, becoming politically active was an early choice. The author of more than 45 novels, she expressed in her 1969 memoir *Journey from the North*, a 'deep unrealised contempt for novel-writing as a serious use for energy and intellect'. 'Serious' for Jameson meant 'politically engaged', a commitment she had come to value more highly than the interior, solipsistic world of the writer. In 1913, she had joined 50,000 suffragettes in the 'women's pilgrimage' to the House of Commons.

Storm brought the same passionate sense of outrage to PEN's concern for those writers who found that the end of the Second World War did not bring the liberation from tyranny it promised. Instead they 'disappeared' or were arrested, in Czechoslovakia, Albania, Romania and Hungary, states in the grip of the Cold War. By 1959, the surge of optimism that had inspired the first PEN Congress after the war, in Zurich in 1947, had melted away as the Iron Curtain descended on Europe and critical voices were silenced.

At the International PEN Congress in Rio de Janeiro on 24 July 1960, the first PEN case list, listing the names of 54 imprisoned writers, was presented to the assembly at the request of David Carver, the international secretary at the time. The WiPC, a committee of just three writers, Jameson, Carver and Victor van Vriesland, was born; four years later Rosamond Lehmann of English PEN became the first chair. This development was the formal expression of the solidarity that had lain at the heart of PEN since 41 writers got together in London in 1921 to form the PEN club, electing John Galsworthy as their president.

A strong thread of continuity links those early meetings to the foundation of the WiPC. The threat of fascism and the burning of books in Germany led to the arrival of Jewish exiles in London, and prompted the adoption of the 1933 PEN Charter, which proclaimed that 'literature knows no frontiers' and that the club would fight to protect a free press. An historic marker for human rights, the charter would influence the United Nations Declaration of Human Rights 15 years later. In London, HG Wells, the new president of

Storm Jameson, founder of PEN's Writers in Prison Committee
Credit: Pictorial Press Ltd/Alamy

English PEN, proposed a fund to support writers under threat for the peaceful expression of their views.

The 50 years that followed the birth of the WiPC have witnessed no diminution of danger for writers of conscience around the world. The PEN case book has grown to 600 cases. Many of these cases demonstrate extraordinary courage and endurance; they also show the power of the pen to challenge oppression and contribute to change. Murder is committed with impunity to silence journalists who uncover uncomfortable truths, such as Anna Politkovskaya. Bandazhevsky narrowly escaped an attempt to take him across the border into Ukraine and kill him. Elsewhere, insult and anti-terror laws are used in the bid to gag editors like Hrant Dink, gunned down in the streets of Istanbul in 2007. In Nigeria, the 1995 execution of Ken Saro-Wiwa shows the price writers pay when they take on repressive governments.

'Modern people long for freedom of thought and expression as much as they long for bread and water,' writes Orhan Pamuk. The WiPC struggles indefatigably to support fellow writers who suffer harassment, torture, imprisonment and death, adopting them as honorary members, appealing to governments through the Rapid Action Network, writing letters, sending books, holding demonstrations and launching petitions. The results of direct action have often been surprisingly successful, even more so as the internet feeds people's hunger for information and they find ways of circumventing government firewalls and mobilising the international community.

Sometimes a case seems hopeless, particularly in the cluster of countries, including Burma, China, Cuba and Iran, that still use long-term imprisonment as a means of censorship. But PEN never loses hope that the oxygen of publicity may bring about release, however long it takes, as well as providing psychological support to prisoners. For this reason the WiPC has mounted two demonstrations recently on behalf of Aung San Suu Kyi. In 2009, the inaugural PEN/Pinter Prize for an international writer of courage was awarded to Zargana, the imprisoned Burmese comedian, and a grant was given to support his family. The 2010 award went to Mexican journalist Lydia Cacho (see pp. 72-81). This year, 18 of the journalists imprisoned during Cuba's Black Spring of March 2003 were finally freed, shortly after PEN's Cuba media briefing was launched.

And the journey from prison to presidency made by Václav Havel (who won office in 1989), has been made more recently by Mohamed Nasheed of the Maldives (see pp. 47-50), and was followed by the release of two journalists from Maafushi island prison, where Nasheed was once himself incarcerated. Writer-to-writer contact makes PEN unique in the human rights arena, lending a personal dimension to protest. And we continue to reach out to new cases and countries: last year Eva Hoffman and Alev Adil went to Azerbaijan to support imprisoned journalist Eynulla Fatullayev (see pp. 218-219), an honorary member and another recipient of a Prisoners of Conscience grant.

Yet in Belarus, in China, in Mexico, in the Horn of Africa, the need is critical, for the 21st century has witnessed a growing confidence among authoritarian regimes. Dictators are contemptuous of outside complaints. In September 2010, the journalist Aleh Byabenin, who had spent 15 years of his life fighting Lukashenko's dictatorship, was found hanged in his country home. Few believe the coroner's verdict of suicide. In Mexico, eight journalists have been murdered and three have 'disappeared' since January alone. In China, on Christmas Day 2009, Liu Xiaobo, honorary president of the Independent Chinese PEN Centre (ICPC), was sentenced to 11 years' detention. There is no let up in the Chinese government's persecution of the ICPC or in its censorship of cyberspace.

Talking in 2010 about the writer's journey towards political engagement, Martin Amis remarked: 'you think that you live inside the whale and the ocean is politics. There is no whale.' Politics and writing continue to intersect, throwing up new challenges to those working to protect the rights of poets, playwrights, critics, journalists and novelists. Across the globe people are signing up to PEN's central mission: to promote the freedom to write. It is as important now as it was in 1960. ❐

©Carole Seymour-Jones
39(4): 17/23
DOI: 10.1177/0306422010389359
www.indexoncensorship.org

Carole Seymour-Jones is chair of the Writers in Prison Committee and deputy president of English PEN. She is the author of *Painted Shadow: The Life of Vivienne Eliot* (Constable Robinson) and a regular contributor to *The Literary Review*. She is currently working on a biography of a British female special operations executive during the Second World War

EYEWITNESS

Moris Farhi on
Faraj Sarkoohi

Faraj was born in 1947, in Shiraz. He started writing at the age of 14 and published his first collection of stories, *Red Hand, Green Hand*, when he was 19. He attained prominence with *Long Night of Loneliness*, another collection of stories, and *Perspectives of Our Time*, a compilation of his literary essays.

In 1971, he was arrested by the Shah's security service for his political writing and was sentenced to 15 years of confinement. He was released, together with other political prisoners, in 1979, during the Islamic Revolution led by Ayatollah Khomeini.

In 1985, he co-founded the monthly literary magazine *Adineh*. In 1994, he emerged as one of the principal initiators of 'The Declaration of 134 Iranian Authors', which promulgated the writer's inalienable right to freedom of expression. Between 1984 and 1996, during the respective presidencies of Ayatollah Khamenei and Ayatollah Rafsanjani, he was arrested several times and systematically tortured.

On 4 November 1996, as he was about to fly to Germany from Tehran airport to visit his wife, he disappeared. He 'reappeared' 48 days later, on 20 December, recounting that he had indeed travelled to Germany – a story blatantly concocted by the Iranian authorities. In reality, he had been taken into custody by the secret police and subjected to physical and psychological torture in solitary confinement.

On his release, he managed to smuggle a letter out of Iran that related the facts of his disappearance, stressing the dangers that writers and intellectuals faced under the regime of the Islamic Republic. In January 1997, following the publication of this letter in the West, he was re-arrested. (Ghazi Rabihavi later adapted Faraj's smuggled letter into a documentary play, *Look, Europe!*, which was performed at the Almeida Theatre under Harold Pinter's direction in October 1997.)

Charged with 'espionage' in a secret trial, he was sentenced to death. This verdict provoked intense international pressure and compelled the authorities to contrive an arraignment. In a new trial, the charge of espionage was modified to 'anti-state propaganda' and his death sentence commuted to a year's imprisonment. Faraj served the full term of his imprisonment and was released on 28 January 1998. After weeks of bureaucratic hindrances, he was finally allowed to leave Iran and visit his family in Germany on 6 May 1998. (The then new president of Iran, the reformist Mohammad Khatami, might well have been instrumental in this unexpected decision.)

Since then, Faraj has been living in exile in Frankfurt. He has never severed his links with his country. He continues to strive indefatigably to promote human rights and freedom of expression, not only in Iran but also wherever they are under threat.

Our brotherhood started with the announcement of Faraj's 'death sentence'. At the time, I was chair of both English and International PEN's Writers in Prison Committees (WiPC). Both committees were still in shock from the fact that, barely a year earlier, despite all our efforts to save him, the great Nigerian writer Ken Saro-Wiwa, who led a non-violent movement against the multinational petroleum industry for causing severe environmental damage to the lands and waters of his people, had been hanged on the orders of his country's military dictator, General Sani Abacha. Suddenly confronted with yet another iniquitous execution, we at English PEN agreed to campaign as effectively as we could for Faraj's release. We decided that the best means available to us was persistent demonstrations – at least once a week. So many of us – invariably bolstered by Iranian exiles – gathered every Monday outside the Iranian embassy in London. Brandishing banners and photographs of Faraj, we maintained this campaign until his release.

Our brotherhood was sealed when I went to meet Faraj in Berlin days after his arrival there. The then German WiPC chair, Rajvinder Singh, organised a party for the occasion. Standing amidst the gathering, I didn't see Faraj come in. But he spotted me and rushed over. We embraced and shed tears. I recognised him immediately from his photographs. But how had he recognised me? He told me his guards in prison would often hector him about the campaign on his behalf in London and mock the fact that videos taken by the embassy personnel showed a fat, white-haired old hippy at the forefront of every demonstration.

Thereafter, Faraj and I met regularly at various conferences in Europe. At one significant meeting, in September 1998, in London, he told us: 'Though I was held incommunicado in prison, news of your activities somehow reached me. That gave me the strength to keep going.'

Another significant meeting took place in Paris, in December 1998, the day after we heard about the brutal murders, in the space of two weeks, of four eminent Iranian writers: Mohammad Mokhtari, Mohammad Jafar Pouyandeh, Dariush Forouhar and his wife, Parvaneh Eskandari. We sat, in a hotel foyer, numbed, holding hands, chain-smoking and wiping away the occasional tear, for almost a whole day. Then Faraj jumped up and said: 'Let's go and work even harder!'

For me the quintessence of our brotherhood was the 65th International PEN Congress in Helsinki, Finland. I was on the platform and had just given my annual report to the assembly of delegates. I summed up by stating that we had been blessed by two miracles during the year: the deliverance from execution of the Yemeni writer, Mansur Rajih, and of the Iranian writer, Faraj Sarkoohi. One of the miracles, Faraj, I told them, had come to the congress to address the assembly. (Mansur Rajih, too, had been at the conference but had had to return to Norway where he was given asylum – he still lives there.)

I invited Faraj on to the platform. The hall plunged into silence. Eyes turned this way and that. Faraj is a wiry man, not tall, and was not noticed by the delegates until he reached the platform. Then a deafening applause erupted. I have never seen – nor am likely to see again – so many faces glowing with rapture and awe. I thought: here, in microcosm, is the proof that humanity always celebrates life and will always defeat tyranny.

Faraj began to speak. Good enough English, expressive, often poetic and from the heart; the articulation of a natural storyteller.

As he related the horrors of his experiences, as he thanked his brothers and sisters in PEN for their efforts on his and his fellow writers' behalf, I felt the delegates attain an extraordinary bonding. I felt, in some mystical way, that we had become Faraj and Faraj had become us; that by defending freedom of thought and expression we were in effect defending all life's right to life. That, after all, is the raison d'être of the creative arts. ❐

© Moris Farhi
39(4): 24/26
DOI: 10.1177/0306422010388576
www.indexoncensorship.org

Moris Farhi's books include *A Designated Man* (Telegram, 2009) and *Children of the Rainbow* (Saqi Books). He won the 2007 Alberto Benveniste Prize for the French version of his novel *Young Turk* (Saqi)

TWO FOR THE ROAD

Maureen Freely on Harold Pinter and Arthur Miller's infamous trip to Turkey and the pitfalls of intervening in another country's troubles

The human rights field is crowded: when PEN campaigns for the right to free expression, it shares the stage with many others. But because it is an international writers' organisation that promotes world literature, it tries to look beyond the horrors of the prison and the courthouse to take an interest in the words that get writers into trouble in the first place. The conversations that begin outside those courthouses may result in lifelong friendships.

Like all friends, they will have their ups and downs. And sometimes they will argue. At the worst of times, the prosecuted and persecuted writers will grow tired of always being at the receiving end of a helping hand. They will stop saying thank you. They will take offence at a remark that perhaps could have been phrased more thoughtfully. They will have one drink too many, and then they will accuse their foreign friends of being human rights tourists, of meddling in a country they do not begin to understand. 'You just came here to convince yourselves your own country is superior,' they will say. 'And, of course! Let us not forget. You are also gathering material for your next book. Well, I hope you found what you wanted. I hope you have fun railing against all the injustices you'll never suffer…'.

Just about anyone who has ever gone on a mission for PEN will have heard such words at one point or another. And they are hard to forget, because the danger is there. The power imbalances are real. A foreigner can never understand a country well enough. It is so very easy to offend. And it's true. Writers who have flown in for a few days to observe a nasty trial will never feel the full force of its consequences. As well-meaning amateurs, they may well create new problems for the writers they have left behind.

In December 2005, for example, a number of international human rights organisations and several PEN centres sent observers to Orhan Pamuk's trial after he was charged with insulting Turkishness by acknowledging the mass killing of both Armenians and Kurds. I was inside the court building when ultra-nationalist lawyers insulted, threatened and assaulted the dozen or so European Union parliamentarians also attending Orhan Pamuk's trial, and I saw how the ultra-nationalist lawyer Kemal Kerinçsiz used the very presence of such observers to 'prove' to the nation that Turkey was being insulted and humiliated. He used this and many other show trials to present his case on television, denouncing Pamuk and the hundred-odd other writers being similarly prosecuted as traitors who were selling their countries to Europe to advance their careers. During the months that followed, free-speaking writers and activists with profiles abroad were, if anything, in greater danger than before.

But by and large, the western media remained blind to their plight. Obsessed as they were at that time with Islam, they assumed the danger to Pamuk and other writers came from Turkey's moderately Islamist ruling party. In fact the danger came from Turkey's hugely powerful military and its pro-military state bureaucracies, which propagate a monolithic ideology that they defend with draconian laws curbing free speech. Anyone seeking to understand the wars of words now raging in Turkey (on Armenian Kurds, Islam, the EU, or human rights) would do well to study the history of this young republic, which owes its very existence to the army commanded by Mustafa Kemal Atatürk in the aftermath of the First World War, when much of what is now known as Turkey was occupied by that war's European victors. It was the might and reputation of the same army that guaranteed the success of Atatürk's fast-track westernisation programme (known in Turkey as the 'revolution from above') over the decades that followed.

Largely thanks to our conversations with Turkish friends, those of us working on human rights issues in Turkey are well aware of the power of the

Orhan Pamuk trial, Istanbul, December 2005
Credit: Sipa Press/Rex Features

army and of the punishments that the Turkish state has visited on its critics almost from the very moment of its inception in 1923. But for the most part, we have not found a way to translate this complex history into words that make sense to a larger audience. It is hard to explain why Turkey, the most democratic republic in the region, is in fact not all that democratic, just as it is hard to connect the vibrant, economically thriving country that people might have seen as tourists with these dark accounts of writers being persecuted and prosecuted for insulting the memory of Atatürk, questioning the power of the military, acknowledging the Armenian genocide, or seeking to advance a historical understanding of the Kurdish conflict. But the hardest job falls to the persecuted and prosecuted writers: from the moment they receive their first mention in the European press, their phones start ringing, as non-governmental organisations of many and dubious persuasions rush in to 'help', as well-meaning human rights groups from all over Europe offer help without having an accurate overview of the country's political complexities.

When producer Gemma Newby and I travelled to Istanbul in March 2010 to record interviews for our BBC Radio 4 documentary on the trip that Harold Pinter and Arthur Miller made to Turkey for PEN in 1985, I took these memories and concerns with me. I remembered the splashy coverage in the British press afterwards. The first trip of its kind to Turkey, it remains its most celebrated. Thanks to the fracas the two playwrights caused at the tail-end of their visit to the US embassy in Ankara, it made for perfect literary gossip. But I feared that those they'd gone to help might have more complicated feelings. I was ready to listen and stand corrected, apologise and qualify and explain.

Quite a few of those who briefed and entertained Pinter and Miller were old friends of mine. With one exception, they'd never spoken to me of the visit. I was soon to discover that this was only because I'd never asked. And the story they went on to tell me began long before I thought it did. The catalyst in this instance was an article published in Turkey in 1975 in the ur-establishment *Cumhuriyet* newspaper, given its name by the founder of the republic. Its author was a diplomat named Mahmut Dikerdem, who had decided to use the occasion of his early retirement to air his views on Turkish foreign policy in general and the role of the military in particular.

He had a great deal to say about Turkey's invasion of Cyprus a year earlier, in 1974. The island, he said, should be demilitarised. The same went for Turkey, then studded with Nato bases to fend off the Soviet threat. It could, he believed, find a better future in nonalignment. Dikerdem's unorthodox proposals caused a great stir. It was just not done in those days for a prominent member of the establishment to challenge foreign policy in public. But others in the establishment were receptive to his ideas, and a new sort of conversation was born.

In 1978, Dikerdem and other leading figures formed the Turkish Peace Association (TPA). Together they launched numerous initiatives to broaden the discussion, at the same time reaching out to like-minded groups in other parts of the region. In so doing, they again broke new ground, as Turkey's US-bankrolled military liked to justify its great size by telling the country's citizens that their lives depended on it, seeing as the republic was ringed by enemies.

The military kept a close eye, too, on the enemy within. The Turkish penal code, drawn from Benito Mussolini's Italy, had long made it dangerous to lean to the left. When the army staged its third coup in 20 years on 12 September 1980, its expressed aim was to save the nation from communism. But the generals were also mindful of the greater threat posed by establishment figures arguing for a rolling back of the military and greater space for democratic debate. Seventeen months after the takeover, warrants went out for the entire executive committee of the TPA to be arrested.

Two years later, the trial was still dragging on, with the executive committee wasting away in prison. Mahmut Dikerdem's son Mehmet Ali, who was studying for his doctorate in London, had joined with several others to set up a defence campaign, but to little avail. The western media had failed to show much interest in the 1980 coup and its aftermath, the most brutal regime this nation had ever known. And – not for the first time, not for the last – Turkey's Nato allies seemed happy to overlook its suppression of democracy, so long as it also staved off (or was seen to stave off) the communist threat.

Then Mehmet Ali hit on the idea of writing to Harold Pinter. Pinter responded promptly, inviting Mehmet Ali to his house for drinks. Mehmet Ali was surprised, though in retrospect Pinter's interest does not seem so surprising. A conscientious objector in early life and a tireless, eloquent defender of free speech forever after, Pinter took a particular interest in writers and peace associations seeking to move beyond the nostrums of the Cold War.

When Gemma Newby and I interviewed Mehmet Ali in March 2010, he recalled his first impressions of Pinter, sitting in his study under a painting that 'was almost like a visual representation of relativity. It was brown and there were things sort of disappearing into it. And so he was sitting under that and he was serving me lots of Chablis.'

Other meetings followed. Pinter wanted to know everything Mehmet Ali could tell him about the situation in Turkey, which was, in the words of Anne Burley, then Amnesty International's researcher on Turkey, 'as bad as it ever has been'. When she went on fact-finding missions to Turkey, it was 'very difficult to find people who would speak to me ... I'd make appointments to see people and they'd just not turn up, they were too frightened.'

We now know why. According to the Human Rights Foundation of Turkey, roughly 650,000 people were detained for political reasons between 1980 and 1984; 210,000 of those detainees were tried in military courts, of whom 65,000 were convicted. More than 500 people received death sentences. Of these, 50 were executed, while 460 people died under torture and 180 were disappeared. Martial law commanders removed 4,891 civil servants from office, sending 4,509 into exile and forcing another 20,000 to retire or resign. Of the 30,000 people who had to flee the country, half were stripped of citizenship. Newspapers and journals that were not shut down were closely watched. Tens of thousands of books were burned and 937 films banned.

All political parties and trade unions were shut down, along with 23,667 associations. More than 1,000 villages were evacuated, wrecked, or burnt to the ground. The Kurdish language was banned. And torture got more creative. In addition to the visible methods (beating, blindfolding, humiliation, electric shocks, isolation, death threats, suspension on a hanger, restriction of food and water, sexual abuse, pulling out nails, mock executions, forced consumption of salt and more) there was 'torture without marks' (forcing detainees to watch others being tortured, dropping them into sewer pits, or leaving them outside in the cold without clothes and then depriving them of medical treatment).

When we interviewed the human rights activist Murat Belge in March, he repeated what he'd been told by a former prisoner in the mostly Kurdish city of Diyarbakir: 'Every morning they came with a new idea and one day they said, "Everybody is to catch 100 flies until night-change time" and, being used to doing any crazy thing which was an order, they did. ... In the evening they came in and counted the flies and if you didn't have 100 they made you swallow them – 97 flies for instance – and how can you sleep after hearing something like this?'

It was Mehmet Ali who first explained to Pinter why the Turkish state refused to acknowledge that Kurds even existed, preferring to describe them as Mountain Turks. The more Pinter heard, the more convinced he became that he had to make a stand. Things seem to have come to a head at a party also attended by the philosopher and writer Roger Scruton, who had been writing approvingly of the Turkish military in the press.

Scruton brought with him two Turkish friends who were, Pinter later recalled, 'extremely attractive and intelligent young women'. But when he asked them about the TPA trial, they said: 'Oh, well, it was probably deserved … they were probably communists. We have to protect ourselves against communism.' Pinter then pressed them for facts. 'They of course had no facts at all at their fingertips. They were ignorant, in fact.' When he went on to ask them whether they knew what Turkish military prisons were like, they said: 'Well communists are communists, you know.' 'But what do you have to say about torture?' Pinter asked. 'Oh, you are a man of such imagination,' they replied. 'Do you mean it's worse for me than for the victims?' Pinter asked. They shrugged their shoulders. 'Yes, possibly,' they said. Whereupon, 'instead of strangling them', Pinter went home, sat down, 'and, it's true, out of rage, started to write…'.

This marked the beginning of *One for the Road*, Pinter's play on torture. But it was not enough. He wanted to do something to draw the

Harold Pinter and Arthur Miller on their trip to Turkey, 1985
Credit: The Wylie Agency

world's attention to those suffering in Turkey's prisons. So he approached Arthur Miller, who was as active in American PEN as Pinter was in English PEN. In March 1985, the two playwrights set out on a fact-finding mission to Turkey.

Their first stop was Istanbul. Things got off to a bad start, Pinter later recalled, with the airline losing one of his two suitcases: 'Apart from other things, this left me with no socks. So Arthur lent me his. Bloody good ones they were too. Made to last.'

Waiting for them outside the baggage hall was a shy young novelist named Orhan Pamuk and also Gündüz Vassaf (now a celebrated writer, then a professor of psychology), who represented Amnesty International in Istanbul. Over the days that followed, they would introduce Pinter and Miller to many leading members of the intelligentsia – those, that is, who were not at that moment in prison. When we spoke to him last March, Vassaf likened Pinter and Miller to 'two schoolboys having a good time with each other. ...

They did see the suffering. But the two of them got on amazingly well. It was a wonderful friendship to be able to witness.'

Pamuk, who was new to the spotlight, was more uneasy. In his 2006 Arthur Miller Memorial Lecture, he recalled a moment at the Istanbul Hilton when he and Vassaf were whispering darkly in a shadowy corridor, only to look down the corridor and see Pinter and Miller whispering to each other inside shadows just as dark. It distressed Pamuk that these two great writers were seeing only the worst of his country. The acclaimed playwright Ali Taygun, who was one of the 24 TPA defendants, and whom English PEN had made an honorary member, expressed the same sentiments in a letter to Pinter and Miller:

> When I first heard of your visit … my reaction was that of 'stage fright'. I imagined you two standing across from me in the booth, smiling at me; waving perhaps as you saw me approach … and then would come the moment of truth! What would I say? Two of the greatest playwrights alive visit this country. I, a director full of admiration, of awe in their presence, have so much to hear from them, to ask, to discuss and, no, we do not talk of how their plays should be produced, … but of trials and prisons and of plight. Such a waste!

Sadly, he never got to meet them. Ali Taygun was then entering the third year of his prison term. But his fiancée, the opera singer Yekta Kara, invited them to her home with Mahmut Dikerdem and Melek Ulagay, the wife of the artist Orhan Taylan, another TPA defendant. Both Kara and Ulagay recall the evening with gratitude and affection. When we met them in March, Yekta Kara spoke of the ostracism she had endured from the first moments of the trial. Not even her closest colleagues would speak to her, and now the world's two greatest playwrights had come for supper. Melek Ulagay remembered Miller as cool and calm, speaking 'slowly and thinkingly, whereas Pinter was a very exuberant character, speaking to three people at the same time … and telling different stories and listening to everything.' He struck her as a man with 'a lot of empathy'. Describing the evening to his son, Mahmut Dikerdem described Pinter as a 'chevalier' and Miller as an 'alchemist of souls'. And in his memoirs, Miller wrote how 'there was something surreal about sitting … in a large and lovely apartment with a tremendous view of the Bosphorus at night, with the silent ships, many of them Soviet, sailing past below, and having to remember that this young woman's fiancé was not far away in a room with eight or 10 other prisoners, kept there for thoughts they had held in their heads.'

As he and Pinter travelled on to Ankara the next day, Miller would also have been thinking of the visit's low moments. The argument late one evening with a group of leftists who told them they should leave Turkey to the Turks. The story Murat Belge had told them about the torturer who, after sitting him down to sign his confession, had brushed against his knee and politely apologised. Miller would also have been thinking of the offence he'd caused just afterwards, when he'd asked, without thinking, if there was something in the Turkish nature that drove it to torture. Was he not aware that the coups of 1960, 1971 and 1980 had all had the green light or the active approval of the USA?

It was with all this in mind that the two playwrights arrived at the residence of the US ambassador in Ankara. It was, from the outset, a tense occasion. 'I had hardly taken my first bite at the hors d'oeuvres,' Pinter later recalled, 'when I found myself in the middle of a ferocious row with the US political counsellor about the existence of torture in Turkish prisons'. There followed another altercation with the deputy chief of mission, whom Miller later described as sitting 'behind his tinted glasses with an expression of irremediable grimness'. The conservative columnist Nazli Ilıcak soon joined the fray, accusing Pinter of Orientalism, and of preaching about a country he knew nothing about: they had no commitment to Turkey, they were just looking for material.

Pinter went out to the corridor to look at the paintings and cool off. The ambassador followed him out. Pinter later recalled what happened next:

> The ambassador said to me: 'Mr. Pinter, you don't seem to understand the realities of the situation here. Don't forget, the Russians are just over the border. You have to bear in mind the political reality, the diplomatic reality, the military reality.' 'The reality I've been referring to,' I said, 'is that of electric current on your genitals.' The ambassador drew himself, as they say, up to his full height and glared at me. 'Sir,' he said, 'you are a guest in my house.' He turned, as they also say, on his heel and his aides turned too. Arthur suddenly loomed up. 'I think I've been thrown out,' I said. 'I'll come with you,' Arthur said, without hesitation. Being thrown out of the US embassy in Ankara with Arthur Miller – a voluntary exile – was one of the proudest moments of my life.

March 12th, 1985

Dear Arthur, Dear Harold,

When I first heard of your visit from PEN American Center, and then from Jeri Laber, my reaction was that of 'stage fright'. I imagined you two standing across from me, in the booth; smiling at me; waving perhaps as you saw me approach... and then would come the moment of truth!

What would I say?

"Hello Mr Miller, hello Mr Pinter"? (I know I should address the older one first)

Or should it be: "Hi! Arthur and Harold"?

Or would something humorous be in order:

"Sorry to have kept you waiting, gentlemen. Busy time of the year"? —to impress you with the stiff upper lip!

I even thought of: "Welcome, great masters of my profession!" And would have stuck to that if it wasn't for the archaic flavour making it sound corny....

And that's the problem with a meeting of this sort: anything one says seems to be either corny or self-conscious... awkward!

But this is so because the situation is awkward, I think.

Two of the greatest playwrights alive visit this country. I, a director full of admiration, of awe in their presence; have so much to hear from them, to ask, to discuss and, no, we do not talk of how their plays should be produced, what they think of the 'Beckett Brouhaha', can the small bare room be changed

into a deserted subway station, does a designer have the
right to do that..., or of a million other things members of
this profession talk about when they are together; the theatre;
but of trials and prisons and of plight.

Such a waste!

Such a waste of energy, effort...and time!

Yes, it seems "time doth waste" us now.

But is this because we "have wasted time"? We, ~~are~~ wasting it?

No, I do not think so. I think, time will waste us; not only
us, not only others like us, but nearly all value created by man
as well, if we do not now bear time's waste.

We are not wasting time: I am where I am, instead of that
room with the beautiful view where you are, and you, graciously so,
there, instead of where you would normally have been.

We are not wasting time: My reason tells me what theirs told
those who shared the same predicament; the agony we put the
oppressors through by my being here and your being there is
our triumph. Time's triumph.

That's why I felt no dejection when I heard you wouldn't
be permitted to see me. Why should I? It's their shame! I wear
my prison denims with pride. They fear you seeing me in them...
They are guilty. And they want to hide their guilt behind the bars.

What they do not understand, what they can not comprehend is
that I am now in that room where you are, with you. We are
more "together" now than we would ever have been, had we been
together physically. I know that.

A toast, then, my friends: "To the triumph of human dignity!"

Fraternally,

Ali

Vassaf remembers how elated they still were when they changed planes at Istanbul airport on their return journey. And so the story spread. It wasn't long afterwards that the Turkish press offered its own version: 'They ate, they drank and then they vomited poison.' The row with the US ambassador had made their visit a talking point, at long last bringing the world's attention to bear on Turkey.

And the story didn't end there. Pinter's friendship with Mehmet Ali continued. When his father was again free to travel and came to London to see his son, Harold Pinter and his wife, Lady Antonia Fraser took them out to a splendid lunch. They did the same for other writers Pinter had met during his 1985 visit. Pinter continued to correspond with the playwright Ali Taygun and he took a keen interest in Orhan Pamuk as his reputation grew.

I was present at the lunch when they met again 21 years later. Pinter had won his Nobel Prize by then. Pamuk would win his several months later. As I watched them from the other end of the table, they did indeed look as excited as two schoolboys. It was as if they had last spoken to each other just yesterday.

The Turkish press offered its own version: 'They ate, they drank and they vomited poison'

Pinter's commitment to Turkey's persecuted minorities never flagged. As vice president of English PEN, he spoke often and eloquently on their behalf. The last time I saw Pinter was in January 2007, when he came with Fraser to attend a vigil outside the Turkish embassy to protest against the assassination of the Turkish-Armenian journalist and human rights activist Hrant Dink. Pinter had been very ill, and it was a very cold day, but he wanted to meet the people who had organised the protest. He wanted to talk to them.

It was, perhaps, because Pinter is one of my great heroes that I was afraid of what I might hear when we went to Istanbul for our documentary. I knew that many of the people he and Miller had met 25 years ago were still being prosecuted and persecuted. I knew of the friends they had lost, I knew how many battles they had yet to win, so I was afraid to hear them say that it was a deluded enterprise from the very beginning – this idea that you could parachute writers into a country they hardly knew to help writers they had never met and expect any good to come of it. But I promised myself I would be balanced. I promised myself I would ask. And so I did, though I kept my questions general. I got lots of good answers. Mehmet Ali reminded me that it was not long after Pinter and Miller's visit that the Turkish Peace Association defendants were acquitted. Murat Belge noted that those who took a dim view of such visits had rarely felt the full brunt of the military: when he'd been in prison himself, he'd taken comfort in the knowledge that he had friends abroad campaigning for his release.

One evening, I decided to go one step further. We were sitting with Melek Ulagay and Orhan Taylan, enjoying a glass of wine in his Beyoğlu studio, when I plucked up the courage to say it straight. Had they ever felt uneasy about Pinter and Miller's visit? Had they ever thought of them as human rights tourists?

No, said Orhan Taylan. No. It had given him confidence to think that there were others in the world who thought as he did, and to know 'they existed all over the world' and that 'some of them were courageous enough to come over to a country ruled by the military where they shoot people in the streets'. It took 'great courage on their part', he repeated. That they had done so 'just to show their solidarity for our position – that was a great feeling for us. This is how things should be, this is how all intellectuals all around the world should be. ... We are grateful for Harold Pinter and Arthur Miller for their actions.'

I took these words with me when I travelled to Turkey on behalf of English PEN in September 2010 to observe yet another trial, this one involving the publisher Ragıp Zarakolu and Mehmet Güler, author of a book on the history of the Kurdish conflict. Both are charged with printing and publishing material for a terrorist organisation.

The Beşiktaş courthouse was buzzing that morning. In the rooms upstairs, prosecutors were taking statements for a series of controversial trials implicating more than 200 people (among them generals, air force commanders and admirals previously in active service) in a state-sponsored terrorist organisation. But the crowds of unkempt men filing in and out of the downstairs lobby were, for the most part, charged with drug smuggling. When it came time for our hearing, the courtroom was half-empty: even Zarakolu had chosen not to attend. But there were four judges in attendance, and one of them seemed almost half interested when Mehmet Güler stood up to give them a very fine lecture on the origins of the Kurdish conflict. Later on, Güler told me that he planned to attend every hearing, even though he was only required by law to attend one. 'Each time I shall give the judges a new lecture from a different part of my book.' It was his job, he said, to add to their education.

In the conversation that followed, he added to mine – as did the many other writers and journalists and activists we met in the course of our visit. Though they did fill us in on the latest twists and turns of Turkish politics, the best conversations were about the books they were writing, the initiatives they had launched and the international conference they'd organised, at which they would imagine a world in which the right to free expression had been fought and won. If that day ever arrived, what would they do next? What would any of us do? As always it is difficult to explain why such confident conversations can happen in full view of a courthouse where justice is routinely obstructed, or how the long shadow of a courthouse can prompt people to speak all the more imaginatively. These conversations are the seeds of the small miracles that can happen when writers travel from one country to support writers in another ... if, that is, they can converse as equals, and as equals share their ideas. ❐

© Maureen Freely
39(4): 27/40
DOI: 10.1177/0306422010389282
www.indexoncensorship.org

Maureen Freely is a writer, translator and professor at Warwick University. Her latest novel is *Enlightenment*, published by Marion Boyars

SURVIVAL IN PRISON

Detained writers suffer from violence, humiliation and loneliness. Writing, often in secret, helps make sense of these terrible experiences, writes **Anne Sebba**

I have seen close up how wrongful imprisonment and torture can affect a human being. I have also seen incredible bravery and resilience. As journalist and editor Kunle Ajibade has observed, the 'strength of the human spirit seems to come from nowhere'.

Kunle had worked on a number of Nigerian newspapers, but in May 1995 was arrested and jailed for life for refusing to reveal the source of a story published in the *News* magazine. The regime did not like this: he was held for three years in Makurdi prison, acknowledged as the worst in Nigeria. For two years he was not allowed the use of a bed or a mosquito net and eventually contracted malaria. There had been something about his case, it was such a grotesque travesty, that although I knew little about Nigeria and nothing about him, I immediately felt a connection and wrote to him for a year or so before his release. I too had started out as a journalist, and thought: what if? He was released in 1998 under a nationwide amnesty, partly thanks to international pressure.

In the autumn of 1999, I volunteered to help put on a fundraising gala in aid of English PEN's Writers in Prison Committee (WiPC). PEN was not a charity in those days, had no sponsors and was permanently short of funds. I blithely wrote to anyone with whom either I or others on the committee had any connections, and was staggered by the response: Timothy West, Prunella Scales, Fay Weldon, Janet Suzman, Sue Lawley, Antonia Fraser, Harold Pinter and Rachel Billington, who was then president of English PEN, all volunteered their services, as did many others.

In the midst of all the organising, I received a letter from Kunle Ajibade. He told me that he was planning to come to London en route to Los Angeles – he had been awarded the Villa Aurora Feuchtwanger Fellowship and was to spend 10 months at the prestigious Getty Research Institute to write, reflect, read and lecture. This was fantastic timing and I invited him to attend the gala as guest of honour.

He wanted neither to read a poem nor to prepare a written speech, just to speak as the mood took him. As it turned out, he was the star performer. He spoke passionately from the heart about what it means to be in prison when you know you are innocent, wondering if anyone knows you are still alive, imagining you may never see your children grow up, agonising about how your family is managing. Kunle explained that night how vital it was to be remembered by fellow writers at PEN. He told of how receiving letters from abroad increased his standing among the jailers, even though it was impossible to reply. He survived by persuading his captors to allow him to sleep during the day and scribble secretly at night, just notes on scraps of paper, sketching out what he wanted to write when he emerged from prison. Somehow he never stopped believing that he would emerge and bear witness to his ordeal. It was electrifying to be in the audience to hear him that night. From the moment I met him there was something infectiously joyous about Kunle's spirit.

Asked what kept him going during his detention, Kunle, now executive editor at the *News*, has said more recently: 'The strength of the human spirit when it is confronted with something that wants to annihilate it – you never know until it happens. That is what is called epiphany. To be honest with you, it wasn't as if there was anything in my life that prepared me for it. It's just an elemental force; it is difficult to describe.'

A few years later I had the privilege of meeting another young journalist, this time while her fate was still unknown. Asiye Guzel Zeybek was 26 and newly married when she was arrested as she attended a workers' demonstration. When she refused to confess to being a member of the Marxist-Leninist party, a crime that in Turkey carried a maximum sentence of 18 years, she was tortured and gang raped. She had been shot during prison riots and dragged down stairs by her hair. As a result, she suffered constant pain in her back, which was compounded by mental anguish and nightmares. She was acutely depressed by not being able to see her parents and three siblings, who supported her throughout her ordeal, or her husband Sardar, also in prison, who was desperately sick from a prolonged hunger strike. While Asiye awaited a verdict on her own case, she was moved to his prison for four weeks. Guards brought Sardar in a wheelchair to see her, separated from her by a partition of thick bars.

Depressed and suffering from weight loss, Asiye was almost broken by this. But what kept her going was the decision to write secretly during her time inside about what was happening to her. This was especially courageous in a society such as Turkey's, where rape destroys a woman's reputation. Equally courageously, she smuggled her manuscript out, chapter by chapter. It was eventually translated into English by Richard McKane in 2003.

I had first seen Asiye in Istanbul, where I went in September 2001 to observe a hearing. Her pain and suffering were indelibly written into every crease of her skin. The hearing – it could not be described as a trial – was one of several court appearances she made during the five years she was held in prison before being formally charged, and it made a mockery of international laws on human rights. Her lawyer, Ercan Kanar, was doing what he could but told me how defendants were constantly moved from one prison to another, which meant that documents disappeared and needed to be replaced, requiring extra time. 'But mostly,' he explained, 'it's difficult because there is so little time to discuss a case. I may be given one and a half hours each week to see 12 or 13 clients in a given prison, but generally I have to wait 40 minutes before even one arrives. There are so many restrictions and obstacles.' I could not speak to Asiye herself on this occasion but I did meet her family in the courtroom mêlée.

I saw Asiye shortly after her release from prison in Turkey in 2002. When she was finally given asylum in Sweden, I flew to Stockholm for our first meeting. I found her living in a modern government apartment surrounded by a group of Kurdish refugees trying to help her adjust. Still pretty, not surprisingly, she looked pale, dazed and unhappy. Shortly after, she came to London to celebrate the publication of her book in English, again with a Kurdish friend who helped translate for her. But although she was free she could never return to her homeland, where she had been sentenced in absentia to twelve and a half years' imprisonment for membership to an illegal organisation. Her parents were in Turkey, she was unable to be a journalist in Sweden

(from L-R) Asiye's sister-in-law, Elisabeth Zila Olin from Swedish PEN,
Asiye Guzel Zeybek and Anne Sebba, 2002

as she could not speak the language and Sardar was still in prison. On her last visit to him before she left, Asiye told him that she would be back in a month, unable to contemplate permanent exile or possible asylum in an unknown country.

Asiye said that writing about what happened to her had the effect of lifting and altering her burden – though it did not, could not, remove it entirely. 'I hadn't thought I would let it out. I was going to keep it a secret … If I hadn't done it, I would have been dead, not physically but psychologically. You can't live with a burden like that.' I asked her if she was ever angry with Sardar, who now suffers from a total and definitive loss of memory as a result of fasting. 'I try to understand him', she said.

Prison changed Asiye: 'I feel stronger because it was a school for me, where I learnt to analyse and build a perspective on life.' In 2009, she got married for the second time, to a man she had known in Turkey, and they now live in Malmö with their baby son.

'Prison as school' is a description used by many of those who survive it. In July 2010, the Cuban government agreed to release 52 political prisoners, including 22 writers, journalists and librarians who had been on the PEN case list. Ricardo González Alfonso, one of those released and living in exile, explained why being out of prison did not mean he was free. He spoke of the lessons prison offered in zoology (learning to live with rats and spiders) and in cosmic solitude (months of silence and darkness). He said: 'A large part of the programme of study consisted in the defence of one's rights. There was no theoretical option, only the very Cuban practice of the hunger strike.

Writing can be of vital cathartic importance. But sometimes prisoners are so shocked they cannot find a voice to express what they have lived through. Sheila Hayman, coordinator of the 'Write to Life' workshop run by the Medical Foundation for the Care of Victims of Torture, says those she works with find writing helps them to make sense of their experiences and to process the painful elements. Her group meets every two weeks, and although some may have been journalists, they mostly write autobiographical poetry or short stories. 'People who have been tortured and humiliated begin to think they don't exist, but the response to what they write proves they do, it's an echo … The response to their writing works as an indirect way of learning to trust people again.'

In *Survival in Auschwitz*, Primo Levi writes: 'Even in this place one can survive, and therefore one must want to survive, to tell the story, to bear witness; and that to survive we must force ourselves to save at least the skeleton, the scaffolding, the form of civilisation.' He not only survived, miraculously, but wrote some of the most powerful literature of the 20th century. For the rest of us it's hard to imagine how any prison experience might affect our ability to write. Does anything else ever matter again? ❐

© Anne Sebba
39(4): 41/45
DOI: 10.1177/0306422010388687
www.indexoncensorship.org

Anne Sebba is a biographer. *That Woman: The Life of Wallis Simpson, Duchess of Windsor* will be published by Weidenfeld and Nicolson in August 2011

LIBERATING LANGUAGE

Mohamed Nasheed on how the Maldives has rejected the lexicon, along with the rule, of decades of dictatorship and rediscovered freedom of expression

The English author and journalist George Orwell railed against politicians and bureaucrats who perverted language 'to make lies sound truthful and murder respectable'. In *Nineteen Eighty-Four*, Orwell describes how an authoritarian regime selectively uses words to maintain control. The regime develops a new language, a slimmed-down version of English called 'Newspeak', in which all terms pertaining to freedom or rebellion are excised. The new language limits people's capacity to think critically, helping to prevent 'thought crimes' against the state. *1984* is a work of fiction aimed at exposing the horrors of Soviet authoritarianism. But Orwell's depiction of regime propaganda doesn't just apply to Stalinist Russia: it also rings true in the Maldives's recent past.

The Maldives, an island nation in the Indian Ocean, has been a brutal authoritarian regime for much of its recent history. Former president Maumoon Abdul Gayoom, who ruled with an iron fist for three decades until democratic elections in 2008, maintained his grip on power through fear, intimidation and violence. Under the former president's rule, political parties were banned, the press was tightly censored and political freedoms

Mohamed Nasheed takes part in a sit-down protest against President Gayoom's government, Malé, 2005

severely restricted. The president was also omnipotent: head of the armed forces, the judiciary and, through his appointed proxies, the legislature. Amnesty International reports spanning the 1980s to the 2000s detail the arrests, beatings and torture of dozens of political prisoners. I was arrested some 15 times over a 20-year period, spending close to six years in jail for speaking out against the regime.

Overt repression was accompanied by a more sinister and invisible form of control: language was also under arrest. The dictatorial narrative, spewed out via government propaganda outlets, sought to maintain the political status quo and discourage dissent. Appeals to 'national unity', 'stability' and 'sovereignty' were none too subtle demands for obedience to the regime. Anyone who sought to criticise the government was immediately accused of attempting to 'destabilise' the country and labelled a traitor to the nation.

Prior to the start of the democracy movement in 2005, there were no words in Dhivehi, the Maldivian language, to describe 'peaceful protest' or 'civil disobedience'. There was also no word to describe a detainee who may or may not be guilty of an offence. The regime labelled people arrested during human rights protests as *quvvarin*, which means 'criminal'.

It was not just verbal language that was used to suppress the people: body language also played a part. The former president developed a calculated persona to make him appear untouchable and god-like: he was aloof and during TV interviews appeared rigid, expressionless and unflappable. He also used a mixture of Dhivehi and Arabic, which most Maldivians do not understand. This fed a perception that the everyday person did not have the knowledge, or intelligence, to criticise a president they were unable to comprehend, let alone appreciate.

President Gayoom also portrayed himself as a learned religious scholar. The regime developed a cult of personality, with the president framed as the father of the nation and the defender of the faith. The implication was that if Gayoom fell, so would Islam in the Maldives. Any attack on the president was therefore regarded as a direct attack on Islam itself. When fellow activists and I founded the Maldivian Democratic Party in exile in Sri Lanka, it was no surprise that the regime attempted to portray us as a threat to religion.

From the start of the democracy campaign, it was clear we would never beat the regime if we used their version of Maldivian 'Newspeak'. We had to write a different narrative about the Maldives, so people saw the president not as the father of the nation but as a tyrant holding people back. To free the Maldives from authoritarianism we first had to liberate language.

The democracy movement expanded the scope of critical thought by resurrecting long-forgotten words associated with freedom and independence. The movement borrowed words from Arabic and Urdu, such as *quidee*, which means 'detainee'. These words are now a common feature in human rights reports and news articles in the Maldives.

Since the new administration took office in late 2008, the lid on political freedoms has been finally lifted. Prisoners of conscience and journalists wrongly imprisoned by the former regime have been freed. Defamation has been decriminalised, so that journalists no longer have to fear they will go to jail for anything that they write. And limits on freedom of association, assembly, free speech and political participation have been scrapped. These developments have been closely monitored by several international human rights NGOs: last year, Freedom House promoted the Maldives from a 'not free' to a 'partially free' country. Four years ago, Reporters Sans Frontières (RSF) labelled the Maldivian president a 'predator of press freedom'; today, the Maldives stands just eight places behind France in RSF's global press freedom index.

Perhaps most encouragingly, members of the former regime have adopted notions of freedom and democracy in their own political discourse. I am often criticised – unjustly I would hasten to add – by members of the former regime for acting 'like a dictator' or 'against democracy'. The opposition's embrace of the new political lexicon suggests that the preservation of democratic principles is becoming sacrosanct.

As Orwell understood: 'If thought corrupts language, language can also corrupt thought.' ❐

©Mohamed Nasheed
39(4): 47/50
DOI: 10.1177/0306422010388710
www.indexoncensorship.org

Mohamed Nasheed is president of the Maldives, after being elected in the country's first multiparty presidential elections in October 2008

DIALOGUE WITH DARKNESS

Arthur Koestler's imprisonment marked a turning point in his thinking, writes **Michael Scammell**, and was one of the first campaigns to be a cause célèbre

Arthur Koestler regarded himself as something of a connoisseur of prisons. His first and worst incarceration occurred at the height of the Spanish Civil War in 1937. While working as a journalist covering the Battle of Malaga, he was arrested by General Francisco Franco's Falangist forces and transferred to a military jail in Seville, where he was held for just over three months. Listening as his fellow prisoners were hauled out for execution one by one, he was convinced that he too had been given a death sentence and waited for his end to come at any moment.

Two years later, having been released and allowed to return to Paris, he was arrested again by the French security services and sent to the concentration camp of Le Vernet in southern France. The camp regime was harsh enough, but more relaxed than Seville's, and towards the end of his time there he was actually able to work on the novel that became *Darkness at Noon*. No sooner had he been released and returned to Paris than the police appeared at his apartment yet again and arrested both him and his novel. The German manuscript of *Darkness at Noon* disappeared forever, but a translation into English had been mailed to London just days before the raid and thus saved it from oblivion. Koestler escaped, this time by bluffing his way out of the police station and going underground, after which he spent the next five months on the run.

He eventually made his way to England, where he was arrested for a fourth time and ended up in Pentonville prison. By now he was able to joke about it, calling Pentonville a 'three-star' prison, 'the most decent jail I have been in', compared with his others, but the execution of a German spy shook him to the core and reminded him where he was. He was still there in December 1940 when the English version of *Darkness at Noon* was published.

The key event in this odyssey was his imprisonment in Spain. The Spanish Civil War was an international *cause célèbre* in the mid-1930s, marking the first major clash in Europe between the forces of the left and the right, of socialism and fascism, and proved in effect to be a rehearsal for the Second World War – except that in the 1930s the fascists won. It was also a conflict that, even more than the later Korean or Vietnam wars, assumed huge symbolic importance in the eyes of public opinion, and held a special attraction for artists and intellectuals. Dozens of noted writers and journalists flocked to Spain either to fight on behalf of the left (Orwell, Malraux) or to report or write in its defence (Auden, Spender, Hemingway, Dos Passos, Neruda, Ehrenburg, and many others).

Koestler, unlike these figures, was virtually unknown at the time, but he was the only writer to be captured and jailed, and apparently to face a death sentence. He was also one of the first writers to become the object of an international campaign (by PEN, among others) to free him, inspiring a wave of publicity, protests, petitions and back door negotiations unprecedented in their intensity, paving the way for the innumerable international protest campaigns that have been conducted ever since.

The first indication of what was in store for Koestler came in the form of a telegram from Sir Peter Chalmers-Mitchell, the British consul in Malaga (with whom Koestler had been staying) immediately after Koestler's arrest: 'Do everything to save Koestler,' it said. The recipient was the news editor of the progressive *News Chronicle* in London, one of the newspapers Koestler worked for as a foreign correspondent. The *News Chronicle* immediately launched a campaign that reached through newspaper and diplomatic channels into the Vatican and the League of Nations, and drew in even pro-Falangist newspapers, like those of the Hearst press. Questions were asked in the British and French parliaments, while the PEN centres of England, France, America and Italy were all enlisted to provide support. The campaign was given a human face by Koestler's first wife, Dorothee, who travelled from Paris to London to plead with influential British politicians and public figures for help.

It was never clear whether Koestler actually faced a death sentence or not, but he was extricated through a prisoner exchange managed by the International Red Cross, and the campaign was hailed as a model exercise of democratic public opinion in defence of an innocent victim. The truth, however, is a bit more complicated than that. Koestler was a communist at the time of his arrest, and had earlier visited Spain as an agent of the communist front organisation, the Comintern. His arrests in France were also prompted by his communist past, and it was these affiliations that assured his arrest in Britain.

Sir Peter Chalmers-Mitchell, the man who first raised the alarm on Koestler's behalf, was a fellow traveller of the Communist Party, and the recipient of his telegram, the news editor of the *News Chronicle*, was a party member. Dorothee herself was a member of the party, and her urgent pleas for mercy – and indeed much of the campaign – was micromanaged by the Comintern. Such were the sympathies accrued by the left in Europe at that time, especially among intellectuals, and such the skill of the Communist Party in manipulating public opinion, that its role in the protests went entirely unnoticed. PEN itself had come heavily under the influence of the Popular Front of the 1930s and had many communists among its members, so that those who knew what was afoot kept silent, while the unsuspecting were happy that the left had scored another victory.

The successful campaign turned Koestler into a celebrity, but the irony of his situation was that he had experienced a series of epiphanies in his Spanish jail that had started him on a path away from communism and towards a very different spiritual and intellectual position. One of these epiphanies carried the insight that human ethics drew on psychological and intellectual wellsprings that were far more profound than any provided by any political doctrine or ideology. Another was the recognition that fascist violence was no different in kind from communist violence, and a third convinced him that the sanctity of human life took precedence over any kind of religious or political dogma. These maxims eventually coalesced into a conviction that evil means could never be justified by benevolent ends, and it was this belief that would eventually drive him out of the party altogether.

They remained in his subconscious for a while after his release, but as they blossomed in his mind they changed his whole worldview and helped transform him from an unusually talented journalist into an author of distinction. Like Orwell, he realised that Spain marked a turning point in his life, and that 'every serious line' he wrote after that was the fruit of his experiences there. He worked out the implications of this new understanding in works that plumbed his prison experiences for their deeper meaning and applied the lessons he had learned to other areas of life.

The first of these was *Dialogue with Death,* a memoir about his Seville experiences that he published almost immediately, but continued to edit and refine as his insights deepened and developed. The second and most profound fruit of his conversion was *Darkness at Noon,* the story of a Communist Party leader's arrest, interrogation and condemnation to death, in which Koestler drew on his memories of a fascist jail to illustrate with uncanny accuracy the mental state of a prisoner in a communist jail. In doing so he was one of the very first to draw a comparison between the inhumanity of the two competing political movements, and to conclude that, in regard to their savagery, there was little to choose between them.

In *The Scum of the Earth,* his next memoir, published in 1941, chronicling his imprisonment in France and his flight to Britain, Koestler drew on his experiences at Le Vernet for yet another portrait of prison life, but broadened his perspective in the story of his escape south to present a devastating picture of France in collapse and a Europe in shambles. The narrative is bathed in an air of doom and disillusionment, and Koestler dedicated his book to five fellow exiles who had committed suicide rather than surrender to the Germans. His story, he later said, was 'a requiem for European civilisation'.

There were echoes of this apocalyptic tone and despairing pessimism in Koestler's 1943 novel, *Arrival and Departure,* about the Second World War, which contained one of the first (if not *the* first) descriptions of the Holocaust in a work of literature, and he revisited the subject of a disintegrating Europe in his two autobiographies, *Arrow in the Blue* and *The Invisible Writing.* Written in the early 1950s, they presented his tempestuous life and career as the 'typical case history' of a 20th-century European intellectual, and treated prison as a natural (if not inevitable) part of an intellectual's life. Not long after that, Koestler turned to writing about science, but his experiences in Seville undoubtedly inspired the writing of *Reflections on Hanging,* his fiery polemic against the death penalty in Britain, and even, to a certain extent, of *The Ghost in the Machine,* his exploration of the sources of man's inhumanity to man.

Like many writers past and present, Koestler came to regard his prison experiences as enlightening and a blessing. Prison had opened his eyes to truths that he might not otherwise have perceived, or would have taken much longer to arrive at, and enriched his understanding of both himself and others. But he never made the sentimental mistake of thinking they were a general good, or couldn't mean disaster for the prisoner. He realised he was one of the lucky ones, and devoted a great deal of time and money to helping other political prisoners who had suffered such a fate. Later in life, he helped start the Koestler Trust to help *all* prisoners endure their sentences with dignity, and never forgot what a jail sentence was like. Meanwhile we can rejoice that in 1937 PEN, the Communist Party and the Red Cross were successful in getting him out, not only for Koestler's sake, but also for our own as readers. ❐

©Michael Scammell
39(4): 52/57
DOI: 10.1177/0306422010389114
www.indexoncensorship.org

Michael Scammell edited *Index on Censorship* from 1972–80 and was the first chair of PEN's Writers in Prison Committee. He teaches writing and translation at Columbia and is the author of *Solzhenitsyn* (WW Norton & Co Ltd) and *Koestler: the Indispensable Intellect* (Faber & Faber)

DON'T TELL US WHAT TO WRITE

Margaret Atwood on why the mark of a truly free society is one that allows writers to speak with their own voice, not for causes, however worthy

Formal Invocation to the Reader:
Dear (Mysterious) Reader, Whoever You May Be:
Whether near or far, whether in the present or the future or even – in your spirit form – in the past,
Whether old or young, or in the middle of your life,
Whether male or female, or located somewhere along the continuum that joins these two supposed polarities,
Of whatever religion, or none; of whatever political opinion, or nothing much definite;
Whether tall or short, whether luxuriously-haired or balding; whether well or ill; whether a golfer or a canoeist, or a soccer fan, or the player or devotee of any number of other sports and pastimes;
Whether a writer yourself, or a lover of reading, or a student forced into reluctant readership by the necessities of the educational system;
Whether reading on paper or electronically, in the bathtub, on a train, in a library, school, or prison, under a beach umbrella, in a cafe, on a rooftop garden, under the covers with a flashlight, or in a myriad other manners and possible locations;

It is you whom we writers address, always, in your unknown singularity.
Oh Reader, live forever! (You – the individual reader – won't live forever, but
it's fun to say, and it sounds good):
We writers cannot imagine you; yet we must,
For without you, the activity of writing is surely meaningless and without
destination,
And therefore it is by its very nature an act of hope, since writing implies a
future in which the freedom to read will exist:
We conjure and invoke you, Mysterious Reader; and Lo: You exist! The proof
of your existence is that you have just read about that existence of yours,
right here.

There. That's what we're talking about: the fact that I could write these words, and that you, via the go-between of paper or screen, can read them.

Which is by no means a foregone conclusion: for this is the very process that all governments and many other groups – religious, political, pressure lobbies of all shades and varieties, you name it – would like to harness, control, censor, bowdlerise, twist to their own purposes, exile, or extirpate. The extent to which they can implement this desire is one of the measures on the graduated line that extends from liberal democracy to locked-down dictatorship.

The publication of this special commemorative issue of *Index on Censorship* is a noteworthy occasion – and it is an important one, for often PEN and Index on Censorship have been the chief witnesses and recording angels of the erasures of books, as well as other acts against our shared writing-and-reading activity – the murders of journalists, the closing down of newspapers and publishing houses, the trials of novelists.

Neither organisation wields any power apart from the power of the word: what is sometimes called 'moral suasion'. Thus both organisations can exist only in societies that allow a fairly free circulation of words. I say 'fairly free', for there has never been a society that sets no limit at all on what can legally be made public, or 'published'. A country in which anyone could say anything he or she chose would be one without any legal recourse for the slandered or traduced. 'Bearing false witnesses' is probably at least as old as language, and no doubt so are the prohibitions against it.

But a brief history of censorship would by no means be brief. Cast your mind over the various laws, past and present, here and there, against hate speech, child pornography, blasphemy, obscenity, treason, and so forth, all of which come with the best of justifications – preserving public order, protecting the innocent, enhancing religious toleration and/or orthodoxy, and so forth, and you'll see there's been no end of effort. It's the balance between forbidden and permitted, however, that is one of the litmus tests of an open democracy in progress. Like the coloured water in a tube barometer, this balance is in constant flux.

In honour of this special *Index on Censorship* issue, I've been asked to write some words about 'the writer as political agent'. This is a little difficult for me to do, because I don't believe that writers necessarily are political agents. Political footballs, yes; but 'political agent' implies a deliberately chosen act that is primarily political in nature, and this is not how all writers work. Instead, many writers stand in relation to politics as the small child does to the Emperor with No Clothes: they remark on the man's nakedness not to be bratty or disruptive, but because they just can't see any clothes. Then they wonder why people are yelling at them. It can be a dangerous kind of naivety, but it's common. No one was more surprised than Salman Rushdie by the fatwa issued against him for *The Satanic Verses*: here he thought he was putting immigrant Muslims on the literary map!

There are of course many different kinds of writers. Journalists and non-fiction authors frequently write deliberately as political agents – that is, they want to further a specific end, often by making known facts that are inconvenient to those with power. It's frequently these kinds of writers who are gunned down in the street, like so many Mexican journalists, or assassinated where they live, like the crusading Russian reporter Anna Politkovskaya, or have air-to-surface missiles lobbed at them, like the al Jazeera broadcasters during the American invasion of Baghdad. Such deaths are intended to shut down dissent, both by silencing individuals and by sending a message to any others who might feel the temptation to get mouthy.

Government crackdowns on the media have now been circumvented to some extent by the internet. You can take the guts out of the investigative journalists, both figuratively and literally, but so far no one has been able to completely suppress the human urge that's at least as old as the Book of Job: the need to tell. Catastrophes strike Job's family members, one after the other; but each of them produces its messenger, who says: 'I only am escaped alone to tell thee.' The urge to tell is balanced by the urge to know. We want the story, we want the true story, we want the whole story. We want to know how bad things are, and whether they might affect us; but also we want to make up our own minds. For if we don't know the truth of a matter, how can we have any valid opinions about it?

True or not true: these are the primary categories that we apply to reporting journalism and political non-fiction. But I am primarily a fiction writer and a poet, so it's the suppression of these kinds of writing that concerns me the most. What we expect from journalists is accuracy, but the 'truths' of fiction and poetry are other. Let's just say that if you can't make a novel plausible in its detail, engaging in its language, and/or compelling in the story it is telling, you will lose the Mysterious Reader.

Novelists, poets and playwrights have had varying stated intentions over the years: the re-enactment of a society's core myths, the flattering of the aristocracy, the holding of a mirror up to Nature so that we might see our own natures in it. During and after the Romantic era it became a truism that the 'duty' of a writer was to write in opposition to whoever was in power, as such incumbents were assumed to be corrupt and oppressive; or to expose abuses, as in Charles Dickens's take on the kill-a-boy Dotheboys Hall schools of his time; or to tell the stories of the oppressed and marginalised, as in *Les Miserables*, an approach that has subsequently launched millions of novelistic ships; or to champion a cause, as *Uncle Tom's Cabin* did for abolition.

But this is very far from saying that novelists and poets *have* to write with such intentions. To judge novels on the justness of their causes or the 'rightness' of their 'politics' is to fall into the very same kind of thinking that leads to censorship.

Many is the revolution that has ended by eating its writerly young, as their once-acceptable productions are pronounced heretical by the victors in the inevitable power struggles. As a red-diaper friend of mine said recently of her parents' communist group: 'They were always so hard on the writers.'

For revolutionaries, reactionaries, the religiously orthodox, or simply the passionate adherents of any cause whatsoever, the writing of fiction and poetry is not only suspect but secondary – writing is a tool to be employed in the service of the cause, and if either the work or its author doesn't toe the line of the moment, or worse, goes directly against it, the author must be denounced as a parasite, ostracised, or disposed of, as Federico García Lorca was by the fascists in Spain – shot without trial, then dumped into an unmarked grave.

But for the fiction and poetry writer, the writing itself – the craft and the art – is primary, whatever other impulses or influences may be in play. The mark of a society approaching freedom is the space allowed to the far-ranging human imagination and to the unfettered human voice. There's no shortage of folks standing ready to tell the writer how and what to write. Many are those who feel impelled to sit on panels and discuss the 'role of

Harriet Beecher Stowe's novel championed a cause, but it is
dangerous to demand that writers always be political (following page)
Credit: Pictorial Press Ltd/Alamy

135,000 SETS, 270,000 VOLUMES SOLD.

UNCLE TOM'S CABIN

FOR SALE HERE.

AN EDITION FOR THE MILLION, COMPLETE IN 1 Vol., PRICE 37 1-2 CENTS.

" " IN GERMAN, IN 1 Vol., PRICE 50 CENTS.

" " IN 2 Vols,. CLOTH, 6 PLATES, PRICE $1.50.

SUPERB ILLUSTRATED EDITION, IN 1 Vol., WITH 153 ENGRAVINGS,

PRICES FROM $2.50 TO $5.00,

The Greatest Book of the Age.

the writer' or the 'duty of the writer', as if writing itself is a frivolous pursuit, of no value apart from whatever external roles and duties can be cooked up for it: extolling the fatherland, fostering world peace, improving the position of women, and so forth.

That writing *may* involve itself in such issues is self-evident, but to say that it *must* is sinister. 'Must' breaks the bond between the writer, such as me, and you yourself, Mysterious Reader: for in whom can you place your readerly trust if not in me, the voice speaking to you from the page or screen, right now? And if I allow this voice to be turned into the dutiful, role-fulfilling sock puppet of some group, even a worthy one, how can you place any faith in it whatsoever?

Both Index on Censorship and PEN defend the word 'may' in this connection, and oppose the word 'must'. They defend the open space in which writers may use their own voices freely, and readers may then read freely. Thus I was happy to write something for them; though it may not be exactly what they had in mind. ❐

© Margaret Atwood
39(4): 58/63
DOI: 10.1177/0306422010388981
www.indexoncensorship.org

Margaret Atwood's books include *The Handmaid's Tale, Cat's Eye, The Blind Assassin* and *Oryx and Crake,* all published by Bloomsbury. Her latest book is *The Year of the Flood* (Random House)

British Muslims protest the publication of Salman Rushdie's
The Satanic Verses outside the Houses of Parliament, 1989
Credit: Roger Hutchings/Alamy

WORDS WITHOUT BORDERS

As ideas move freely around the world, attacks on
writers continue, reports **Lisa Appignanesi**

On the morning of 12 July 1991, the body of 44-year-old Professor Hitoshi Igarashi was found in the corridor near his seventh-floor office at Tsukuba University, 40 miles northeast of Tokyo. The translator of Salman Rushdie's *The Satanic Verses* and himself a Muslim convert, Igarashi had been stabbed to death by an assailant carrying out the murderous orders laid down in Ayatollah Khomeini's notorious fatwa on Rushdie and his publishers.

Igarashi's murder, in an environment so distant from the Britain where Rushdie's book had first appeared three years earlier, made me viscerally aware of what the fatwa of 14 February 1989 had set in train: the edicts of religious and state power, and indeed of criminal undergrounds, had a lethal resonance on writers and translators well beyond any geographic frontiers. The world had emphatically become a 'global village'. In one of those ironic synchronies that history is prone to, 1991 was also the year that the world wide web first went live, though it would take another decade for it to acquire its current prominence.

Borders have, of course, long been permeable to writing and ideas. They have also been permeable to fear. In its *Index Librorum Prohibitorum* (List of Prohibited Books), established in 1559 and only abolished four centuries later in 1966, the Catholic Church proscribed a host of works dangerous to the morals of the faithful – from Johannes Kepler's astronomical writings in the 17th century, to Immanuel Kant's *Critique of Pure Reason* (1781) and Thomas Paine's *Rights of Man* (1791), to Simone de Beauvoir's *The Second Sex* (1953). But the targeting of writers, as well as their writings, by religious and state authorities both outside and inside domestic frontiers has taken on a particular virulence over the past 20 years. The speed of communication the internet permits, its blindness to geography, seems to have stoked the fires of prohibition. The freer and easier it is for ideas to spread, the more punitive the powers that wish to silence or censor become. Then, too, in much of the world, outside the liberal enclaves of secular Europe, God has never died and seems to need increasingly arduous protection from purported blasphemers.

The events surrounding *The Satanic Verses* were prophetic. After 9/11, the anger of conservative believers, Muslim or Christian, over the way they and their beliefs were represented was even more readily sparked. Skins had grown thin. In 2004, the Dutch filmmaker Theo van Gogh was murdered because his film about the subjection of women in Islam, *Submission*, insulted Muslims; threats to his collaborator, Ayaan Hirsi Ali, then an MP, led to her needing long-term police protection. When the conservative Danish newspaper *Jyllands-Posten* published cartoons of the Prophet Mohammed in 2005, it resulted in protests throughout the Muslim world, some 100 deaths, attacks on Danish embassies and a brutal assault on Kurt Westergaard, the best known of the Danish cartoonists.

Both the teaching of Darwin in schools and performances of the purportedly 'blasphemous' *Jerry Springer: The Opera* have attracted protests by militant Christians both in Britain and the USA. Films of Dan Brown's *The Da Vinci Code* and Philip Pullman's *Northern Lights* came in for similar protest. Meanwhile, Christian librarians in the USA saw fit to keep books as innocuous as *The Wizard of Oz* off their shelves, for fear of contaminating young minds.

Secular power, as we've long known, can be as jealous as religious power and react as adversely to criticism, silencing writers in brutal ways. In 2006, the Russian journalist Anna Politkovskaya, whose bold reports on Chechnya hardly endeared her to Vladimir Putin's hierarchy, was murdered. In the same year, this time in Italy, the writer Roberto Saviano began receiving the death threats that forced him into a hidden, itinerant life under police protection, following the publication of his bestselling book *Gomorrah*, which details the workings of the Neapolitan-based Camorra and its mafia-like international reach.

Strange to say, while evidently recognising the importance of literature, ideas and investigative journalism, the censorious seem to be blind to the fact history so flagrantly illuminates: that ideas and writings outlive both their makers and their censors. The works of Kant, Paine and Flaubert are still with us, but we have long forgotten the particular papal committee that sought to ban them. The power of words trumps temporal expedience.

But writers, themselves, are made of flesh and have families. They can be silenced – by death, by imprisonment, by the conditions of exile and by fear itself. That fear, in countries such as Britain, where free expression is invoked as a right, can come from a variety of sources. It can be as general as an atmosphere of political correctness – a sense of pressure from an ethnic or religious community or publishers alert to these; or as specific as the possibility of a libel suit. And where free speech is chilled, where access to information, ideas and literature is severely restricted, the very fabric of our lives is impoverished.

When I took on the position first of deputy president of English PEN in 2004 and then of president in 2007, it was clear to me that the permeable, globalised world in which we live meant that campaigning to protect endangered writers abroad, though crucial, was no longer a sufficient undertaking. We had to clean up our own stables as well. How could we deplore the cry of blasphemy by Muslim leaders, the harsh penalties of Islamo-fascist regimes, when an antiquated statute outlawing blasphemy still existed in our own books? Meanwhile, the Turkish regime, which we criticised for its law criminalising any denigration of Turkishness, could point to the continued existence here of 'seditious libel'. We were often reminded that many of the countries of the old commonwealth base their legislation and jurisprudence on British law and cite our example when carrying out repressive measures.

It was evident that our defamation laws needed attention. Blasphemy was top of the agenda for rescinding. Some Muslim groups had been campaigning ever since the Rushdie affair to have it extended to include offence to Islam. Far better, it seemed to us, to establish parity by abolishing the hoary old law altogether.

Achieving change in legislation is ever slow and never easy. Campaigns need partners and growing momentum. They also need a political moment. Ironically, our sense that the blasphemy laws needed repealing coincided with the Labour government's wish to extend the limits of offence. Trapped in worries about security and confusion about the meaning of 'respect', on 24 November 2004 it introduced a law banning incitement to religious hatred. In large part a response to conservative Muslim pressure, the law was loosely framed. Enacted in its original unamended form, it would have placed impossible limits on expression as well as thought. It would have criminalised any questioning of belief – itself a system of ever-changing ideas – and left any satirist open to protracted court proceedings. It would also have criminalised a good part of what contending religions themselves teach about each other. Had the law existed back in 1989, Rushdie, instead of being protected by the state, would have found himself censored by the courts.

The very promulgation of the law seemed to give minority faiths the licence to protest and shout 'offence', often against writers who shared their own homeland, imaginary or real. A group of Birmingham Sikhs rioted in December 2004 in protest against Gurpreet Kaur Bhatti's play *Behzti* and closed it down, while the government – ever ready to make concessions to minority action in the name of a bureaucratised multiculturalism – applauded their exercise of free speech. A contingent of Bangladeshis in London's East End, in 2006, protested against the filming of Monica Ali's *Brick Lane*, with the result that many of the Brick Lane scenes had to be filmed elsewhere.

But the gathered vocal force of opposition to the legislation, our 'Free Expression Is No Offence' campaign, together with the help of experienced parliamentarians such as Evan Harris MP and Lord Lester, won through. The PEN amendment, eventually introduced into the bill, resulted in making it unworkable. It marked the first robust protection of free expression in our statute books. Offence cannot be protected by law, which nonetheless protects individuals from harm.

English PEN, Sense About Science, and Index on Censorship
launched a campaign for libel reform in 2009 (following page)
Credit: Brett Biedscheid

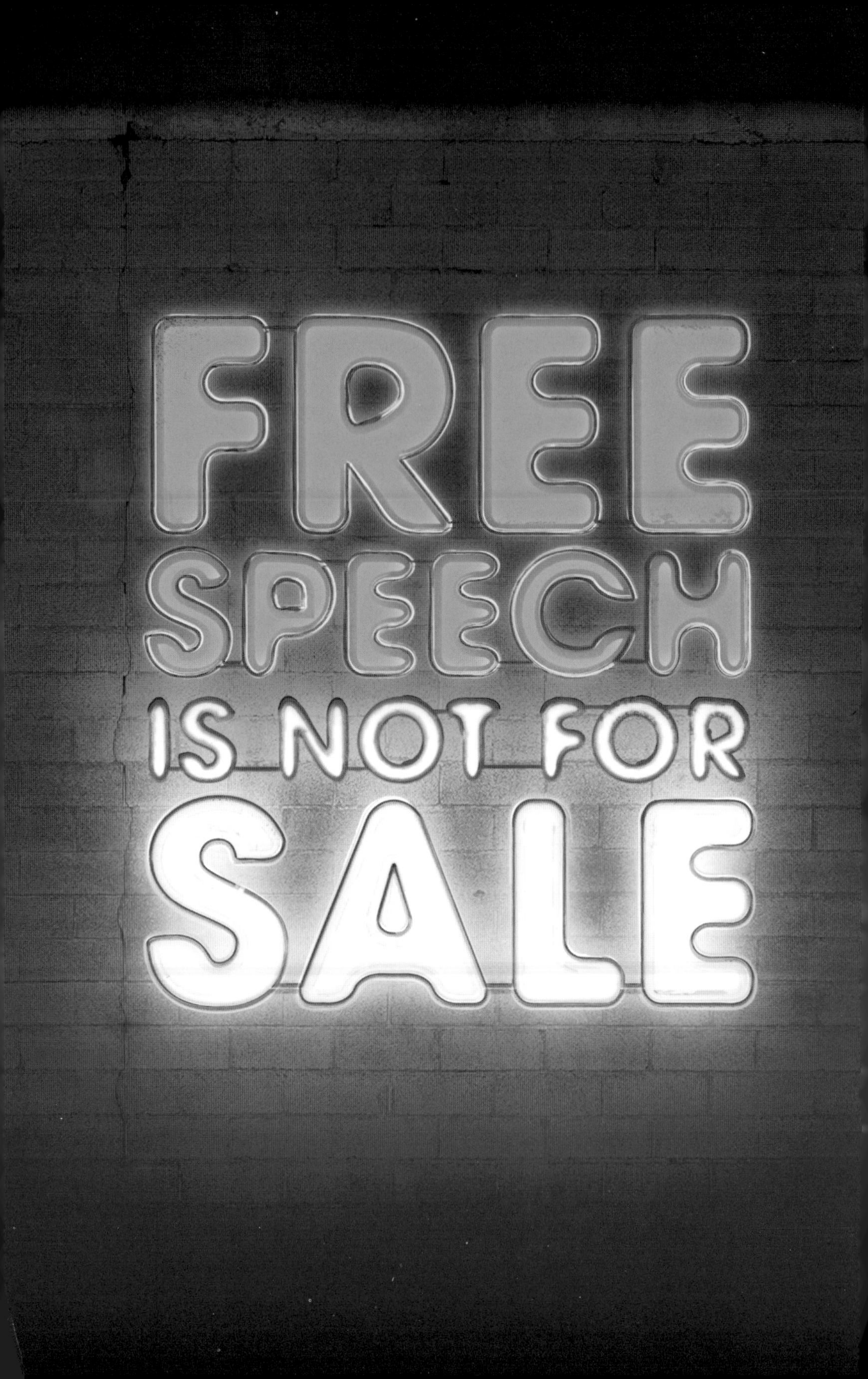
FREE
SPEECH
IS NOT FOR
SALE

Reform of the civil libel laws was next. These laws promulgated at a time when wealth and reputation were thought to walk arm in arm and have accrued in precedents. Libel courts thrive on conditional fee agreements open alike to a Sudanese businessman angered by the memoirs of the young woman whom he and his wife had, in effect, enslaved; to an oligarch seeking to silence a journalist alleging corruption in a Ukrainian newspaper with only a hundred subscribers in Britain; and to the British Chiropractic Association attesting that its reputation had been tarnished by Simon Singh's queries about its wide-ranging claims.

Thanks to the campaign run jointly by Index on Censorship, English PEN and Sense About Science, momentum to reform the laws reached a sufficient pitch for the Labour, Conservative and Liberal Democrat parties to commit to change in their manifestos. Following Lord Lester's private member's bill in the Lords in May 2010, the government has promised to publish its proposals for reform in the coming year. We will keep them to it.

Although Britain seems to welcome the world into its libel courts, its new points-based visa system adamantly works to keep writers, artists, academics and students from non-EU countries out. The system, which at borders has the effect of turning everyone into a suspected terrorist or asylum seeker, also endangers our status as a cultural hub and centre for the knowledge industries. Impeding the free circulation of ideas and art in this way is an attack on citizens and their freedom to hear, to learn and to see. Living behind walls of unrestricted bureaucracy makes prisoners of us all.

As I near the end of my term as president of English PEN, I would like to think that we have accomplished something. But keeping the terrain of expression free is a continual challenge and one that hardly affects writers alone. In this permeable and stratified world, where injustice abounds, we neither want to be threatened into restrictive practices nor intimidated into false respect. We all need fresh ideas, open exchange and imagination to keep our plural democracies robust. We also need them to make life worth living. ❏

©Lisa Appignanesi
39(4): 66/71
DOI: 10.1177/0306422010389251
www.indexoncensorship.org

Lisa Appignanesi is the author of *Mad, Bad and Sad: Women and Mind the Doctors from 1800 to the Present* (Virago) and editor of *Free Expression Is No Offence* (Penguin). Her new book is *All About Love: Anatomy of an Unruly Emotion*

RELUCTANT HEROES

International recognition offers a degree of protection to investigative reporters. But, writes **Lydia Cacho**, being in the limelight presents a new set of dilemmas

The first call is the one you never forget. The person uttering the death threat has spent days preparing for this moment – to let you know that your fate is sealed. Up until this phone call, or email, threats were something ethereal and alien, something that happened to other people.

Over time, I learned what many journalists and writers have learned before me: that becoming the news is a double-edged sword. It can weaken and wound; it unsettles us and sets us apart from our colleagues and loved ones. The threats somehow become as important as the original story.

This dilemma dominates the rest of our lives, because for us to come through safely we need to be out there, in public, and never be silenced. At the same time, we have to always remain on guard, watching our backs, alert whenever we see a police or military patrol, reacting instantly to any sound resembling a shot, tensing every time a motorcycle accelerates or approaches, permanently on the lookout for a weapon in case the rider is a hit man. And on and on, we have to proclaim to the four winds, until we're fed up with doing so – and everyone else is fed up with us too – the name of the *mafioso*, the politician, the policeman or the corrupt businessman who has put a price on our heads. Yet we yearn for the privacy and anonymity that would allow us to move around without being recognised, for those times when we used to have no need to conceal the names of our family members (for they are now vulnerable too).

As well as the threat of death, there is the threat of imprisonment. Many of my colleagues, from Iraq to Colombia, Cambodia to Kenya, have published memoirs that deal with post-traumatic stress they have suffered as a result of their experiences in jail. Once out of jail, there is the coming to terms with working and earning money, no longer now simply to feed our children, to pay for fuel and water, or for cinema tickets, but to pay lawyers in whose hands, like a small fish out of water, our conditional freedom rests. We spend years in courtrooms, gathering evidence and convincing witnesses to risk their lives by coming on board with us. Cases of defamation are regularly brought against us with the intention of exhausting us emotionally and financially. The courts become yet another weapon the mafia or corrupt politicians can use against us.

There are lessons to be learnt here. As more journalists become victims of the courts, those whose plight they are trying to expose also become victims. We must learn how to interview a victim without obliging them to relive their suffering. Let us learn to show compassion for those who dignify us with the confidence of their personal histories. Let us discover how to conduct investigations so that we do not hurt further those who have already suffered. Let us develop methods of inquiry that protect those victims (of war and the mafia, of natural disasters and domestic violence) whom we interview.

We need to learn to operate in a world where much of the media have been captivated by the spectacle of cruelty, by a morbid fascination with pseudo-pornography, in which there is no pain without blood. In the fabulous world of ratings, to survive and maintain one's dignity is hardly good news. There are always those who demand drama: a few tears from the Mexican journalist who was tortured and imprisoned, then raped in order to ensure her silence, feeds the morbid desire for titillation, not for indignation. In Uganda, the reporter whose hands were mutilated by the military in order to stop him ever writing again is asked to display his stump as if begging for pity. The media ask the Iraqi journalist to recount a hundred times over how US soldiers murdered her children to quell her voice, and how she herself washed their little bodies alone in her house. They insist the South African poet stops reading his verses of love and hope and instead relives the darkness of his cell, shows the camera the marks of the torture he has spent the last 10 years trying to forget, and explains how the love of his family faded to the point where, one autumn afternoon, nobody at all came to visit him in prison. And they ask the Russian woman journalist – only two months before she dies – 'Are you afraid that they'll kill you? Have you ever thought what might become of your children?' To which she stoically replies, as one who recognises her struggle as moral as well as political must reply, that for as long as the lives of others are not secure, then neither is our own. Later, alone in her hotel room, she calms her sobs by burying her head in a feather pillow. In her dreams, she begs her children's forgiveness and visualises a world in which those who tell the truth – about shameful acts of war and humanity's incapacity to negotiate conflict, about the rapaciousness of the powerful, who use war to exterminate or for the acquisition of material goods – do not pay with their lives.

Why do we tell our tales? Why do we move on from being the narrators to becoming the subjects of our narratives? What do we do about our dual role of playing both narrators and characters in the same drama?

I have put such questions to more than a hundred people, both writers and journalists, with whom over the past six years I've done what we smilingly call the 'tour of heroic celebrity'. We are awarded prizes; invited to hold round tables reflecting on investigative journalism, on war and peace, or on human rights; we are asked to write for online and print publications, translated into Zulu, Spanish, Turkish or in French, English or Italian. As we are not – nor have any desire to be – preachers, we look to share our convictions openly and honestly.

Without knowing it, we have become part of a global fraternity. We are the survivors of a war without barracks, a war bent on eliminating freedom of expression by every means possible. By becoming the story, we have silenced many other voices and stories. We go about the world talking of our tragedies as if they had become a symbol of those of our country, or of other people's countries. This fraternity would not exist without the human networks that protect us from within their own stable and secure bases.

This revelation is what impelled the author of *The Satanic Verses*, Salman Rushdie, to renounce the bodyguard who made false claims about him in a book, to dare to live free of ties, fed up with going through life the prisoner of his own words. It is what inspired the Russian journalist Anna Politkovskaya to make a political act of leaving the supermarket alone, as a free citizen, reminding her president every single day that if she was killed, she and so many among us would know it was he who, whether by omission or commission, would be responsible for the murder. And this revelation impelled the young Italian journalist, Roberto Saviano, to dare to denounce

Roberto Saviano addresses a demonstration defending media rights under a sign that reads 'No to the leash', Rome, 2 October 2010
Credit: Gregorio Borgia/AP Photo

his government earlier this year for attempting to pass a gagging law, knowing that his outspokenness could mean the removal of the national policemen there to protect him from the mafia, hell-bent on killing him for treating them so wonderfully in the pages of his book, *Gomorrah*.

It is what inspired a group of young people in Sudan and Uganda, whose hands had been mutilated or cut off by soldiers, to take up radio journalism for which 'hands are not necessary: one only needs a voice and a will'. It is the concept of being free within the ideological prison of an island, where the young woman Yoani Sánchez reveals a Cuba that Che Guevara himself would have fought against for being a dictatorship.

This paradox is woven into our daily lives. International recognition sustains us with life, and our dignity demands that we never cease denouncing our persecutors. Their acts of aggression are intended to silence us, wear us out, or distract our attention from what's really important. Prizes and accolades are converted into shields to protect and forums to express the messages others are trying to conceal.

For every time our body rebels and says 'not again!' to another 15-hour flight, eating badly, sleeping worse, in order to repeat the story told a thousand times over, a little inner voice replies: 'You are alive, you have to do it.' When others insist that we are heroes or heroines, we are genuinely reluctant to believe them. I've never known of a single colleague who has been tortured, or who lives with the threat of death and persecution for their work, in such a confused state of mind that they believe that working in the defence of individual and collective freedoms is an act of heroism. We know full well that it is nothing more than an exercise in survival and shared dignity. We also understand, for we are constantly reminded of it, that the world demands its heroes to be examples who defend human rights with their voices, their words and their culture – those rights that prompt us to demand access to water, food, land, justice and, ultimately, the right to lead a happy life, free of violence. So it is we can proceed anew to the forum of the survivors: like optimistic chroniclers, we document the tragedy and nourish the possibility that all this will disappear if we persevere together in making it so.

To reveal the opprobrium of power requires a monumental effort, yet it's a daily task. For inside the world of the persecuted there are more and more who seek to pass themselves off as professional victims. They include those who have already surrendered; who fight only their own battles; who understand that at times suffering makes for good business. Even though they may be few in number, they are the ones who have a tremendous power to render us invisible to the media on our home patch. They are the ones who give up, or carry on negotiating with the forces of power, even so far as to seat themselves at their table, sharing their bread and salt, frequently steeped in blood. They are those who collaborate in the message that death threats are merely boring; those who, greased by the palms of corrupt politicians, make strenuous efforts to discredit us. Little by little, rumours filter out: 'so many prizes … maybe that's what's behind her denunciations' or 'if they really wanted to kill her, they would have done so', or 'he's just another martyred poet'. There are those set out to wear us down, and to render the dispensation of justice impossible. It is they and no one else who know, deep down, that some of us survive because we strive for this every day of our lives; because thousands of eyes are upon us, because our visibility has succeeded in raising the political stakes if we are removed. Until one day our luck runs out.

The maestro of Mexican journalism, Jesús Blancornelas, the founder of the weekly news magazines *ABC* and *Zeta*, survived a hail of bullets in 1997 and spent the rest of his days (he died of cancer in 2006) blockaded in his house in Tijuana, ringed by armed soldiers. He carried on working with an immeasurable capacity to inspire. One afternoon I went to speak to him, with the ingenuous idea of learning the secret of living under the constant threat of death, in his case the result of revelations of collusion between politicians and a drugs cartel. In mine, it was the mafias trafficking young girls and the politicians who protect them. We compared notes on the price set on each of our heads by the *mafiosi* (a sense of humour is essential to drive out fear). The maestro told me: 'Show them a good man, and they'll ask you to bring in a thousand more to prove that good truly exists; show them an evil man and they'll tell you he brings all human evil with him.' 'Never give up on calling the good together,' Jesús recommended. 'Even if it should cost you your life, you must trust, believe and approach those who, without knowing you, will know the importance of what you see and document, the importance of what you write.' At the end of the discussion, I realised that my grandmother was right when she told me: 'Inspire what is good in order that what's good may inspire you.' The Polish journalist and writer Ryszard Kapuscinski put it differently: 'This is no task for cynics.' And he's right. It is not.

Because thousands of eyes are upon us, the political stakes are raised

A young reporter once asked me what I have done to overcome the threats. 'It is not a matter of saving your life, but of ensuring that every moment is worthwhile for as long as you are alive,' I responded. He took a sheet of paper out of his briefcase. It was the printout of an email containing a death threat for his investigations into drug trafficking in Durango. He told me he was convinced it came from local officials and stashed it away again, as if it were something to be treasured. I advised him to go to the capital, that we'd kick up a fuss within the international community, that we would denounce the drugs traffickers he was investigating. 'I don't think they'd dare,' he said with a smile. Three months later, his inert body was found a few blocks away from the office of the newspaper where he worked. That newspaper, like so many in my country, gave up publishing news about organised crime. They kill one to silence the many, which is why we insist that so many of us speak out, so that the few can never silence us.

Mexican president Felipe Calderón persists in berating the press, and in a vein of the purest George W Bush-speak, assures us: 'Those who are not with me are against their homeland.' Like those journalists who denounce institutional corruption, military violence against civilians and journalists, police forces colluding with kidnappers and sex traffickers. Because we are the ones who demonstrate the ineffectualness of the Mexican government in the face of the violence and deaths of thousands of Central American migrants, we are deemed to be the enemies of our country, still pretending to be a democracy.

We are the enemy, and truth is the enemy of a nation refusing to engage in self-criticism and assume responsibility for its own tragedy. This is why the public prosecutor whose job it is to protect journalists repeatedly fails to investigate attacks against them, does not acknowledge the dangerous conditions in which they work – and has tried to ruin the reputations of several journalists.

Now there are 19 colleagues whose deaths the Mexican authorities refuse to investigate. Sixty-four journalists have died in my country. Not one of these murders has been explained.

When a colleague loses their life, the authorities sow rumours that they are in the pay of organised crime, or else it must have been a crime of passion; if a woman has disappeared, then they say she must have run off with a man. My grandfather, a soldier, used to say that an enemy is killed twice over. First the bullet puts paid to a man's life, closely followed by the humiliation that destroys his humanity: the latter is his true annihilation. That is why, when Jesús Blancornelas died, and society demanded a funeral worthy of such a great journalist, the then mayor of Tijuana, Jorge Hank Rhon, said that his life was not worthy of commemoration, that people die every day.

Each time I am asked what is the most original slander targeted at me, I explain how the governor of Puebla, who threw me into prison to protect the mafia, ordered his press chief to proclaim that I was a guerrilla fighter, and my book a tactic to destabilise the state. So it was that the guerrilla leaders published a disclaimer in the daily papers across the country, stating that I most certainly did not belong to their organisation, and that my work was of critical importance to the children of Mexico.

In my country, journalists operate as reporters, investigators, security strategists and therapists. We know our phones are tapped and speak in code. The vast majority of reporters never agree to appointments or meetings by phone, in order not to reveal sources. There are villages where journalists work semi-clandestinely, just as in Zimbabwe. There are cities where my women friends report with the same trepidation as my colleagues in Baghdad. There are nights when the phone rings and a premonition takes my breath away, my mind immediately trying to ascertain from the prefix of the number on my screen which part of the country the call is coming from. I respond slowly, in a low voice. Please let it not announce a death, not of yet another person, nor even my own.

The last two occasions on which I travelled to Spain, after giving talks about freedom of expression in my own country, I received news of the murder of colleagues who had already told me of the threats they had received. They had ignored my advice. One of them told me, before his murder, that he did not wish to live as I did, underneath the glare and the harsh criticisms of those powerful and corrupt moguls, always following my every step and every word, anticipating an error and ready to discredit me when I fumble. He admitted that so many prizes had tarnished my image, that numerous editors were protesting that I only denounce the threats I receive because I enjoy celebrity; that journalists should not be the news, but make the news. I replied that as fame is a life-saving tool, I have no problem with being famous and he should therefore have no problem either; in this country, under these circumstances, our names shall eventually appear in the media, either as a survivor or as a mortal victim.

In his obituary there was a tiny mention of the manner of his death, but it failed to mention that he was threatened with murder in exactly the manner in which it occurred. Fear has a great many faces. It makes some active and some responsive; others keep themselves to themselves. Many give in and go along with the system they formerly denounced, and who can blame them? There is no one to protect them. Self-censorship plunges us all into darkness, and opens the door to uncertainty.

In my home country, more and more journalists subject themselves to self-censorship. The younger ones start to lose heart when their publications decide that their columns should appear unsigned, in order not to put them at risk. They say if their work has to appear anonymously, there's no point in them making efforts that will go unrecognised. Others, mostly young women, insist that what's most important is that they provide news. It doesn't matter whose name appears at the bottom of the page: what counts is that society

Photographs of murdered reporters at a demonstration in Mexico City, 7 August 2010
Credit: Henry Romero/Reuters

has access to this information. Most of them feel abandoned by the owners of the press, who refuse to protect them, or to provide adequate training for them to assess the risk for themselves; or even to acknowledge their worry and stress when they receive death threats. In recent months, some editors have united to defend the sector as much against the drug cartels as against the attacks of corrupt politicians. International solidarity has played a key role in achieving this.

In Mexico, death threats are hardly newsworthy. Nor is death, or the struggle to remain alive. Maybe this is why my father, in solidarity and with great emotion, asks me why I refuse to accept the idea of living in another country for a while, one where I would not be considered an enemy of the state because I defend human dignity.

Six years ago, when I was imprisoned and tortured by a mafia who trafficked in minors and child pornography, parts of the Mexican media exclaimed: 'A woman who opposes mafia power!', as if in surprise. Thanks to their reaction, society looked at and listened to me, but most importantly, it reacted and demanded justice for the hundreds of children who are the victims of sexual tourism and child pornography. Legislators created new laws to protect children, and when I was cleared of defamation charges, women on the streets, old and young, applauded and embraced me. They stopped me in public places to congratulate me on having reminded them that truth has power – and so do women who refuse to subject themselves to macho violence.

Only the other day, as I was pushing my trolley along the supermarket aisle, two older women approached me and asked, 'Are you the writer?' Timidly, I said, 'Yes'. One woman threw herself at me for a typically Mexican-style embrace, informing me that her granddaughter wrote an essay at primary school on her chosen heroine. It was me. 'Why did she choose me?' I asked, and she answered: 'Because we are all a little bit like you, and you remind us of it, when you refuse to give in, when you won't hold your tongue, and when you smile and tell us that the world is also ours.'

Perhaps that's what it comes down to in the end. Journalism brings it all together. We can't ask others for something we are not inclined to give. There are moments to listen and others to be listened to. It is not enough to arouse empathy, it is not our job to make people cry. What we have to do is to reflect an outrageous reality with such power that it inspires the hope that all people want to participate in and be responsible for change. Objective journalism does not exist: we are not objects. We are subjects, so we write subjective journalism, and to do that well, everyone's rights and everyone's lives are of equal importance. Sometimes we tell the story. And at other times, we are the story. ❐

Translated by Amanda Hopkinson
©Lydia Cacho
39(4): 72/81
DOI: 10.1177/0306422010388594
www.indexoncensorship.org

Lydia Cacho's most recent book is *Slaves of Power: A Journey into Sex Trafficking around the World* (Debate). She was awarded the PEN/Pinter Prize for an international writer of courage in October 2010

CARTAGENA
BEIRUT
BELFAST
HAY
ZACATECAS
BRECON
SEGOVIA
NAIROBI
MALDIVES
KERALA
and more to come in 2011...

BONNE ANNÉE

HAPPY NEW YEAR

Feliz año nuevo

HERI ZA MWAKA MPYA

SREČNO NOVO LETO

BLWYDDYN NEWYDD DDA

新年快樂

VOORSPOEDIGE NUWE JAAR

A LICENCE TO WRITE

Classroom rules provide first lessons in censorship.
Ngugi wa Thiong'o looks back on a childhood debate
and recalls his early brushes with a repressive regime

At the Alliance High School in the colonial era in Kenya, 1955-58, I found
the English language continued to fascinate me. I discovered that the grammar I had picked up in my elementary and middle schools had more than
prepared me for high school. Conjugation and the adjectival and adverbial
clauses and phrases that made the simple subject-predicate structure into a
complex sentence, which seemed to bother others, came easily to me. This
was always handy when taking English language tests. I would start with
the section on grammar and complete it quickly, thus ensuring that I had
50 per cent of the test right, then use the rest of the time to write the essay
section and go over it carefully. Literature for me was an enjoyable extension
of my language classes. Ironically, it was during a literature class that I first
experienced tension between my teachers and me.

James Stephen Smith, Scotsman, Bachelor of Science, Glasgow, first
arrived on the Alliance scene in 1927, to join George A Grieve, who became
the first headmaster of the school, his wife, and their African assistant,
Carpenter Kinuthia. The students had nicknamed him Muturi, the Gikuyu-
language equivalent of Smith. He was literally the second master after Grieve.

Trained in biology, he had been recruited to teach practical agriculture, a hundred acres of land at his disposal. He allotted his students a quarter of an acre to grow crops and carry out experiments under his watchful eye, the students finding, in the school, a ready market. A bachelor, Smith was soon absorbed in the practical work of breeding Ayrshire cows for milk, keeping Rhode Island hens for eggs, and pigs for bacon. Early in the morning, before classes, he would milk the cows with his own hands and have the milk bottled, a new phenomenon in the area at the time, and then delivered it in person to the school and to the Church of Scotland Mission on the other side of the valley. In his very first delivery to the Anderson family, he stood outside, a little bit confused, looking at the missionary's daughter, Janet Hamilton, who had opened the door. She too must have found music in the clinking bottles the young man held out. Four years later, she would become Janet Smith, or Janet Muturi.

The couple would come to embody the school's continuity through its lean and fat years. He was the only deputy and acting principal the school would ever have, up to and including our times. With the literary eventually edging out the vocational, practical agriculture became a thing of the past. Smith ended up teaching biology and other subjects, among them literature, besides his involvement in scouting matters. One day he was discussing our essays, dwelling on the tendency of students to use big words to suggest a profound grasp and knowledge of the language. He read out a sentence a student had written: 'As I was perambulating on the road, I countenanced a red garmented boots-appareled gentleman mounted on a humongous four-legged creature of bovine species.' This became the poster sentence for how not to write English. Avoid words with Latin roots, he would say. Use the Anglo-Saxon word. Above all, learn from the Bible. It has the shortest sentence in English: 'Jesus wept.' Two words. So follow the example of Jesus. He spoke very simple English.

I was puzzled. I was not trying to be clever or correct him when I raised my hand and said that Jesus did not speak English. The Bible was a translation. It elicited laughter in the class and a sheepish silence from Smith. Then he gave us a little sermon on willingness to learn. 'Remember you have come here to learn, not to teach. Or do you want to change places with me?' he asked, holding out the chalk to me. There was tense silence. He now explained that he was talking about the King James Version of the Bible, a version that had excellent English. It had inspired many writers of English prose and poetry. Smith had the effect of freezing out both questions and differing perspectives.

Smith's testiness made me start thinking of Kenneth Mbūgua in my primary school. I recalled our readings, our frank and often heated debates with disagreements that left no rancour – yes, our acceptance of difference. The most intense differences we ever had were over whether one needed a licence to write. I argued that one needed one: that if one did not have a licence to write, he would be imprisoned. Kenneth disagreed with me. One did not need a government permit, like a driver's licence, in order to write. He felt so strongly about his position that in our last days in Kinyogori Middle School, he had started to write what he called a book. He had not shown me any chapters, for soon after we left for different institutions – he to a teacher training college, and I to Alliance High School.

In my first few weeks I had looked, in vain, for someone with whom I could argue the way Kenneth and I used to do. I was convinced that Kenneth could have more than held his own against any of my fellow students and this made me start thinking about English and educational opportunities. It was almost by chance that I was in a high school and he was at a teacher training college, both of us on journeys that pointed to different destinations. Even more disturbing was the case of Kagwe from Banana Hills. We were together at Kinyogori. He was not one of the top students but he was close behind. But the results of the Kenya African Preliminary Examination, a terminal exam after only eight years of elementary schooling, were stunning. He was the only student with distinctions, 'A' in nearly all the subjects, including mathematics.

The entire exam was in English. Kagwe spoke English much more fluently that any other person in class. But Kagwe had failed in the English language paper. The person with the best results could not find a place in any secondary school or teacher training college because of that 'F' in English. My performance in English, more than any other subject, had gained me entry into the best of the African secondary schools of the time. English language grammar had become the biggest decider of a person's future. It was the censor of an African student's dreams of a meaningful future.

I had not heard from Kenneth since he left for Kambui. I missed him, more so now, after the confrontation with Smith. And then one day I got a large envelope from him. I grabbed the accompanying letter first. He did not tell me tidbits about how he was faring at the teacher training school, nor ask how I was liking it at Alliance. He just wanted to let me know that he had started on the book that he had vowed to write to prove that I was wrong in thinking and arguing that one needed a licence to write or that one could be arrested for writing without a licence. He had sent the pages as proof that he had embarked on the project.

The story of a boy who goes to the city to look for work so he can pay school tuition for himself and his two siblings but gets lost in its corrupt ways was captivating but too short. Immediately I noted one serious flaw in the telling. He used big words and long sentences. Earlier I would have been impressed by the weight of his vocabulary. Now I was looking at his work through Smith's eyes.

So despite his sarcastic response, Smith's call for us to learn from the example of English prose in the Bible must have left a mark. The King James Version remained one of my best reads. I relied on the simple sentence. I learned to mix the simple, the compound and the complex for different effects. Smith had given me my first critical tool in evaluating a piece of work, which I now used to critique Kenneth's work.

'Give me some more pages,' I wrote back. 'But don't use big words. Read the Bible again and see how English is used.' I was about to write that Jesus spoke simple English but caught myself. Alas I did not hear back from Kenneth. I soon forgot about it. I was caught by the fever of learning but was now more cautious in what I said in the classroom.

Years later I did write and publish books without a licence: *Weep not Child* (1964); *The River Between* (1965); *A Grain of Wheat* (1967); and *Petals of Blood* (1997). No policeman ever came to my door or stopped me in the streets to demand to see my writing permit. Was my friend right after all?

In 1977, I took part in the writing of a Gikuyu-language play, *I Will Marry When I Want*. Police raided my home on 31 December 1977. I woke up in a cell in a maximum security prison, where I would stay for a year without charge. No trial. In 1982, three truckloads of armed police raided Kamirithu Open Air Theatre, where my Gikuyu- language plays had originated. They razed it to the ground. I was forced into exile. In 1983, in exile in London, I published a novel, *Matigari*, in the Gikuyu language. In Kenya, the then Daniel arap Moi dictatorship sent police to arrest the main character, thinking that he was a real living person. Failing, they literally arrested the book, taking it away from bookshops and the publisher's warehouse.

Had I been right after all? I have always thought about our argument in the light of what happened to writers in Kenya during the colonial and post-colonial periods; indeed, what has happened to so many writers in history. One does not need a licence to write, but what one writes or says may have consequences. Authorities in the classroom or within the state do not always tolerate words from writers. What is important is that democratic institutions are in place that defend and protect the right to differ. But even then, writers and their institutions have to remain watchful. ❐

©Ngugi wa Thiong'o
39(4): 83/87
DOI: 10.1177/0306422010390169
www.indexoncensorship.org

Ngugi wa Thiong'o is a novelist, playwright and critic, writing in English and Gikuyu. His book *Matigari* was banned in Kenya in 1986. He was awarded the 2001 Nonino International Prize for Literature and is a professor of Comparative Literature and English at the University of California, Irvine. His latest book, *Dreams in a Time of War* (Harvill Secker), is supported by English PEN's Writers in Translation programme. This is an excerpt from a work in progress

BLOGGING DANGEROUSLY

The next generation of censorship is in full force. **Ron Deibert** reports on new tactics and argues that only a global movement can protect free speech online

In no other time during the internet's history has it been as dangerous to publish on the web as it is now. How recent it seems that dissidents, scholars, and activists were trumpeting the power of blogs to break free of traditional media. New tools of anonymity would ensure a safety net for those for whom it is too risky to speak openly. Free blog services, offered in an increasing variety of local languages, would provide a cheap platform to reach global audiences. RSS feeds would link communities of bloggers in a web of mutual support. A distributed army of ants would outflank heavy-handed and slow-moving repressive regimes. But what was once considered to be an unstoppable force for the democratisation of publication is quickly turning into a jeopardy trap. What has happened?

To understand the growing threats to bloggers, one must understand a major sea change that has occurred around cyberspace in the last several years. Whereas once governments were either incapable of, or chose not to, regulate the internet, today they are reasserting themselves dramatically and forcefully. More than 30 countries engage in internet filtering world-wide, including filtering access to many blog-hosting services. Although filtering can be bypassed with circumvention technologies, the new road-blocks erected by governments and internet service providers (ISPs) make it inconvenient and potentially dangerous to do so. Using circumvention technologies is now explicitly illegal in Vietnam, Burma and Iran.

But governments are not just blocking access to information through filtering. In our research, we have documented a burgeoning number of what we call 'next generation' controls that go beyond denial of access. These next generation controls are more subtle and offensive, aimed at shaping cyberspace and creating a climate of self-censorship and fear. They include the implementation of new and more rigid laws around slander, libel, and copyright protection, denial of service and malware attacks against adversaries and arrests, threats and intimidation of bloggers.

No longer is it possible for bloggers to write in the relative sanctuary of cyberspace as if it were a world apart. State authorities have brought the activities that happen in cyberspace under increasingly rigid and very tangible police and intelligence control.

The tactics of governments are being complemented by the increasingly stifling policies of ISPs' online hosting companies. It is important to remember that cyberspace is owned and operated by the private sector. Decisions taken for market reasons can end up having major political consequences, though often without public accountability or transparency. There have been a growing number of cases where blogging and other social networking accounts have been terminated because of supposed violation of terms of service. More nefariously, complaints issued to companies have become a favourite tactic to silence opposition and human rights groups. Fearing liabilities, companies are either ill-equipped or afraid to resist these complaints and take the easy road of compliance. Some companies routinely share information with authorities without public accountability or oversight; others, like Research in Motion (the maker of BlackBerry mobile phones), are being increasingly pressured to do so.

More generally, though, the environment for bloggers is changing because of the ways in which we communicate. Ironically, the great innovations in social networking and information sharing that have led to a proliferation of voices have also produced a much deeper exposure of personally incriminating information. No longer is it easy to hide from slow-moving and inept bureaucracies in the vast pools of information flows. New technologies of data mining, analysis, and deep packet inspection that erupted out of the cyber security sector have given authorities unprecedented capabilities to monitor the digital traces that individuals leave behind. We are entering a new dot com boom in the market for digital repression techniques and services.

What can be done about all of this? Unfortunately, the forces described above are not easily contained because they are not isolated instances but components of an epochal shift involving powerful social forces on a global scale. Cyberspace has become an object of intense geopolitical contestation, characterised by cyber crime, espionage, and warfare. Such a massive shift will make it much less propitious for the flourishing of blogging as we have seen to date. Much like a change in sea temperature affects the vitality of certain marine species, the changes to the cyberspace ecosystem are strangling free expression, access to information and privacy.

The first step in rectifying these matters is to recognise the scope of the challenge. No internet freedom technology, policy, or programme will solve these problems alone. Awareness raising and lobbying efforts on behalf of imprisoned arrested bloggers is essential, but incomplete. New transparency initiatives among internet companies is welcome, but only a first step.

One way to think about it is to extend the ecological analogies and draw lessons from the environmental movement. Cyberspace is an environment that we have created, albeit an artificial one. It is under intense degradation, much like the natural environment, from a multiplicity of interactive and mutually-supportive causes. What is required is no less than a broad global movement, involving like-minded citizens, governments and private sector actors, to protect the net in the same way that we think about protection of the global environment or the movement to rid the world of nuclear weapons. The job is not easy and will not happen in the short term. Until such time, activists and others are going to be facing a growing number of years of blogging dangerously. ❏

©Ron Deibert
39(4): 88/90
DOI: 10.1177/0306422010389889
www.indexoncensorship.org

Ron Deibert is the director of the Canada Centre for Global Security Studies and the Citizen Lab at the Munk School of Global Affairs, University of Toronto. He is a co-founder and principal investigator of the OpenNet Initiative and Information Warfare Monitor projects, and was a founder and former vice president of Psiphon Inc. He was one of the authors of the Tracking Ghostnet and Shadows in the Cloud reports, documenting global cyber-espionage networks, and is co-editor of *Access Controlled* (MIT Press)

Bloggers in jeopardy: recent arrests

Bahrain: Ali Abdulemam. Status: Arrested on 5 September 2010. Leading Bahraini blogger and Global Voices Advocacy author, he was accused of spreading 'false news' on the BahrainOnline.org portal, one of the most popular pro-democracy outlets in Bahrain

China: Liu Xiaobo. Status: Arrested on 8 December 2008 for co-authoring Charter 08, a manifesto calling for greater freedoms and democracy in China, which was signed by hundreds of citizens. Awarded the 2010 Nobel Peace Prize

Iran: Hossein Derakhshan. Status: Arrested in 2008. Influential Iranian-Canadian blogger arrested after returning to Iran. Convicted of collaborating with enemy states, propaganda against the Islamic Republic, propaganda in support of counter-revolutionary groups, 'insulting what is holy' and creating immoral websites

Russia: Irek Murtazin. Status: Arrested in November 2009. He was accused of spreading false rumours about the death of the president of the republic of Tatarstan, Mintimir Shaimiev, and sent to a penal colony

Saudi Arabia: Hamoud Bin Saleh. Status: Arrested in 2008. He was arrested after he criticised the kingdom's judiciary and made an announcement on his blog that he had converted from Islam to Christianity

Syria: Tal al Molouh. Status: Arrested in December 2009. Arrested by Syrian state security agents for posting poems about Palestine on her blog. Currently detained with no charges and no trial; her whereabouts are unknown

Thailand: Suwicha Thakor. Status: Arrested in 2009. Serving a 10-year jail sentence, handed down on 3 April 2010, for criticism of the monarchy

Thailand: Chiranuch Premchaiporn. Status: Arrested on 24 September 2010. Webmaster of the independent online journal Prachatai, he was arrested on charges of insulting the monarchy

Tunisia: Zouhaïer Makhlouf. Status: Released in 2010. On 20 October 2009, the human rights activist and writer for Assabil Online was arrested for publishing an online video investigating the social, economic, and environmental problems in Nabeul (Dar Chaabane el Fehri), a coastal town in northeastern Tunisia

Yemen: Mohammed al Maqaleh. Status: Arrested in 2009. The editor of the opposition Socialist Party's website, al Eshteraki, was apprehended by security forces

Sources:
The Arabic Network for Human Rights Information, Global Voices, the New York Times, *Reporters sans frontières*

EYEWITNESS

William Boyd on
Ken Saro-Wiwa

I first met Ken Saro-Wiwa at a British Council conference in Cambridge in 1986. While he had been a student in the 1960s at the University of Ibadan, in Western Nigeria, he had been treated by my late father, who then was running the university's health services. Ken had recognised my father in the thinly-disguised portrait of him in my first novel, *A Good Man in Africa* (he appears as 'Dr Murray'), and was curious to meet his son.

As a result of that meeting, a strong friendship ensued. I wrote a profile of Ken for *The Times* and we took to having regular lunches whenever he was in London, usually at the Chelsea Arts Club, a place he came to relish. We talked about books and writing in the main – Ken was a prolific author: novels, plays, children's books, journalism, TV soap operas were all part of his oeuvre – and of course about Nigeria.

But I became aware as the 1990s arrived that an increasing radicalisation was taking place in him. It was all to do with oil and the despoliation of his tribal homeland, Ogoniland, in the Niger River delta by, among others, the multinational oil companies – Shell in particular. The wanton disregard for ecological good management had condemned the Ogoni people – whose livelihood was farming and fishing – to live in a pestilential circle of hell. The lush forests and the winding creeks of their homeland in the delta had been transformed by massive oil spills and 24-hour gas flaring into one of the most noxious and polluted places on earth. Ken was determined to do something about it and, with other Ogonis, created the Movement for the Survival of the Ogoni People (MOSOP). A highly-organised, scrupulously non-violent protest campaign was initiated – and Ken's troubles began to multiply.

Nigeria was then ruled by a succession of corrupt military governments sustained, in every sense of the word, by the huge revenues that Nigeria's oil provided. Any protest movement, however internationally recognised, that threatened the flow of petro-dollars was in harm's way. Ken and MOSOP's agitation was proving highly successful – a fact measured by the amount of state persecution they attracted, the most sinister form of compliment.

Ken endured a period of house arrest in 1992 and in June 1993 he was arrested again and jailed without charge (the period is recorded in his prison diary, *A Month and a Day*). I came back from my summer holiday that year to find a series of messages on my answer phone from MOSOP organisers, asking if there was anything I could do to help publicise Ken's ordeal. Amnesty International had made him an official Prisoner of Conscience but MOSOP was finding it hard to keep up the pressure.

In the light of Ken's global posthumous fame it's perhaps worth recalling that in 1993 MOSOP and the Ogoni people's suffering was barely known abroad. The scandal of Shell Oil's devastation of the Niger River delta hardly figured in the world's news bulletins. I decided to ask *The Times* if they wanted an article. The profile of Ken I had written had been a lavish multi-page colour spread in the magazine. I thought the newspaper might be intrigued to learn that their interviewee was now languishing in a noisome jail in Port Harcourt.

Peter Stothard, then editor of *The Times*, came to our aid. He commissioned the piece and ran it with due prominence in the paper. It was sufficiently obvious to attract the attention of BBC Radio 4's *Today* programme. I was invited on one morning and spoke about Ken, the fact that he was in jail and about MOSOP's campaign against the Nigerian military and multinational, all-powerful oil companies. The military dictator at the time in Nigeria was General Ibrahim Babangida. Babangida – the name is resonant – was mentioned a great deal in the broadcast.

Ken was released on 22 July, free to return to the UK. Many people were agitating for Ken's release at the time and indeed it was the editorial teams at *The Times* and *Today* who decided to run the story that really swung things our way. The media events surrounding the case of Ken Saro-Wiwa in July 1993 have always seemed to me to illustrate the positive power of unwelcome publicity. If there's a lesson to be learned it is that the key media outlets in this and any other country – those with the highest profile and influence – have an additional responsibility in the field of human rights: they are not simply there to report. They would be astonished at the significant difference they can make.

This point was reinforced when I saw Ken again in London and he told me a story – which must remain apocryphal as it can never be verified. He had been told, so rumour had it, that General Babangida's wife was in London at the time of the article's publication and the broadcast, on a

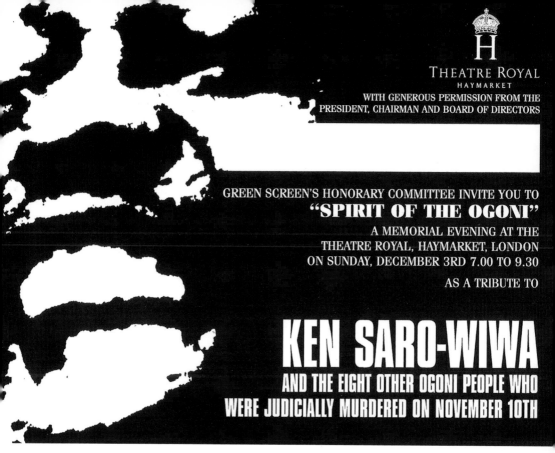

THEATRE ROYAL
HAYMARKET
WITH GENEROUS PERMISSION FROM THE
PRESIDENT, CHAIRMAN AND BOARD OF DIRECTORS

GREEN SCREEN'S HONORARY COMMITTEE INVITE YOU TO
"SPIRIT OF THE OGONI"
A MEMORIAL EVENING AT THE
THEATRE ROYAL, HAYMARKET, LONDON
ON SUNDAY, DECEMBER 3RD 7.00 TO 9.30
AS A TRIBUTE TO

KEN SARO-WIWA
AND THE EIGHT OTHER OGONI PEOPLE WHO
WERE JUDICIALLY MURDERED ON NOVEMBER 10TH

Flyer for a memorial evening in honour of Ken Saro-Wiwa, 1995

discreet shopping spree. Mrs Babangida had been shocked and alarmed to hear her husband's name mentioned blithely and without contradiction as a despot and a criminal on the BBC (and ashamed of the guilt by association) and had urged him to release this Saro-Wiwa man immediately. True or false, the anecdote does illustrate that a little bit of notoriety and publicity – particularly when it is communicated through the mainstream media – can go a long way. Subsequently, in future agitations on Ken's behalf, as his situation became progressively more dire, *The Times* and the *Today* programme proved the most loyal of supporters of MOSOP and the Ogoni cause, something Ken recognised and for which he was always grateful.

It is the bitterest irony that when Ken was arrested again, accused of murder in a kangaroo court, condemned to death and eventually executed in 1995, the cries of outrage were both loud and universal in the world's media – not just in Britain – but proved ultimately powerless. Ken Saro-Wiwa, MOSOP and the ecological devastation caused by Shell were on everyone's agenda by then. But in Nigeria, Babangida had gone, replaced by another general – Sani Abacha – whose cocaine-fuelled paranoia, fear and ignorance overrode all political pragmatism. Ken and his eight co-accused were hanged on the morning of 10 November 1995. I genuinely believe that had Babangida still been in power Ken would have been reprieved, but to some corrupt, warped minds no amount of press exposure makes a difference. Abacha himself, the most ardent and wholesale plunderer of Nigeria's state coffers, died less than three years later in highly suspicious circumstances. He may well have been poisoned by one of the Egyptian or Indian prostitutes he consorted with – and his tiny footnote in history will be his baleful, criminal responsibility for the unjust and lamented death of Ken Saro-Wiwa, a real and actual good man in Africa. It is little consolation. ❏

©William Boyd
39(4): 93/96
DOI: 10.1177/0306422010388839
www.indexoncensorship.org

William Boyd's novels include *A Good Man in Africa* (Penguin), *Any Human Heart* (Penguin), which won the Prix Jean Monnet, and *Ordinary Thunderstorms* (Bloomsbury)

THE PRICE OF TRUTH

Following his release in May 2010, newspaper editor **Lewis Medjo** writes about the horrors of his 20-month ordeal in a Cameroonian jail

After the damning classification of Cameroon as the most corrupt country in the world by Transparency International in 1998 and 1999, we at the weekly *La Détente Libre* took a decision to expose corrupt officials in the republic. For years our editorial team carried out investigations into sensitive areas of the administration. We published dossiers that caused a stir in high places and led to us being blacklisted.

The chance to nail me came in September 2008 when we published a series of stories on corruption in the judiciary, in particular its collusion with the executive. I was arrested on 20 September 2008, barely a week after the story appeared. The authorities asked the head of communications in the Littoral region of the country, where the newspaper is based, to invite me to a press dinner. Little did I know that the invitation was a trap. At 11.45pm, when the dinner ended, I was accosted outside the hotel by the commissioner of the judicial police, Minkoa Nga, who announced that I was under arrest. I was whisked off to his police station where I was grilled throughout the night.

That was just the start of my ordeal. For seven days I was tortured in an attempt to force me to reveal my source. After making no progress, I was taken before the state counsel. The late Pius Njawe, an editor and campaigner for press freedom, rushed to the court to plead for my release in vain. It was later that afternoon that he told me the terrible news. The authorities in the capital Yaoundé had decided to send me to prison, sending a strong message to other journalists who were disturbing the peace of the republic with their stories on corruption. Pius Njawe, who had been arrested 126 times, encouraged and advised me and gave me some money.

I was taken straight to the New Bell prison in Douala. There was excitement when I arrived; all the workers wanted to see the journalist who dared to write about their boss. A wardress ordered me to undress before crossing the gate of the prison. She had drunk herself into a stupor. I refused to be naked in front of her. Two of her male colleagues descended on me with their whips, beating me mercilessly. A crowd of inmates looked on, excited to see a journalist they recognised from television being humiliated like a common thief.

This treatment lasted for about 30 minutes until Pastor Ngassa, who preaches in the prison, arrived on the scene. He sent someone to pay 200,000 francs (US$400) as a bribe to the prison officials not to send me to the quarter inhabited by hardened criminals. It was this pastor who escorted me to my 'special cell 18'. I had to walk past about a thousand prisoners who rained invectives and threats at me because I was a journalist whose colleagues regularly showed pictures of their arrests, spiced with negative comments about them. They hated me.

Once inside my cell, it was three days before I ventured out, and only in the company of four bodyguards I had hired for my protection. As time went on I learned to adapt to my new environment. The other prisoners needed my help to write letters for them; that is how I become integrated and began to be able to participate in prison activities. Letters addressed to me from different parts of the world, through PEN, began arriving. These letters made the prison officials afraid of me; they reasoned that I could use these contacts abroad to denounce the torture, extortion and other vices that are the stock-in-trade of the New Bell prison.

Confronted by the large-scale misery and the regular deaths of inmates at the jail, I decided to be at the service of the most vulnerable prisoners, especially minors from war-torn countries such as Congo, Chad, and Sudan, who have no family in Cameroon. Most of them are forced to prostitute themselves for a bowl of porridge or get involved in hard drugs.

The quantity of hard drugs that enter the prison is alarming. Though illegal, prison workers are at the centre of the drug trafficking. Cocaine, heroin, marijuana and other drugs are circulated freely. It is big business.

L@ Detente

Libre 13ème année

Directeur de Publication : Levis Medjo - B.P. : 1221 Douala - N° 356 du 17 août 2010 - Cél. : 99 93 77 96 / 77 48 30 18 - E-mail : ladtentelibre@yahoo.fr - Prix : 400 Fcfa

SCANDALE EN HAUTE MER

Des bâteaux camerounais détournés

- Des milliards en fumée
- Notre enquête en Espagne, Brazzaville, Douala, Yaoundé

P. 3

IMPOTS LITTORAL
Vaste détournement
des recettes de la pêche maritime
P. 4

RDPC DOUALA 2
La maison du parti transformée en auberge
P. 9

FINANCE
La subvention à la CTPL n'est pas suspendue
P. 4

BABOUANTOU

L'adieu au combattant Njawé
Pp. 5,6,7,8

FRAUDE DOUANIÈRE
Nestlé condamné à payer 740 millions
P. 10

How to survive in this overcrowded place? A former military camp built in the 1930s for 500 inmates, the New Bell prison, in Cameroon's economic capital of Douala, is home to 4,000 inmates, a large majority of whom are in pre-trial detention. On Sundays, during church services, women who have been abandoned by their husbands accost you with their pathetic stories. How can I forget Marie Ngone, serving 10 years for stealing a baby from the Douala hospital because she could not have any of her own, or the death of Alexis on 25 December 2009 after a visit from his fiancé? He was stabbed by other inmates during a dispute over cards.

My encounter with the dean of the inmates, Samuel Ndin Ndin, who has already served 34 years in the jail, was emotional. He told me that he indulges in homosexuality with other inmates to cool his sexual urge; he admits that it is unnatural but says he has no choice. 'I lost my father, mother and only brother and could not attend their funerals; if I had listened to the advice of my parents I would not be in this condition. I was involved in armed robbery, committed crimes. You are a journalist, tell the world my story. I am begging for forgiveness for all I have done.'

Torture is a daily occurrence. Some inmates are taken to a torture chamber known as the *bureau interieur* where their legs are tied to a metal window, their heads facing down for long minutes. Each time I found myself in this area, the warders stopped their torture session for fear that once out of jail I would report the story. Other inmates are kept in chains for months.

Visiting loved ones in prison is a nightmare for family and friends. Besides the humiliating body searches, you have to pay to sit in the waiting room and for your loved one to be called from the cell. Wives, daughters and sisters of inmates are often victims of sexual harassment.

Falling ill in prison was the most difficult experience of my life. Here I would like to pay special homage to Alain Gauthier Fanyep who, noticing that my temperature was rising and that I was suffering from acute pain on the right side of my head, immediately informed the nurses of my condition. For three days he assisted me as we waited for the prison doctor and nurses to attend to me. It took the intervention of Lapiro de Mbanga (a popular musician in jail on trumped-up charges) before Dr Amougou could attend to me. Instructions had been given that I should be allowed to die to please the regime of President Paul Biya. It was only after my family paid a huge bribe to the prison authorities that I was taken to see a specialist, who diagnosed a serious ear problem. I needed urgent and special treatment. The prison officials refused to admit me to the hospital. I was taken back to prison where I resorted to painkillers and some palliatives. My condition worsened and I had difficulty hearing, as well as additional problems with my nerves and heart. Today my right ear is seriously damaged and I need a hearing aid to help me use my left ear. Twenty months in New Bell prison has left a permanent scar on my life. ❏

© Lewis Medjo
39(4): 97/101
DOI: 10.1177/0306422010389665
www.indexoncensorship.org

Lewis Medjo is publisher and editor of *La Détente Libre*

EYEWITNESS

Ania Corless on
Uzbekistan

The cities of Bukhara and Samarkand conjure lost images of opulence and learning; Tashkent was once considered the richest city in Central Asia. Yet Uzbekistan today is a land that time has forgotten and the world has abandoned. Its significance for the West lies in its proximity to Afghanistan, not in its situation on the Great Silk Road, between Europe and Asia. Following 9/11, Uzbekistan found favour with Washington by allowing the United States to set up an airbase in the country, which served as a hub for missions to Afghanistan. However, the airbase was vacated in 2005, following the Andijan massacre, when security forces opened fire on protesters, killing and injuring hundreds.

In 2007, as the West searched for alternative energy sources, the European Union eased its sanctions on the country and the World Bank reversed its decision to suspend loans and slash aid. According to the International Crisis Group, the United States also gave aid to Uzbek secret security law enforcement agencies. Yet, despite this renewed support from the West and the fact that the country is rich in natural gas, oil, gold and cotton and was once known as a centre for science and engineering, Uzbekistan is rife with poverty and unemployment. An authoritarian, corrupt, paranoid state with no legal political opposition, its educational system is at a standstill. Under Joseph Stalin, the Cyrillic alphabet was imposed on Uzbekistan. However, after gaining independence from the Soviet Union, President Karimov insisted on reforming the alphabet so that Latin script was revived. This made the majority of academic texts and general educational materials obsolete so that the country suffers from a dearth of educational publications and has a cavernous gap in schooling.

In 2004, Lucy Popescu, then programme director of the Writers in Prison Committee (WiPC) of English PEN, and I, a member of the committee, had come to Tashkent to meet with four Uzbek writers, novelist Mamadali Makhmudov and journalists Ruslan Sharipov, Muhammad Bekzhon and Yusif Ruzimuradov, who had all been made honorary PEN members. They were serving average sentences of 14 years' imprisonment for defending their right to freedom of expression under a regime that was, and still is, repressive in the extreme. We had been writing letters to the prisoners, but this had not yielded much information. The aim of our visit was to gather details that would better equip us to mount an effective campaign for their release and to inform the world about what was going on in this closed society. We also aimed to find out what support we might usefully offer to the prisoners' families, who were living on the edge of despair.

During our time there, we were watched and followed, our rooms were searched, our hotel telephones didn't work and it was an accepted fact that informers attended our meetings with dissidents. All of this was intended to intimidate and it did, not least by making us aware that we might be endangering the very people whom we'd come to help.

We met with Otanazar Orifov, leader of the disbanded opposition party, *Erk* (Freedom), who maintained that in 2004 there were 800 newspapers – and 800 censors. It's doubtful whether the number of censors has diminished, since so little else has changed in the country. According to the defence lawyer who handled the PEN cases, Russia, once that monolith of repression, often provides the first refuge for Uzbek dissidents. Ruslan Sharipov himself began his journey to the West by seeking asylum in Russia in June 2004.

Political opposition in Uzbekistan is crushed, often through torture: prisoners have been thrown out of windows, forced to end their days as invalids; many are committed to mental asylums; they receive regular beatings and are deprived of basic needs. There have also been reports of political prisoners being boiled alive, which was brought to international attention by Craig Murray, the British ambassador to Uzbekistan from 2002–2004. We spoke to him during our time in the country, and he described photographs he had seen, shown to him by the mother of one prisoner, Mirzakayam Avazov. The pictures showed a body covered in burns, which the authorities maintained had been caused by other prisoners spilling hot tea over him, causing his death. Murray sent the photographs to the Foreign Office in London, where a forensic report stated that the burns were consistent with the body having been immersed in boiling liquid. Human Rights Watch (HRW) also gives a description of this case in its briefing paper to the United Nations in 2003. In a subsequent detailed report dated 2007, entitled *Nowhere to Turn,* there are further eyewitness accounts of how criminal detainees are paid to beat and rape those serving political sentences.

Sabit Madaliev, a dissident writer, was our translator and constant courageous companion. The lawyer representing the writers, who was himself the victim of many attacks and an abduction, made it possible to contact the prisoners' families. Conditions in the prisons were horrific, with outbreaks of tuberculosis and other diseases. We could not visit the prisoners themselves. Instead, we met with nieces, nephews, mothers and wives; we gave them money and brought back information; and we picked up one new case, that of Gayarat Mekhlibaev, a journalist accused of supporting an Islamist group. His arrest followed the publication of his article, critical of the government, entitled 'The Scales of Justice'.

Our activities seemed to us to add up to so very little, yet they brought some respite to the families of prisoners, many of them living alone and in fear. They were ostracised, forced to live on the margins of society and unable to find work; their children were excluded from schools. We swore to the families that we would not publicise any names since that could put them in danger, leading to further repercussions. However, the stories of those who can be named paint a picture of what dissent can mean in this country.

Journalists Muhammad Bekzhon and Yusif Ruzimuradov were accused of involvement in a series of explosions in Tashkent, but it is thought that they were incarcerated because of articles they had written for the opposition movement's newspaper, which Ruzimuradov edited. Jailed for threatening the president, it is widely believed that novelist Mamadali Makhmudov was actually arrested for having links with *Erk* too. He was jailed in 1999 and sentenced to 14 years' imprisonment. 'The possibilities are tied. The eyes are tied. The tongues are tied. The walls are wandering all around,' he wrote from prison. Now on crutches after being tortured, he is allowed a four-hour visit every other month. He writes in Uzbek and his first novel, *The Immortal Cliffs*, was published in 1981. He craves contact with foreigners and every communication from abroad is a source of pleasure and pride.

In the bare flat that is his home, his wife pulled out tattered boxes filled with cards and notes from PEN correspondents, the ink on some grown faint. When we arrived, at what in England would be called a tenement, the entire family were waiting to greet us. Makhmudov's wife was in tears. A lavish lunch they could ill afford was set and as a present we were each handed a carved wooden box fashioned in prison by dissident writers. I still have that box. We stayed an hour or two, but could offer little comfort except for our presence, proof that Makhmudov was not forgotten and that those in whom he'd placed his faith knew of his bravery. It seems sometimes that is enough to keep the spirit alive.

Internet journalist Ruslan Sharipov received a five-year prison sentence for homosexuality – though the more likely reason is that he formed an independent union of journalists. He'd been tortured and made to watch as others underwent torture. Later he was transferred to an open prison where he worked as a librarian and had relative freedom of movement. After a number of abortive attempts and following a series of complicated journeys, assisted by his lawyer, we finally met with him. The venue was a cafe in Tashkent. Sharipov had feigned sickness and been given a day away from work. His English is very good and he insisted that we should not bring our translator – one of the successes of President Karimov's repressive measures is that Uzbeks are deeply distrustful of one another; everyone is a possible informer. One reason HRW has made as much headway as it has in Uzbekistan is that it employs foreigners exclusively, so that those who consider themselves to be part of the opposition feel a degree of safety with these representatives and are more likely to confide in them.

Sharipov spoke of his arrest and of the beatings he'd received. In jail he'd had no contact with other prisoners of conscience – all his fellow inmates were violent men inside on criminal charges. He wanted a foreign passport for protection once he left prison, believing it would give him immunity while he continued his activities at home. Finally, he saw the impossibility of this position and travelled to America via Russia. Away from Uzbekistan, his life lost its meaning and he had a complete mental collapse. Following treatment made possible with PEN's assistance, he now works as editor-in-chief of an online magazine reporting on human rights abuses in Central Asia.

In Uzbekistan, people, especially writers and political activists, learn to live with fear and suspicion. The relatives of prisoners who agreed to see us during our time there took great risks; their bravery was unquestionable. Because the 2004 trip made it possible for us to have a connection with these prisoners, they were made aware that we had travelled there and that we would not abandon our campaign on their behalf. As long as President Karimov casts his shadow over this beleaguered nation, the WiPC will continue to fight for the rights that have been taken away from Mahmadali Mahmudov, Muhammad Bekzhon, Yuzif Ruzimuradov and Gayarat Mehliboev, who remain incarcerated. Meanwhile, Ruslan Sharipov yearns for home. ❐

©Ania Corless
39(4): 102/105
DOI: 10.1177/0306422010389378
www.indexoncensorship.org

Ania Corless is a literary agent at David Higham Associates. She was deputy chair and acting chair of the Writers in Prison Committee and a founder member of the publishing network of Amnesty International

Amnesty and ARTICLE 19 campaigning for the release of Eynulla Fətullayev, June 2010
Credit: Robert Sharp

LONE STAR

As activists shift focus, **Salil Tripathi** reminds us that the battle for universal rights is not yet won

I grew up in independent India and took Indian democracy – with all its flaws – for granted. We may be poor, but we could vote, unlike our neighbours. China had never known democracy; Nepal and Bhutan were monarchies; Pakistan oscillated between dictatorship and democracy with more of the former; and a bloody coup ended Bangladesh's nascent democracy in 1975.

But we could not be smug; a few weeks before the Bangladesh coup in 1975, we flirted with authoritarianism. Indira Gandhi responded to a court judgment against her by declaring an emergency, jailing political opponents and journalists, suspending parts of the constitution, and offering India a 20-point programme for economic development. 'Work more, talk less,' was one of the slogans emblazoned on billboards in major cities.

Her pithy point was that fundamental rights – civil liberties, political rights, and the right to protest – must take the backseat if India was to meet its socioeconomic goals. To remove poverty, protests had to be stopped first. The individual's needs must make way for the collective good. A few respectable lawyers and academics even agreed with that view. The needs of the many were to take precedence over the rights of the few, who should mind their own business anyway, instead of criticising the government.

Nineteen months later, Indira Gandhi called elections, certain that she would win. Instead, her party lost, and she herself suffered a humiliating defeat in her own parliamentary seat. Indians were still poor, hungry, and continued to suffer from diseases – but they valued their individual freedoms.

Human rights groups have traditionally fought for civil and political rights, but in recent years they have begun campaigning more vigorously for economic, social, and cultural rights. They are drawn into such campaigning because their supporters want it that way. And in developing countries, where they wish to spread their wings, local civil society groups often say that tackling poverty is the single most important task. As they broaden their reach and widen their interest, there is a risk that the distinction between individual rights and collective good may blur.

That would be a mistake. Today, more countries regularly hold elections. But writers continue to be jailed, tortured and, in some cases, killed. The inspiring image of a lone individual, writing something that reveals what those in authority wish to conceal, is a powerful one. Throughout history, writers have stood firm, remained unrepentant, stayed stubborn, said exactly what they have felt, written just as they have imagined, and forced the state and others with power to go on the defensive.

During the emergency, every Indian did not express criticism of the state; only some did. But they all felt the pinch of authoritarianism. The actions and resistance of the few mattered; they set the example, and when elections were called, they collectively liberated India.

There is utilitarian logic in the argument that the state should pursue the greatest good for the largest number of people. But such logic can have extreme consequences, where the end becomes important and the means don't matter. Governments occasionally use the phrase 'you have to break an egg to make an omelette', but human rights groups must not let them get away with it. They must keep reminding governments that human rights are indivisible, universal, complementary and inalienable. Human rights groups are appalled by the division between civil and political rights on the one hand, and economic, social and cultural rights on the other. But in their zeal to fix problems of poverty and disease, they should not forget the basics.

While the Universal Declaration of Human Rights identifies 30 rights, with none taking priority over another, the two covenants that codify and elaborate on those rights are divided on political and economic grounds. During the Cold War, the West could admonish the East for detaining its thinkers; the East condemned the West for failing to provide universal education or health. Amnesty International and Human Rights Watch had emerged from the West. They emphasised the universal nature of human rights, but their initial focus was on grave abuses committed behind the Iron Curtain, and in authoritarian regimes.

After the Cold War ended – which also coincided with the end of apartheid in South Africa and the emergence of China and India as major economies – human rights groups began working on economic, social, and cultural rights. Until then, those rights had been the preserve of development agencies and other groups, and there was an unseemly tussle to get attention. I remember, at the World Economic Forum some years ago, the head of an international charity that specialises in delivering food aid saying, 'We are fighting the wrong war', after the representative of a human rights group made an eloquent plea for safeguards against torture in the war on terror. The development expert contrasted the rights specialist's narrow approach with his organisation's work on more chronic issues, like world hunger. He implied that his cause – hunger – was right; I thought he had missed the point altogether.

Nevertheless, human rights groups have begun taking economic and social rights more seriously. Instead of championing political prisoners, they are paying attention to people imprisoned by poverty. That phrase is instructive, as is the use of the passive voice – 'by poverty' – for it does not say who is doing the imprisoning (because it cannot be said with any clarity), and what is to be done about it (besides increasing development assistance). One of Amnesty International's major current campaigns is called 'Demand Dignity', and focuses on the rights of the poor. Indeed, the poor face discrimination and innumerable hurdles to access justice. And Amnesty has published reports on forced removal of people living in slums, the treatment of the mentally ill in state-run hospitals, and maternal mortality. Human Rights Watch has produced excellent reports on the mistreatment of domestic workers in Southeast Asia and construction workers in the Middle East, and the bullying of people because of their sexual orientation.

These are important issues; none should be overlooked. But as human rights groups widen their coverage, they will find that structural issues defy simplistic solutions, and there is the risk that some of the older concerns – like the writer in jail – will get less attention.

Think of the simple image of a writer jailed for his beliefs. It is easy to find out who has placed him in detention. And it is also easy to fix the problem – get the writer out of jail. The violation is clear, as is the violator, and the remedy is known, too. Try doing that with poverty or starvation. It is complicated to figure out who the violator is – or, as is often the case, who the violators are. And the remedy? Further resources? Will that stop the abuse?

Blurring has occurred because of the shift from the individual to the collective. The early cases that human rights campaigners fought for revolved around individuals – the dissident being tortured; the cartoonist being detained; the columnist beaten up; the editor in jail. With economic, social, and cultural rights, the stories become undifferentiated. Thousands may be in a similar situation. The response the human rights groups seek is collective. But a campaign to liberate an individual who has risked jail by speaking out empowers many more, and that may lead to systemic change. The power of the individual cannot be underestimated. Think of aid agencies' campaigns for complex problems like child poverty. It is a collective crisis, but they focus on an individual case, using a child's photograph to tug at the consciences of donors, to raise funds to alleviate the crisis.

As human rights groups take on bigger battles, there is the real risk that the small vital voice will get short shrift. The focus shifts from the man who stands in front of the tank at Tiananmen Square to the millions suffering from HIV/Aids. China has also jailed people who provide information about HIV/Aids online. It wants to fight the disease while preventing information from reaching the people. Without information and transparency, those efforts are doomed.

When we fight to get those individual activists free, we are fighting for that precedent, that example. Their freedom empowers many others, because it boosts the strength of the powerless against the powerful. When Aung San Suu Kyi is truly free, Burma will be truly free; if Anna Politkovskaya's killers are finally brought to account, then everyone will feel safer.

The Soviet Union and China tried to dismiss human rights as a western norm. Several East Asian governments echo China, saying that if people want their rice bowls full, they should keep quiet. But for every China, there is a North Korea and a Burma, where generals have offered that Faustian bargain – rice bowl in exchange for freedom – without filling that bowl and while fattening themselves. Which is why it is all the more important not to forget those writers in jail. They are the conscience-keepers. Their presence in jail shows that those old battles are not over.

That old man from India, Mohandas Gandhi, who was jailed many times for many things, including seditious writing, was right: 'When I despair, I remember all through history the way of truth and love has always won. There have been tyrants and murderers and for a time they seem invincible, but in the end, they always fall. ... Think of it, always.' ❐

©Salil Tripathi
39(4): 106/110
DOI: 10.1177/0306422010389742
www.indexoncensorship.org

Salil Tripathi is a freelance journalist and writer based in London. He is the author of *Offence: The Hindu Case* (Seagull Books), and a trustee of English PEN

EYEWITNESS

Antonia Fraser on
meeting Irina Ratushinskaya

In selected extracts from her diary, written between 1986 and 1988, **Lady Antonia Fraser** *recalls her involvement, together with her husband Harold Pinter, in PEN's campaign for the release of the political prisoner Irina Ratushinskaya, a Russian poet and writer who was a prominent dissident in the former Soviet Union. Ratushinskaya was released in October 1986.*

24 May 1986

'Try everything, expect nothing.' I always think that is the right motto of the demonstrator, one who lives safely in a country where there are no penalties to be paid for demonstrating other than evoking annoyance – or worse still, indifference. In this mood, Harold and I went to the Bayswater Road on Saturday afternoon to stand about as near as we could get to the Russian embassy (not very near in fact, across the road from the gates to the wide palatial street where the embassy actually lies). The idea was to listen to readings of Irina Ratushinskaya's poems and also to the Amnesty International report on conditions at the women's prison in zone 4. Then there would be extracts from her smuggled samizdat diary: on the one hand unbearable details, like the women's boots, jackets and slips being removed when they were taken into the punishment cell, made of concrete, temperatures as low as $8°$ F; on the other hand, by putting all these special women prisoners together, the Soviet authorities unintentionally created a strong and supportive unit so that the women took turns to hunger-strike in favour of whoever was in the punishment cell.

The composition of the demo was like a literary cocktail party, but unlike such a party, we all stood around listening to great poetry, not making small chit chat. Since I first read them, I've always loved Irina's poems. This is not true of every prisoner for whom I've demonstrated – how could it be? – and of course it shouldn't make any difference. However, we're all human and it does. I wish I could believe I would ever meet Irina. But I don't. This is the best I can do, meet her poetry on a Saturday afternoon in Bayswater.

Irina Ratushinskaya was released from prison in October 1986.

12 December 1986

Ann Morgan, of the Irina Trust, had suggested that we call Irina on the telephone: she's 'lonely' and awaits her visitor's visa in Kiev to come here for medical treatment. The first time we tried, Harold suddenly asked me to inquire from the operator the time in Kiev, just as we were about to get through. Three hours ahead! My goodness, we're idiots! We could have been the KGB telephoning in the middle of the night. Finally did it at a more sociable hour the next day. Waited for 20 minutes and the operator rang back: 'Irina's on the line.' Trembled as I realised I was actually going to speak to her. Then her voice: strong, even vigorous, measured, lovely deep Russian lilt. Babbled my name, then introduced 'my husband the playwright'. Harold talked of our desire to see her here and welcome her. I talked of my feeling for her poetry. Irina: 'I have written poetry since my release.' And she referred me to Alyona Kofvanikov, who had the poems in London, reeling off the telephone number. I asked her if she would go to mass on Christmas Day. Irina: 'There is nowhere here.' Me: 'Then I will pray for you in London.' Irina, drily: 'I hope it does some good!' She added that she did feel lonely, was glad she was not forgotten, and sent her greetings to PEN.

I was still trembling when I rang off. Later, Alyona confirmed that all these telephone calls, naturally monitored by the KGB, helped to establish Irina's continued importance in the eyes of the West.

13 December 1986

Alyona telephoned: Irina will be here for Christmas! Harold and I read her poems to each other after dinner. And I re-read *No, I'm not afraid*.

23 December 1986

We watched Irina on TV, a person bearing witness to the truth, we both felt: a little Russian doll of a girl, broad face, wide-apart dark eyes, pale skin, square-cut fringe, dowdy (and touching) dark dress as my grandmother might have worn. Irina: 'I have been put in prison for my rhymes.' She uses the word 'rhymes' all the time for 'verse'.

10 February 1987

Met Irina! At the Poetry Society. (I had begun to think that Irina was a mythical white unicorn who I would never actually see.) Harold: 'She's there, *she's here*.' I looked and looked and couldn't see – because the little Russian doll of

Sally Soames

Writers protest to free top Russian poet

by Norman Lebrecht

WRITERS gathered outside Russian missions, embassies and consulates in London, New York and Chicago yesterday to recite the works of a young poet who is dangerously ill in a prison camp in the Soviet Union.

Irina Ratushinskaya, 32, is serving seven years' hard labour for alleged anti-Soviet propaganda, and is fast becoming the Kremlin's most troublesome symbol of oppression. This weekend Lord Whitelaw, who is leading an Inter-Parliamentary Union delegation to Moscow, plans to raise her case with officials there.

The archbishop of York, Dr John Hapgood, who is in Moscow with a British Council of Churches group, is also pressing for her release. A similar call will be made by Dr Robert Runcie, the archbishop of Canterbury, when he meets Leonid Zamyatin, the new Soviet ambassador to London.

Ratushinskaya was imprisoned in 1983 for writing verses in defence of human rights. She is reported to have been beaten, force-fed and kept in icy solitary confinement at a women's camp 300 miles southeast of Moscow. Her husband has not been allowed to see her for three years. She is suffering from a

talent. David McDuff, a British authority on Russian literature and the translator of a new collection of her verse, believes she is the finest poet to emerge in the Soviet Union for 20 years. "She was marked out by the KGB for her mixture of talent, fearlessness and intelligence," he says.

Joseph Brodsky, one of the foremost Russian poets-in-exile who is now based in the

Ratushinskaya: fears for her life

United States, describes her as "a remarkably genuine poet, a poet with faultless pitch who hears historical and absolute time with equal precision".

Ratushinskaya was born in the Black Sea port of Odessa. Her parents were conformist but at an early age Ratushinskaya became a Ro-man Catholic, then militant

In 1979 she married Igor Gerashchenko, a human rights activist, moved to Kiev and applied to emigrate. "From birth," her husband writes in McDuff's book, "she found the psychology of Soviet man and the Soviet religion unacceptable." She was arrested for the first time in 1981 at a demonstration in Moscow for Andrei Sakharov.

Most of her finest poems have been smuggled out of the labour camp. One reads:

I will live and survive and be asked:
How they slammed my head against a trestle,
How I had to freeze at nights,
How my hair started to turn grey...
I will smile. And will crack some joke
And brush away the encroaching shadow.

"Through her sufferings she has developed as a poet," says McDuff, "but in her present condition I don't know if she can still write."

Among the London writers demanding her release yesterday were Frederic Raphael, Ian McEwan, Marina Warner, Alan Sillitoe and Christopher Logue. In New York, science fact and fiction joined hands as the novelist Kurt Vonnegut joined Dr

my imagination didn't exist. Irina is really quite tall – 5ft 7in at a guess – tall and slender, a good supple figure. One got the height wrong because her husband, seen on TV looming above her, is actually enormously tall – 6ft 4in or so. She has a smooth pale olive complexion, short dark curly hair like a child's mop, but I saw the threads of grey to which, at the age of 32, she refers in one of her poems. She wore a high-necked grey tunic and skirt, flat-heeled black shoes.

Edna O'Brien at my side points out that when Irina looks away, there's a look of torment, or at least apprehension, about her. It was true, I noticed, as Irina turned to the side, coughing.

When we met, Irina was being indignant about the press: 'I just want to read my poems,' she said in that wonderful Russian voice, both soft and strong. 'I don't want to talk politics.' Nevertheless, she feels a loyalty to give press interviews in order to help those still in prison.

25 February 1987

Went to Lambeth Palace for Irina's reading in the chapel. Irina seemed luminous in the austere, grey chapel, with a couple of Russian ikons adjacent, which I had imagined had been imported for the occasion (wrongly as it turned out: Dr Runcie [the then Archbishop of Canterbury] used to be in charge of the Christians in Russia and retains strong links). She looked just a little fuller and less ill; her clear voice came at us out of the hall, once again the voice of a witness. Elaine Feinstein read the first translations very softly, but as a poet would; later Fiona Shaw, as an actress, was much more audible and expert but lacked a poet's magic. All the same, it was an occasion of great beauty and well-handled by Dr Runcie, who recalled gracefully to our attention, without naming him, Terry Waite's [a Church of England envoy held hostage in Lebanon] continued captivity. In the middle of the performance, a man connected to a great many members of the audience had a heart attack and had to be carried out. I looked at Irina and realised that such violent transitions from life to death on public occasions were no surprise to her.

31 May 1988

Irina Ratushinskaya came to International PEN. Siobhan Dowd, eyes shining (as mine did at the prospect of seeing Irina again), arranged a room at the Africa Centre in Covent Garden, where International PEN has its tiny offices. The room, although very dingy with little of the hoped-for 'African' colour, was lit up by Irina.

My first reaction was *amazement* at how she had changed. The emaciated woman, with complexion of grey porridge, in grey clothes to match, of the Lambeth Palace reading has become a sparkling-eyed, pink cheeked, very pretty girl. *Try everything…* I certainly never expected this.

Irina also speaks really good English. She laughed when I told her how much she had changed. Described her own similar reactions at seeing other women in New York, such as Verushka who had been in the small zone [prison] with her: 'Verushka,' she told her, 'we were good people, we were fine people, but no one could have said we looked very nice. But now, Verushka, you are a preeetty woooman!' ❏

©Lady Antonia Fraser
39(4): 111/114
DOI: 10.1177/0306422010388980
www.indexoncensorship.org

Lady Antonia Fraser is a historian and crime novelist. Her books include *The Gunpowder Plot: Terror and Faith in 1605* (Weidenfeld & Nicolson), *Marie Antoinette: The Journey* and *Mary, Queen of Scots* (Random House). Her most recent book is *Must You Go?: My Life with Harold Pinter* (Weidenfeld & Nicolson)

NEVER FORGOTTEN

In July 2010, several Black Spring dissidents were released after years in detention. **Val Warner** reflects on the highs and lows of writing to Cuban prisoners

In 2007, I sent seasonal greetings cards to the families of all the Cuban prisoners on PEN's caselist. I received a reply from one of them, the journalist Léster Luis González Pentón.

Léster was the youngest of the 75 people arrested in the Black Spring clampdown of 2003, which included journalists, librarians and trade union activists. The strongest impression from his letters is the waste of life and time. In December 2008, he wrote: 'Very soon we will have spent six years unjustly imprisoned, separated from our loved ones. My daughter was born and has grown up without knowing the warmth of her father – I can only see her for two hours every 30 days.'

For Christmas 2009, he sent a beautiful handmade card to the PEN office; in New Year 2010, he said: 'Being behind bars at this time is very difficult to bear because I am losing years of my life without being able to do anything.' In that letter, he also wrote: 'Even when I am doing a boring task, it helps to remember that we are not alone, nor forgotten, as our captors would like us to think.' He added that his mother had framed the letter from PEN informing him he had become an honorary member, and hung it on her wall.

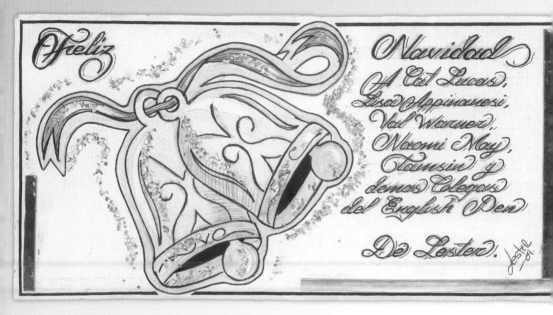

González Pentón's Christmas card to the PEN office, 2009

Although, like all the prisoners, Léster had serious health problems, often exacerbated by jail, Normando Hernández González, who became one of the best known of the Cuban political prisoners, seemed always to be perilously sick. I had become his minder when he was first elected an honorary member, which meant that I was responsible for writing to him and his family and for raising public awareness of his case. I heard from his wife only once – not surprising, as she received many letters from organisations and individuals around the world. In an email sent in June 2006, she wrote: 'I'd like you to know that Normando was very happy to learn that he was a member of PEN and that people like you think about him and the rest of the journalists who are imprisoned. The situation is very difficult; he is very ill at the moment and losing weight considerably. He has an illness that means he does not absorb food properly. He also has chronic gastritis and jejunitis; these illnesses cause him much pain, colic, acidity, constant diarrhoea and constipation. Imagine that if it is difficult to be imprisoned, how much more difficult it is to be both a prisoner and an invalid.' An attachment contained some poems written by her husband on rough paper in jail, including 'Conviction':

> The unbearable hatred
> that you leave behind when treating me,
> makes your meanness
> break the decibels of your rage.
> And while you make me suffer further,
> and while you make me endure further,
> and while I carry this cross further:
> a penetrating patience
> will assail me
> cramming me
> with conviction,
> courage
> love ...,
> and that is why,
> I forgive you

The Writers in Prison Committee (WiPC) probably had more contact with prisoners in Cuba than it has had with prisoners of conscience from other countries featured on their case list, which lists almost 600 writers in prison or under threat. The Cuban postal system can be unreliable and we assumed there was some intervention by authorities, but certainly some of the letters, packets and books sent got through. The prisoners' toughness, which came through in their communications, was humbling.

It was surprising how rapidly technology had an impact on our communication with prisoners. We were able to have regular online contact with Jorge Olivera Castillo, who was released on health grounds in December 2004, and with the family of Adolfo Fernández Saínz. Technological developments and new media made campaigning easier – political prisoners are now publicised all over the web – but technology alone cannot bring about change for dissidents. There were thousands of references to Normando Hernández González online, but the man himself, often in solitary confinement, was barely alive. I recall one bleak discussion at a WiPC meeting about how we would mark the first death among Cuban honorary members, if it came to that.

Of course, this kind of campaigning is very safe in the UK, in stark contrast with Cuba, where the wives of prisoners have been very active on their husbands' behalf, despite the trouble they may bring on themselves.

Normando Hernández González's wife, Yarai Amparo Reyes Marín, was in regular contact with human rights organisations campaigning for the prisoners. Adolfo Fernández Saínz's wife, Julia Esther Núñez Pacheco, was one of the *Damas de Blanco* (Ladies in White) who protested continuously for their husbands' release and who were selected to receive the Sakharov Prize for Freedom of Thought from the European Union in 2005. The Cuban government banned the group's leaders, including Núñez Pacheco, from travelling to Strasbourg to collect the prize. However, it is hoped that they will be able to attend the prize ceremony this year to collect their prize in person, alongside the 2010 winner, Cuban dissident Guillermo Fariñas.

In February 2010, prisoner Orlando Zapata Tamayo died after 85 days on hunger strike. Tamayo's death appeared to expedite the release of a number of prisoners; the Roman Catholic Church and the Spanish government also played a seemingly crucial role. As of November 2010, it is estimated that over 100 political prisoners remain in jail, with 39 released, including many of the Black Spring dissidents. Six of English PEN's seven Cuban honorary members, including those mentioned here, have been freed; Pedro Argüelles Morán is still in prison, having refused to leave Cuba in exchange for his freedom. Those who were released agreed to live in Spain and, for the foreseeable future, will apparently not be allowed back into Cuba. They are unpopular with many Cubans who regard them as collaborating with the United States as it continues the deeply damaging embargo imposed in 1962. ❑

©Val Warner
39(4): 115/118
DOI: 10.1177/0306422010389745
www.indexoncensorship.org

'Conviction' translated by Susana Medina

Val Warner's poetry collections include *Tooting Idyll* and *Before Lunch*, published by Carcanet. She translated Corbiere as *The Centenary Corbiere* (Carcanet) and edited Charlotte Mew's Collected and Selected (Virago and Carcanet)

The darkest of places

Léster Luis González Pentón

In the midst of the uncertain darkness of a Cuban prison, I was forced to serve seven years and four months of an illegal prison sentence, simply for writing about the realities of life in Cuba and the form of slavery imposed by the communist dictatorship of the Castros, whose government has ruled the country for more than 50 years.

Although I was sentenced to 20 years in prison, I was released and exiled to Spain in July 2010, with no right of return to my lovely Caribbean island, my Cuban birthplace, since its dictator, Fidel Castro Ruiz, has banned me even from visiting my homeland.

During my detention inside that jail, I was the victim of serious human rights violations merely for my defence of democracy, and subjected to humiliating behaviour, psychological torture, beatings and other forms of maltreatment. Throughout this time I was held in a dark cell, in solitary confinement, and in the course of a year and a half, only allowed a family visit every three months.

There in the dark depths of my cell, I received support from numerous international organisations and individuals, who showed their solidarity with me by sending letters and postcards. By giving me their moral support they let me know that I was neither alone nor forgotten behind those thick prison bars, stripped of my freedom and my human rights.

Most particularly, throughout those long years, I received strong support from English PEN, a London-based organisation, and this modest association took me up, awarding me the accolade of welcoming me into the ranks of its honorary members.

Its members sent me postcards and letters and further support, also in the form of letters and cards, to my family; these communications were and are most important to me, for they showed me at that time I was not forgotten in the darkest of places, where prisoners lose all hope, including the will to live, and where many are tempted to commit suicide, for we were treated as if we were utterly worthless.

The recognition of being made an honorary member of English PEN was so important to me inside that prison cell, it was one of the best things that has happened in all my life, the more so because it came at such a difficult time. It brought me great joy and spiritual strength.

I have brought all those cards and letters with me to Spain and they are guarded as closely as treasure. They are a wonderful memory I will never forget, given that they helped me to survive in the darkness of despair.

©Léster Luis González Pentón
Translated by Amanda Hopkinson

50 YEARS
50 WRITERS

From Cold War novelists to bloggers in 2010, we highlight some of the key cases championed by the Writers in Prison Committee

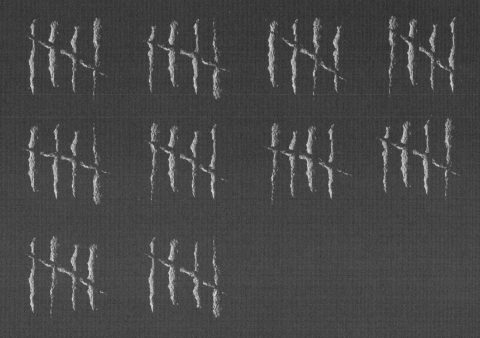

Anatoly T Marchenko

Country of origin:
Russia

Occupation:
Writer and activist

Status:
Died in prison in 1986

Anatoly T Marchenko was a Soviet dissident, author and human rights activist. Born in 1938 in Siberia, he spent 20 of his 48 years in prison and internal exile.

Marchenko was first arrested in 1959 after a fight broke out at a workers' hostel. Police arrested everyone present, and Marchenko was imprisoned near Karaganda. He escaped but was then arrested for 'treason' and sentenced to six years in a labour camp. Both his parents were illiterate and he had not finished his schooling, but Marchenko learned from intellectuals imprisoned with him.

Following his release in 1966, Marchenko wrote his most famous work, *My Testimony*, a vivid account of life in a prison camp. He was arrested again in 1968, after anticipating the invasion of Czechoslovakia and protesting against the Soviet government's treatment of the country. Charged with violating passport regulations, he was sentenced to one year in a labour camp. Around the scheduled time of his release, he was instead sentenced to a further two years for defamation. Many believe this was a punishment for the publication of *My Testimony* in the West. In 1971, Marchenko was internally exiled with fellow dissident Larisa Bogoraz, whom he later married. He co-founded the influential human rights organisation Moscow Helsinki Group in 1976.

Following the publication of his third book, *To Live Like Everyone*, Marchenko was charged with 'anti-Soviet agitation', and given a 15-year sentence. During the last years of his life he went on several hunger strikes, calling for the release of political prisoners across the USSR and an end to torture. His health deteriorated and he died in Chistopol prison in 1986.

Marchenko is the only person to be posthumously awarded the Sakharov Prize for Freedom of Thought.

from *My Testimony*

by Anatoly Marchenko

Everybody must know, including those who would like to know the truth and instead are given lying, optimistic newspaper articles, designed to lull the public conscience; and also including those who don't wish to know, who close their eyes and stuff up their ears in order to be able at some future date to justify themselves and to emerge from the dirt with their noses clean. If they have a single particle of civic conscience or genuine love for their country they will stand up in its defence, just as the true sons of Russia have always done.

I would like my testimony on Soviet camps and prisons for political prisoners to come to the attention of humanists and progressive people in other countries – those who stick up for political prisoners in Greece and Portugal and in Spain and South Africa. Let them ask their Soviet colleagues in the struggle against inhumanity: 'And what have you done in your own country to stop political prisoners from being "re-educated" by starvation?'

I don't consider myself a writer, these notes are not a work of art. For six whole years I tried only to see and to memorise. In these notes of mine there is not a single invented personage nor a single invented incident. Wherever there is a danger of harming others I have omitted names or remained silent. I am prepared to answer for the truth of every detail recounted here. Each incident, each fact can be confirmed by dozens and sometimes by hundreds or even thousands of witnesses and their comrades in the camps.

It seems a likely supposition that the authorities will try to be revenged on me and to escape the truth that I have told in these pages by an unprovable accusation of 'slander'. Let me declare, therefore, that I am prepared to answer for it at a public trial, provided that the necessary witnesses are invited and that interested representatives of public opinion and the press are allowed to be present. And if instead we are given yet another masquerade known as a 'public trial', where representatives of the KGB stand at the entrance in order to repel ordinary citizens and secret policemen dressed up in civvies are used as the 'public', and where the correspondents of all foreign newspapers (including communist ones) are forced to hang around outside, unable to get any information – as happened at the trials of the writers Sinyavsky and Daniel, Khaustov and Bukovsky and the others – then that will merely confirm the justice of what I have written.

© *Penguin/translator Michael Scammell*
39(4): 122/123, DOI: 10.1177/0306422010390836

Ruth First

Country of origin:
South Africa
Occupation:
Journalist, writer,
campaigner, academic
Status:
Imprisoned in 1963; murdered in 1982

Born in Johannesburg in 1925, Ruth First was a journalist and activist committed to the struggle against apartheid in South Africa.

First started her career on the weekly newspaper the *Guardian*. Throughout the 1950s, her investigative journalism exposed conditions for farm workers, migrant labourers and other members of the country's underclass. She was a founder member of the Congress of Democrats, which brought together the African National Congress and other organisations to work for political and human rights. First helped to draft the seminal Freedom Charter in 1955 but was prevented from attending the Congress of the People in Soweto. During the same period, she became editor of the pro-alliance journal *Fighting Talk* and acted as a consultant to the United Nations, focusing on political, social and economic issues across southern Africa.

In 1956, Ruth First and her husband, Joe Slovo, were arrested and charged with treason, along with 154 other defendants. The trial lasted four years, after which all were acquitted, although First was banned from working as a journalist. In 1963, she was detained and held in solitary confinement for 117 days without charge or trial.

After her release, First and her three daughters joined her husband in England, where she worked as an academic and writer. Between 1978 and 1982, First was research director of the Centre for African Studies at Eduardo Mondlane University in Maputo, Mozambique. She was killed on 17 August 1982 by a letter bomb sent to her office at the university. It later emerged that orders for the bomb had come from an apartheid-era spy.

from *117 Days*

by Ruth First

I was in Pretoria Central Prison for 28 days. It was like being sealed in a sterile tank of glass in a defunct aquarium. People came to look at me every now and then and left a ration of food….In Marshall Square my sooty surroundings and the general air of gloom about the old police station would have justified melancholy, but I had been buoyant and refractory. Pretoria shone of bright polished steel and I grew increasingly subdued….I reflected on the new-found skill of the security branch in subjecting people to an enforced separation, a dissociation, from humanity. I felt alien and excluded from the little activity I saw about me; I was bereft of human contact and exchange. What was going on in the outside world? No echoes reached me. I was suspended in limbo, unknowing, unreached.

I read the Bible, day-dreamed, tried to shake myself into disciplined thinking. I devised a plot for a novel. The characters were me and my friends, all cast in heroic mould. We planned and organised in opposition to the government, called for strikes and acts of civil disobedience, were harassed and chivvied by the police, banned and arrested. I spent hours getting behind the political declarations of my characters, dissecting their private disillusionments and idle talk. I was ravenous for reading matter. One day during the early part of my stay in Pretoria I was in the yard during exercise hour and saw a scrap of paper in the dustbin for cinders from the kitchen high combustion stoves. I fished it out and held it between my thumb and forefinger to devour the words. It was a prison card and recorded prisoner's name, number, crime and sentence. Perhaps a dozen words in all but to me they were like an archaeological find, proof that some people in this society recognised the value of written language and were able to use it. Even better than this find was the ration of brown sugar that started to arrive every few days, for the six or eight ounces were rolled in a cone of paper, printed paper, torn from old magazines. This way I feasted on a few torn paragraphs from the *War Cry*, organ of the Salvation Army, and once only, tantalisingly, I got a short jagged piece from the *Saturday Evening Post*… I tried to improvise a version of a serial a la James Bond in which all the action centred round a jail break from Pretoria Central — my cell. Generally, though, my sugar ration was wrapped in an advertisement.

© *Ruth First/Bloomsbury.* 117 Days *will be republished by Virago in 2011*
39(4): 124/125, DOI: 10.11770306422010387565

Jorge Valls Arango

Country of origin:
Cuba

Occupation:
Poet and activist

Status:
Released in 1984; living in exile in
USA

Jorge Valls Arango was born in Cuba in 1933. A well-known activist and poet, he was arrested in 1964 for his political activities. He spent more than 20 years behind bars in several Cuban prisons and was finally released in 1984. After his release, he moved to Miami, Florida, where he published *Twenty Years and Forty Days: Life in a Cuban Prison*, making a significant contribution to the social and penal history of Cuba. He became a Cintas Foundation fellow in 1986, celebrated for his artistic accomplishments. His poetry collections include *Donde estoy no hay luz y está enrejado* (Where I am there is no light). He is currently the international secretary of the Democratic Social-Revolutionary Party of Cuba. Although it is no longer illegal in Cuba to form or participate in political parties other than the Communist Party of Cuba, the party is not allowed to campaign or engage in political activity within the country. 'Without civil rights, the best intentions turn into a trap, and societies become prisons and asylums', Valls wrote in 2000.

© Index on Censorship/English PEN
39(4): 126, DOI: 10.11770306422010391881

Credit: Darren Whiteside/Reuters

Pramoedya Ananta Toer

Country of origin:
Indonesia
Occupation:
Author (1925-2006)

Pramoedya Ananta Toer was born in Java in February 1925. Educated at the Radio Vocational School in Surabaya, he worked for the official news service under the Japanese occupation. During the revolution he joined the Indonesian Republic army, where he reached the rank of lieutenant.

Pramoedya wrote nationalist propaganda pamphlets and short stories during the 1940s. In 1947, he was imprisoned by the Dutch colonial authorities for two and a half years, during which he wrote his first major novel, *The Fugitive*.

Upon returning from a brief visit to China in 1956, he struggled to find employment in the mainstream press and at publishing houses, and began to work for various left-leaning publications in Indonesia. He later lectured at the University of Res Publika and co-founded a literature academy.

In 1965 President Suharto assumed power; one month later Pramoedya was arrested. He was detained in Sulemba prison for four years without trial, and then moved to the prison colony of Buru Island in 1969. There he began to tell stories to fellow prisoners, and in 1973 was granted permission to write in prison. He penned *The Buru Quartet: This Earth of Mankind, Child of All Nations, Footsteps* and *House of Glass*, all of which were subsequently banned in Indonesia. They were published abroad and have been translated into more than 25 languages.

Although he was released into house arrest in November 1979 it was not until 28 years later, in 1992, that Pramoedya was freed.

from *The Fugitive*

by Pramoedya Ananta Toer

The sound of footsteps became more distinct. The gambler put down the ear of corn he had been roasting and stood. He walked to the gate, where he peered to the right and the left and then returned to the hearth and the corn.

The wind brought him a muffled cry. 'He's probably at his father's hut.' The gambler jumped up and looked wildly around him. The sound of a wall in his hut being stretched and torn caused his head to jerk back. He heard the sound of corn stalks behind the hut being trampled and broken. The gambler listened more carefully. 'Thunder and lightning!' he barked. 'What was that?' He jumped to his left and ran to the side of the hut. Then he turned to search the right side before taking his place once more before the doorway. The light from the moon and the fire revealed the confusion on his face and the movements of a man not sure of what to do...

...As the voices closed in a dog yelped as if it had been kicked. Suddenly the gambler awoke from his shock. He turned around and ran into his hut. The floor creaked beneath his weight. Then he stopped. The hut was empty. The beggar was no longer there. All he could see were the slivers of light from the fire outside that pierced the hut's wall and disappeared like shooting stars in a darkened sky. In the back wall of the hut, beneath the dancing stars of firelight, was a hole, and through the hole he saw the ground outside, pale beneath the yellow light of the moon.

The sound of pounding feet grew louder. The gambler suddenly thrust his hand out in a gesture, but then let it fall weakly to his side as he settled into a crouch on the floor. His head dropped. From outside came the sounds of human cries. 'My son, my boy' he whispered. He was still as the wind picked up and the stars of firelight danced furiously on the walls. He poured out his confusion in a stifled moan. 'Where are you? Are you alive? Will the Japanese hunt you forever? If you are my son, I pray to God that He always watches over you. Was it for nothing that I brought you into this world?'

© Pramoedya Ananta Toer/HarperCollins/William Morrow
39(4): 128/129, DOI: 10.11770306422010390607

Yuli Daniel

Country of origin:

Russia

Occupation:

Writer, poet and translator
(1925-1989)

Yuli Daniel was jointly tried alongside his colleague Andrei Sinyavsky in 1965 for publishing satirical articles outside the Soviet Union. Credited with being the founders of an anti-censorship movement, they were convicted on charges of disseminating anti-Soviet propaganda.

Yuli Daniel was born in Moscow in 1925 and fought during the Second World War on the eastern front, where he was seriously wounded. In 1956 he graduated from Moscow Pedagogical State University and went on to become a teacher and member of the Gorky Institute of World Literature. He began to write satirical novels about life in Soviet Russia and, like Sinyavsky, had them published in Paris, using the pseudonym Nikolai Arzhak. His collection *This is Moscow Speaking and Other Stories* was also published in the United States in 1969.

At a closed trial, both Daniel and Sinyavsky pleaded not guilty – unprecedented in the USSR – and were sentenced to five and seven years of hard labour respectively. The trial was said to be symbolic of the end of the 'Khrushchev thaw' and the beginning of the Brezhnev era, and has been cited as the root of the Soviet dissident movement. Daniel spent four years in Mordovia labour camps and a further year in Vladimir prison. During his incarceration, he and five other dissident writers joined in a formal protest against prison conditions. He also met fellow political prisoner and author-to-be Anatoly Marchenko.

After reforms instigated by Mikhail Gorbachev in the late 1980s, Daniel was semi-rehabilitated. Refusing to leave the country as many Soviet dissidents did, some of his poems were published in Russia. He died at the age of 63, on 30 December 1989.

An Air

by Yuli Daniel
Translated by David Burg and Arthur Boyars

Week after week
Dissolves in smoke from cigarettes
In this curious establishment
Everything's dream or else delirium.

Birds stray along the ledges,
Keys sing in the locks.
The world of unreality is steeped
In urine's pungent smell.

In here the light doesn't go off at night,
In here the light isn't too strong by day.
In here silence, the managing director,
Has taken me over.

You can choke with nothing to do,
Or beat your head against the wall,
Week after week
Dissolves in blue smoke.

Tirelessly, you're counting here
How many days are still to go.
Here in your frenzied fantasy you dream
Of her, of her, always of her.

In here the thump of the warders' steps –
Or is it the thumping of your heart?
In here you don't know as you would outside
Who's your friend and who's your foe.

This evil terrifying dream
Limbo between 'yes' and 'no',
Week after week
Dissolves in smoke from cigarettes.

Dissolves in smoke…

———————————————

9 November 1965, from *Prison Poems*

© *Yuli Daniel*
39(4): 130/131, DOI: 10.11770306422010391693

Credit: Caro/Alamy

Adam Michnik

Country of origin:

Poland

Occupation:

Writer

Status:

Released in 1986

Adam Michnik was born in October 1946 in Poland. In 1964 he was suspended from his studies at Warsaw University for distributing an open letter to members of the Polish United Workers Party (PUWP) calling for reforms to the Polish political system. He was suspended a second time in 1966 for organising a discussion with expelled former members of the PUWP.

In March 1968, Poland was rocked by student protests across campuses and major cities. For his involvement, Michnik was once again excluded from university and sentenced to three years in prison for 'acts of hooliganism'. He was released the following year under an amnesty.

After a brief period in Paris, Michnik returned to Poland in 1977 and became involved in the Workers Defence Committee (KOR), editing several underground publications, including *Biuletyn Informacyjny, Zapis* and *Krytyka*. He also became advisor to the independent trade union Solidarity.

In December 1981, Michnik was taken into custody, accused of attempting to 'overthrow socialism'. He was released in 1984, but was sent back to prison the following year for attempting to organise a strike in the Gdansk shipyard. He was sentenced to three years' imprisonment but released in 1986 under another amnesty.

In 1989, Michnik helped organise the Round Table talks between the authorities and opposition and, after the fall of the communist government, went on to found and edit *Gazeta Wyborcza* — one of Poland's leading newspapers. His books include *Letters from Freedom: Post-Cold War Realities and Perspectives, Church and the Left*, and *Letters from Prison and Other Essays*.

© Index on Censorship/English PEN
39(4): 132, DOI: 10.1177/0306422010390837

Akinwande Oluwole 'Wole' Soyinka was the first African writer to be awarded the Nobel Prize for Literature, which he received in 1986. He has been a prominent figure in drama, literature and politics in Nigeria for almost half a century and continues to speak out against injustice, corruption and human rights abuses across Africa.

Soyinka was born near Ibadan in 1934, the son of an Anglican clergyman. He studied at Government College in Ibadan and later completed a doctorate at the University of Leeds.

He was first arrested in 1965 after a radio broadcast in which he demanded that rigged regional elections in western Nigeria be cancelled. He escaped sentencing on a technicality, but was again incarcerated in 1967 when he tried to negotiate peace between the Nigerian and Biafran parties during the Nigerian Civil War. Held in solitary confinement for nearly two years, he began writing poems on toilet paper. Following his release, he published *Poems from Prison* and *The Man Died: Prison Notes of Wole Soyinka*.

During the rule of General Sani Abacha, Soyinka escaped Nigeria on a motorcycle and in 1997, was sentenced to death in absentia, after publicly criticising the regime. He continued to use his influence abroad to call for sanctions against Abacha's government, which was finally democratically deposed in 1998.

Soyinka's published work includes plays, poetry, fiction and essays. He was elected an honorary fellow of the Royal Society of Literature in 1983 and has been a Unesco ambassador since 1994. He has been a visiting professor at the universities of Cambridge, Sheffield and Yale, and is currently an emeritus professor at Obafemi Awolowo University, Ile-Ife.

Credit: Martina Salvi/Rex Features

Wole Soyinka

Country of origin:
Nigeria
Occupation:
Writer, dramatist and poet
Status:
Released in 1969; went into exile in 1997

© *Index on Censorship/English PEN*
*39(4): 133, DOI: 10.1177030642201039061*2

Yannis Ritsos

Country of origin:
Greece

Occupation:
Writer, poet and translator
(1909-1990)

Yannis Ritsos was born in May 1909 in Greece. In 1934, the same year he joined the Communist Party of Greece, his first collection of poems, *Tractor*, was published. Two years later, his second collection of poems, *O Epitaphios*, was published, followed by *The Song of My Sister* in 1937 and *Symphony of Spring* in 1938. His early writing was described by the authorities as 'militant' and 'doctrinaire' and copies of *O Epitaphios* were symbolically burned in front of the Acropolis under the fascist Ioannis Metaxas government.

During the Greek civil war in the 1940s, Ritsos joined the anti-fascist resistance and was eventually arrested. He spent four years in detention camps in Greece, during which time he continued to write poetry, with the collections *Romiosyni* being published in 1947 and *The Moonlight-Sonata* in 1956.

Under the military junta, which ruled Greece from 1967 to 1974, he was interned on the Greek islands of Yaros, Leros and Samos before being moved to house arrest in Athens. Despite being banned from publication until 1972, he continued to write and paint.

Ritsos died in Athens on 11 November 1990. Over his lifetime, he published 117 collections of poetry, novels and plays, and is believed to be Greece's most widely translated poet. He was nominated for the Nobel Prize for Literature nine times in his career and in 1975 was awarded the Lenin Prize for Peace.

© *Index on Censorship/English PEN*
39(4): 134, DOI: 10.1177/0306422010391946

Oppsite - Credit: Yannis Behrakis/Reuters

Angel Cuadra

Country of origin:
Cuba

Occupation:
Poet

Status:
Living in exile in the USA

Angel Cuadra was born in Havana in 1931 and started composing poetry when he was eight. In 1956 he graduated from the University of Havana with a degree in Law and Dramatic Arts, and began to participate in the activities of anti-Batista organisations. Two years later, his poem '*Lamento a Jose Marti en su Centenario*' (A Lament to Jose Marti on his Centenary) won a prize from the Circle of Iberian-American Poets and Writers in New York.

After the Cuban revolution of 1959, Cuadra began to gain recognition as a poet; his articles and poems appeared in national newspapers and his collection *Peldaño* was also published. He worked as a government lawyer but soon grew disillusioned with Castro's Cuba and became involved with the anti-communist underground movement.

In April 1967, Cuadra was arrested and charged with being an enemy of, and spreading propaganda about, 'the people's government'. He was sentenced to 15 years in prison, and was reportedly only spared the death penalty due to a 'lack of proof' that he was guilty.

When he was granted early release from prison in December 1976, Cuadra sent his poems to the poet Juana Rosa Pita in the USA. In 1977, he was re-arrested and sent back to prison to serve out his original sentence as punishment. Whilst incarcerated he was awarded the Miami Pluma de Oro prize in 1982.

Cuadra was released later that year and went into exile in Miami, where he continues to write poetry, as well as working as an international jurist. He is president of the Cuban Writers in Exile PEN centre.

The Unavoidable Voice

by Angel Cuadra

Translated by Luis Ignacio Larcada. Edited by Sarah Hesketh and Cat Lucas

My friends, I say,
I did not want
to have to write these poems.

After so much death
 – daily deaths in cells, from anguish, from impotence –
you would have expected from me
a Hymn to Life, a promising song
to raise your spirits.

But I could not,
my friends.

I left the bars behind –
minutes or centuries ago… I cannot tell –
but I still carry the pain of chains,
I am dragging them through the streets.

Streets where I loved years ago,
where I walked with books, with haste,
with fights and with dreams:
with everything that, on my return, I wanted to recover.
But there is only boredom.

I promised myself to shut up.
But I could not, my friends.

These are poems of another truth,
from someone who gathers it and suffers.

And, my friends, I could not
set it behind bars,
in the silence.

© *Angel Cuadra*
39(4): 136/137, DOI: 10.11770306422010391952

Alexander Solzhenitsyn

Country of origin:
Russia
Occupation:
Novelist (1918-2008)

Dramatist and historian Alexander Solzhenitsyn was born in Kislovodsk in 1918. After graduating from Rostov University in mathematics, he took a correspondence course in literature. At the same time, he was selected for the army, where he served as the gunner and artillery officer, and reached the rank of captain.

In 1945, while serving in East Prussia, Solzhenitsyn was arrested and charged with making critical remarks about Joseph Stalin. He spent the next eight years in labour camps and was released in 1953, after Stalin's death, but had to remain in exile for a further three years before returning to Russia.

Solzhenitsyn's acclaimed novel *One Day in the Life of Ivan Denisovich* describes life in a prison camp in Karaganda in northern Kazakhstan. The author submitted the novel to *Novy Mir* magazine for publication in 1960, but there were divisions within the central committee of the Communist Party about whether it should be published. On the orders of Nikita Khrushchev, it was eventually published in 1962 and sold out immediately.

In 1970, Solzhenitsyn was expelled from the Soviet Writers' Union. Later the same year he was awarded the Nobel Prize for Literature.

In 1974, after the publication of his novel *The Gulag Archipelago* in Europe, Solzhenitsyn was deported to West Germany.

In Germany, Solzhenitsyn continued to write, publishing *From Under the Rubble*, *The Oak and the Calf*, and *Lenin in Zurich*. In 1975, he settled in Cavendish, Vermont, where he remained for twenty years.

In 1990, the writer's Soviet citizenship was restored and, in 1994, he returned to Russia. His last novel, *Two Hundred Years Together*, was published in 2003. Solzhenitsyn died near Moscow on 3 August 2008.

From *One Day In The Life Of Ivan Denisovich*
by Alexander Solzhenitsyn

A prisoner was allowed to wear a shirt and an undershirt — he was to be stripped of anything else: such were Volkovoi's instructions, passed down the ranks by the prisoners. The teams that had been frisked earlier were in luck. Some of them had already been passed through the gates. But the rest had to bare their breasts. And anyone who had slipped on an extra garment had to take it off on the spot, out there in the cold.

That's how it started, but it resulted in a fine mix-up — a gap formed in the column, and at the gates the escort began shouting 'Get a move on, get a move on.' So when it was the turn of the 104th to be frisked, they had to ease up a bit: Volkovoi told the guards to take the name of anyone who might be wearing extra garments — the culprits were to surrender them in person at the camp stores that evening with a written explanation of how and why they had hidden the garments.

Shukov was in regulation dress. Come on, paw me as hard as you like. There's nothing but my soul in my chest. But they made a note that Tsezar was wearing a flannel vest and that Buinovsky, it seemed, had put on a waistcoat or a cummerbund or something. Buinovsky, who'd been in the camp less than three months, protested. He couldn't get rid of his commander's habits.

'You've no right to strip men in the cold. You don't know Article 9 of the criminal code.'

But they did have the right. They knew the code. You, chum, are the one who doesn't know it

'You're not behaving like Soviet people,' Buinovsky went on saying.

'You're not behaving like communists.'

Volkovoi had put up with references to the criminal code but this made him wince and like black lightning he flashed:

'Ten days in the cells.'

And aside to the sergeant:

'Starting from this evening.'

They didn't like putting a man in the cells in the morning: it meant the loss of his work for a whole day. Let him sweat blood in the meantime and be put in the cells in the evening.

© Victor Gollancz/Orion
39(4): 138/139, DOI: 10.11770306422010391944

Reza Baraheni

Country of origin:
Iran

Occupation:
Novelist, poet, critic

Status:
Living in exile in Canada

Reza Baraheni was born in Tabriz, Iran in 1935. He is the author of more than fifty books in Farsi and English and his works have been translated into a dozen languages. After completing a PhD in Istanbul, he became professor of English at Tehran University. Along with fellow writers, Baraheni helped initiate the Writers Association of Iran in 1967. In 1972, his first novel, *The Infernal Days of Mr Ayaz* was banned in Iran. He was arrested along with other writers and intellectuals in 1973; his book *God's Shadow: Prison Poems* is based on the 102 days he spent in solitary confinement during the Shah's rule.

As E L Doctorow writes in his 1977 introduction to *The Crowned Cannibals: Writings on Repression in Iran*, Baraheni is 'chronicler of his nation's torture industry and poet of his nation's secret police force.' He left Iran to live in the United States in 1975, but returned to teach at Tehran University after the fall of the Shah in 1979. In 1981, he was once again arrested for a brief period, followed by another arrest in 1982. Baraheni continued to write novels and essays in the 1980s and early 1990s, and was a signatory to a 1994 open letter calling for artistic freedom and an end to censorship.

In 1996, he was forced to leave Iran and settled in Canada. In 2000, he was one of two scholars to join the new Scholars-at-Risk Program at University of Toronto's Massey College and later became a professor at University of Toronto's Centre for Comparative Literature. Baraheni was president of PEN Canada between June 2001 and June 2003. He was awarded the Sepass Award in Canada for Lifelong Achievement in Literature and was honoured by the International Freedom to Publish Committee of the Association of American Publishers.

Cemetery
by Reza Baraheni

The criminal prison autumn
has arrived outside without
us seeing its signs
If we were
in Darakeh now
we could see
the cemetery of yellow leaves
And now that we are not there
we had better put
our heads on the cold tiles of the cell
and sleep until
the sounds of shooting startles us
and we rush
to the hole in the cell's iron door
and if the windowlet is open
watch the silent caravan of the innocent
like Ardaviraf who saw
pre-Islamic hell dwellers
The identity of the caravan of the innocent
will not be proven in the course of time
Future archaeologists
will remove the firing squad's last bullet
rattling in the empty skull like a peanut
and send it to the laboratory
so that at least
the geological stage of the crim
will be brought to light
And the bald scholars of the future will write
two or three dissertations connecting this peanut
to a dark prehistoric time
which is our present

© *Reza Baraheni/Indiana University Press*
39(4): 140/141, DOI: 10.11770306422010391945

Breyten Breytenbach

Country of origin:
South Africa

Occupation:
Novelist, poet, writer

Status:
Released in 1982

Born in 1939 in Bonnievale near Cape Town, South Africa, Breyten Breytenbach is considered to be the finest living poet of the Afrikaans language. Whilst living and teaching in Paris in 1961, he came into direct confrontation with the injustices of his homeland. At the time he married his French wife of Vietnamese descent, interracial marriages were illegal in South Africa and he was unable to return home. He became more active in his opposition to the apartheid regime and helped to found the resistance group Okhela, the activities of which he organised from abroad. Upon his return to South Africa in 1975 using a false passport, he was convicted of terrorist offences and imprisoned for seven years. His incarceration, which included two periods of solitary confinement, is documented in the second part of his four- volume memoir, *The True Confessions of an Albino Terrorist*. Although his most renowned works are his widely translated memoirs, on his return to France following his release he resumed writing Afrikaans poetry and took up painting. Many of his widely exhibited subjects are depicted in a state of captivity and his post-apartheid writing has continued to analyse South African society. Breytenbach has received global recognition in the form of accolades for literature and art, including the APB Prize, CAN Award and the Hertzog Prize. Breytenbach continues to publish and teaches at New York University, the University of Cape Town, and the Gorée Institute in Senegal. Recent books include *Mouroir: Mirror Notes of a Novel* (2008), *Intimate Stranger* (2009) and *Notes From The Middle World: Essays* (2009).

from *The True Confessions of an Albino Terrorist*
by Breyten Breytenbach

When first I came out of prison I was thrown into emptiness and I found all space around me cluttered. For so long had I been conditioned to the simplification of four walls, the square of a barred window, a double square door, a square bed, emptiness, nowhere to hide the smallest illegal object, nowhere to hide the crust of bread to which you were not entitled, nowhere to efface yourself, or tuck away the soul or to protect your three dreams from prying eyes and acquisitive fingers, nowhere to hide your anguish: all these had been erased by being made apparent. It just became language. So that when I found myself ejected into what you would consider to be the normal world, I found it terribly confusing. Why are there so many people moving through the theatre décor of streets? How come the air is so bloated with useless words? Why on earth do people have so many objects in their houses? Why do they have to hang things on the wall, or have to have more than one set of clothes? Why do they collect possessions? You should know by now that one can never possess anything, and when The Law strikes you will lose everything anyway. And I remember, because now it is passing, that whenever I entered a new space I lifted my feet very high and I pulled my head down between my shoulders from fear of the unexpected step or beam.

What else must I describe? Do you really want to know what it's like to be free?

Freedom is not knowing where to stop. It is a gargantuan appetite; it is a need to burn clean, with whatever is spicy and hot, the taste of dullness which has encrusted your memory and your appetite; it is the unquenchable thirst; it's the need to absorb, to take, to grasp, to experience, to renew and to drink, because it is simultaneously the necessity to deaden the nerve ends. I have not the slightest measure of what ought and ought not to be done and when and how. I should eat whatever you put before me. I read on the wall 'Mangez-vous les uns les autres', and I discover all kinds of lusts: a yearning for seafood; I must have mustards; I must have pickles. I must exercise the regrets and the shame and the guilt.

Ah, Mr Investigator, don't you think I'm guilty? Yes, I have the guilt of the survivor.

© *Breyten Breytenbach/Faber & Faber*
39(4): 142/143, DOI: 10.11770306422010391954

Alicia Partnoy

Country of origin:
Argentina
Occupation:
Poet, academic, translator and
human rights activist
Status:
Released in 1979;
living in the USA

Alicia Partnoy was among 30,000 Argentineans who were 'disappeared' after the military coup in 1976. She was secretly imprisoned from 1977 to 1979. Following her release, Partnoy claimed asylum in the United States. She has been active in testifying before international human rights organisations against those involved in Argentina's military dictatorship.

At the time of her disappearance, Partnoy was a literature student and a member of the Peronist Youth movement, clandestinely disseminating information about the regime. On 12 January 1977, she was arrested by the army along with her infant daughter.

Partnoy was imprisoned at a concentration camp known as La Escuelita (The Little School), where dissidents were 'taught' their 'lessons' through torture. After three months she was moved to the Villa Floresta prison, where she spent two and a half years without charge or trial. She was separated from her child and repeatedly tortured, but managed to smuggle out stories and poems, which were published anonymously. Partnoy's first book, *The Little School: Tales of Disappearance and Survival in Argentina*, provides a poignant insight into her life as a 'disappeared' person.

Partnoy was released in 1979 thanks to international pressure. Following an Inter-American Commission on Human Rights monitoring mission to Argentina in 1979, she left for the USA, where she was granted refugee status and reunited with her daughter and husband.

Once in the USA, Partnoy became involved with PEN as a writer in exile. She has worked on behalf of other persecuted writers and served on the board of PEN USA.

Ruth v the Torturer

by Alicia Partnoy

For a while now I've been trying to recall how Ruth's face looks. I can remember her big eyes, her almost non-existent little nose, the shape of her mouth. I recall the texture of her hair, the warmth of her skin. When I try to put it all together, something goes wrong. I just can't remember my daughter's face. It has been two months since I've seen her. I want to believe she's safe.

'Vasca! Do you remember my daughter's face?' I whisper.

'Of course I do, she's so pretty.'

I think I'll turn over in my bed. That will help me reorder my thoughts. No, it doesn't work. It's funny. I can recall the things we did together, even when I'm not thinking about them all the time; but I want to imagine her face, to put together the pieces of this puzzle.

Perhaps if I try to bring to mind some scenes when we were together; for example, that day while coming back from my parents: I was pushing her stroller along the street when suddenly she looked up at the roof of a house. An immense dog was impatiently stalking back and forth. Ruth pointed to the dog with her little finger. 'Meow,' she said, since she was used only to watching cats climb up high. Thrilled, I kissed her – but how did her face look? I can only remember her small, triumphant smile.

Night is coming. The radio is on, not very loud this time, playing Roberto Carlos's song again. When the newscast starts, they turn the radio off.

One morning, while on the bus, I heard on the radio:

Fellow citizens, if you notice family groups travelling at odd hours of the day or night, report them to the military authorities. The number is…

I was one of a few passengers on that early bus. It was 6.30am. I was travelling to a suburban neighbourhood with my baby and two bags. For a short while I thought the driver was going to stop the vehicle and run to the nearest phone to alert the army. He just glared at my reflection in the rear-view mirror. The night before some friends of mine had been kidnapped. Since they knew where I lived, I thought of moving out for a few days, just to be safe. But I can't remember my daughter's face on that bus. I know that she was wearing the pink jacket, and that I had the bag with stripes, the one my mum used to take to the beach. I have a perfect recollection of everything in the bag. But try as I might, I still can't remember my daughter's face.

© *Alicia Partnoy*
39(4): 144/145, DOI: 10.1177/0306422010387867

Vasyl Stus

Country of origin:
Ukraine

Occupation:
Poet

Status:
Died in prison in 1985

Vasyl Stus was sentenced to a total of 23 years' imprisonment and exile during his lifetime, and his poetry was banned by the Soviet regime. In 2005, he was posthumously given the title 'Hero of Ukraine' by order of the state.

Born in the Vinnytsia Oblast in 1938, Stus studied philology at the Donetsk Pedagogical Institute, and his first poems were published in 1959. After graduating he worked as a teacher, served in the army and briefly edited the newspaper *Sotsialistychnyi Donbas* (Socialist Donbas). In 1963, he began studies at the Institute of Literature in Kyiv, and had some of his work published in journals. But after participating in a protest that denounced the arrests and closed trials of Ukrainian intellectuals that year, Stus was dismissed from the institute.

The struggling poet was arrested in 1972 with fellow dissident writers Ivan Svitlychny, Yevhen Sverstiuk, and Ihor and Iryna Kalynets. He was sentenced to five years in a labour camp and three years' exile. Returning to Kyiv in 1979, he joined the Ukrainian Helsinki Group. He was arrested again just eight months later and sentenced to ten years in prison and five years' exile.

Conditions at the Perm Oblast labour camp were severe. Stus was not allowed visitors, was continually harassed by the authorities, and suffered from chronic stomach ulcers and heart problems. His letters and everything he wrote in the camp were confiscated.

During a hunger strike in September 1985, Vasyl Stus died in solitary confinement. He was buried in the camp cemetery in a grave marked 'Number 9' before his remains were interned at Baikove cemetery in Kyiv in 1989.

© Index on Censorship/English PEN
39(4): 146, DOI: 10.11770306422010391962

Imprisoned without trial for nearly 17 years by Singapore's government, Said Zahari holds the dubious distinction of being the country's second longest-serving political prisoner.

After working as a journalist during the 1950s and 1960s, Zahari became editor-in-chief of *Utusan Melayu*, an influential Malay-language newspaper. In 1961, he was exiled to Singapore for leading journalists in a strike against the takeover of the paper by United Malays National Organisation, the ruling party.

In 1963, shortly after being appointed president of the Singapore People's Party, Zahari was arrested during 'Operation Cold Stone', a joint action by Malaysian and Singapore security forces to silence trade unions and opposition voices. He was detained by Lee Kuan Yew's government under the Internal Security Act, along with more than 100 others who were opposed to the creation of Malaysia — the merging of Singapore and the Federation of Malaya.

Zahari was kept in solitary confinement and threatened with death if he did not confess to being a communist, but unlike many of his fellow detainees he refused to cooperate with the authorities. Conditions in prison were harsh and Zahari's health suffered badly during his incarceration.

Following his release in 1979, he published a memoir, *The Long Nightmare: My 17 Years as a Political Prisoner*. He also participated in a documentary about his prison experience, which was criticised by Malaysian authorities for its allegedly exaggerated account of prison conditions. Zahari published *Dark Clouds at Dawn: A Political Memoir* in 2001, and now lives with his family in Malaysia, though he retains his Singapore citizenship.

Credit: Claes Grundsten/Scanpix/Press Association Images

Said Zahari

Country of origin:
Singapore

Occupation:
Journalist

Status:
Released in 1979

© Index on Censorship/English PEN
39(4): 147, DOI: 10.11770306422010391849

Václav Havel

Country of origin:
Czechoslovakia

Occupation:
Playwright, poet and activist

Status:
Released in 1983

Václav Havel was born in Czechoslovakia in 1936 and studied drama at the Academy of Performing Arts in Prague. His first play, *The Garden Party*, was published in 1963, and was soon followed by *The Memorandum* and *The Increased Difficulty of Concentration*. During the Prague Spring of 1968, Havel became chair of the Independent Writers Club and a member of the Club of [Politically] Engaged Non-Partisans. Czechoslovakia consequently banned his plays and confiscated his passport.

In an open letter to President Gustáv Husák in 1975, Havel accused the regime of 'sacrificing the country's spiritual future for the sake of their present power interests'. In 1977, he co-founded the human rights organisation Charter 77, which criticised the government for failing to implement its own commitments to human rights.

In April 1979, Havel helped to establish the Committee for the Defence of the Unjustly Prosecuted. He was charged with subversion later that year and sentenced to four and a half years in prison. During that time, he wrote *Letters to Olga*. He was released in 1983 due to illness.

During the Velvet Revolution of 1989, Havel formed an opposition group, Civic Forum. In November, he was elected president of the Czech and Slovak Federal Republic, and became the first president of the new Czech Republic in 1993.

Having retired from office in 2003, Havel continues to campaign for democracy and liberty worldwide, and is now chair of the Human Rights Foundation's International Council. In 2008, his first play for 20 years, *Leaving*, premiered at Prague's Archa Theatre.

Mistake
by Václav Havel
Translated by George Theiner

Dramatis Personae:

>XIBOY
>KING (a trustie)
>FIRST PRISONER
>SECOND PRISONER
>THIRD PRISONER

As the curtain rises, we see a door, left, with the FIRST, SECOND, and THIRD PRISONER crowding the doorway, KING in front. All four have shaven heads and a variety of tattoos on their arms and torsos – KING most of all. They are dressed in prison uniforms and are gazing intently at XIBOY. On the opposite side of the stage there is a tier of three iron bunks; XIBOY is sitting on the top one, like the others in prison garb and with shaven head but no tattoos. XIBOY is a newcomer and he looks with some apprehension at the group in the doorway. A long, tense, silence…

>KING (to XIBOY)

I hear you lit a fag after slop-out…
>(short pause)

>FIRST PRISONER (to KING)

'e did – I saw 'im.

>KING (to SECOND PRISONER)

That right?

>SECOND PRISONER

Sure, that's right.

>KING (to XIBOY)

Don't you know when we fall out for breakfast?
>(short pause)

FIRST PRISONER (to KING)
Sure, he knows… Ten minutes after slop-out.

KING (to SECOND PRISONER)
Does 'e know?

SECOND PRISONER
Sure he knows! They tell all the new boys, don't they…

KING (to XIBOY)
Now listen 'ere, friend. We have ten minutes between slop-out and breakfast. In that time we've all gotta get dressed, those as wants can wash or 'ave a piss, there's no objection to that, you understand, everyone's got a perfect right to do it, if they wanna, you can even start making your bed so we don't all start at once and get in each other's way. And we open the windows to get rid of all the farts first thing. That's the custom 'ere, that's the way it's done and always 'as been. Then we all grab our caps and food bowls and wait for the order to fall in. And when they yell 'fall in' we gotta look sharp and line up outside the cell. If we don't get out there quick enough, they send us back and we gotta wait our turn again. So we don't want anybody fartarsing around holding things up, looking for his things or tipping a fag-end or anything like that – and the rest of us get in the shit on 'is account. Understand? Because of one lousy slowcoach we ain't all gonna go back and 'ang around waiting. I 'ope that's clear. And if anyone thinks it ain't, we'll soon put 'im right!

FIRST PRISONER (to KING)
It's clear, all right, and everyone does it just like you said.

SECOND PRISONER (to XIBOY)
That's right – and if some cunt thinks 'e can mess us about, 'e'll do it just once and never again…

KING (to XIBOY)
So, as I said, there's a hell of a lot to do between slop-out and breakfast. No time for fartarsing around. Much less for smoking. That's not the way we do things 'ere. Now, *after* breakfast, that's something else again, *then* you can light up if you've got any fags, that is. Then

there's time and nobody gives a shit. But not before breakfast. That's how it's always been in this pad, and it's going to stay that way. Nobody's gonna tell me they can't wait a lousy twenty minutes for a smoke. That ain't asking too much, is it?
　　(to SECOND PRISONER:)
Am I right?

　　　　　　SECOND PRISONER
Sure you are.

　　　　　　FIRST PRISONER (to KING)
We can wait.

　　　　　　KING (to XIBOY)
So, from now on remember – no smoking before breakfast...

　　　　　　FIRST PRISONER
'specially as we're trying to air the fucking place...

　　　　　　KING (to XIBOY)
Yeah, that's right. And some people just can't stand the smell of smoke first thing in the morning. They don't like it, their lungs don't like it, they can't stand it. As is their right. Is that clear?
　　(XIBOY says nothing, looks embarrassed and shrugs)

　　　　　　SECOND PRISONER (shouts at XIBOY)
Didn't you hear what 'e said?
　　(XIBOY says nothing, looks embarrassed, shrugs)
Anyone we catch smoking after slop-out gets a fistful, see?

　　　　　　KING (to XIBOY)
What they do in other cells, that's their business. But nobody smokes in this one after slop-out. That goes for everybody, 'specially for new boys like you. That's all I wanted to say to you, friend. And not just for myself but for all of us.
　　(to SECOND PRISONER)
Right?

SECOND PRISONER

Right.

FIRST PRISONER (to KING)

That's what we all say – right…

KING (to XIBOY)

Everybody saw you smoking first thing, and everybody yakked about it. But I told 'em: 'e's a new boy, doesn't know the ropes yet. And so they stopped yakking. So you're OK for today. But next time just remember we don't hold with nobody trying to be clever and going it alone. Not on your life…

FIRST PRISONER (to KING)

As long as I been 'ere, nobody ever had the nerve to light a fag before breakfast.

KING (to XIBOY):

So, as I said, you got away with it this time, but see it don't 'appen no more. Is that clear?
(XIBOY says nothing)

SECOND PRISONER (yells at XIBOY)

What're you gawping at, you cunt? King asked you a question!
(Silence)

KING (to XIBOY)

We're trying to be nice to you, see? So we'll skip it this once – but now you know and kindly keep your nose clean.
(Longer silence)
Oh, and while we're on the subject… From tomorrow, you'll make your bed exactly like all the rest of us. If the others can do it, so can you. We don't want to lose a point every day just because some stupid bastard doesn't know how to make his bed properly, do we? We don't want the whole lot of us to get it in the neck on account of one miserable rookie what doesn't know how to make his bed. So you'd better hurry up and learn, 'cos if tomorrow your bed isn't just like everybody else's, we'll make you practice all evening.

SECOND PRISONER (to XIBOY)
We'll make you do it ten times in a row, see if we don't.

KING (to XIBOY)
Blanket's gotta be two inches from the edge on both sides, the sheet neatly folded over, and so on and so forth… The boys'll show you how it's done.

FIRST PRISONER (to KING)
I'll show 'im…

KING (to XIBOY)
Is that clear?
(Silence)
Everybody in 'ere gets the 'ang of it sooner or later, so no reason why you shouldn't get the 'ang of it. Understand?
(Silence)

SECOND PRISONER (to XIBOY)
Bloody hell! Cat got your tongue, you bastard? Speak up when King asks you something!

FIRST PRISONER (to KING)
What's the matter with 'im? Stupid idiot!

KING (to XIBOY)
Did you clean the washbasin?
(Silence)
Your turn to scrub and clean this week, so you'd better look smart! And if you think you're just going to tickle the floor with the brush and that's it, you're bloody well mistaken. You get down and scrub the floor under the bunks, 'specially in the corners by the wall – the screws shine their torches down there. You dust everywhere, and the washbasin's gotta be washed, wiped dry and shined – and the same goes for the kaazie. Today it's a mess, so you can thank your lucky stars we haven't had the screws round 'ere. They'd 'ave shown you a thing or two. Tonight, before inspection, I'll come and look personal like. We're all in the same boat 'ere, nobody gets any privileges, 'specially not a rookie whose fag-end is still burning outside the prison gate!

SECOND PRISONER (yells at XIBOY)

So why don't you come down off of there, you cunt, when King's talking to you!

(XIBOY remains sitting on his bunk, smiling in embarrassment. Tense silence. SECOND PRISONER is about to lunge at XIBOY and drag him down but KING stops him)

KING (to SECOND PRISONER)

Wait a sec!

(Silence)

(to XIBOY)

Now look 'ere, me lad! If you've got it in yer 'ead that you're going to do as you bloody well please 'ere, or maybe play at being King, you've got another thing coming! We know how to deal with the likes of you. Understand?

(Silence)

FIRST PRISONER (to KING)

What a stubborn bastard!

SECOND PRISONER (to XIBOY)

Come down off that bloody bunk, and be quick about it!

(Silence – XIBOY doesn't move)

SECOND PRISONER (to XIBOY)

Well…?!

(Silence – XIBOY doesn't move)

KING (to XIBOY)

Now then, you, I don't take kindly to them as tries to make a monkey out of me. So don't get any ideas!

FIRST PRISONER (to XIBOY)

Down you come this minute and apologise to King!

(Silence – XIBOY doesn't move, just sits there smiling in embarrassment)

SECOND PRISONER (yells at XIBOY)

You fucking mother-fucker!

(SECOND PRISONER leaps forward and catches XIBOY by one leg, pulling him down. XIBOY falls on the floor, SECOND PRISONER kicks him and returns to KING's side. XIBOY rises slowly, looks at the others, puzzled. Silence.)

THIRD PRISONER (softly)

'ere lads...

(Silence – they all gaze at XIBOY)

KING (without turning to THIRD PRISONER)

What?

(Silence – they all gaze at XIBOY)

THIRD PRISONER (softly)

Know what? He's some kind of a bloody foreigner...

(All three look questioningly at KING. Tense silence)

KING (after a pause, softly)

Well, that's his bloody funeral...

(KING starts out menacingly towards XIBOY, followed by FIRST, SECOND and THIRD PRISONER. They slowly edge closer to him. Curtain falls)

(CURTAIN)

First published in Index on Censorship, 1984

© Václav Havel
39(4): 148/155, DOI: 10.11770306422010391878

Martha Kumsa

Country of origin:
Ethiopia

Occupation:
Journalist

Status:
Released in 1989; living in Canada

Martha Kuwee Kumsa was born in Dembi Dollo, Ethiopia. During the 1974 Ethiopian revolution she was a university student in Addis Ababa when, following the end of Haile Selassie's rule, a Soviet-backed Marxist military junta established a communist state. The junta closed all universities, leading Kumsa to train as a journalist at the Lutheran World Federation in Addis Ababa.

Under the dictatorship of Colonel Mengistu Haile Mariam in a period which became known as the 'Red Terror' (1977-1978), those deemed enemies of the state were arrested, tortured and executed, among them hundreds of Oromo people. Kumsa's husband, Leenco Lata, who was one of the founders of the Oromo liberation movement, was arrested and tortured on four separate occasions, after which he fled the country.

In 1980, Martha Kuwee Kumsa was herself arrested at the office of the Oromo newspaper where she worked. This followed an article she had written calling for Oromo women to reclaim their cultural heritage and encouraging them to speak out about their experiences.

Kumsa was imprisoned without charge and subjected to physical abuse and torture. Despite the harsh conditions, she was able to teach and learn in the prison school established by fellow inmates. PEN and Amnesty International campaigned for her release and, on 10 September 1989, she was freed as part of general amnesty for prisoners.

Following her release Kumsa was reunited with her children. However, living in Ethiopia was still unsafe for her and she eventually moved to Kenya before being granted asylum in Canada. She has since gained a PhD at the University of Toronto and now teaches at the Wilfrid Laurier University.

from *The Taxi Project*
by Martha Kumsa

The Taxi Project (Scirocco Drama, 2010) is based on the lives of writers in exile, including Martha Kumsa. It was co-written by Kumsa, Sheng Xue, Goran Simic and Emma Ari Beltrán

SCENE 20: AWARD CEREMONY

SEEYYEE is at a large auditorium receiving an award.

> EMCEE
>
> Ladies and gentleman, we are honouring a very special woman this evening. She spent ten years imprisoned for fighting for equal rights for the Oromo People in Ethiopia who were persecuted for their ethnicity. She was forced into exile and sought refuge in Canada. Tonight we honour Seeyyee Sera.

> SEEYYEE
>
> Thank you very much.
> (She looks at her notes.)
> I am very honoured to be...
> (A long pause.)
> I had a speech prepared but...I'd like to ask my baby brother to be here with me tonight.

She lights a candle.

> The last time I heard my brother's voice, I was crying into the phone. I could see the turbulent billows of smoke rise over my homeland. I could see the fire spread and the flames dance all around him. Agitated tongues of flame lashed out to lick my brother. Yet he stood there smiling, so sure.

We hear drums.

BABY BROTHER

Stay put my big sister, stay put. I'm home: you are the one in exile.
Stay put till you come home to freedom.

SEEYYEE

But, what is home and what is exile? Oh, I enjoy home in exile, when
you are rendered homeless at home.

In my homeland, Baby Brother, in my homeland,
The grass shades me from the scorching sun;
but in exile, Baby Brother,
the sun burns me in the thickest shade of the biggest tree.
In my homeland, Baby Brother, in my homeland
The meat of a flea feeds a multitude;
but in exile, Baby Brother,
Two friends fight over the meat of an elephant.

BABY BROTHER

Home is freedom, my big sister, home is bilisummaa (freedom). Home
is dignity. Home is justice. Exile is wherever home is not.

SEEYYEE

Exile is wherever they plough the fields with guns and sow the seeds
with blood. In an unjust world, home can only be in the struggle to
restore freedom and justice.

BABY BROTHER

Yes, that's why I took to the woods with the village youth.

SEEYYEE

Our father took to the woods, and I am not coming home
Our father's brother took to the woods, and I am not coming home
Our mother's brother took to the woods, and I am not coming home
I saw the injustice
And my heart howls.
Oh my heart howls with rage.

Drum stops. SEEYYEE is back in reality.

SEEYYEE
(To the audience)
Thank you.

© *Martha Kumsa/Scirocco Drama*
39(4): 156/159, DOI: 10.11770306422010388460

Mansur Muhammad Ahmad Rajih

Country of origin:
Yemen

Occupation:
Writer and poet

Status:
Released in 1988; living in Norway

Writer and poet Mansur Rajih was born in North Yemen in December 1958. He attended the University of Aleppo in Syria between 1978 and 1980, and then went to the University of Beirut between 1980 and 1982. During this time, Rajih was active in student politics and held the positions of president of the Yemeni Student Union and secretary general of the Organisation of Arab Students. He also became active in the National Democratic Front, a coalition of Yemeni opposition parties.

In January 1983, just days after getting married, Rajih was arrested. He was initially held for six months without trial and then released before being re-arrested eight days later. He was eventually tried in March 1984 for the murder of a man from his village and was given the death penalty. However, it was widely believed that he was held because of his political activities as a student; the evidence was regarded as spurious, the trial was rife with irregularities, and witnesses were not able to identify Rajih as a suspect. Rajih later reported that he had been tortured and forced to make a confession.

Rajih's wife Afrah, who had been allowed to leave Yemen earlier, was a tireless campaigner for his release. She worked closely with PEN, who arranged missions to Yemen, where writers met with the government to appeal for his release. Rajih was released on 7 February 1998, after 15 years in prison. He joined his wife in Stavanger, Norway, where he continues to live with his family. He has published three poetry collections, including *So Far: So Close* and *My Brother's Pain*.

Eiganes
by Mansur Muhammad Ahmad Rajih
Translated by Ren Powell and Mansur Rajih

Here, in this quiet, the trees are proud of themselves
Longing eats at the heart
There is no life in exile
Here, the sound has no echo
The poem flees from between your hands,
flees to the heat of Yemen
Love is blocked by questions
What does get through is strangled by frost
A new morning over you, the silent city
Pain wars pain within the heart
This stretch of time eats at the mind

The wind bring nothing to the banished man,
and leaving, it carries nothing hence

The title, Eiganes, refers to a neighbourhood in Stavanger, Norway,
and the final couplet (in italics) is An Arab proverb

© *Mansur Muhammad Ahmad Rajih/Profile Books*
39(4): 160/161, DOI: 10.11770306422010391940

Anti-Apartheid rally, 1989
Credit: Ulli Michel/Reuters

Zwelakhe Sisulu

Country of origin:
South Africa

Occupation:
Journalist

Status:
Released in 1988

Zwelakhe Sisulu was born in 1950 into a political family, the son of anti-Apartheid stalwarts Walter and Albertina Sisulu. His father was imprisoned for more than 20 years, along with Nelson Mandela.

Sisulu began writing as a trainee journalist for *Rand Daily Mail* in the mid-1970s, during a time of rising unrest in his home town of Soweto. As a member of the Release Mandela committee, he was put under house arrest from 1981-1983. Upon his release, he became political editor of the prominent daily newspaper the *Sowetan*, before founding and editing the strongly leftist *New Nation* in 1986.

With South Africa under a state of emergency, Sisulu was detained without trial from 1986-1988. He was held in solitary confinement and subjected to harsh interrogation. Denied any information, his family did not know where he was, or whether he was alive or dead. An international campaign for his release was spearheaded by PEN and other free expression organisations, and he was awarded the Louis Lyons award by the Niemann Foundation while in prison.

Sisulu was eventually released without charge, and when Mandela was finally freed, Sisulu became his personal assistant and spokesperson. He became chief executive of the South African Broadcasting Corporation in 1994, and now works in the corporate sector, as chief executive of a mining company called Savannah Resources. He maintains interests in the media, energy and agri-business sectors, and is executive chairman of Afriminerals and Universal Media.

Sisulu was founding president of the Writers Association of South Africa and of the Media Workers Association of South Africa, both of which campaigned against censorship and in support of a free media.

© Index on Censorship/English PEN
39(4): 162, DOI: 10.1177/0306422010380832

Opposite - Credit: Roger-Viollet/Rex

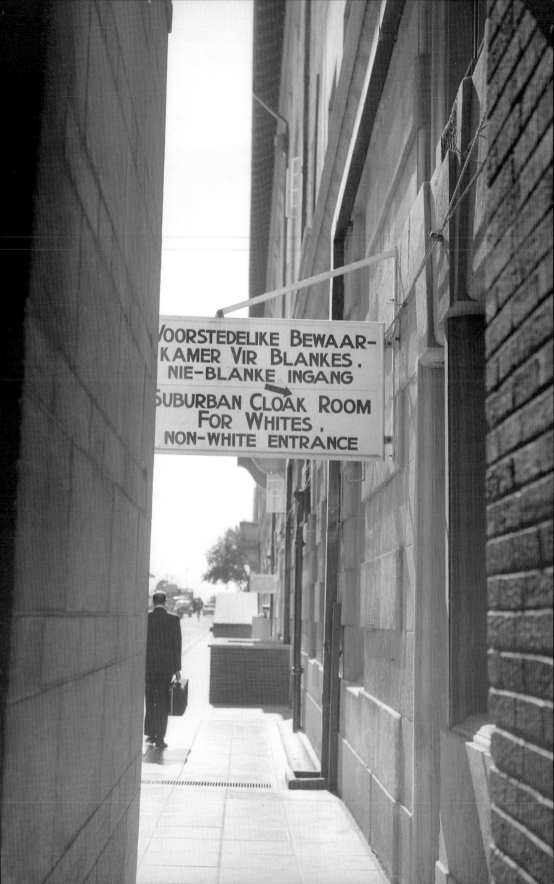

Chris Abani

Country of origin:

Nigeria

Occupation:

Novelist, playwright, poet, musician

Status:

Released in 1991; living in the
United States

Chris Abani was a political prisoner in Nigeria between 1985 and 1991. The author was accused of inciting a coup because his novel *Masters of the Board*, which he wrote when still a teenager, realistically portrayed a neo-Nazi takeover in a year when one coup and another attempted coup had already taken place in the country. He was detained initially for six months in two three-month stretches.

In 1987, Abani joined a university guerrilla theatre group, which performed plays in front of public buildings and government offices. He was re-arrested and held in the notorious Kiri Kiri maximum security prison, where he was tortured. He was later released without charge or explanation and returned to his university studies. His play, *Song of a Broken Flute*, written for the 1990 convocation ceremony for the university, led to his final period of incarceration, for 18 months. He spent six months in solitary confinement. Abani was sentenced to death for treason – without trial – and held on death row, where he was again tortured.

Abani was able to leave Nigeria in 1991, moving to the United Kingdom and later Los Angeles in the United States, where he teaches creative writing at Antioch University and University of California, Riverside. He is the author of five poetry collections, including *Kalakuta Republic*, in which he documents his treatment in prison. His novel *GraceLand* was published in 2004 and met with critical acclaim, winning the PEN Hemingway Book Prize. He is also winner of the Prince Claus Award and a Hurston/Wright Legacy Award. His novel *Becoming Abigail* was published in 2006.

from *Song for Night*

by Chris Abani

Ijeoma shook her head.

'Good. If you don't want me to split your head open, you should follow orders!'

That was that. We followed orders, did what we were told, even when the training seemed at odds with what we thought soldiers should know, like the feet exercises, mostly from ballet. To make our feet sensitive, we were told, which was funny because we weren't going to be issued boots. The rebel army didn't have any, but even if they did, we wouldn't get them because they needed our toes to be exposed all the time. Then we were taught to use our toes almost like fingers. One exercise which was cruelly ironic was tying our training officer's shoelaces with our toes.

Having learned to walk across different terrain with my band of fellow elite, feeling for the carefully scattered lumps in the ground, being careful not to step on them as per instruction, clearing the earth around the buried mines with our toes, we learned to bend and insert a knife under the firing mechanism and pull out the valve. We practised on live mines and we realised the value of the one-legged balancing when we accidentally stepped on one, arming it. We balanced on one foot, reached down, and disabled the mine. We were discouraged from helping each other in these situations – if things went wrong it was better to lose one instead of two mine defusers, John Wayne explained, almost kindly.

A week before graduation he took us all into the doctor's office. One by one we were led into surgery. It was exciting to think that we were becoming bionic men and women. I thought it odd that there was no anaesthetic when I was laid down out on a table, my arms and legs tied down with rough hemp. John Wayne was standing by my head, opposite the doctor. I stared at the peculiar cruel glint of the scalpel while the doctor, with a gentle and swift cut, severed my vocal chords. The next day, as one of us was blown up by a mine, we discovered why they had silenced us: so that we wouldn't scare each other with our death screams. Detecting a mine with your bare toes and defusing it with a jungle knife requires all your concentration, and screams are a risky distraction.

What they couldn't know is that in the silence of our heads, the screams of those dying around us were louder than if they still had voices.

© *Chris Abani/Telegram*
39(4): 164/165, DOI: 10.11770306422010391880

Jack Mapanje

Country of origin:
Malawi
Occupation:
Poet, editor, linguist and human
rights activist
Status:
Released in 1991;
living in the UK

Born in Malawi in 1944, Jack Mapanje, one of Africa's most distinguished poets, studied in England before returning to teach at the University of Malawi.

His first collection of poems, *Of Chameleons and Gods*, published in the UK in 1981, was banned in Malawi in June 1985 due to its being 'full of ... coded attacks' on the ruling dictatorship of Hastings Kamuzu Banda. Two years later, in September 1987, he was imprisoned without trial or charge by the Malawian government.

Many writers, linguists and human rights activists campaigned for his release, including Harold Pinter and Wole Soyinka, and in 1990 he was awarded the PEN/Barbara Goldsmith Freedom to Write Award. Despite this international pressure, Mapanje served almost four years in Mikuyu prison, where he composed his second collection of poetry, *The Chattering Wagtails of Mikuyu Prison*, and most of his third collection, *Skipping without Ropes*. He was finally released in May 1991.

Following his release, Mapanje wrote to PEN, stating, 'I was told personally that it was the efforts and pressure from certain distinguished bodies in the UK which made my release possible. One such body is English PEN.' Mapanje later settled in England with his family and is now a senior lecturer in creative writing at the University of Newcastle.

Between 2002 and 2004, Mapanje was poet in residence at The Wordsworth Trust and in 2007 he was shortlisted for the Forward Poetry Prize (Best Poetry Collection) for *Beasts Of Nalunga*. Other works include *The Last Sweet Banana*, *Altar Boy at Sixty*, and *Gathering Seaweed: African Prison Writing*. His prison memoir *And Crocodiles Are Hungry At Night* will be published by James Currey in 2011.

On His Royal Blindness Paramount Chief Kwangala
by Jack Mapanje

I admire the quixotic display of your paramountcy
How you brandish our ancestral shields and spears
Among your warriors dazzled by your loftiness
But I fear the way you spend your golden breath
Those impromptu, long-winded tirades of your might
In the heat, do they suit your brittle constitution?

I know I too must sing to such royal happiness
And I am not arguing. Wasn't I too tucked away in my
Loin-cloth infested by jiggers and fleas before
Your bright eminence showed up? How could I quibble
Over your having changed all that? How dare I when
We have scribbled our praises all over our graves?

Why should I quarrel when I too have known mask
Dancers making troubled journeys to the gold mines
On bare feet and bringing back fake European gadgets
The broken pipes, torn coats, crumpled bowler hats,
Dangling mirrors and rusty tincans to make their
Mask dancing strange? Didn't my brothers die there?

No, your grace, I am no alarmist nor banterer
I am only a child surprised how you broadly disparage
Me shocked by the tedium of your continuous palaver. I
Adore your majesty. But paramountcy is like a raindrop
On a vast sea. Why should we wait for the children to
Tell us about our toothless gums or our showing flies?

© Jack Mapanje/Pearson/Heinemann
39(4): 166/167, DOI: 10.11770306422010390616

Salman Rushdie

Country of origin:
India

Occupation:
Author

Status:
Fatwa declared in 1989

Salman Rushdie was born in 1947 in Mumbai. He attended Cambridge University and, after a brief period in Pakistan, made the UK his home. His novel *Midnight's Children*, published in 1981, quickly became a bestseller and went on to win numerous awards, including the Booker and the 'Best of the Booker' prizes. The book's protagonist, born at midnight on 15 August 1947, the moment of India's independence, finds that he has telepathic links with 1,000 other children born at the same time, all of whose destinies are linked with that of India's politics.

The 1988 publication of his fourth novel, *The Satanic Verses*, met with protests, book burnings and death threats, and Rushdie was accused of blasphemy, apostasy, and insulting the Islamic faith and the Prophet Mohammed. Some Muslim organisations in the UK called for the author to be prosecuted. The book was subsequently banned in Bangladesh, India, Sudan, South Africa and Sri Lanka. The following year, Ayatollah Khomeini of Iran issued a *fatwa* calling for Rushdie's execution. This, along with other threats, forced the author into hiding, where he continued to produce critically acclaimed works of both fiction and non-fiction. The *fatwa* was extended to apply to others involved in the book, including publishers, translators and booksellers. The novel's Japanese translator, Hitoshi Igarashi, was stabbed to death in 1991, and attempts were made on the lives of two other translators. Almost 10 years later, Rushdie began to emerge from hiding, and from 2004 to 2006 served as president of PEN's American Centre. He has received eight honorary doctorates and was awarded a knighthood in 2007 for services to literature. In December 2010 he received the Golden PEN Award for a Lifetime's Distinguished Service to Literature.

© Index on Censorship/English PEN
39(4): 168, DOI: 10.1177/0306422010390619

Faraj Bayrakdar

Country of origin:
Syria
Occupation:
Poet and journalist
Status:
Released in 2000; living in exile

Faraj Bayrakdar was born in Homs, Syria in 1951. By the age of 26, he was working as contributing editor of a literary journal representing the work of young Syrian writers. He was arrested twice on vague charges believed to be connected to this journal, which ceased publication after only 12 issues. In 1979, Bayrakdar published his first collection of poems, *You Are Not Alone*, followed by the second in 1980, written in homage to an imprisoned Iranian poet. His third collection, *A New Dance at the Court of the Heart*, was published in 1981.

In 1987 Faraj Bayrakdar was arrested by Syria's Military Intelligence on suspicion of being a member of the Party for Communist Action. He was imprisoned for almost seven years without charge. During his incarceration Bayrakdar was subjected to a form of torture known as 'the German Chair', a metal contraption that causes hyperextension of the spine and stress to the neck and limbs. The publication in Beirut of his collection *A Dove With Wings Outspread*, penned in prison, publicised his case outside Syria, and prompted PEN to campaign for his release.

In October 1993, Bayrakdar was finally brought before the Supreme State Security Court, where he was charged with belonging to an illegal political organisation and sentenced to 15 years in prison. He was released on 16 November 2000 under a presidential amnesty, 14 months before the end of his sentence, which was unprecedented for a political prisoner in Syria. He subsequently left the country to take up an academic post in the Netherlands and now lives in Sweden.

In 1999, Faraj Bayrakdar was awarded the PEN/Barbara Goldsmith Freedom to Write Award.

Visit
by Faraj Bayrakdar

Finally —
unlike what hadn't been usual for him —
my darling smiled at her name.
The universe celebrated by adding two extra skies
and butterflies
wore wings
of pure freedom —
Thanks,
said the forests
as they combed their hair with the wind —
Thanks,
said the seagulls
as they shook the fatigue of those first migrations
off their wings —
Thanks, said the waves,
as they performed their dance
in an oceanic key of passion —
Wheat fields stirred
and dreams tamed the storms
and God retook his throne again
Finally,
and like what had been usual till then,
the guard's voice gurgled
making known the end of the visit
the prison grilles close her
eyes
and the walls don
a hue of deep shame

---

26 January 1993, Saydnaya Prison

© *Faraj Bayrakdar, http://www.icorn.org*
39(4): 170/171, DOI: 10.11770306422010390621

Zargana

Country of origin:
Burma

Occupation:
Comedian, poet, director,
human rights activist

Status:
Imprisoned for 35 years;
due for release in 2043

Zargana is Burma's leading comedian and an accomplished poet, writer, and director who throughout his career has used his artistic talents to draw attention to political repression in Burma.

Zargana was first arrested in 1988 following the pro-democracy demonstrations, in which he played a leading role. As reading and writing were forbidden in his cell in Insein Prison, he mixed dust from the bricks in his cell with water and wrote poetry on the floor, committing the poems to memory and sweeping away the evidence. He was freed after six months.

He was arrested again in 1990 while making jokes at a political rally, and was returned to Insein, where he spent five years in solitary confinement. Following his release, he was increasingly involved in social activism and worked closely with international NGOs. During the 'Saffron Revolution' of 2007, Zargana was one of the key figures to lead public support. This led to a further three weeks in detention.

Zargana's arrest in June 2008 resulted from his criticism of the Cyclone Nargis relief effort. He had personally organised support from the Burmese arts community and oversaw its delivery to the delta. He was angered by the neglect and corruption he encountered and spoke out about this in interviews. In November 2008, he was convicted of 'public order offences' and sentenced to 59 years in prison, later reduced to 35 years.

In late 2008, Zargana was moved to Myitkyina Prison in northern Burma, 1,500km from his family home, where he remains today. Zargana was awarded the inaugural PEN/Pinter Prize for an International Writer of Courage in 2009.

Untitled
by Zargana
Translated by Vicky Bowman

It's lucky my forehead is flat
Since my arm must often rest there.
Beneath it shines a light I must invite
From a moon I cannot see
In Myitkyina.

Myitkyina Jail, 2010

39(4): 172/173, DOI: 10.11770306422010390622

Nizar Nayouf

Country of origin:
Syria
Occupation:
Journalist, poet, activist
Status:
Released in 2001

Born in 1962, Nizar Nayouf is a founding member of the banned Committee for the Defence of Democratic Freedoms and Human Rights and former editor-in-chief of the monthly publication *Sawt al Democratiyya*. In early 1992, he was sentenced to ten years in prison and hard labour for his membership to the organisation and for being involved in the production and distribution of a leaflet calling for human rights reforms in Syria. Much of Nayouf's work, including his poetry, is overtly political in content and he has written about Lebanese citizens who 'disappeared' in Syria during the Lebanese civil war.

While in prison, Nayouf was tortured and his health suffered dramatically. He was often kept in solitary confinement. Nevertheless, he was able to smuggle letters and other writing out of the prison and also had occasional access to letters from supporters. In 2000, he was awarded the Golden Pen of Freedom award for his commitment to press freedom.

Nayouf was released from prison on the night of 6-7 May 2001, after nine years in detention; President Bashar al Assad ordered his release just as the Pope embarked on a visit to the country. He was initially held under house arrest, but following considerable international pressure, he was allowed to travel to France for medical treatment in July 2001. He successfully sought political asylum in 2002. He continues to be politically active, speaking out on human rights violations in the Middle East. He is a member of the Syrian Democratic Coalition, which calls for democratic change in the country.

© Index on Censorship/English PEN
39(4): 174, DOI: 10.1177/0306422010393452

Aung San Suu Kyi

Country of origin:
Burma

Occupation:
Politician, writer

Status:
Released in November 2010

Credit: English PEN

Aung San Suu Kyi was born in June 1945 in Rangoon, the daughter of General Aung San, who formed Burma's first army and negotiated independence from Britain in 1947 only to be assassinated the same year.

Suu Kyi graduated from Oxford in 1969 and returned to Burma in 1988 to care for her sick mother. Upon her return she became involved in the setting up of the National League for Democracy (NLD) and was appointed to the post of general secretary of the party. On 20 July 1989, Aung San Suu Kyi was placed under house arrest without trial after Burma was placed under martial law. The following year the NLD won national elections, despite the incarceration of many of its leaders. However, the result was ignored by the ruling regime.

Aung San Suu Kyi was in and out of prison or under house arrest in Rangoon for decades, from where she addressed her supporters. In 1991 she was awarded the Nobel Peace Prize. Her book *Freedom from Fear and Other Writings* was published in London in 1992.

On 14 May 2009, Suu Kyi was charged with breaching the terms of her house arrest. On 11 August of that year she was found guilty and sentenced to a further 18 months' detention. On 13 November 2010, just days after the first election in Burma for two decades, this sentence expired and Aung San Suu Kyi was released.

© Index on Censorship/English PEN
39(4): 175, DOI: 10.1177/0306422010391875

Taslima Nasrin was born in East Pakistan (now Bangladesh) in August 1962. She began writing poetry from an early age, and her work appeared in literary magazines when she was a teenager. She went on to publish six collections of poetry between 1986 and 1993.

In 1989, Nasrin began writing on women's rights for various magazines and newspapers and soon became a popular columnist. She produced several collections of essays and novels before her most famous work, the novel *Lajja* (Shame), published in 1993, changed her life and career dramatically.

Lajja, written in just seven days, is the controversial story of a Hindu family that is attacked by Muslims. Its publication provoked the previously unknown group, Soldiers of Islam, to call for her execution. Already under attack, in May 1994, her situation became more extreme when an interview was published in an Indian newspaper in which she was quoted as calling for revision of the Quran. This led to mass protests on the streets of Dhaka, which at their height were said to have numbered 300,000 people. In August 1994 she was officially charged with 'making inflammatory statements' and went into hiding before going into exile. She was sentenced to one year in prison in absentia.

In 1998, Nasrin gained permission to return to Bangladesh to visit her ailing mother, who died in January 1999. Two weeks later, she was forced to flee once more, after receiving further death threats. She has spent the last decade in exile, living in both France and Sweden. She currently lives in India.

Simon Walker/Rex Features

Taslima Nasrin

Country of origin:
Bangladesh
Occupation:
Novelist, poet and journalist
Status:
Living in exile

Preface to *Lajja* (Shame)

I detest fundamentalism and communalism. This was the reason I wrote *Lajja* soon after the demolition of the Babri Masjid in Ayodhya on 6 December 1992. The book, which took me seven days to write, deals with the persecution of Hindus, a religious minority in Bangladesh, by the Muslims who are in the majority. It is disgraceful that the Hindus in my country were hunted by the Muslims after the destruction of the Babri Masjid. All of us who love Bangladesh should feel ashamed that such a terrible thing could happen in our beautiful country. The riots that took place in 1992 in Bangladesh are the responsibility of us all, and we are all to blame. *Lajja* is a document of our collective defeat.

Lajja was published in February 1993 in Bangladesh and sold over 60,000 copies before it was banned by the government five months later – their excuse was that it was disturbing the communal peace. In September that year a fatwa was issued against me by a fundamentalist organisation and a reward was offered for my death. There have been marches on the streets of Dhaka by communalists clamouring for my life. But none of these things have shaken my determination to continue the battle against religious persecution, genocide and communalism. Bangladesh is my motherland. We gained our independence from Pakistan at the cost of three million lives. That sacrifice will be betrayed if we allow ourselves to be ruled by religious extremism. The mullahs who would murder me will kill everything progressive in Bangladesh if they are allowed to prevail. It is my duty to try to protect my beautiful country from them and I call on all those who share my values to help me defend my rights.

The disease of religious fundamentalism is not restricted to Bangladesh alone and it must be fought at every turn. For myself, I am not afraid of any challenge or threat to my life. I will continue to write and protest persecution and discrimination. I am convinced that the only way the fundamentalist forces can be stopped is if all of us who are secular and humanistic join together and fight their malignant influence. I, for one, will not be silenced.

© *Taslima Nasrin/ Penguin India/Dhaka, March 1994*
39(4): 176/177, DOI: 10.11770306422010390756

Grigory Pasko

Country of origin:
Ukraine
Occupation:
Journalist and poet
Status:
Released in 2003

Grigory Pasko was born in 1962 in the Kherson Oblast region, in what is now Ukraine. He studied journalism at Lvov University and, after graduating in 1983, worked as an investigative journalist and editor for the in-house newspaper of the Russian Pacific Fleet, *Boyevaya Vakhta*. He also worked as a freelance reporter for the Japanese media.

During his time at the paper, Pasko exposed the Russian Navy's dumping of nuclear waste in the Sea of Japan in 1993. As a result, he was arrested by secret service agents in 1997, accused of possessing state secrets with the intent to spread them abroad. Due to a lack of evidence he was instead convicted on the charge of abusing his official position, and was released under a general amnesty. Pasko appealed against the conviction to the Supreme Court, wanting to clear his name, but the prosecution also appealed, pushing for retrial. In 2001, Pasko faced another military court, and was found guilty on one of the ten charges of treason brought against him. He was sentenced to four years in prison.

During his imprisonment he wrote prolifically and received over 500 letters of support. His case also attracted the attention of international human rights organisations. In 2001, Pasko was elected an honorary member of English PEN and was adopted as a prisoner of conscience by Amnesty International. In the same year he was also awarded the Index on Censorship International Whistleblower award and the following year, 2002, received the Reporters Sans Frontières Fondation de France prize.

Pasko was released in January 2003, when a civilian court overturned the original military decisions. He was only allowed to travel abroad 18 months later.

Pasko now edits and writes for the magazine *Environment and Rights*.

from *Singing to the Deaf*
by Grigory Pasko

Banya! The bathhouse! The word's enough to make any prisoner quiver in anticipation, frantically collect his soap, loofah and towel, smooth the hair stuck to his scalp and grin ear to ear.

I remember when I first arrived in the common cell in prison, I waited to hear the word for more than 30 days. I got there in the end but it was too late, my body was already covered in scabs. And the memory of the bathhouse (over 30 people under 4 showers in 10 square metres of space) still makes me flinch.

And now it's banya-time again! The first shower in 17 days of isolation in the penal wing. They say that it was announced 10 days ago but the water was ice-cold so they didn't bother me. Luckily I managed to heat water in my tiny kettle (big ones were forbidden) and wash in the lavatory pan in my cell. This time, they said, everything was fine.

I was the only one left in solitary in the penal isolation wing; Zhora had been moved a few days before. The bathhouse attendants in penal isolation aren't the same as in the common bathhouses – here you get your own banya – so once again my wash began with the usual interjections: 'Take a look at that! He's on his own! Must be dangerous!' There's nothing you can do. Not everyone reads the papers and if you're in prison it stands to reason you're a criminal. But being alone proved a privilege. I washed on my own, longer than the others. But 'wash' is an overstatement. After soaping myself I'd leap under a stream of boiling water for a few seconds and risk scalding my privates. Perhaps 'longer' is an exaggeration, too: everyone else got ten minutes to wash, I got 15.

I suppose I must be beginning to understand something about life. After the murder of state deputy Galina Starovoitova in 1998, I was expecting them to announce an increase in the powers of the interior ministry and the FSB. They did: by presidential decree. Now the murderers can be caught. Or rather handed over. The murder was necessary so that the authorities could have carte blanche for the implementation of repressive measures. In my (not necessarily biased) view, the FSB plays a role that cements crime rather than controls it. With KGB/FSB help, Russia became – and now definitively is – a criminal state. With FSB help, a government and parliament will be established ('elected' for the benefit of the West) which will assist in the revival of the former power of the KGB. A totalitarian police-informer state with a thin stratum of private business, a few millionaires at the top and a mass of grey, silent people working like dogs for a few kopeks. The number of prisons, prison camps and internal troops will grow, as will the number of police schools and institutes. There will even be competition to get in. Police privileges will be increased. The first to be armed and fed will be the militia, the FSB, internal troops, tax office employees, customs, public prosecutor's offices and the law courts. Then the army, or rather what's left of it.

People are downtrodden and fearful. They are afraid of everybody: the authorities, deputies, militia and particularly the FSB. As soon as someone outstandingly able, with independent judgment, appears on the scene, he or she immediately comes to the FSB's attention. After that there are four options: become an informer, be killed, be imprisoned or be put away in a psychiatric hospital. All are time-honoured methods, approved by silent public acquiescence. Gorbachev's thaw is long over. The next, if it happens, will not come for 30 years.

Now, just before the parliamentary elections [December 1999], there will be several very public murders, a few dozen less public ones and hundreds that won't even be noticed by journalists.

But the FSB will notice journalists. They will all be bought, bribed, terrorised and made to sing along with the FSB. There will be scarcely any opposition – anyone who opposes will be killed.

The gap between us and the West will grow. They need our raw materials, but not our criminal ways, which are also spreading west. Financial aid, like any other, will only help to strengthen the personal position of the criminals in power.

The arrogance and cynicism, the shabby insidiousness of the generation taking over from the KGB dinosaurs and the party nomenklatura will astonish everyone: the people who will be silent, the oldest dinosaurs who will have their privileges taken away, and the entire western world whose affluence will be threatened.

And I can see no force that can halt the onset of the KGB's and the interior ministry's criminal and chaotic rule.

---

published in Index on Censorship, 2001

Alison Spedding

Country of origin:
United Kingdom
Occupation:
Novelist and academic
Status:
Released in 2000

Harvesting coca leaves, South Yungas.
Credit: David Lomax/Robert Harding/Rex Features

Alison Spedding is an anthropologist and fantasy novelist, best known for her *Walk in the Dark* trilogy.

In 1989, she moved to Bolivia, where she taught at the Higher University of San Andreas in La Paz, specialising in the study of the coca-growing communities of the Andes. She learnt the Aymara language and in 1994 published *Wachu Wachu: Cultivo de coca e identitad en los Yungas de la Paz*, considered the most complete ethnographic account of Bolivia's Yungas region.

During the 1990s, the Bolivian government aligned itself with the USA's controversial 'War on Drugs' campaign and sought to eradicate the coca-leaf (from which cocaine may be derived). Spedding became an outspoken critic of this policy, which drove thousands of people into poverty.

In 1998, Spedding was charged with drug trafficking after 2kg of cannabis was discovered at her house after a late night police raid. Despite a lack of evidence, the Bolivian court convicted her of drug trafficking and handed down a ten-year prison sentence. Spedding's academic colleagues in Bolivia and the UK were outraged, believing the harsh sentence to be a convenient way to silence a critic. A campaign for her release was launched and her sentence was eventually commuted, on payment of a surety.

Throughout her incarceration, Spedding was allowed to receive visitors, and so she continued to teach tutorials from her cell until her contract at the university was terminated.

© Index on Censorship/English PEN
39(4): 181, DOI: 10.1177/0306422010391933

Jiang Qisheng

Country of origin:
China

Occupation:
Pro-democracy campaigner

Status:
Released in 2003; living
in China

Jiang Qisheng is a pro-democracy activist who has been arrested and imprisoned by the Chinese authorities on many occasions.

In 1989 he was head of the Beijing Student Autonomous Federation and formed part of the delegation that met with Prime Minister Li Peng in the hope of resolving the Tiananmen Square protests peacefully. After the bloody crackdown on 4 June 1989, Jiang was imprisoned for 17 months for his part in the demonstrations. Upon his release he was denied employment by the Chinese government.

Ten years later, in 1999, as the anniversary of the Tiananmen Square massacre approached, Jiang Qisheng wrote and distributed an open letter to commemorate the victims, and called on the Chinese people to light candles in memory of those killed in the suppression of the pro-democracy movement. He also gave interviews to the *Boston Globe* and Radio Free Asia. He was arrested soon afterwards and charged with 'propagating and instigating subversion'. The courts deliberated over the case until 27 December 2000, when he was finally sentenced to four years' imprisonment. Jiang served his full sentence in Beijing's No 2 prison, a victim of 'arbitrary detention', before being released on 17 May 2003 on the expiry of his sentence.

Jiang Qisheng continues to suffer harassment at the hands of the Chinese state. In 2009, twenty years after the Tiananmen Square massacre, he was arrested by the Beijing Public Security Bureau and interrogated over his involvement in Charter 08, the pro-democracy statement signed by over 8,500 activists. Despite this pressure, he continues to campaign tirelessly for democracy in China.

From 'A true story of April Fool's Day', *My life in Prison*

by Jiang Qisheng

Translated by Ben Carrdus

It was almost ten o'clock on 1 April when we heard the sound of the electric steel gates being opened, and a line of some 70 immaculately dressed bank personnel filed into the prison. Under the careful planning and detailed organisation of the prison, no one saw any electric cattle prods, and no one heard any screams. Instead, they all stepped onto a cleanly swept path where the first thing they saw was a building hung with the signs 'Library' and 'Psychological Counselling Room', while in the corner of one of the rooms inside was a 34-inch colour television. They continued on and saw the bright and clean toilets and washrooms; they went through the dormitories, signposted from 'Group One' through to 'Group Eight' and all identically arranged around study areas where prisoners in uniform sat pressed together in silence, concentrating on their 'studies'. No one looked up or around; no one so much as whispered.

This whole series of eight sweatshops had been immaculately swept and 'converted' into prison dormitories. All of the workbenches and machines had been stowed away. Even the sharpest eyesight would have missed the minuscule clues that showed this was in fact a workshop. Every single mattress on the prisoners' beds was exactly the same position at the foot of the bed. There was something even more military than the military about the scene.

But the good bank workers would never have noticed such details; and nor could they have possibly known that stuffed into the space under each of the beds was the bedding that the prisoners actually used. Sadly, those threadbare and faded bedrolls could not speak; sadly, the prisoners in those rooms who knew the truth of it all were too terrified to speak. And so it was that these young white collar merchants, these handsome young men and beautiful young women, were publicly duped on April Fool's Day.

An extract from his prison diary, 1999-2003

© Jiang Qisheng/Profile Books
39(4): 182/183, DOI: 10.11770306422010391937

Akbar Ganji

Country of origin:
Iran

Occupation:
Journalist, democracy campaigner

Status:
Living in exile in the USA

Akbar Ganji has been a thorn in the side of successive governments in Tehran, and as a result has spent much of the past decade in Iran's notorious Evin Prison.

Ganji is the author of the bestselling book *Dungeon of Ghosts*, a collection of newspaper articles he wrote in early 2000, which accused the former president Akbar Hashemi Rafsanjani and other leading conservative politicians of being involved in a series of political assassinations. The book is said to have contributed to the conservative defeat in parliamentary elections in February 2000.

Ganji was arrested by the Iranian regime in April 2000, following his participation in a political and cultural conference in Berlin. At his trial he was sentenced to ten years in prison – in part for his participation in the conference, and in part for allegedly 'spreading propaganda' against the regime, a reference to the impact of *Dungeon of Ghosts*. While Ganji was in prison, the government pursued a sustained vendetta against him, delving into his journalistic record and bringing retrospective charges for articles published prior to 1998.

During his time in prison, Akbar Ganji continued to campaign for freedom of expression in Iran. He wrote *A Republic Manifesto* in 2002, urging democratic reforms for Iran, which was published online. In June 2005 he went on hunger strike, a move that further galvanised human rights groups to campaign on his behalf. During this period he wrote two letters to 'the free people of the world' and a second manifesto, which called for a popular boycott of the presidential elections.

Ganji was released from prison in March 2006 on grounds of ill health, and fled Iran soon after. He now lives in New York.

From *The Road to Democracy in Iran*
by Akbar Ganji

What can be done to fight gender apartheid? We must begin on three fronts: culture, law and politics. But we need to work on culture more than anything else. Discriminatory laws against women have their genesis in traditional images of men and women. As long as these images pervade our society, the status of women will not improve much. They have deep roots in religious as well as non-religious literature, so our first task is to become conscious of them and subject them to criticism. In my view, we must recognise that the following deeply embedded, traditional views on gender are not 'natural':

Boys and girls do not have the same ability to master technology. According to this view, women do not have sufficient rational and logical faculties, and tend to be more emotional and instinctive;

Differences in body, mind and psyche should dictate men's and women's roles in society and family; therefore, it is natural that men take the lead in these social hierarchies;

Boys should be raised for roles that are natural to their capacities (like management, supervision and leadership) and girls for naturally feminine roles (like bearing children, housekeeping and taking orders). The poet Sa'edi describes the 'ideal good woman' as one who obeys her husband's orders, keeps herself for her husband, and has, as the ultimate goal of her life, making her husband, and not herself, the 'king';

Since in the traditional vision women are naturally inferior to men, they cannot enjoy equal rights with them. Any change in the 'natural' order can only bring about ruinous consequences for everyone, including women.

Given these deeply entrenched ideas about gender, we must begin our cultural effort in the household, in schools, in our textbooks, and in the way we raise our children. In the context of the family, we must recognise that in the nature of familial relationships and division of labour, injustices hurt women. Assigning social roles and responsibilities can be considered just only when men and women are afforded an equal chance to take them on; when they accept roles commensurate with their individual abilities and talents; and when their choices are made freely.

© *Akbar Ganji*/Boston Review/MIT
39(4): 184/185, DOI: 10.11770306422010391932

Ibtissam Berto Sulaiman al Dakhil

Country of origin:
Iraq

Occupation:
Journalist

Status:
Released in 2003

Ibtissam Berto Sulaiman al Dakhil was imprisoned in June 1991 for allegedly writing for an Iraqi government newspaper during the occupation of Kuwait. Although born in Iraq, she had lived in Kuwait all her life and it was not until the invasion in 1990 that she was regarded as an Iraqi.

Al Dakhil had been working as a journalist for a newspaper in Kuwait City, but during the occupation all of the paper's articles were written by Iraqi journalists and sent from Baghdad. Despite this, staff were told to continue going to the office, to keep up appearances. The instruction was allegedly given with the full knowledge of Kuwaiti authorities, but soon after Iraqi forces left the country, the newspaper's 45 original journalists were arrested. Their trial lasted only one day, and they were forbidden to speak in their own defence. They were all sentenced to 20 years in prison on charges of collaborating with Iraqis.

Still in detention, al Dakhil began a hunger strike in September 2002. On the third day, she was told she would be allowed to leave if she could find a country to accept her. Fearing the repercussions of repatriation to Iraq, and without alternative asylum, she was forced to remain incarcerated.

PEN's Writers in Prison Committee made contact with al Dakhil's family in France, with high-profile French politicians and with other human rights organisations. The family of her daughter's husband agreed to sponsor her asylum application, and in early 2003, al Dakhil was granted refugee status by the United Nations Human Rights Committee. She was finally released in May that year.

© Index on Censorship/English PEN
39(4): 186, DOI: 10.1177/0306422010391955

Brigadier General José Gallardo

Country of origin:
Mexico
Occupation:
Army officer, writer
Status:
Released in 2002

In November 1993, Brigadier General José Gallardo, who had served over 30 years in the Mexican army, was arrested for the publication of an excerpt from his thesis. The piece, entitled 'The Need for a Military Ombudsman in Mexico', called for an independent civilian to investigate human rights abuses committed by military personnel. Judicial proceedings were initiated against him for damaging, libelling, and slandering the army, and on 18 December 1993 a military court issued a written order stating that he was to remain in custody until further notice.

In 1996, the Inter-American Commission on Human Rights (IACHR) declared that Gallardo was imprisoned 'without reason and legal justification' and recommended his immediate release. Nevertheless, he remained in detention, and in March 1998 was sentenced to more than 28 years in prison.

Frustrated by the Mexican government's refusal to comply with its recommendations, the IACHR petitioned the Inter-American Court to grant Gallardo emergency measures. The court accepted the case and ordered the Mexican government to appear at a hearing in Costa Rica in February 2002. A week before the hearing, Gallardo was released, having served more than eight years in prison.

Gallardo and his family were special guests at the PEN Congress in Mexico City in November 2003. They arrived with several boxes containing the thousands of letters and books he had received from all over the world. In his address, Gallardo stated that 'Without the work of the Writers in Prison Committee, it would have been so difficult for the Mexican government to open up the gates for my release... I owe them my freedom.'

© Index on Censorship/English PEN
39(4): 187, DOI: 10.11770306422010391956

Jorge Olivera Castillo

Country of origin:
Cuba

Occupation:
Journalist, writer

Status:
Released in 2004

Jorge Olivera Castillo worked as a television editor between 1983 and 1993, but was forced to resign after making public his disagreement with the government's censorship policies. From 1995, he worked as a journalist at *Havana Press*, rising to director in 1999. In 2003, he was one of 35 journalists, writers and librarians to be arrested during a crackdown on alleged dissidents, and in April was sentenced at a one-day, closed trial to 18 years' imprisonment.

On 6 December 2004, after 20 months and 18 days in prison, often in solitary confinement, Olivera was released on health grounds. He had lost 30 pounds and was suffering from high blood pressure and serious infections. His release was conditional and he was threatened with re-arrest if he resumed his political journalism.

Since 2004, Olivera has therefore focused on writing poetry and short stories. His prison poetry, including 37 poems on love and politics, was published by the Independent Libraries Project in 2005. In 2006, his poems were included in the Italian anthology *Verses Behind Bars* and, in 2008, Czech PEN published a bilingual version of his collection of poems, *En cuerpo y alma* (Body and Soul). In February 2007, a collection of his short stories was published in Spain, including ten stories based on his prison experiences. His journalism has been published in newspapers in Sweden, Argentina, the United States and the Czech Republic.

Olivera lives in Havana with his wife Nancy, where he continues to write. Following a PEN nomination, he has been invited to take up the post of Visiting Writer in the Department of Literature and Comparative Literature at Harvard University for the 2010-2011 academic year.

Emergency Exit
by Jorge Olivera Castillo
Translated by Cat Lucas

Get out of the fire of hypocrisy
from the edge of barefoot verse

Look for an avenue to throw down these necessities
and don't delay on the threshold of pearls and rain.

Enter like a shooting star.
Break the protocol
and teach the remnants of your soul
chained to the last collection of poems.

None will dare call you a marionette, wretch or fool.
You will be – for ever more – safe
from gloomy reflections
from voices from beyond the grave
from the threads that support the mask

Escape from falsity and heaviness.
At the end of the passage there is a door.
Escape this minute.
Before nightfall.
Before they trap you again
and force you to howl like a goat
or to jump like a fool.

© *Jorge Olivera Castillo*
39(4): 188/189, DOI: 10.11770306422010387562

Ali Reza Jabari

Country of origin:
Iran
Occupation:
Translator, freelance writer, poet
Status:
Released in 2004

Ali Reza Jabari was first arrested on 28 December 2002, following a critical interview he gave to a Farsi language newspaper in Canada. His house was searched and his computer hard drive was seized; he was held in solitary confinement until February 2003.

The following month, Jabari was arrested and sentenced to four years' imprisonment, 253 lashes and a fine of six million rials for 'consuming and distributing alcoholic drinks' and 'adultery and incitement to immoral acts'. However, it was widely believed that he was in fact targeted for his membership of the Iranian Writers' Organisation and for contributions to foreign-based news websites, on which he was critical of the Iranian authorities. His lawyer was not allowed to attend the trial.

On 17 June 2003, an appeals court upheld the conviction against Jabari, but reduced the prison term from four to three years. Despite being more than 60 years old and suffering from a heart condition, Jabari reportedly received 174 lashes in detention and was denied medical care.

Whilst in prison, Jabari received letters from PEN members and later spoke of how it was 'a great mental support to have such friendly contacts with so many fellow writers'. In 2004, those with whom he had been corresponding decided to contact renowned Chilean author Isabel Allende. Jabari had translated her book *The Stories of Eva Luna* into Farsi before his imprisonment. Allende reportedly lobbied the highest authorities in the Islamic Republic of Iran — including the then president, Mohammad Khatami — calling for the ailing journalist to be freed. Jabari was granted early release shortly afterwards, on 14 October 2004. In 2006, Jabari addressed an International PEN conference in Stockholm, outlining Iran's violations of human rights and oppression of 'free thinkers'.

The Sun Smiled

by Reza Jabari

Translated by Ali Reza Jabari and Val Warner

*To honour the memory of the martyrs of the summer 1988
Iranian national tragedy*

To say that we were buried means nothing,
We rose to heaven on the sun's gold wings,
The sun smiled when we were in love's domain,
Ragged-shirted and with anthems to sing.

Hearts given to tomorrow, band of knights
Running, our feet's exhaustion like a blight,
Running at night, dawn's banner in our hands,
Battalion of free people, to the light.

Ours, this garden's music soon flowering,
Ours is the song the nightingale now brings.
Don't ever abandon our memory,
Ours is this odour in winter of spring.

How good's melodious flight, as on wine's wings!
How good in winter's this odour of spring!
Your clamour's offering rare promises!
How good's the song this nightingale trills, flings!

Our names on people's lips all through the day,
Each place you walk, our presence on the way —
What happened to the dawn, the melody?
The lyric nightingale has gone away.

© *Ali Reza Jabari*
39(4): 190/191, DOI: 10.1177/03064222010391951

Paul Kamara

Country of origin:
Sierra Leone
Occupation:
Journalist
Status:
Released in 2005

Editor of newspaper *For Di People* since 1983 and chairman of the National League for Human Rights in Sierra Leone, Paul Kamara has been repeatedly detained by the country's rulers. Despite continual harassment and intimidation, *For Di People* has continued to fight against corruption and campaign for press freedom and human rights.

Born in 1956 in the district of Kambia, Kamara went on to study at the University of Sierra Leone, and took a senior diploma in journalism at the Thomson Foundation in London. He served as secretary general of the Sierra Leone Association of Journalists, and when *For Di People* was banned in 1993, Kamara continued to campaign for human rights. He defied the ban in 1995, despite receiving death threats.

Kamara was persuaded to take the position of Secretary of State for Land, Housing and the Environment ahead of elections in 1996, but he left the government when the junta began to sabotage democratic processes. He was ambushed, shot and left to die on the day of the election. Flown to London for treatment, he returned to Freetown in 1997. Following the AFRC-RUF coup later that year, Kamara was violently attacked several times for writing articles critical of the rebels.

In 2004, Kamara was convicted of seditious libel for an article he wrote in 2003 that criticised President Ahmad Tejan Kabbah. He was sentenced to two years in prison. After campaigns from human rights groups across the world, and a long court battle, he was released in November 2005.

Kamara was named the US Press Review's Editor of the Year in 1999 and awarded the Civil Courage Prize in 2001.

© Index on Censorship/English PEN
39(4): 192, DOI: 10.1177/0306422010391959

Shi Tao

Country of origin:

China

Occupation:

Journalist; poet

Status:

Imprisoned,
due for release in 2014

In the run up to the 15th anniversary of the military crackdown in Tiananmen Square in 2004, the Chinese government issued journalists with guidelines, advising them on how to report on events and warning them not to publish articles about pro-democracy activists returning to the country to mark the occasion. Using his Yahoo! email account, Shi Tao sent a summary of the directive to US-based website Democracy Forum. On 24 November, he was arrested at his home and his personal belongings were confiscated, among them samples of his writing.

In April 2005, Shi Tao was sentenced to ten years' imprisonment and two years' deprivation of political rights for 'revealing state secrets'. It later emerged that Yahoo!'s Hong Kong division provided detailed information to the police, enabling them to link Shi Tao's message to his personal account and the address of his computer. The sentence was upheld on appeal in June 2005.

Twelve months into his sentence, Shi Tao's health had deteriorated considerably as a result of forced labour. In 2007, he was transferred to another prison, where conditions improved, and later that year, Yahoo! settled a lawsuit lodged by Shi Tao's family, pledging to provide an undisclosed amount of 'financial, humanitarian and legal support'. In May 2010, he was transferred to Yinchuan Prison in the Ningxia Hui Autonomous Region. It is believed that the improvements in his prison conditions, which have in turn improved his health, are a result of continued international pressure.

June

by Shi Tao
Translated by Chip Rolley

My whole life

Will never get past 'June'
June, when my heart died
When my poetry died
When my lover
Died in romance's pool of blood

June, the scorching sun burns open my skin
Revealing the true nature of my wound
June, the fish swims out of the blood-red sea
Toward another place to hibernate
June, the earth shifts, the rivers fall silent
Piled up letters unable to be delivered to the dead

In 2008, the year of the Beijing Olympics, PEN members translated Shi
Tao's 'June' into 100 different languages, ranging from Adnyamathanha
(an Australian indigenous language) to Tamazight (a Berber language
spoken in Algeria) for the PEN Poem Relay. As the Olympic Torch was
lit and began its journey across Greece, the poem virtually left Taiyuan
City, Shi Tao's home town, and began its journey around the world, from
centre to centre, language to language, adding new translations as it
went and ending up back in Beijing for the 2008 Olympics.

© *Shi Tao*
39(4): 194/195, DOI: 10.11770306422010387563

Coming back to life:
written for the 'Tiananmen mother'

by Shi Tao

Translated by Frances Wood

I creep into the ear of the deaf man
And wake him with a burst of rifle-fire
I creep in front of the blind man's eyes
To paint him a picture of death

I creep amongst shadows
To stroke the cold palpitating heart
I creep amongst the crowds in the supermarket
To find myself a body to keep me from the cold

I creep into the deserted classroom
To learn what the truth sounds like
I creep in front of my lover's window
To watch her dancing with her thoughts

I creep onto the roof of the classroom
Thinking I'll hear the breath of penitents
I creep amongst the grasses of the garden of the martyr's grave
Thinking I'll see myself come back to life like wildflowers in early summer

I open Whitman's *Leaves of Grass*
Read it line by line — each word, each sentence
Fills my young, vibrant blood
My eyes come back to life in the light of rows of candles!

My hand, touching the pianola, the keyboard playing the 'Ode to Joy'
I'm the hero of the funeral dirge
But I was once the King of human happiness!

All night long, all night long
I curl up by my mother's bed
Listening to her calling to the empty wall
For her beloved children to come back

I didn't disturb her, I also
Could not hear the sound of her crying, couldn't hear
Time reducing her Pain. Listening, I leave her…

I'm afraid I can hear frightening things in the song.
I close the window, letting the moonlight
Dodge into the locked wardrobe
Records of childhood songs are deeply etched in the mother
A 'Diary of growing up' with my name on it
But after that nothing, no further entry
The date: June 4th, 1989
It can't be written, it will never be written!

A line of tears falls to the ground
I trample them, tread them into the ground
I don't want other people to see
The cold hatred hidden in the sound of weeping

I stand in the square which is strictly guarded
Shouting at an indifferent crowd, 'I haven't gone mad!'
My two feet still stand firmly on the hard bricks of the ground,
In the lake of blood

I stand here, I am the spokesperson for youth
Keeping close the heart-scent of childhood
The white swing going backwards and forwards between the white
flowers will
Never let my mother keep watch alone.

© *Shi Tao*
39(4): 196/197, DOI: 10.1177/0306422010387563

Nurmuhemmet Yasin

Country of origin:
China/Xingjiang Province
Occupation:
Writer, poet
Status:
Imprisoned;
due for release in 2014

Nurmuhemmet Yasin has an established literary reputation among Uighur readers around the world. An award-winning freelance writer, prior to his detention in 2004, he published many highly acclaimed literary works and prose poems, including the poetry collections *First Love*, *Crying from the Heart*, and *Come on Children*.

Yasin was arrested at his home in Kashgar on 29 November 2004, shortly after his short story 'Wild Pigeon' (*'Yawa Kepter'*) appeared in the Uighur-language *Kashgar Literary Journal*. Upon his arrest, the authorities confiscated Yasin's personal computer, which contained around 1,600 poems, commentaries, stories and one unfinished novel.

The charges against him are believed to be based on the publication of 'Wild Pigeon', a tragic and beautiful tale of a bird captured by humans. Yasin's story was widely circulated and nominated for an award by a prominent literary website in the Xinjiang Uighur Autonomous Region. It also attracted the attention of the Chinese authorities, who considered the fable to be a tacit criticism of the work of their government in the region, portraying people as deeply unhappy with life under Chinese rule.

After a closed trial in February 2005, at which he was reportedly denied a lawyer, Yasin was sentenced to 10 years in prison for 'inciting Uighur separatism'. His sentence was upheld on appeal by the Kashgar Intermediate Court, and, on 19 May 2005, he was transferred to Urumqi's Number 1 Prison where he remains detained today. He has been permitted no visitors since his arrest and there are serious concerns for his well-being. In 2009, Yasin was awarded the Vasyl Stus Freedom to Write Award by PEN New England in recognition of his courage in the face of censorship and oppression.

from 'Wild Pigeon'

by Nurmuhemmet Yasin

Translated by Dr Dolkun Kamberi

A familiar smell comes to me, and then I see my mother – her eyes gleaming, anxious, noting in turn my loosened feathers, my broken mouth, my pathetic, twisted wings.

The soul's release

'Forgive me, mother,' I start to say. 'I wasn't equal to the trust you placed in me. I am not fit to be your son.' I lower my head, like a condemned criminal in the dock. Why couldn't I have died before she arrived here?

'You did everything in your power,' she replies. 'Now you must end this.'

'But mama, I cannot,' I tell her. 'I am a prisoner – without energy, without strength. Much as I would like to die, I cannot.'

'That is clear,' she tells me. 'And so I have come to bring you freedom.'

'I no longer deserve freedom,' I say. 'I am no longer worthy of being your child.'

'Then I shall tell you again – I have brought you freedom. You are still my brave child – you must not be forced to live like a slave but must be allowed to die bravely, with dignity,' she says, pushing a bit of food toward me.

A high price for freedom

'This strawberry is the poisonous variety – eat it, and it will set you free. Restore the honour of our flock. And remember always that true freedom comes only at a high price. Here, move your mouth closer to me.'

I gaze at my mother for the last time. She seems peaceful, and brave. I stretch my damaged mouth out toward her. My beak, my only remaining weapon – an enemy to the humans, it protected and fed me, and then led me into the humans' trap. It is broken now, shattered by my failed collision with the iron bars.

The poisons from the strawberry flow through me like the sound of freedom itself, along with gratitude that now, now, finally, I can die freely. I feel as if my soul is on fire – soaring and free.

I see everything clearly now – the sky is still such a deep blue and the world remains so beautiful, and everything is so quiet and still. A group of pigeons gathers at the edge of cage around me, watching me, puzzled and surprised.

© Radio Free Asia, 2005
39(4): 198/199, DOI: 10.11770306422010387566

Ali al Dumaini

Country of origin:
Saudi Arabia
Occupation:
Poet, novelist, activist
Status:
Released in 2005

Saudi writer and poet Ali al Dumaini was among 12 leading intellectuals to be detained in March 2004. A Ministry of Interior official announced that the detainees were suspected of issuing 'statements which do not serve the unity of the country and the cohesion of society...based on Islamic religion', after they had signed and circulated petitions that called for political reform. They were also accused of criticising the National Commission on Human Rights (NCHR) and for planning to set up their own human rights organisation.

The NCHR, the country's first human rights watchdog, was approved in early March 2004 by the Saudi government as part of limited steps towards political reform. However, many liberal and opposition figures, including al Dumaini, wanted to see speedier and more radical change.

Most of the detainees were released shortly afterwards, but Ali al Dumaini remained in detention – he refused to sign a pledge promising not to engage in further political activity because he believed that pro-reform lobbying was in the interests of his country. More than 12 months after his initial arrest, al Dumaini was sentenced to nine years in prison. He was charged with threatening 'national unity', promoting a constitutional monarchy and using western terminology in his demands for more wide-ranging political reform.

While in prison, al Dumaini wrote the first part of his memoirs, *Time for Prison, Times for Freedom*, which was published on 30 November 2004 in Beirut. Following an International PEN campaign, and shortly after receiving the 2005 PEN/Barbara Goldsmith Freedom to Write Award, al Dumaini was granted a royal pardon on 8 August 2005. Al Dumaini is the author of three collections of poetry and a novel.

I am Fatima
by Ali al Dumaini
Translated by Amira Kashgary

I am Fatima
To Fatima and Mansour, who have been forcibly divorced against their will on the grounds of un-equivalent lineage; to their two children who will endure the pain and agony of this divorce

I am Fatima
I call not for waging wars
I pray not for new delusions
Suffice it
To hold on to my little share of humanity
To fiddle with my right to life behind bars.
I claim not that my vision's always right
But I stand by my right to my destiny.
Have I not the right to breathe like all humans?
Isn't my existence worthy of having its share of oxygen
Imaginary as it may be?
Am I made of a nature different from other human beings?
I don't go far in my dreams
But I hold on to every ounce of my being to be who I am.

I am Fatima
A woman from the land of arid desert and oil
A woman from the land of traditions and holiness
A woman who places her hands, soaked in darkness, on a dream:
To merely live
With her daughter, Nuha; With her son, Sulaiman; and With her husband, Mansour

I don't ask for more
I don't settle for less

I am Fatima, small but strong on her own
Big with sympathisers in my long journey in the darkness of jail I'm living in!

And with the light of the innate right I carry within all my senses!

Only to live with my small family
Kept in my heart
After my big family, stretching from sea to sea, has lost me.

When I put my little son in my lap
Along that endless prison wall
When I lull him to sleep so that I have some solitude
When I sleep lonely, scattered and isolated
I feel more love for the life I have chosen,
For the husband I have accepted and
For the little children I've begotten.

I am Fatima
Never begging for a bite or for dignity
Never summoned my tears to join that river of larger tears
Never waiting for pity from a soul.

I am Fatima
Only waiting for fellowmen to open a door to my simple rights
To live together with my son, daughter and husband in our little house,
To open our eyes in the morning to a clear sun
As tender on us as young flower buds in this universe.

To fix my daughter's uniform before she sets off to her nursery school close to my heart

To relieve her father from carrying her on his shoulders throughout the times
I was lost in the dungeons and charities

For Sulaiman and Nuha to laugh listening to their father's songs

Or to have them laugh to a family love quarrel between their parents

I am Fatima
I seek not to wage war on anybody

I hope not for a fight between the trees and their branches
Or between the flowers and their roots

I merely march on towards my humanity
Which has been written in the lines of a true love story
Towards a marriage blessed by my father
Together with my future husband!

 I am Fatima
A tree in this open space
I monopolise neither 'righteousness' nor truth,
I explain not why the stars sleep near dawn
I open my eyes on nothing but what makes the world happier, more
transparent, and more just,
I am the innocent daughter of this country
And its true seed
I don't take of its air more than I need
I don't see of the sky further than what's enough for me
And for my simple freedom
I don't open my eyes on more dewy blueness than I need
To embrace my son, my daughter, and my husband.

Dhahran, Saudi Arabia, 19 July 2007

© *Ali al Dumaini*
39(4): 200/203, DOI: 10.11770306422010391943

Dolma Kyab

Country of origin:
China/Tibet
Occupation:
Writer and teacher
Status:
Imprisoned,
due for release in 2015

In March 2005, writer and teacher Dolma Kyab was sentenced to ten and a half years in prison. Although authorities have never confirmed this, the charges against him are thought to be based on the suspicion that he endangered state security in his manuscript *Sao dong de Ximalayasha* (The Restless Himalayas). Writing from prison in November 2005, Kyab attributed his conviction to this unpublished book, in which he writes in detail about Tibetan geography, history and religion.

The book alone does not justify such a sentence under Chinese law, but, according to Kyab, the Chinese government accused him of espionage or 'stealing state secrets' because of another of his manuscripts, which includes information on the location and number of Chinese military camps in the Tibet Autonomous Region. Espionage is one of the most serious political offences in China.

Motivated by the desire to express the opinions of Tibetan youth, Kyab has written about a range of issues pertinent to present day Tibet, including human rights, democracy, literature and culture. He is gravely concerned about the destruction of the Tibetan environment under Chinese policy, particularly the pollution of rivers and land by uranium mining. His work remains unpublished.

There have been serious concerns over Dolma Kyab's health and he reportedly contracted tuberculosis during pre-trial detention. In July 2007 he was transferred to Seilong prison, a labour camp 400km from Lhasa, where prisoners undergo 're-education through labour'. He remains there today.

from *The Restless Himalayas*

by Dolma Kyab

Translated by The International Campaign for Tibet/Ben Carrdus

In the world famous epic (Tibetan poem) King Gesar there is the famous axiom 'If I know not myself, how can I know this land?' It is only when we understand ourselves that we then have the power to understand this land that belongs to us. In fact, such an understanding is a great unifying force behind a spirit of rejuvenation. It pushes us a step further towards understanding ourselves, and initiates an understanding of the world. And as such our hopes will no more be dreams.

I remember when China's Deng Xiaoping said to a western leader 'There are people who want to split Tibet from China, to take Tibet away, but I don't think they are able.' We were so simple in those days, and we too firmly believed that there was no one to take Tibet away. But today, my generation of Tibetans who have grown up in a colony firmly believe in another truth, that Tibet will always belong to Tibetans; and if China believes an 'ability' is needed to take Tibet away then our generation of Tibetans has that ability and our next generation will have that ability too. Tibetans believe that there are no tigers in this world that cannot be slain, only people who dare not slay them.

We Tibetans are rallying our strength with every passing generation, and even with their guns the Chinese government won't be able to deal with us. It is our wish that both parties will wisely choose dialogue, and that too is the wish of the Chinese government and people. The key to this beautiful, peaceful wish lies with the Chinese government, and not with us, the children of this colony.

A spirit of unity – an attitude of being able to conquer everything that ails us – does not help if we are passive. A far more welcome and greater undertaking is being able to see more clearly a correct strategy.

The importance of unity [therefore] outweighs all other current duties and decides our future missions. With resolve and bravery, and even with principles of steel, it must be understood why unity is so essential. Cohesion is unity, and unity is success! This is such a self-evident truth!

© *International Campaign for Tibet/Ben Carrdus, www.savetibet.org/documents/reports/raging-storm* 39(4): 204/205, DOI: 10.11770306422010394079

Orhan Pamuk

Country of origin:
Turkey
Occupation:
Novelist
Status:
Charges dropped in 2006

Orhan Pamuk, winner of the 2006 Nobel Prize for Literature, is Turkey's most celebrated author. Born in Istanbul in 1952, he published his first novel, *Cevdet Bey and His Sons*, in 1982. *The Black Book* was published in 1990, bringing him international recognition. It was followed by the publication of *My Name Is Red* in 1998. *Snow*, which Pamuk describes as his only political book, was published in 2002.

Pamuk was brought before an Istanbul court on 16 December 2005, charged with 'insulting Turkishness' under Article 301 of the Turkish penal code. He faced up to three years in prison for an interview published in Swiss newspaper *Das Magazin* on 6 February 2005, in which he acknowledged the Armenian genocide at the hands of Ottoman forces in 1915-1917. 'Thirty thousand Kurds and a million Armenians were killed in these lands and nobody but me dares to talk about it', he said, commenting on the silence around both the massacre and the conflict between Turkish forces and Kurdish separatists that began in 1984.

News of the interview for which Pamuk stood trial led to protests and copies of his books were burned. He also suffered death threats from extremists. The case against the writer, widely seen as a test of Turkey's commitment to the democratic principle of free speech and crucial to its bid for European Union membership, was dropped in January 2006 on a technicality.

Pamuk's books have been published worldwide in 46 languages. Among his many awards are the Le Prix Médicis étranger award, the Orhan Kemal literary prize and the Richarda Huck Prize. *The Museum of Innocence* was published in 2010.

© Index on Censorship/English PEN
39(4): 206, DOI: 10.1177/0306422010391887

Opposite - Credit: Fatih Saribas/Reuters
Protesters demonstrating against the French National Assembly's approval of a draft bill that would make it a crime to deny the Armenian genocide, 2006